Praise for Nancy Jo Sales's

American Girls

"Based on interviews with hundreds of teens from thirteen to nineteen, this exploration of the hypersexualized, social-media-ruled world girls grow up in today is eye-opening and sobering."   —*People*

"Social media is life; social media destroys life. For *American Girls*, Ms. Sales spent two and a half years investigating this paradox. . . . She's exquisitely unobtrusive as she does it. Conversations that are not safe for adults seem to open like apps under her fingertips. She has sophisticated methods of infiltration."   —*The Wall Street Journal*

"Sales painstakingly draws on scholarly research and numerous interviews with girls from New Jersey to California to offer a harrowing glimpse into a world where self-esteem, friendships and sexuality play out, and are defined by the parameters of social media."   —*USA Today*

"This intelligent, history-grounded investigation by journalist Sales (*The Bling Ring*) finds dismaying evidence that social media has fostered a culture 'very hostile' to girls in which sexism, harassment, and cyberbullying have become the 'new normal.'. . . Parents, educators, administrators, and the purveyors of social media platforms should all take note of this thoughtful, probing, and urgent work."

—*Publishers Weekly* (starred review)

"Readers are afforded the opportunity to understand what is really going on in the lives of teenagers, especially our girls. . . . This book stands apart from other books targeted at understanding the concerns and current plight of teenage girls. . . . A must read for all parents."
—*The Examiner* (Missouri)

"This book is an ice-cold, important wake-up call."
—*Kirkus Reviews*

Nancy Jo Sales

American Girls

Nancy Jo Sales is an award-winning journalist and author who has written for *Vanity Fair, New York, Harper's Bazaar,* and many other publications. She is known for her reporting on youth culture and crime and for her profiles of pop-culture icons. She won a 2011 Front Page Award for "Best Magazine Feature" and a 2010 Mirror Award for "Best Profile, Digital Media." Her 2013 book, *The Bling Ring: How a Gang of Fame-Obsessed Teens Ripped Off Hollywood and Shocked the World,* tells the true story behind the Sofia Coppola film *The Bling Ring,* which was based on Sales's 2010 *Vanity Fair* piece "The Suspects Wore Louboutins." Born in West Palm Beach, Florida, Sales graduated summa cum laude from Yale in 1986. She became a contributing editor at *Vanity Fair* in 2000. She has a daughter, Zazie, and lives in the East Village in New York City.

www.nancyjosales.com

Also by Nancy Jo Sales

*The Bling Ring: How a Gang of Fame-Obsessed Teens
Ripped Off Hollywood and Shocked the World*

American Girls

American Girls

Social Media and the Secret Lives of Teenagers

NANCY JO SALES

VINTAGE BOOKS
A Division of Penguin Random House LLC
New York

FIRST VINTAGE BOOKS EDITION, JANUARY 2017

Copyright © 2016 by Nancy Jo Sales

The Cataloging-in-Publication Data for the Knopf edition is available from the
Library of Congress.

Vintage Books Trade Paperback ISBN: 978-0-8041-7318-6
eBook ISBN: 978-0-385-35393-9

Author photograph © Jayne Wexler
Book design by M. Kristen Bearse

www.vintagebooks.com

Printed in the United States of America
10 9 8 7 6 5 4 3 2 1

For Alyson

Contents

American Girls

Introduction

Ever since I was a little girl, I've read myself to sleep. Often throughout my life I've awakened to find the light still on and a book resting in my hand after I've dozed off reading a few more pages. When I was ten and twelve it was *The Chronicles of Narnia, To Kill a Mockingbird,* and *Jane Eyre.* I've always been crazy for the great noir writers Raymond Chandler and Patricia Highsmith and James M. Cain. Reading has always been like breathing to me, necessary for existing and thinking. But recently, I find, as I try to make it through the pages, my mind keeps wandering to my phone. What's happening there? What am I missing?

One possible reason for my sense of distraction is that for the last two and a half years I've been researching a book on girls and social media. I went on a sort of picaresque journey, visiting ten states (New York, New Jersey, Virginia, Florida, California, Arizona, Texas, Indiana, Delaware, and Kentucky) and talking to girls, ages thirteen to nineteen, about their lives on and off social media. After I met the girls and talked to them, I followed them on their accounts, seeing what they posted, checking on how they were doing. And even though they knew I was one of their followers on these public forums, sometimes the watching still felt, as girls call it, like "stalking," and sometimes I would ask myself, What am I doing? What are we doing?

I followed apps girls said they liked, such as Yik Yak, the so-called anonymous Twitter. Yik Yak, launched in 2013 by two young men who met at Furman University in South Carolina, is popular with high school and college kids. Like many anonymous apps, it has appeared in the news in connection with cases of cyberbullying, and some school districts and colleges have banned it. But in the five-mile radius in which I'm able to view posts, an area including some New York City high schools and New York University, Yik Yak users are most often heard voicing concerns which echo those of young people throughout the ages: Am I attractive? Will anyone ever love me? How can I be expected to put up with my annoying roommate?

There are a lot of Yik Yak posts about sex. And many of these seem to be describing something different from what we know of young people in the past. There are posts about wanting sex, and seeking sex, even just cybersex, immediately, it doesn't seem to matter with whom. ("Anybody wanna fuck?") Technology makes such instant sexual connections possible. There are threads in which users exchange their names on other anonymous apps known as places for sexting and the sharing of nudes. Sometimes the language of such posts is reminiscent of the language of porn, riddled with disparaging words for women and girls. At first I found such posts jarring, but after a while I sort of got used to them, and they didn't seem that remarkable anymore. On social media, things which once might have been considered outrageous or disturbing come to seem normal very quickly through widespread repetition.

And then, one Saturday night in October 2015, I was on my phone, scrolling through Yik Yak and not reading a book, when I heard about something which even blasé Yik Yakkers were finding shocking. "Oh my God, Syracusesnap." "LMFAO Syracusesnap." "What's Syracusesnap?" people asked. Everybody wanted to know. Everybody had to know.

Syracusesnap was a Snapchat Story, a series of pictures or videos on Snapchat which stay viewable for twenty-four hours rather than the usual one to ten seconds per Snap. On Snapchat, famously launched in 2011 by three fraternity brothers from Stanford, Stories have become the most popular feature, with more than a billion viewed daily, according to the company. But few go viral. Within hours of its creation, Syracusesnap was being followed by college students and teenagers across the country. "Notoriety for the Story circulated faster than a *Gossip Girl* post," said The Tab, a college news website, and the only news organization to write about this. In an era which has seen an almost total erosion of privacy, there are still things which exist only in the world of young people, hiding in plain sight, online, and Syracusesnap was one of them.

"Soon it wasn't just Syracuse [University] students jumping on the bandwagon," said The Tab. "Snaps from schools like Pitt, Cornell, and NYU were added to the story"—meaning that other schools were following Syracusesnap and contributing pictures to it. " 'Cuse is lit!' and 'Wish we went to 'Cuse!' were among some of the captions featured," said The Tab. "Everyone add @Syracusesnap on Snapchat. You're welcome," someone tweeted. What was causing the excitement?

Syracusesnap featured pictures of kids in college dorm rooms drinking and doing drugs, but what was getting it all this attention were its many images of naked girls. Girls having sex. Sex with boys, sex with girls. The sex with boys was almost always in a standing, bent-over position, the girls' heads pointing toward the ground. Some of these shots were adorned with cartoon pictures of footballs and references to Syracuse's annual "Orange Central" homecoming and reunion week. It was as if some twisted public relations expert had melded pornography and school spirit to make Syracuse look like the best party school ever. But more on that later.

There were pictures of girls' breasts and girls' behinds, many where the girls were lying prone on a bed or on the floor, their faces hidden. There was a picture of a boy holding two girls' bodies on his shoulders, their behinds, in identical black thongs, facing the camera, his dumbstruck face encased with butt cheeks. "Snap whore," said a picture of a girl Snapchatting, her cleavage prominently showing.

There had been scandalous college Snapchat Stories before; in fact, such accounts can be found at colleges across the country. They're a sort of rebellious parody of Snapchat's Campus Stories, another feature on the app which many schools sponsor and monitor, and which typically shows students in their fun-filled and inspiring moments—looking joyful in the stands at winning football games, attending lectures.

In 2015, Arizona State University's SunDevil_Nation became notorious for its shots of students brandishing bags of weed and snorting cocaine. UCLAyak, named in homage to Yik Yak, had sexually explicit photos and videos cycling "every few seconds," according to the *Daily Bruin,* the University of California–Los Angeles paper. The anonymous psychobiology student who created the account told the *Bruin* he wasn't surprised at the nudity: "It was just a matter of time. That's what Snapchat is for." He said he suspected that some of the videos on other rogue campus accounts were staged, created to shock. Snapchat's Community Guidelines prohibit sexually explicit content, and the company routinely deletes Snapchat Stories that violate its policies, but as soon as they're banned, they often just reappear with a different handle.

So what made Syracusesnap go viral? As the Saturday night wore on and more kids were alerting one another to its scandalous appeal, the Story became more hard-core. There was a picture of boys doing coke off girls' behinds. There was a picture of two girls doing what are known as "butt things" to each other. "Syracusesnap is insane lmao," tweeted @Alexus_x30. "Okei, everyone on Syracusesnap need JESUS," tweeted @vmankss. "If my parents saw syracusesnap they would make me transfer immediately," tweeted @lexhallmark. "I've been scarred for life by adding syracusesnap omg my eyes," tweeted @t__victoria.

As I watched the story of this Story playing out on my phone, I was struck by how rife it was with themes that had been coming up in my reporting on girls and social media. There was the viral element, the wildfire aspect of something that races around online, the feeling that there's something out there that must be known and shared, lest you be left out of the conversation. There was the sexual nature of what was being shared, and the fact that it was centering on the naked images of young women, some of them perhaps teenage girls. There was the commenting on this content in a gossiping, derisive way, criticizing the girls for their sexual behavior, or "slut-shaming."

On Yik Yak, users discussed the "ho-ishness" of the girls. It was the girls in the shots, rather than the boys, who were called out for their alleged indecency. Yik Yak is anonymous, but it seemed to be both young women and men who were either directly or indirectly judging the girls for acting "slutty." The girls were mocked and psychoanalyzed. "Going to guess that the girls on syracusesnap don't have very good relationships with their fathers," tweeted @chief_keef_jon. Of course all of this was being said without anyone ever asking how it was that the sexually explicit pictures of these girls had been obtained. Had they been leaked? It was another subject that had come up frequently in my interviews with girls—the cyberbullying of girls for the sending of nudes which might have been intended only for an intimate partner.

When a picture appeared of two girls having a physical fight, Syracusesnap began to show signs of being different from other unofficial Campus Stories. Violence was not a typical characteristic of such accounts, but girl-on-girl aggression is a common theme in today's popular movies and TV shows, and some social media users seemed to find it entertaining. "OMFG catfight LOL." But when Syracusesnap showed a picture of a boy seemingly threatening a girl with violence (their faces were not shown), even nonchalant Yik Yakkers started to recoil. "To the guy that put his hands on that girl on Syracusesnap, I hope you get your ass beat," someone posted.

And yet when Snapchat shut the Story down and banned it, sometime the following day, there was a scramble to find out where it had gone—where could it be seen, this thing that everyone was talking about? "Yeti," "Yeti," Yakkers posted on threads. "What's Yeti?" people asked.

Yeti - Campus Stories is a mobile app launched in 2015, a sort of hybrid of Snapchat and Yik Yak, seemingly inspired by the trend of salacious Campus Stories. Its page on the Apple iTunes store warns that users must be seventeen to download it (but who checks?), and advises that its content may include "Infrequent / Mild Realistic Violence" and "Frequent / Intense Mature / Suggestive Themes," as well as drug use. When Yeti was launched, The Daily Dot website called it "an X-Rated Snapchat clone" and predicted it would "[set] the stage for inter-college competition. Which frat rages hardest? Whose spring break is bawdiest? And whose coeds are the hottest?" Tumblr blogs soon appeared of "Yeti babes" and the "hottest" "Girls of Yeti - Campus Stories," with pages of nudes and semi-nudes the blogs' creators claimed were "snapshots" and "screenshots" from the app. When I e-mailed Yeti's director of communications, twenty-three-year-old Ben Kaplan, asking whether these photos had actually appeared on Yeti and were consensually shared there, he said he'd never seen these blogs before and that Yeti had "no involvement in them, whatsoever."

Kaplan said, "Unfortunately there is no software in the world (that I'm aware of) that detects whether or not the subject of a photograph gave consent to the photographer." His response made me wonder, Well, why wasn't the question of whether nudes were consensually shared being addressed by software developers?

What's weird about all this is that when you actually look at Yeti, its content seems relatively mild. Browsing through the accounts of NYU, Texas A&M, Penn State, and other schools, I saw reams of the usual sexy selfies (duckface and cleavage), as well as pictures of food and students acting silly, and, yes, showing off their drugs (bongs and cocaine). But there weren't any outright nudes or images of sex acts that I could see. In fact, when Syracusesnap announced that it had moved to Yeti after its wild debut, the shocking images never showed up there. So what did it all mean?

A source in the Syracuse University administration says he believes that Syracusesnap was actually created by Yeti. No one on social media seemed to suspect this; however, as soon as it was suggested to me, it didn't seem impossible. The final image on Syracusesnap displayed the Yeti logo—vertical multicolored bars like a television test pattern. "Snapchat is banning our account," the message over the logo said. "We are moving the story over to YETI CAMPUS STORIES, Available in the Apple/Google Playstore." It looked like an ad.

So was Syracusesnap just a marketing ploy? Had Yeti instigated the discussion about the account on Yik Yak and Twitter? Ben Kaplan said on e-mail that Yeti had nothing to do with Syracusesnap; he said he'd never heard of it. He said he thought the use of the Yeti logo was "possibly to decrease confusion during the transfer?" "Mature Yeti sites" were handled by campus "moderators" who edited out "distasteful content," Kaplan wrote—which might account for why the pornographic images on Syracusesnap had vanished. When I asked him about the contrast in Yeti's rather tame content with its warnings of sex and violence, Kaplan became emphatic. "Yeti was in no way designed to be an 'X-Rated Snapchat,'" he said. "Yeti is a live feed of EVERYTHING happening on campus."

So who made Syracusesnap? When I talked to Hannah Malach, a Syracuse student and the writer of the piece in The Tab, she said that no one on campus had been identified as the creator of the account, as far as she knew. I asked if she had heard of Yeti before Syracusesnap, and she said, "I hadn't, and many people are still unaware of it." Some of the college students I'd interviewed also said they'd never heard of Yeti - Campus Stories. Its Twitter and Instagram accounts, on that

October night, had fewer than 6,000 and 3,000 followers, respectively, although it had been around for almost a year.

But however the account was generated, it didn't seem to matter to those who had enjoyed its pornographic images. "The Syracusesnap Story was the epitome of 'fun at college,'" a freshman named Chris told The Tab. "It illustrated the usage of drugs, glorified pornography, and sexual exploits, as well." It's clear that what had made Syracusesnap a hit were its many pictures of naked girls—girls having sex, a girl being threatened with assault, and girls assaulting each other. There's no proof of where any of these images came from, from this side of the screen. But there they were. And they got people talking, and watching, and clicking, and wanting more.

What do we mean when we talk about the culture of social media? I think it's important to talk about it, because, for most American girls, social media is where they live. "We're on it twenty-four/seven," said a thirteen-year-old girl in Montclair, New Jersey. "It's all we do." As a teenage girl might say, this isn't *literally* true. Girls go to school, they play sports and hang out with their friends, they take care of siblings; many have jobs; they volunteer and pursue hobbies and read—although kids are reading a lot less, which some studies blame on their increasing engagement with technology.

The complaint you hear from parents and teachers is, "They're on it all the time." When pressed, many of these same adults will admit that they're checking their social media quite often, too. We've all become tethered to our mobile devices in ways we never would have imagined possible just a few years ago. But of all groups of Americans, teenage girls are in fact the number one users of social media.

In 2015, 88 percent of American teens ages thirteen to seventeen had access to a mobile phone, and 73 percent had smartphones, according to the Pew Research Center. Ninety-two percent were going online from a mobile device daily, and 24 percent were online "almost constantly." Girls ages thirteen to seventeen are slightly more likely than boys to have access to a smartphone, computer, or tablet; and "teenage girls use social media sites and platforms—particularly visually-oriented ones—for sharing more than their male counterparts do," according to Pew. The numbers of girls on social media on a daily basis run high regardless of race, education, and household income, or whether they are living in urban, rural, or suburban areas. In 2015, Facebook, Instagram, Snapchat, Twitter, and online pinboards such as Pinterest were the most popular sites for girls. Girls in 2015 were exchanging anywhere from 30 to more than 100 texts per day, according to studies.

Just why girls are on social media "all the time," and what they're doing there, are the subjects of my investigation; but that they're on it an inordinate amount of the time is important to note before beginning to explore these questions. Are girls addicted to social media? If you ask them, many will say they are. The words "addicted" and "addiction," "obsessed" and "obsessing," came up again and again in my interviews with more than 200 teenage girls as they talked about their use of their smartphones and consuming media and using social media. How else can you characterize an activity that, depending on which study you reference, occupies from nine to eleven hours of your day?

Among researchers, the jury's still out on whether social media addiction is truly an addiction in the way of dependence on drugs and other substances, although it's becoming increasingly well established that social media use lights up the reward centers in our brains, causing our hormones to dance. Girls talk about the "dopamine jolt" some researchers say their brains experience when they get "likes" on their posts and photos; and if they don't know of the studies, they know the feeling of pleasure associated with seeing their pictures reap online rewards; they also know the feeling of letdown they get when their posts are ignored or, worse, are ridiculed or attacked.

It's an extraordinary new reality, and it's happened so fast; for the first time, most American girls are engaged in the same activity most of the time. And this seismic shift in how girls spend their time is having a profound effect on the way they think and act, as well as on how they make friends, the way they date, and their introduction to the world of sex. But what are the effects? When we talk about social media, we say we're "going on" it, similar to the way we talk about going on a trip. We seem to experience it as a sort of mental journey to another place; but this isn't a neutral place, it's one created by businesspeople, and much of it emanates from Silicon Valley.

I don't think we can talk about the culture of social media, this place where girls are spending most of their time, without talking about the culture of Silicon Valley. In popular myth this is a place where boy geniuses create magical communication tools which bring us all closer together, tools which prove so irresistible to masses of people across the globe that the boy geniuses earn millions and billions of dollars— money with which they then invest in the ideas and futures of other boy geniuses. The popular myth isn't very far from reality. According to the Department of Labor, 70 percent of the workforce at the top ten Silicon Valley firms in 2012 was male and 63 percent was white. Of the executives and top managers at those companies, 83 percent were male and white.

A 2015 study by LinkedIn found that "software engineering teams in tech have proportionally fewer women than several non-tech industries: namely, healthcare, retail, government, education, and nonprofits." In 2009, the National Center for Women & Information Technology reported that 56 percent of women with STEM expertise leave the industry midway into their careers. "They are seeing they cannot have the careers they want in this industry," Karen Catlin, a former vice president of Adobe Systems, told *Fusion* in 2015. With the exception of some notable examples, such as Sheryl Sandberg, COO of Facebook; Marissa Mayer, CEO of Yahoo!; and Meg Whitman, CEO of Hewlett Packard, there are few highly placed female executives in Silicon Valley. In the digital revolution, which has provided so many job opportunities and seen the start of so many businesses and empires, men have reaped most of the profits.

And the culture of Silicon Valley is a male-dominated culture, some say a "frat boy" culture, populated by "brogrammers" and "tech bros." "In inverse ratio to the forward-looking technology the community produces, it is stunningly backward when it comes to gender relations," wrote Nina Burleigh in a 2015 *Newsweek* piece, "What Silicon Valley Thinks of Women." "Google 'Silicon Valley' and 'frat boy culture' and you'll find dozens of pages of articles and links to mainstream news articles, blogs, screeds, letters, videos and tweets about threats of violence, sexist jokes and casual misogyny, plus reports of gender-based hiring and firing, major-league sexual harassment lawsuits and a financing system that rewards young men and shortchanges women." In

2014, a group of female leaders in the tech industry penned "An Open Letter on Feminism in Tech" in which they described the hostile atmosphere they'd encountered in the industry. "We've been harassed on mailing lists and called 'whore'/'cunt' without any action being taken against aggressors," the letter said. "We're constantly asked 'if you write any code' when speaking about technical topics and giving technical presentations, despite just having given a talk on writing code. We've been harassed at these same conferences in person and online about our gender, looks, and technical expertise."

"It's a community in which the porn-inspired, 'drading,'" or drunken, "college tweets of Evan Spiegel, the CEO of Snapchat, go public," Burleigh wrote, "where a CEO's history of domestic violence has no repercussions but female executives get fired for tweeting about sexist jokes they overhear. It's a place," she continued, "where companies routinely staff conference booths with scantily clad 'code-babes' and where women are so routinely sexually harassed at conferences that codes of conduct have become de rigueur—and the subject of endless misogynistic jokes on Twitter." Burleigh likened Silicon Valley today to the egregiously sexist world of the go-go '80s depicted in *The Wolf of Wall Street*, noting that while Wall Street these days seems "tamer," in Silicon Valley, "misogyny continues unabated."

So what impact does the culture of Silicon Valley have on the place that girls are experiencing all day, most days, on their phones? While not every one of the thousands of social media sites and apps reflects the tech industry's frat house atmosphere, of course, it would be blind to say that none of them do; and it would be naïve to say that some of the most popular apps, some of the ones most often used by girls, don't.

You could start with the concept of "hot or not." "Hot or not" is a prevailing social media conceit, first seen online in 2000, with the launch of the photo-rating site Hot or Not by two Silicon Valley–based software engineers and Berkeley graduates, James Hong and Jim Young. The site grew out of an argument the two were having about whether a certain woman was attractive, or "hot." Hong and Young created a way for strangers to look at a picture of a woman's face and vote on how she measured up. The idea was also the basis of Facemash, the precursor to Facebook, a campus rating site created by Mark Zuckerberg in 2003, when he was still a Harvard sophomore. Two of the founders of You-

Tube, guy Silicon Valley software engineers who met at the University of Illinois at Urbana–Champaign, have said that Hot or Not was the inspiration for what they originally thought would be just a video version of the game, as well. Much of the culture of social media is, in a way, an ongoing expression of "hot or not," liking or rejecting people and things, and the physical appeal of women and girls.

So embedded in the culture of Silicon Valley is "hot or not" that it became the subject of satire with Titstare, a fictional mobile app that was presented at TechCrunch's annual Disrupt Hackathon in San Francisco in 2013. Its creators, two young men in their twenties, described Titstare as "an app where you take photos of yourself staring at tits." Titstare incited a brief uproar online for its outlandish theme, but some on Twitter called the joke "brilliant" and "pretty funny." "Sexism is a major problem in the tech industry," acknowledged TechCrunch, the tech industry news website owned by AOL, apologizing for the "misogynistic" presentation.

"Beautiful," "gorgeous," "sexy," "hot" are conventional responses to selfies in the culture of social media, responses which many girls seek as they spend minutes or hours of their day preparing themselves to be photographed and photographing themselves to the best advantage. There are typically more graphically sexual comments, too, which many girls feel they are expected to show appreciation for, or just ignore. And then there are different kinds of comments, critical or degrading assessments of how a girl appears on-screen, all based on an array of motivations, from personal animus to jealousy to slut-shaming.

For many girls, the pressure to be considered "hot" is felt on a nearly continual basis online. The sites with which they most commonly interact encourage them to post images of themselves, and employ the "liking" feature, with which users can judge their appearance and, in effect, rate them. When girls post their pictures on Instagram or Snapchat or Facebook, they know they will be judged for their "hotness," and in a quantifiable way, with numbers of likes. Social media, which gave us selfies, seems to encourage an undue focus on appearance for everyone, but for girls, this focus is combined with a pervasive sexualization of girls in the wider culture, an overarching trend which is already having serious consequences.

A landmark 2007 report by the American Psychological Association

(APA) found girls being sexualized—or treated as "objects of sexual desire . . . as things rather than as people with legitimate sexual feelings of their own"—in virtually every form of media, including movies, television, music videos and lyrics, video games and the Internet, advertising, cartoons, clothing, and toys. Even Dora the Explorer, once a cute, square-bodied child, got a makeover to make her look more svelte and "hot." The APA surveyed multiple studies which found links between the sexualization of girls and a wide range of mental health issues, including low self-esteem, anxiety, depression, eating disorders, cutting, even cognitive dysfunction. Apparently, thinking about being hot makes it hard to think: "Chronic attention to physical appearance leaves fewer cognitive resources available for other mental and physical activities," said the APA report.

It isn't that girls and women haven't been exploited for their sexuality before; of course they have; but sexualization has become a prevailing mode, influencing how girls see themselves, as well as how they present themselves. The APA did not account for why this damaging sexualization of girls has occurred; it's another one of the questions I'll be exploring here; but the immediate and most prominent influence to consider, I think, is online porn.

The adoption of the Internet in American life is inextricably tied to porn, an industry with revenues that jumped into the billions of dollars when it moved online. In 2015, porn sites were among the most popular in cyberspace, accounting for up to 35 percent of Internet traffic. Porn is more available now than it has ever been, and for the first time it is readily available to everyone, including kids. Studies have reported that American children start seeing online porn as young as age six, and the majority of boys and girls have watched it before they turn eighteen. Some research says the number of kids who have viewed online porn, either deliberately or accidentally, is about 40 percent, while some puts the number as high as in the 90 percent range for boys and the 60 percent range for girls. No one seems to think the size of porn's underage audience is insignificant.

A normalizing trend minimizes porn's effects. American researchers, hindered in conducting studies by the fact that in the United States it is illegal for children to view porn, argue that not enough is known.

"We need a lot more research to keep tabs on this phenomenon and to separate hype from reality," sociologist David Finkelhor, director of the University of New Hampshire's Crimes Against Children Research Center, said on the APA website. Finkelhor pointed to positive developments in teenage behavior by way of questioning whether viewing porn has an adverse influence on kids; for example, the teenage pregnancy rate is down, and some studies say that teenagers are having less sex.

But teenage pregnancy rates began to drop significantly in the 1990s, with safe-sex education and increased condom use (although American teens are still getting pregnant more often than in other industrialized countries). Moreover, some research has found that respondents in studies are inclined to misreport the number of sex partners they have had, for a variety of reasons, including women's fear of being judged or exposed. And the more important question here may be not how many sex partners teenagers are having, but what attitudes about sex they have, and how they are treating each other in a sexual context, both on and off social media. In other words, how is porn affecting teenage sexual behavior?

Porn itself isn't necessarily the problem; since the 1970s, feminists have argued that female-centric porn can be a source of sexual liberation. But much of the online porn children and teenagers are most likely to see is characterized by what looks like violence against women—not necessarily the violence of bondage or sadomasochistic sex, but violence in which men dominate and control women, insult them, and sometimes hurt them physically. The words the porn industry itself uses to describe the scenes in its videos tell the story: women are "pounded," "railed," and "jackhammered," called "cunts," "sluts," "bitches," and "whores." Choking, slapping, and "cum shots to the face" are standard moves.

"A lot of online pornography is violent," said a 2014 article in *The New York Times,* "Does Porn Hurt Children?" "Much of it merely demonstrates the astounding breadth of sexual appetites out there." Online porn is also characterized by fetishism. When people say, "Kids see everything today," it's true, they do, online, including, sadly, child porn. A 2008 study in *CyberPsychology & Behavior* found that "considerable numbers of boys and girls had seen images of paraphilic or criminal sexual activity, including child pornography and sexual violence, at least once before the age of 18." Disturbingly, many of the actresses in popular online porn are in fact teenagers or styled to appear as young as teens. In 2014, the mega porn site Pornhub, with 18 billion visits and 79 billion videos viewed that year, reported that its number one search was for "Teen."

Rape and gang rape are common scenarios in online porn as well. A search for "violent sex" on the Internet turns up millions of results, including videos tagged "violent rape porn" and "cruel sex." In 2013, *The Washington Post* reported on Rapetube, a site "urging users to share what it called 'fantasy' videos of sexual attacks." Garth Bruen, a security fellow at the Digital Citizens Alliance, said the *Post*, had "discovered dozens of similar sites offering disturbing variations—attacks on drunken women, on lesbians, on schoolgirls—to anyone with a credit card. Some made clear that the clips were fictional, but other sites had the word 'real' in their titles. At least a few touted videos that he feared might show actual crimes."

Some psychologists worry about the effects of such porn, or any porn, on boys' attitudes toward women and girls, as well as girls' view of their own sexuality. "Perhaps the most troubling impact of pornography on children and young people is its influence on sexual violence," wrote Michael Flood, a sociologist and Future Fellow at the Australian Research Council. "A wide range of studies on the effects of pornography have been conducted among young people aged 18 to 25, as well as older populations," Flood said. "Across these, there is consistent and reliable evidence that exposure to pornography is related to male sexual aggression against women . . . In a study of Canadian teenagers with an average age of 14, there was a correlation between boys' frequent consumption of pornography and their agreement with the idea that it is acceptable to hold a girl down and force her to have sex . . . Among U.S. boys and girls aged 11 to 16, greater exposure to R- and X-rated films was related to stronger acceptance of sexual harassment." This is all the more troubling when considering how, for many teenagers, porn seems to have become a kind of sex ed. In Britain and Australia, researchers have found that kids turn to porn to get information about sex.

There's a great deal of pressure on teenage girls today to be considered "sex-positive," a term arising from the sex-positive movement encouraging sexual pleasure and experimentation; being sex-positive is often seen as free and feminist. But being "sex-positive" and "porn-positive" aren't necessarily the same things, although they are sometimes conflated by sex-positivity advocates. "You can spin it any way you want, but porn has an effect on how people behave sexually," asserts John T. Chirban, a clinical instructor in psychology at Harvard Medical School and psychologist who treats adolescents in Boston. "With porn, you're not looking at the meaning and value of a whole human being. Girls take away from it the message that their most worthy attribute is their sexual hotness." The primacy of hotness can be seen in the familiar popularity among girls of a kind of porn-star look, apparent in selfies hallmarked by glistening pursed lips and the exposure of butts and cleavage, or "booty pics" and "tit pics."

In many other countries, the effect of online porn on children is of widespread concern. In 2013, Britain's four largest Internet service providers agreed to institute "family-friendly filters" that automatically block pornographic websites unless households chose to receive them. The initiative was inspired in part by studies done in Britain on the impact of porn on kids, and promoted by the government of former Prime Minister David Cameron, who in 2013 gave a controversial speech in which he spoke of an alarming "corrosion of childhood" he claimed was the result of children being exposed to pornography. Whatever one thinks of Cameron's conservative politics, his speech echoed talks I've had with teachers and school administrators across the country, including a Brooklyn principal, Maura Lorenzen, who lamented, "Childhood is gone. They have access to this world of adults they feel they have to participate in." Cameron also spoke of the trend of "young people who think it's normal to send pornographic material as a prelude to dating." What he was referring to, I think, was a link between porn and the culture of social media.

Is there sexism in the lives of American girls? I wasn't aware of just how much until I started talking to girls about their experiences online, which happened sort of by accident one night in Los Angeles in 2013. I was there on a reporting trip after my boss, Graydon Carter, the editor of *Vanity Fair*, asked me to do a story on girls for the magazine. There had been a run of high-profile stories in the news about the cyberbullying, campus rapes, and suicides of girls, often with their victimizers filming their crimes and sharing the footage online. Were these isolated cases, we wanted to know, or indicative of a more widespread, menacing atmosphere? Was there a crisis in the world of girls, and if so, what were the factors behind it?

When I sat down with some girls at the Grove, a shopping mall in L.A., all they wanted to talk about was social media. "Social media is destroying our lives," one of the girls said, as you'll read in these pages (where I've included some of my reporting from that story as well as another in *Vanity Fair* on dating apps and their impact on love, sex, and romance). "So why don't you go off it?" I asked. "Because then we would have no life," said another girl. It was one of the first things that was said to me at the beginning of my reporting process, and I think it could still sum up the conundrum many girls today feel they're facing.

As a side note, I use the word "girls" here to refer to interview subjects, again, between the ages of thirteen and nineteen. There's been some debate of late about the meaning and validity of words describing gender; some argue that we should select from a range of choices that would avoid treating gender as an immutable binary. And I get that. And while I acknowledge the feelings of those who say we could even debate what "female" is, I use "girls" in a purely descriptive if not positive way, and with the permission of the girls I interviewed. In considering the effects of sexism and misogyny on the culture of social media, I focus mostly on issues and questions surrounding heterosexual norms of behavior; for while not all the girls I interviewed were heterosexual, they were still dealing with a culture in which these norms exerted influence.

Over the two and a half years I spent reporting, I spoke to girls from different socioeconomic backgrounds, of different races, sexual orientations, and gender identities. I identify their races per the U.S. Census: black, white, Latino, Asian, Asian Indian, Native American, and again, with the permission of the girls so identified. When the subject of race came up in our conversations, I included that in my reporting. I've changed their names and some identifying details as a way of protecting their privacy. Their ages here are their ages when we spoke. Most of the time, when I spoke with girls ages sixteen and under, their parents knew about our interviews and sometimes sat in on them. I met girls in public places, through parents, teachers, school counselors and administrators, and friends. I met them at high schools and middle schools, at malls and movie theaters and Starbucks. I met them on college campuses, at a Houston beauty pageant, and on spring break.

One of the things that continually struck me over the course of my reporting was the similarity of girls' experiences on social media regardless of their race or background. The homogeneity of the technology and widespread use of the same apps seem to be creating, again, a certain culture. And a lot of what girls had to say about this culture involved an experience of what can only be described as sexism— a word of which many girls, especially in the beginning of my process, were unaware. "What's sexism?" asked a girl in Williamsburg, Virginia. "Is that when somebody likes sex?" When I asked her and her friends if they'd ever heard of feminism, another girl said, "Is that when a boy acts like a girl?"

But those same girls are not unfamiliar with these words now, as I learned in a later conversation. In 2014, a surge of feminism rose up online like Hokusai's *Great Wave off Kanagawa*. It all began in January, in the days after Elliot Rodger, age twenty-two, a rich kid from Calabasas, California, killed six people and injured fourteen others before committing suicide in Isla Vista, near the campus of the University of California, Santa Barbara. He had gone there seeking women to punish for their failure to appreciate him and have sex with him, he said. His 141-page manifesto, "My Twisted World: The Story of Elliot Rodger," which he posted online, was a misogynistic screed. Rodger saw women as "flawed," "like a plague," "incapable of reason or thinking rationally," undeserving of "any rights." He envisioned a world in which he would starve women to death in concentration camps.

The response to this event on social media was like an explosion. Suddenly women and girls all over the world were raising their voices, sharing their experiences of sexual violence, harassment, and discrimination. And they were doing it on social media, with the hashtag #yesallwomen. It was a powerful example of how social media could be used as an activist tool, to protest sexism, as much as it was a place where sexism was being felt. Rebecca Solnit, writing on MotherJones .com, described this as a moment in which "you could see change happen." I could see the change myself.

Girls I interviewed in 2013 were much more resigned to the sexism in their lives than girls I spoke to in 2014. As the year went on and women and girls continued to speak out, online, girls seemed to wake up. They were talking about the same things—"savages" and "fuck-boys," slut-shaming and a punishing double standard—but they were expressing themselves with a new and critical perspective which many said they'd learned from posts and articles they'd read on social media.

It's not that anything material in their lives had necessarily changed, but their thinking was changing, and they seemed to feel emboldened to talk about things in a way they might not have, even as recently as a year before, when such talk might have gotten them labeled "feminists"— and nobody wanted to be a feminist, whatever a feminist might be. Many of their favorite celebrities—Katy Perry, Taylor Swift, Kelly Clarkson, Shailene Woodley, and others—shrank away from being labeled feminists back then. "I'm not a feminist," Lady Gaga said in 2009.

But in 2014, something changed, and girls' role models were starting to embrace the word, and, more significantly, the idea that there was inequality in the lives of women and girls that needed to be addressed. Emma Watson delivered a widely publicized speech at the United Nations, saying, "Fighting for women's rights has too often become synonymous with man-hating. If there is one thing I know for certain, it is that this has to stop." Watson urged men and boys to join women and girls in becoming "advocates for gender equality." Taylor Swift switched teams, throwing in with the feminists. And then Beyoncé performed at the MTV Video Music Awards in front of a twelve-foot sign reading FEMINIST. "That was a big, big thing," said a fourteen-year-old girl in New York. "It was like, Beyoncé, wow."

And yet it was in late 2015 that you saw something like Syracuse-snap. The culture of social media churns away, seeming to pay very little attention, so far, to the protestations of feminists or anyone who objects to its troubling aspects. And girls suffer. On a daily, sometimes hourly, basis, on their phones, they encounter things which are offensive and potentially damaging to their well-being and sense of self-esteem. I sat next to a fourteen-year-old girl on a New York City bus one day and asked her to show me what she was looking at on her phone. As we traveled down Second Avenue, the posts on her Twitter timeline included a meme that was circulating of a picture of Albert Einstein emblazoned with the words "WHAT WAS THE SMARTEST THING TO HAVE EVER COME OUT OF A WOMAN'S MOUTH? MY DICK." "I guess it's supposed to be funny," the girl said uncertainly.

This isn't a book about how girls are victims. "Victim" isn't a word I'd use to describe the kind of girls I've seen, surviving and thriving in an atmosphere which has become very hostile to them, much of the time. How can this be, when girls are graduating from college in higher numbers than ever before, when they're becoming leaders in their chosen fields in greater numbers? From what we hear, American girls are among the most privileged and successful girls in the world. But tell that to a thirteen-year-old who gets called a "slut" and feels she can't walk into a school classroom because everybody will be staring at her, texting about her on their phones. "We need to puzzle out why women have made more strides in the public arena than in the private arena," says Elizabeth Armstrong, a professor of sociology at the University of Michigan who specializes in sexuality and gender. Women, and girls as well. We need also to examine the ways in which girls sometimes echo the sexism they experience in their dealings with one another. For it isn't only boys who slut-shame, not only boys who hold girls to a double standard.

As I traveled and reported, stories in the news continued appearing which reflected what I was hearing from girls. As I'm finishing this introduction, another high school, in Cañon City, Colorado, has been "rocked," as they say, by revelations of a "sexting ring"—known to girls as "slut pages." "The high school football team appears to have been ground zero for the scandal," reported the *Deseret News National*. Technology, again, played a key role in the case, with "vault apps" serving to mask the collection of 300 to 400 nude photographs of mostly girls among at least 100 students. The boy with the largest stash of photographs was referred to as "the pimp of pictures," according to *The New York Times*. The mother of a student at the school complained to the paper that her daughter, a junior, "had been 'propositioned by multiple guys' during her freshman year. 'She received unsolicited photos from guys, which she immediately deleted.' "

"Sexism has filtered into new arenas that adults don't see or understand because they're not using social media the same way," said Katie, a student at Barnard. "They think, Oh, how can there be anything wrong here if it's just Snapchat or Instagram, it's just a game." But if this is a game, it's unlike any other we've ever played. And the stakes for American girls could not be higher.

Chapter One

13

Montclair, New Jersey

"SEND NOODZ."

The boy sent the message in the middle of the day, when she was walking home from school. He sent it via direct message on Instagram, in the same shaky, childlike font as the new Drake album ("IF YOURE READING THIS ITS TOO LATE").

Sophia stared at her phone.

"Wait what???" she responded.

No answer.

She continued along the empty streets. It was a warm spring day and the wide green lawns were full of blooming trees. Montclair was a pretty place, and it was safe, so a lot of kids walked home from school. She'd been with friends, but they had already peeled off and gone inside their houses, so she was all alone. She hoped to see someone she knew, hopefully a girl she could tell: "Oh my God, you know Zack, he asked me for nudes!" And: "What should I do?"

But there was no one around. She thought about texting someone—most things, observations, gossip, jokes, were shared right away, but this seemed like something new. Something almost . . . private. Secret. That rare thing, something no one else could know.

She had heard of boys asking girls for nudes before, but it had never happened to her. This was her first time. She didn't know how to respond, or if she should respond. Should she be outraged? Shocked? Her first reaction was: "I was like, *Whoa*, he finds me attractive? *That's* kind of strange. I never knew he found me attractive . . ."

She thought about the boy. He was thirteen, the same age as she, a boy from her eighth-grade class. He was a boy like other boys—he talked loud and rough and wore baggy shorts and snapback hats and had a swaggering demeanor like Justin Bieber, whom he probably would have dissed. He was "cute," "but kind of gross."

She wondered if he liked her. "He never likes anything of mine on Instagram, but why would he ask me that if he hadn't been thinking about me? If I wasn't *in his mind?* Boys aren't gonna come out and just say, 'I like you,' 'cause they don't do that. They have, like, their own *language . . .*"

When she got to her house, a Victorian house with a wraparound porch, the place where boys had once come calling for girls, she went upstairs to her room. Plugged her phone into the charger. It was almost out of juice. She'd been up most of the night texting under the covers so if her mother walked in she wouldn't see—texting friends in her group chat who were still awake, sending words and emojis and giggling over inside jokes. And then during the day she had texted all through school. She woke up tired a lot of the time, but, she said, "I just drink a Red Bull."

She went into the bathroom and looked in the mirror. Peered at herself. Pursed her lips. Stuck her tongue out to the side, Miley-style. Tossed her hair. She knew that she was "attractive," so she wasn't all that surprised that the boy had asked her for nudes. "I get, like, a hundred likes on all my pictures and people comment, like, '*Gorgeous . . .*'"

But she wondered what it would be like if someone actually had a naked picture of her, and she wondered what that picture would be. "Not like I was gonna *do* it—oh my *God*, no—but if you *did*, like, what would you send so it looked good, and not ratchet?"

She wondered if the boy had thought about kissing her. If he was going to be her first kiss. She'd been wondering what it would be like to kiss a boy, to have one want you so bad he would take you into the park or even his room and press his lips against yours, wrapping his arms around you, holding you close.

She heard her phone ding from inside the bathroom. A text alert. She ran to see. It was the boy, responding to her message:

"I really need this 'cause I have to win a bet I wont show anyone," he wrote.

"What serious who else did you ask," she texted, her heart beating fast.

"nobody lol I need it from you please"

"Why"

"so theres this high school kid I think hes a senior who hooks me up with lq"—booze—"he said hell get us as much as we need cause hes rich if me and jack show that we can get nudes no disrespect im just asking you cause youre the prettiest girl and the best person to ask"

She stared at the phone, thought about it a moment, and wrote: "lol"

New York, New York

At the Barnes & Noble on Fifth Avenue in Manhattan in May 2015, Kim Kardashian was launching her latest book, *Selfish*, a collection of selfies and nudes. It was more than 400 pages of Kim staring into the camera, pursing her lips, looking sultry and suggestive. It was Kim naked in a bathroom mirror, naked in a bedroom mirror, clutching her naked breasts, leaning naked over a bathroom sink, sticking her famous behind up in the air; Kim leaning naked over a bed in the grainy dark, Kim in lingerie and bathing suits, lounging beside electric-blue swimming pools, doing "leg shots."

"Oh my God oh my God oh my God oh my God," said a thirteen-year-old girl waiting in the line snaking through the store.

There were pictures of Kim from 2006, when she was still an L.A. party girl and friend of Paris Hilton's, to 2014, after she had become one of the most famous women in the world. In those eight years, which had seen the introduction of the iPhone in 2007, and the global spread of social media through mobile technology, Kim had become social media's biggest star. In 2006, she had just 856 friends on Myspace—where she announced in her profile, "I'm a PRINCESS and you're not so there!"—and now she had 31 million followers on Instagram, second only to Beyoncé, whom she would eclipse in a few months, climbing to number one. She had 34 million followers on Twitter, where she posted more selfies daily, most of which got thousands of favorites and retweets.

"I love her," said another girl in the store.

What was the meaning of Kim Kardashian? Why was she here, and why wouldn't she go? Why did anyone care about her, and how had she become so ubiquitous? Throughout the years of her ascendance, people had been trying to figure this out. Some seemed furious at her success, which in 2015 included TV shows, endorsement deals, makeup, fragrances, clothing lines, one of the most popular of all mobile apps—in which a Kim avatar showed you how to become as famous as she— and a net worth of $85 million. Still, she was called "vain," "shallow," "frivolous," "egotistical," "materialistic," and many other more vulgar insults in endless media pieces and online rants. "I have never heard more anger and dismay than when we announced that the people you are about to see were on our list," Barbara Walters told viewers before airing a segment on the Kardashian family in her 10 *Most Fascinating People* show of 2011. "You are all often described as famous for being famous," Walters leveled at sisters Kim, Khloé, Kourtney, and their mother, Kris, who sat before her in sleek couture. "You don't really act, you don't sing, you don't dance, you don't have any—forgive me—any talent."

The Kardashians tried, in their mild way, but they couldn't quite seem to explain to Walters, who had come of age at a different time, that this was actually the point—talent didn't matter much in becoming famous anymore. Or perhaps what served as talent had transformed. It was now enough to know how to become famous purely for the sake of fame.

"She's amazing," said another girl in Barnes & Noble.

The Kardashians, a family of American girls, had come on the scene, swept forward by the gown of Princess Kim, in a kind of perfect cultural storm: there was the fascination with fame that had always danced at the edges of American identity, and now, with the explosion of a celebrity news industry fueled by Internet blogs and TMZ, had taken over the aspirational longings of the young. A 2007 survey by the Pew Research Center found that 51 percent of eighteen- to twenty-five-year-olds said their most or second most important life goal was to become famous. Sixty-four percent said their number one goal was to become rich.

A girl waiting in line for Kim said, "I want her life."

There was reality television, which stoked a thirst for more and more intimate details of the lives of celebrities and newly minted reality show stars. And there was princess culture. For a generation of girls raised on the Disney corporation's multibillion-dollar line of so-called princess products, the five sisters of *Keeping Up with the Kardashians* were real-life princesses who lived in a Calabasas, California, castle, unabashedly focused on the pursuit of beauty treatments, expensive fun, and luxury brands—the latter a national fixation spawned in the "luxury revolution" of the last thirtysomething years, in which most of the wealth of the country had traveled into the hands of a few, with the rest of the population looking on longingly as the beneficiaries of a new Gilded Age flaunted their high-end stuff. And entertainment media, from *Lifestyles of the Rich and Famous* to *Keeping Up with the Kardashians,* provided them with ample opportunities to do just that.

"I get letters from little girls begging me to adopt them," Kim once told a reporter. The Kardashian lifestyle was the fulfillment of a new American dream that had been embraced by many girls and young women, unsurprisingly enough, at a time when everything around them supported it as an ideal: it was to be beautiful, famous, and rich, and to have amazing clothes, bags, and shoes and tens of millions of followers on social media. It was to get tens or even hundreds of thousands of likes on all your selfies.

"I want to take a selfie with her," a girl in Barnes & Noble said excitedly.

Behind the Kardashians' lifestyle, there was a mother, but it wasn't Kim; it was Kris Jenner, Kim's own mother and tireless manager, who took 10 percent of all her daughters' incomes. "My job is to take my family's fifteen minutes of fame and turn it into thirty," Kris once declared. That her family's fifteen minutes had begun with a leaked sex tape of her daughter and the singer Ray J didn't seem to give her pause; in fact, it was just after the release of the tape that Kris started shopping her family's reality show, a move she likened to "[making] some lemonade out of these lemons." The scandal which Paris Hilton had already endured wasn't much of a scandal anymore. Porn stars were writing best-selling books and appearing on *The Oprah Winfrey Show.*

For the biggest, darkest cloud in the perfect storm that brought Kim Kardashian rising out of the ocean of wannabe celebrities like Venus on a flip phone was the widespread consumption and normalization of online porn. In 2014, Pornhub reported in its "Year in Review" that Kim was number eight in the top ten most popular "porn stars" in the world.

"Kim, you're doing amazing, sweetie," Kris said in an iconic moment on *Keeping Up with the Kardashians,* in which Kim, naked except for jewelry and heels, is on her knees, arching her back, and posing as a photographer snaps pictures—as does Kris, with a little personal camera. The moment is striking in its depiction of another element of the cultural tempest that delivered us Kim: the hypersexualization of American girls and women.

"She's hot," said a boy waiting in line to see her.

"Is Kim Kardashian a feminist role model?" asked Jezebel in 2013. The website answered "no" and "nooooooooooooooooo." But already the worm of popular opinion was starting to turn. Kim was being touted as a "businesswoman." She was being called "powerful"—and didn't achieving power, any kind of power, by any means, make a woman a feminist? So blogs and think pieces argued. Was it Kim's marriage to a powerful music industry player and self-described "creative genius," Kanye West, or their joint appearance on the cover of *Vogue* in 2014— a nod from establishment media moving Kim onto the A-list—that began to mute her haters? Or was it that Kim's true talent, her skill at using social media—the real secret of her success, all along—was finally being recognized for the power it commanded?

"Something about Kim is very appealing to digital natives," Re/code founder Kara Swisher told *Rolling Stone* in 2015. Yes, and that something was becoming very clear: Kim successfully used the technological tools now available to almost everyone to get what everyone wanted. What she'd been doing relentlessly since the introduction of smartphones and before, now everybody was doing—using social media to self-promote, to craft an idealized online self; and girls coming of age in the second decade of the twenty-first century were using it to present a sexualized self. "My little cousin, she's thirteen, and she posts such inappropriate pictures on Instagram and boys post sexual comments, and she's like, Thank you. It's child porn, and everyone's looking at it on their iPhones in the cafeteria," said a seventeen-year-old girl in New York.

Presiding over the pornification of American life was Princess Kim, who'd been crowned the "Selfie Queen." Posting selfies, once thought to be embarrassingly narcissistic, was now as common as brushing one's teeth—or putting on makeup, the subject of many of the selfies in Kim's new book. For the last and loudest thunderclap in this perfect storm, the precipitous rise of narcissism in the American psyche— charted in studies since the 1970s, and accelerated by social media, according to psychologists—was personified and glamorized in the image of a dewy, contoured Kim staring into her iPhone screen.

Slate called *Selfish* "riveting." *The Atlantic*, in a review titled "You Win, Kim Kardashian," gushed, "In declaring herself, against all com- mon sense, as art, she mocks and dares and provokes. She rejects what came before. And with her candor about who she is and what it takes to make her that way, she might also, against all odds, move us forward." Whatever that might mean.

At the Barnes & Noble in Manhattan, Kim, then thirty-four, was wearing a tight, high-necked white lace dress and glistening with prod- ucts. She sat behind a table, signing books for her hundreds of awaiting fans.

"You've inspired me to be hot and famous," a teenage girl told her, blushing.

"Aw," said Kim. "I love you."

Though there had been a ban on selfies at the signing, Kim stood up and took a selfie with the girl. They posed together, staring into the girl's smartphone, pursing their lips.

"You are a role model for my daughters," said someone's mother.

Montclair, New Jersey

Montclair, New Jersey, is a suburb of some 39,000 people, about an hour by train from Manhattan. It's home to many commuters to New York, many with jobs in the arts and entertainment. Stephen Colbert lives there, as do a number of acclaimed authors and journalists from leading news organizations. It's known as a good place to raise kids, with good schools and its own art museum, art galleries, and live theaters. The downtown area of Upper Montclair has the look and feel of a village—a prosperous village, with antiques stores, boutiques, nice restaurants, and yoga studios for mother and baby.

On a spring day in Montclair, in Watchung Plaza, the shopping area in the center of town, children from three elementary schools were giving a musical performance in a grassy square. Parents were standing around in a semicircle, recording it on their phones.

"America, America," the children sang, in their high, sweet voices; some blew on flutes and clarinets, others banged on shiny drums. A cherry tree laden with pink blossoms blazed in the mid-afternoon sunlight. Some of the littlest girls had garlands in their hair. They looked like budding flowers in the grass.

The parents stood with cell phone cameras focused on the children. Almost every parent held a phone. If the children looked out at the crowd, they saw a sea of smiling adult faces, not looking directly at them, but gazing into their screens. One mother darted around, paparazzi-style, getting shots on a Canon DSLR.

"God shed his grace on thee . . ."

The concert trudged through "Do Re Mi" and "Under the Sea." *Bang, bang* went the drums. An American flag flew languidly from a nearby Chase Bank.

Some parents started to discreetly check their e-mails and texts. Some were already posting the children's performance on Facebook. There were sporty moms in Lycra workout clothes, Burberry and Kate Spade bags dangling from their wrists. There were fathers in jeans and patterned button-downs, wearing Merrell hiking sneakers. One encouraged his son, low, "You got this, buddy, focus, focus," when the boy started banging his drum out of sync. A girl blew hard on a flute, which squeaked in the air.

When the performance was over, the parents erupted in applause and cheers as raucous as if the children had won the Super Bowl.

"Mom," said a girl, running over. She pulled at her mother's hand, which held a phone.

Her mother put an arm around the girl, saying, "You were great! You were so good."

"No," said the girl. "I messed up. And I look bad today. Don't post it."

Online

From the earliest days of photography, parents were using this exciting new technology as a way to capture images of their kids. The rapid growth of daguerreotype studios in the United States in the 1850s was fed in part by the craze for portraits of children and babies. Once upon a time, only the wealthy and privileged could afford to have their portraits done by a small, select circle of artists. Now, with photography, shopkeepers, doctors, butchers, and carpenters could appear in pictures that resembled life, and so could their offspring.

Parents, then as now, wanted pictures of their children to record their development, to be able to gaze upon their innocent beauty and charm, and to show them off to family and friends. There was also the anxious consideration of infant mortality; if a child happened to die before she had a chance to be photographed, she might very well be photographed postmortem, posed in a cradle or bed as if still alive, so intense was the desire to retain an image of the loved one, which was already serving as a stand-in for an actual self.

Today, parents use smartphone technology and social media to broadcast images of their children to the world. They cultivate their children's online selves from birth or even before, in the delivery room, even in utero. Social media has given parenting a whole new dimension, and it has provided a publishing tool for parenting as performance. A 2010 study by the Internet security firm AVG Technologies found that 92 percent of American children have an online presence before the age of two. Parents post nearly 1,000 images of their children online before their fifth birthday, according to a 2015 poll conducted by the U.K.-based Parent Zone, an online safety site. The debate, often heard in the early years of social media, about whether posting pictures of children online is safe, from a personal security standpoint—not to mention questions of privacy—has been overwhelmed by a new parental drive to post and the built-in competition to attract the most attention and adulation for one's own kids.

"There are mothers who actually try to help their daughters use social media to get popular," said a mother of a high school girl in Boca Raton, Florida. "It's embarrassing because a lot of these women were not popular when they were in school. But now they're trying to feel popular through their daughters, and they will check the numbers of likes their daughters' pictures get. I have seen mothers take their daughters to have hair and makeup done to do selfies."

The pride and joy which have always inspired the sharing of a photograph of one's child are now accompanied by the anticipation of the pleasure and personal reward of likes from online friends and followers. A video of Baby cooing or having her first bite of banana is a reliable way to get likes and "awww"s; a picture of Junior making his first soccer goal elicits "yay!"s and "go!"s. And in the background is the unseen image of the loving, doting parent, in effect photo-bombing. Parents wrap their children's online identities into their own online selves.

And so many children growing up today experience the world as a never-ending series of photo shoots, for public consumption. "We're raising our kids to be performers," says the author and journalist Donna Freitas, who writes about campus culture. "Kids know their parents want them to make them look good on social media. So they work really hard at becoming good performers. But nobody is really thinking about what this is doing."

As Freitas suggests, one thing this seems to be doing is encouraging kids to repeat the behaviors, not only by posting images of themselves but by sharing personal information. Parents share intimate details of their children's lives online from the time they are born, sometimes overshare. Researchers at the University of Michigan coined the term "sharenting" to describe parents who use social media to communicate with one another about everything from their children's temper tantrums to their eating and sleeping habits and bowel movements. The website STFU, Parents posts submissions of the most egregious examples of social media oversharing by moms and dads, from stories involving "placenta smoothies" to mucus plugs. Created in 2009 by

Blair Koenig, the site, which jokingly calls itself a "public service" blog, exposes an online culture of "sanctimommies" and "mompetitions"—two symptoms of another aspect of American life discussed in the news: "narcissistic parenting."

"The winner-loser dynamic is at the heart of extreme narcissism, and the narcissistic parent is somebody who plays that game through their children," Joseph Burgo, a marriage and family therapist and clinical psychologist, said on CNN in 2015. Parenting as a "winner-loser dynamic" could also describe two wildly popular reality shows of the last decade—*Dance Moms* and *Toddlers & Tiaras*—in which monster mothers fight pitched battles through their daughters. It's been almost twenty years since the brutal murder of JonBenét Ramsey brought attention to the horror of the world of child beauty pageants—the extreme sexualization of the little girls, the skimpy costumes, garish makeup, and risqué dance moves once associated with stripping. In 1996, this was a dark revelation, seen as a national scandal. But since *Toddlers & Tiaras,* these images have become routine and are even seen as "hilarious" (as in a comment about the show on a pop-culture website). Now parents routinely post videos of their daughters suggestively shimmying to Taylor Swift and Nicki Minaj. You can almost hear Kris Jenner saying, "You're doing amazing, sweetie." These videos tend to get a lot of likes.

And if the videos get enough likes on sites like YouTube or Instagram, they can attract advertisers, and the parents who posted them can profit. In 2015, *The New York Times* ran a piece on "Instamoms," or mothers who cultivate their children's online personas with professional photography in the hopes of attracting endorsement deals and "blowing up." One toddler in the story, two-year-old Taylen, had 112,000 followers on Instagram, and her mother, Angelica Calad, said Taylen had "become a brand." The *Times*'s story didn't mention, however, that in 2013 Taylen's mother and father, Josh Biggs, were in the news in Florida voicing their concern that Taylen's baby pictures were being "copied and shared on other Instagram pages," some of a "sexually pornographic nature," Biggs told WPTV in West Palm Beach. "'I was just completely blown away and the morbid words I was reading, I was just, I'm sick to my stomach,'" Biggs said. But Taylen's online presence continued. The *Times* reported that she would be "headlining the holiday campaign for Kardashian Kids Kollection."

Montclair, New Jersey

"Oh my God."

"Oh, no."

"Oh . . ."

The three girls were coming out of the middle school at the end of the day. They were staring at Riley's phone, on which there was a screenshot of a Snapchat from a boy named Zack, asking her for nudes.

"I can't believe him," fumed Sophia.

Kids streamed past them, coming down the steps of the school. It was a redbrick building with tall white windows, an idyllic-looking school, as if from a John Hughes movie. There were black, white, Latino, and Asian kids, most holding their phones or checking their phones, some already texting and talking about what they were seeing on their phones.

Riley looked around, wondering if anybody was talking about her.

Sophia said, "Let's go."

The three girls walked along Bellevue Avenue toward Valley Road, the commercial section of Upper Montclair, where kids hung out on Friday afternoons. Sophia and Victoria maintained a sympathetic silence. Riley said she was "trying really hard not to lose it."

It wasn't that she had never been asked for nudes before; she said she had; in fact, it had been happening a lot lately. "After this rumor spread around, people have been asking her for nudes every day," Sophia explained. "They think Riley gave Danny a BJ so she's probably gonna send them."

The "BJ," or blowjob, rumor had been started by Danny himself, according to the girls, after Danny and Riley had broken up. The breakup, Riley said, had been sparked by another girl who "told him I was flirting with other guys. She wanted to make him break up with me and he did."

Riley and Danny had been dating for about six months. They'd hooked up for the first time at a party at a "free," or a house where the parents weren't there; such parties took place in the afternoons when parents were at work, said the girls. They said there was weed and vodka at the parties—"boys get nudes from girls and give them to high-schoolers and get l.q. in return"—and there was hooking up. No one they knew had had sex yet—except for one "savage" boy from another school who bragged that he had—but there was "making out, blowjobs, handjobs, everything but"; except they had never heard about a boy giving oral sex to a girl.

"It's like, in bed with a bra," Riley said. She'd hooked up with Danny "wearing a shirt and Spandex." "Danny told me he loved me," she said with an embarrassed smile. "I didn't say it back."

She was a green-eyed girl with dark blond hair pulled back in a tight ponytail. She wore short shorts, a white T-shirt, and blue Converse sneakers. Sophia was tall, with straight black hair, and wore a beach wrap and flowing pants, a look she described as "Coachella-y" (a reference to the annual fashion-forward music festival in Indio, California). And Victoria, brown-haired and freckled-faced, wore a flowered romper. She looked young for her age. They were all thirteen and had braces. Riley and Victoria were white, and Sophia was Latina.

Riley's parents were writers. Victoria's mother and father worked in the media, and Sophia's mother was an artist and her father an executive at a big corporation. Victoria's mother and father were divorced; the other girls' parents were married.

After Riley and Danny's breakup, said the girls, Danny took to social media, where he spread the word that Riley had given him oral sex.

"And I obviously didn't," Riley said.

"Like he called her a slut," said Sophia.

"He called me a slut," Riley said, "and everyone thought I was a slut and everyone started to hate me about that on social media. Like on Ask.fm."

On Ask.fm, users post personal information and invite others to ask questions and make comments, which they can do anonymously. The site, which had a reported 150 million monthly users in March 2015, has a history of attracting cyberbullies. Founded in Latvia in 2010, it was acquired by Ask.com, the question-answering Web search engine, in 2014. Ask.fm has been linked in the news to several infamous suicides by cyberbullying—also known as "cyberbullicides"—including that of Jessica Laney, a Hudson, Florida, girl, age sixteen, who hanged herself in 2012 after Ask.fm users called her "a slut" and a "fuckin' ugly ass hoe." "Can you kill yourself already?" one suggested.

"They told Riley to kill herself and stuff, and the school didn't do anything," Sophia complained.

"People were like, So, how many blowjobs did you give?" Riley said in her downcast tone. "Everyone posted about me, You're a terrible person, stay away from my friends. People commented that they don't like me. It was completely humiliating."

"It was horrible, horrible," said Sophia.

"People kept posting about me on all their personal accounts," Riley said. "And I didn't do anything. I really didn't do anything. Everyone just believes what they hear."

"Like I could post that Victoria has a secret mansion underground and everyone would believe it," offered Sophia.

Riley said that she'd tried calling Danny to talk it over with him, but "he hung up. We have never talked about it in person and now he hates my guts . . . He thinks I flirted and am a huge slut, but I'm not a slut. And now he's trying to get revenge."

Instead of talking to her, she said, Danny sent her Snapchats, those picture and video messages of one to ten seconds, which instantaneously disappear. Snapchat's nearly 100 million users were sending 700 million photos and videos a day in 2014, according to the company. When its founders introduced the idea for the app, naysayers said that no one would want to use a social media site where pictures go away; but, as it turned out, that was exactly what proved appealing to people, including, sometimes, people who had something hurtful to say, or who wanted to share nude images.

Sometimes Danny appeared in the Snaps with the girl who'd told him Riley was flirting with other guys. "I was like, Can you stop sending me Snapchats?" Riley said. "And he was like, When you stop being a slut. I got really upset. I didn't come to school for like a week."

When she refused to go to school, Riley's parents demanded to know why, and she finally told them. Until then, they had no inkling of their daughter's problems on social media. Now they supported her totally. "My parents think it's ridiculous," she said. "I was never close with them until this happened." They "got really involved," she said, informing the school that she was being cyberbullied by other students. But her parents were told there was nothing the school could do. The principal said it was a private matter.

"People would come up to me in school, people I didn't even know," Sophia said, "and if Riley missed school they'd be like, Oh my God, did Riley kill herself? Did Riley commit suicide? Did she give Danny a BJ?"

The girls walked along.

Riley looked pensive.

"Riley's gonna send the boys who asked for nudes a picture of a naked mole rat," Sophia said after a moment.

The girls giggled and started running down Valley Road toward the Dunkin' Donuts.

Rochester, New York, and Princeton, New Jersey

In 1845, a photographer made a daguerreotype of a nude. It's housed in the George Eastman Museum in Rochester, New York, the world's oldest museum of photography, located in the former home of the founder of the Eastman Kodak Company. The woman in the picture is lying, naked, on her side with her back to the camera, on a chaise longue draped with lace. The focus of the frame is her round behind. She looks a bit like Kim Kardashian, with her long dark hair and dark eyes, staring off to the right.

The Eastman Museum's title for the daguerreotype is *Odalisque;* the woman has been styled to suggest a harem girl or prostitute from some "exotic" land, with a serpent bracelet and a headdress adorned with coins. In the past, the photograph had also been called *Académie,* a reference to the "academy figures," or nude photographs, used by painters in French art schools in the nineteenth century, ostensibly for the purpose of study.

The photographing of nudes began almost as soon as there were cameras; the justification was the needs of artists. In "Nude Photography, 1840–1920," Peter Marshall wrote, "In the prevailing moral climate at the time of the invention of photography, the only officially sanctioned photography of the body was for the production of artist's studies." However, Marshall went on, "many of the surviving examples of daguerreotypes are . . . clearly not in this genre but have a sensuality that clearly implies they were designed as erotic or pornographic images." "This explains the demand—which lasted far into the twentieth century—for Artistic Photographs of Nudes," conjectured Uwe Scheid and Hans-Michael Koetzle in *1000 Nudes: A History of Erotic Photography from 1839–1939.*

April Alliston, a professor of comparative literature at Princeton who specializes in gender studies and has taught classes on the history of porn, points out that technological advances are often accompanied by a surge in the production and consumption of pornography. "Historically, a spike in interest in pornography is also associated with advancement in women's rights," Alliston says. "What happened at the time of the invention of the printing press was very similar to what's happening now with the Internet. With the printing press you had porn suddenly made available through technology. At the same time you had women getting more rights; there was more literacy and freedom for women." She goes on, "Historians talk about how pornography, as we understand it today, was invented in the era of the printing press in response to widespread cultural anxieties that women could gain more knowledge through reading. With the printing press, pornographic images and texts were circulated among men in a way that excluded women . . . Most early pornography was presented from the point of view of female prostitutes, whose foremost desire was to service men's pleasure, and to profit from it for lack of other means of survival.

"I see the spread of porn in part as a backlash to women's increased independence," Alliston asserts. "I believe that porn has gone mainstream now because women have been gaining power . . . Rather than being about sexual liberation, I see in porn a form of control over sex and sexuality."

The debate among feminists about pornography, also known as "the porn wars," began in the late 1970s. There are anti-porn feminists who see porn as oppressive to women, a form of patriarchal control, and say that it should be banned. Anti-censorship feminists agree that porn is misogynistic but oppose a legal response. And pro-porn feminists regard porn as liberating for women's sexuality, even a cause for celebration. Since online porn seeped into computers and smartphones in the 1990s and 2000s, it has been the latter view which has gained dominance in the mainstream. "4 Reasons Porn Is Actually Really, Really Good for Women," said a post on MarieClaire.com in 2015. Liking porn has become a trait associated with girls and women who are seen as cool and fashionable. "I love porn," Cameron Diaz said on *Jimmy Kimmel Live*. "I watch a lot of it," said singer Lily Allen.

Today, the online porn industry is overwhelmingly controlled by a handful of men, some of them dubbed the "geek-kings of smut" by *New York* magazine for their background in tech. Many of the top online pornography sites, including Pornhub, RedTube, YouPorn, Tube8, and Extremetube, are owned by a single multibillion-dollar conglomerate, MindGeek, the number one producer and distributer of porn in the world. A spokesperson for the company has claimed that it is one of the top five in the world in bandwidth consumption. Three of its founding owners—Matt Keezer, Ouissam Youssef, and Stephane Manos—are tech guys in their thirties from Montreal who originally know one another from attending Concordia University and "the competitive Foosball circuit." Their sleek website describes the company as a "global industry-leading information technology firm," as if likening it to Google or Apple. Nowhere does it mention that the bulk of the company's profits come from pornography. There are none of the images of women being "pounded" and "jackhammered" that one sees when pulling up any of the MindGeek-owned porn sites. There's no sign of the "barely legal" girls who perform in the videos in Pornhub's most popular category.

"When it comes to children," Alliston says, "there's really nothing to argue about. Kids are defined by our laws as not being able to consent to viewing porn. There are few protections against them seeing it, and some people take the attitude that it's inevitable and benign. I think a lot of people who make this argument don't realize what porn today really looks like in terms of how the women are treated." She adds that in recent years there have been reports of kids watching porn at schools

across the country. In 2014, school district officials in Los Angeles discovered that high-schoolers in its iPad program were bypassing the
devices' security settings in order to watch porn. In 2015, in Encini-
tas, California, parents were outraged to learn that second-graders were
using school-issued iPads to watch it.

James City County, Virginia

Nudes. To have a social media account is to at some point see nudes
or semi-nudes—"boob" and "butt" and body shots of teenage girls and
women, many of whom work in porn. Whether or not a young person
seeks out porn online, chances are she will see pornographic images
popping up on her social media accounts, whether in circulated photos that appear on news feeds or as spam for porn sites. Or she can
easily search social media for porn. On Twitter there are hashtags for
"nudes" and "sluts." On Tumblr and Instagram, searches for "porn"
and "nudes" turn up multiple results. There are thousands of links on
the Web to "leaked" nudes—screenshots taken and forwarded by those
who received them, almost always without the senders' knowledge
or consent. You don't even need to be on social media to see porn or
nudes, graphic nudes; you can just Google them.

There are plenty of sex acts to be seen on social media as well. "It's
a thing to find that really outrageous thing and send it around," said
a thirteen-year-old girl in New York. "When I was in seventh grade,
everybody was watching this viral video, '2 Girls, 1 Cup,' of two [teen-
age] girls having sex and they're eating one of them's poop from a cup.
It's beyond disgusting. But if you don't watch it, it's like you're afraid,
or you missed out on what everybody's talking about."

"A girl I know was bragging to me about how she and her friends
were watching porn of this girl they tied up and rammed in the butt,"
said a thirteen-year-old girl in Los Angeles. "She was laughing about it.
It really creeped me out."

"Porn is not going away," says Soraya Chemaly, a writer and the
director of the WMC Speech Project, an initiative by the Women's
Media Center dedicated to fighting the online harassment of women

and girls. "I don't know if people are fooling themselves or burying their heads in the sand. I was talking to a high school principal and he said, Really, you think our kids are looking at porn? And I just didn't even know what to say. Our kids are not only consuming porn, they're producing porn"—by taking and sharing nudes. "I don't really care if a person has a sex-positive view of pornography," Chemaly adds, "but no one is talking about any of it to kids in terms of how it affects their behavior. Whether or not they're looking at it, our culture is permeated by a porn aesthetic."

So what is it like to be a girl growing up in a world inundated with nude and pornographic images of women and girls? How does it affect her conception of her body, her self, her self-worth? Her relationship to boys and other girls? In the spring of 2014, I went to James City County, Virginia (established in 1634 and located on the Virginia Peninsula, some thirty-five miles inland from the Chesapeake Bay), because I wanted to talk to a girl who was in the news after posting nude pictures of herself on Twitter. She had reportedly been arrested.

The legal system seems at a loss to know what to do about children seeing and sharing nudes. It has become so common. The girl, age sixteen, who went unnamed because she was underage, had been charged with a felony, the possession and distribution of child pornography, according to reports in February 2014. That the girl herself was the same child whose naked images were being distributed made no difference under the law. The charge, under a section of the Virginia code, carries a potential prison term of five to twenty years.

When I talked to Nate Green, the Commonwealth's Attorney for Williamsburg and Jamestown (the two cities that make up James City County, population around 70,000), he was already backpedaling from the charge, possibly due to the negative reaction the girl's alleged arrest had been receiving in the media. "We have no interest in criminalizing a juvenile who does something like this," said Green. "We just want to stop it from happening. We don't want these pictures following anyone to college or making them out as easy prey on the Internet." He said the girl would just receive some "education and counseling." Stephanie Williams-Ortery, a spokesperson for the James City County police, told me, "These were fully nude pictures [the girl] tweeted. She acknowledged she was trying to get the attention of some young men. What she did was pretty brazen."

She was sharing nudes. A nude is a type of sext, an electronically sent message, either in pictures or in words, intended to cause arousal or attraction in, or convey one's arousal or attraction to, another person. Sexting is a kind of virtual flirting, also a kind of sex, cybersex. The results of studies on what percentage of kids sext vary so widely as to make even an educated guess difficult, some researchers say; studies are inconsistent in the age ranges surveyed and in their definition of sexting, which can involve everything from sending a fully naked photo of oneself to sharing a link to a porn site to simply texting "I think your body's hot" with no image included. Studies have found that the number of middle-schoolers and high-schoolers who sext, with either words or pictures or both, is anywhere from just 4 percent to more than 50 percent. It's safe to say that sexting is part of the culture of social media; whether or not a girl is sexting, she's most likely aware of the practice.

Snapchat and Kik Messenger, an anonymous instant-messaging service, are two of the apps where kids say they're most likely to share nudes, as well as by texting. "'Got Kik?' means, Do you want to sext?" said a fourteen-year-old girl in New York. Since its creation by students at the University of Waterloo in 2009, Kik has appeared in the news in stories involving pedophiles who say they used the service to communicate with underage girls. In 2014, *The Trentonian* reported that a twenty-seven-year-old man was arrested after allegedly being found with "14 photographs of a female" he met on Kik, identified as a thirteen-year-old resident of Bensalem, Pennsylvania, "in different stages of nudity and one video of that female masturbating."

A woman who works at a middle school in James City County told me that in the last few years they've been having trouble with kids getting distracted because they were sexting during class. "We had a twelve-year-old writing to the boy, Do you want me to touch your D?" she said, sounding appalled. "D" meant dick. "And we've seen boys looking at naked pictures of girls in school," she said. "There was one girl who texted the boy, I'm home watching porn."

Most states have laws against minors sexting, which prosecutors say is appropriate, given that "lewd" images of children are being distributed, albeit by the children themselves, thereby putting others at risk for being in possession of what is defined by the law as child porn. But the policing of sexting has drawn criticism in recent years. Minors being "prosecuted under child pornography statutes for producing or sending images of themselves or other minors . . . is not the proper use of child pornography prosecution, nor is it a solution to the problem of minors sexting," said an article in the University of Michigan *Journal of Law Reform* in 2014.

In *The Atlantic*, writer Hanna Rosin depicted the busting of a teen "sexting ring" in Louisa County, Virginia, in 2014 as much ado about nothing. The case involved a high school in which a group of boys had posted more than 1,000 nude and semi-nude photos and videos of girls, ages about fourteen to seventeen, on Instagram, without the girls' knowledge or consent. In her piece Rosin described the Instagram page as looking like "a porn site"; but in an interview on NPR, she maintained that the naked images of the girls were equivalent to "baseball cards or Pokemon cards" to the boys, a kind of "social currency" for them, "more than . . . a springboard for fantasy."

"There's so much free porn out there that these pictures serve a different role," Rosin said. "These guys look at these pictures for five seconds. They're just not that big of a deal to them. And so sending them along is kind of fun . . . It seems like a prank."

But if the circulating of nudes is a prank, then it's one that has had some tragic consequences. In 2008, Jessica Logan, an eighteen-year-old Cincinnati girl, hanged herself after her ex-boyfriend shared nudes of her, and she was labeled a "slut" and a "whore." In 2009, Hope Witsell, a thirteen-year-old Ruskin, Florida, girl, hanged herself after a boy she liked shared nudes of her.

When the actress Jennifer Lawrence's nudes were hacked, in 2014, she labeled it a "sex crime," and many people were inclined to agree with her assessment. The danger that sexting may result in cyberbullying, or "revenge porn," the nonconsensual sharing of nudes, has been established in many studies. Sexting has also been linked to "sexual objectification and violence, to risky sexual behavior, and to negative consequences like bullying by peers," according to an article in *Cyberpsychology* in 2014; and yet, despite evidence of its negative impact, the article went on, "a normalcy discourse is appearing in the literature that interprets sexting as normal intimate communication within romantic and sexual relationships, both among adults and adolescents who are exploring and growing into adult relationships."

In other words, teenage sexting has already come to be viewed as normal. Movies and television shows have portrayed teenagers sexting as something romantic and cute, like a kind of cyber-hickey. On an episode of *Keeping Up with the Kardashians,* teenagers Kylie and Kendall Jenner giggled at sexts they found on their mother, Kris's, phone, sexts allegedly sent to a younger man. Even as prosecutors try to make an example of sexting teens, sexting is all but accepted as social behavior.

"How to Take a Tasteful Nude Selfie," said a post on Allure.com in 2015 ("Highlight your best bits"). There's even a kind of nude selfie feminism. Comedian Amy Schumer seemed to equate nude selfies with female empowerment in a 2015 tweet: ". . . Spend less time worrying what others have and focus on getting what you want #dicks #nude selfie"; as did *Rookie* magazine founder and actress Tavi Gevinson in 2013, when she was seventeen, and tweeted: ". . . as long as there are reddit threads of secret shots of girls' butts," meaning leaked nudes on the social networking site Reddit, "let them selfie their own butts."

But some girls and young women aren't comfortable with taking or sharing nudes, as routine as it has become. "When did men obtain the right to ask women for such intimate and over-sexualized requests?" asked Lauren Martin on Elite Daily, a website popular with college students, in 2014. "When did demeaning women to nothing more than a naked photograph become so trendy?" On social media sites such as YouTube, Twitter, and Yik Yak, you often see posts by girls complaining about boys and young men asking for nudes. "I can't handle like 20 year old dudes begging for nudes and shit," said a Yik Yakker in New York.

"I was in my feminism class" at Hunter College, said Jenna, a nineteen-year-old New York girl, "and we were talking about how girls sending nudes of themselves through Tinder," the dating app, "or on similar websites made for the exploitation of, often, young women; and most of the people in my class said that it's totally cool to send nudes, because we have the choice to show our bodies to whomever we want—which is true, but everyone thought I was an asshole for objecting and saying, yeah, but it's for a man's benefit. Like, guys don't see nudes and think, Wow, what an empowered woman, good for her for being com-fortable with her body. They go like, Great, boobs; or like, She's a slut for sending me pictures but, like, I'll still sleep with her."

I didn't get to talk to the James City County girl who'd allegedly been arrested for posting nude photos on Twitter (which was of course created by four young men, one an undergraduate at NYU and three Silicon Valley software developers and entrepreneurs, in 2006). I did talk to some boys on the playing field of her high school one cloudy afternoon. They were good-looking white boys, all age seventeen. They seemed like nice young men. I asked them if they knew the girl who'd been in the news. They all pulled out their phones, and one of them showed me a nude picture of the girl, which he said had been forwarded to him by another boy. Each of the boys had nude or semi-nude photos on his phone of girls they knew or had met on social media.

"That's my old girlfriend," said one of the boys, thumbing through pictures on his phone. "That's a girl who wants to get with me, that's a girl I asked for nudes . . ."

The other boys laughed, embarrassed.

When I asked them what they did with these pictures, they were sheepish, grinning, and finally said: "Use 'em to jerk off." "We're horny dudes, you know?"

I went to the New Town mall in Williamsburg one Sunday afternoon and saw a flock of middle-school-age girls from a local church group eating frozen yogurt at the Sweet Frog frozen yogurt store. They were bouncy and loud in brightly colored clothes—a baby-blue hoodie, a pink down vest, lime-green leggings. Almost all of them had cell phones in their hands, which they looked at intermittently, checking and texting, as they obstreperously conversed.

Some of the little girls were sitting at a table, gathered around an iPhone which was playing the trailer for *American Horror Story: Coven,* a critically acclaimed show full of sexual violence whose characters, a coven of witches, include a promiscuous Hollywood starlet and a teen-ager who causes her boyfriend to have a brain aneurysm by having sex with him.

"*Oooooh*, I wanna see that!" the girls exclaimed. "Oh my gosh, it's *sooooo* good."

And there was one girl who sat off to the side, scraping the bottom of her yogurt cup with a plastic spoon. She wore aviator shades and a jaunty pink polka-dotted hat. I asked her why she didn't have a phone.

She smiled up at me and said, "It got taken away 'cause I was being a flirt butt."

A flirt butt? I asked.

She cupped her hand around my ear and whispered hotly, *"Sexting."* Then she drew back coyly and giggled.

Boca Raton, Florida

The four thirteen-year-old girls had gone to spend the day at the Town Center mall. Wearing short shorts and tank tops, Converse and flip-flops, they glided along the air-conditioned halls past all the stores—Saks, Sephora, Victoria's Secret, Tiffany, Louis Vuitton. Their mothers had dropped them off for lunch; they had chicken and waffles at the Grand Lux Café, and now they were stuffed, so they sat down on some couches to check their phones.

As they visited their social media accounts, opening their Snapchats and liking and commenting on the Instagram posts of their friends, a procession of mothers and daughters drifted past, all dressed almost identically in Boca fashions. There was a lot of bronzed skin and bleached-blond hair. There were teenage girls in booty shorts and cleavage-baring tops, and mothers wearing almost exactly the same things, except with heels and bling. They carried shopping bags from Neiman Marcus, DKNY, and Pink.

"They call them 'Boca brats,'" said Julie, one of the girls on the couch, using an unflattering term for rich girls in the area. Boca Raton, a coastal city with a population of around 90,000, about fifty miles north of Miami, is wealthy. According to *Forbes,* it has several of the most exclusive gated communities in America. Andy Roddick has a home there, as does Jon Bon Jovi. Ariana Grande is Boca's homegrown pop superstar of the moment, a ponytailed diva known for her four-octave range, extreme microminis, and more than 50 million followers on Instagram.

I remarked to the girls how strange it seemed to see the mothers in the mall dressed so similarly to their daughters.

"They want to look hot," said Cassy, not looking up from her phone.

"Everybody wants to look hot," Julie said.

"Their daughters look hot and they want to look like their daughters," said Maggie. "They think they're the Real Housewives."

The reluctance of Baby Boomers and Gen-Xers to grow old is not lost on girls. The resistance to aging has been evident in the success the beauty industry has had with "anti-aging" products. The demand for plastic surgery and other cosmetic procedures skyrocketed in the 2000s, with a 98 percent increase in procedures overall between 2000 and 2012, according to the American Society of Plastic Surgeons. The second most popular procedure for women ages forty to fifty-four in 2014 was breast augmentation. The hypersexualization which has enveloped the lives of American girls seems to have also ensnared their moms. The rise of the MILF ("Mother I'd Like to Fuck") and cougar as sexual fantasies spilled over into mainstream pop culture in the 2010s, with TV shows like *Cougar Town* and *Hot in Cleveland*—the latter a sitcom about a group of women from L.A. who want so desperately to be considered hot that they move to a theoretically less competitive Midwestern town, looks-wise.

It was in porn that the MILF was widely fetishized. In describing the success of the porn production company Brazzers—it was the first endeavor of the founders of MindGeek—its CEO, Feras Antoon, attributed it to their mining of the MILF as sex object. "At first," Antoon told *New York*, "they focused on busty women, 'because the big-tits niche was so cheap'"; but then "they realized that the MILF niche—the older-woman niche—is even bigger. And they became the masters of the big-tit-MILF niche."

"MILF" was the third most popular search on Pornhub in 2014. The site's top porn star that year was Lisa Ann, born in 1972 and the so-called queen of MILF porn. (She prefers the term "cougar.")

"All girls think about is trying to look hot," Leah said.

"It's always a competition between girls, like, who has the biggest boobs," said Cassy.

"A lot of people comment on social media, like, Oh my God, she's so flat, if she doesn't have boobs," said Maggie.

As the girls began to talk about girls "trying to look hot," their words came tumbling out, as if they couldn't say them quickly enough; they talked over one another, interrupting one another, their faces becoming urgent and intense.

"And a lot of boys are like, if you don't have boobs and a butt, they don't like you," Maggie said.

"That's most of the boys right now," said Cassy.

"A lot of boys in this generation—boys are not looking at the *personality*," said Julie.

"They're just looking at the boobs and butt," Cassy said. "And if you don't have them they won't date you."

The girls were friends from middle school; they were all in eighth grade. Maggie and Cassy were Latina, and Julie and Leah were white. All of them had long, straight, dark hair, except for Leah, who was blond, and all of them had braces. Cassy's and Maggie's fathers worked in technology; Leah's father was an industrial designer; Julie's mother was an executive in a communications company, and her father was a business owner. All of their parents were married.

"A lot of girls wear really tight shirts to make them look like they have bigger boobs," Cassy said.

"They buy like a bra too big for them to make them look like they have bigger boobs," said Maggie.

"A lot of girls post *this*," said Julie.

She held up her phone, on which there was an Instagram shot of a girl they knew; her behind filled the frame. She was wearing only underwear. "Screenshot if you like my ass," said the caption.

I asked them why they thought some girls posted nude or semi-nude pictures of themselves on social media.

"They're so insecure," Cassy said. "They're looking for attention from boys—like, Damn, you're so hot—to make them feel better about themselves."

" 'Cause it's like if you're not hot—you're *not*," said Julie.

"They have Instagram accounts at our school," Maggie said, "like '[Name of School] Hotties,' where they post pictures of the hot girls. Like they tell you if you're hot or not."

"And they get people's nudes and post them all over, like on 'Broward County Exposed,' " said Julie.

They said there were "a lot" of Instagram accounts where nude and semi-nude pictures of girls were posted. Known as "slut pages" to kids and "sexting rings" in the media, these types of amateur porn sites can be found in schools across the country. Their existence became a subject of national concern in 2012 with a Change.org petition to have a page titled "12 Year Old Slut Memes" removed from Facebook. Soraya Chemaly reported in *The Huffington Post* that "one of the offending page's profile photos is of a pink-lipped and pouty child (she looks a lot younger than twelve) wearing a tank top that reads 'I love COCK.'" The page, which had been created by two nineteen-year-old boys in Brisbane, Australia, was eventually taken off Facebook after an outpouring of protest. But slut pages have persisted in the United States and other countries.

"There's so many," Julie said. "Like 'Boca Barbies,' 'Boca Bitches'—"

"'Boca Hos,'" said Cassy.

"'BocaBiggestHos'—all one word," said Julie.

"It's pictures of girls with their boobs and butts," Maggie said. "The boys take pictures and make an Instagram account. After a while someone flags it and they take it down, but usually it's after everyone's already seen it."

"It's girls that do it sometimes, too, if they wanna get back at someone," Cassy said. "They'll post pictures and hate on people in the comments."

"And sometimes girls do it so, like, they can post pictures of themselves," Julie said. She pulled up one of the accounts they were talking about on her phone. There were about twenty shots of nude and semi-nude girls, all young teens. It was unsettling.

I asked them where the boys posting these pages were getting the pictures.

"If a girl sends nudes, everyone winds up having it," Cassy said.

"Girls send it to a boy and that boy is sending it around," said Julie.

What percentage of girls were sharing nudes? I asked.

"Twenty . . . thirty?" they guessed.

"The thing is, with boys," Cassy said, "if you don't send them nudes, they say you're a prude."

"Or scared," said Maggie.

Had a boy ever asked them for nudes? I asked.

"*Yes,*" they said.

"They blackmail you," Cassy said. "They say, Oh, I have embarrassing pictures of you, if you don't send nudes I'll send them all out on social media."

A 2009 survey by the National Campaign to Prevent Teen and Unplanned Pregnancy found that 51 percent of girls ages thirteen to nineteen said they believed that "pressure from a guy is a reason girls send sexy messages or images." Sixty-six percent of girls who had sexted someone said they did so to be "fun or flirtatious," and 52 percent as a "sexy present" for their boyfriends. So even some of the girls who willingly sent nudes were aware of pressure from boys to send them, in this study.

"Like embarrassing pictures of you when you wake up or something like that," Maggie explained.

"Or they say, like, I know a secret of yours," Leah said. "Or they make up a rumor."

Did any of the parents know about the slut pages? I asked.

"Yes, some do," Julie said. "And I'm sure the school knows from the parents, but the school says it can't do anything 'cause it's happening on social media."

I heard from girls all over that, when difficult situations involving social media occurred in their schools, their principals and school administrators would tell their parents that there was nothing they could do. However, Justin Patchin, a professor of political science at the University of Wisconsin–Eau Claire and the codirector of the Cyberbullying Research Center, told me, "That's completely false. Schools can do something about it; there are federal standards based on Supreme Court cases giving schools the authority to discipline students for anything that happens online. I used to get that comment a lot, 'Not at school, not my problem,' but it's completely wrong. We're going to need more higher-level court cases where schools *don't* intervene when they're supposed to in order to get them to take responsibility."

"And boys send dick pics, too," Cassy said.

"*Yeah,*" said the other girls.

It has become common for girls to receive dick pics from boys—meaning pictures of boys' erect penises—usually unsolicited. It was regarded as shocking in 2011 when the aptly named Anthony Weiner, a New York congressman, was exposed for sending a picture of his penis bulging under a pair of shorts to a young woman who followed him on Twitter. But just a few years later, the congressman's dick pic might be viewed as no big thing. Like nudes, dick pics have become a fact of life for both adults and teens. "We are in the age of the dick pic," said MensHealth.com in 2014. "How to Take a Dick Pic," advised Esquire .com that same year. On Critique My Dick Pic, a well-known Tumblr blog accessible to anyone online, dick pic submissions are posted, assessed, and graded.

There have been blog posts and Reddit threads where women exchange advice about "what to do if you get a dick pic"; but rarely does anyone ever bring up the question of sexual harassment, although the majority of women in surveys say they don't like receiving such images, especially unasked. "Do they think that we want that? 'Cause we don't," said Sally, a seventeen-year-old girl in Boca Raton. "It makes you feel disrespected," said her friend Michelle, seventeen. "I got dick pics in sixth grade. But nobody wants to see it; it doesn't turn me on. It shocked me."

In 2015, the actress Juliette Lewis posted a video on Facebook registering her disgust at receiving an unsolicited dick pic. "So I looked at my direct messages," Lewis said, referring to a message she had received on social media. "So people just send naked pictures to each other and be like, Hey, here's my dick? It's so sad . . . You're sick."

And yet, many of the same feminists who condemn street harassment and online harassment can't be heard calling the sending of dick pics "harassment," if they talk about it at all, although sending an unsolicited dick pic could reasonably be compared to the crime of flashing. On social media, dick pics are treated in a jocular way; a YouTube video, "Women React to Dick Pics!" has gotten millions of views. "Please stop sending me pictures of your dick," one of the young women in the video pleads in a comical tone. In 2013, Cosmopolitan.com ran "In Defense of the Dick Pic," saying, "It's kind of romantic, actually. Like a Hallmark card made of skin."

When I asked the boys in James City County if they sent dick pics, they said they had, usually as a way to try to get nudes in return. "Sometimes it works, like thirty percent of the time," one boy said. "I send them my dick, so they'll show me something of theirs."

"Yes, I have gotten one," Julie said, "and I didn't ask for it. I thought he was my friend, but he changed. It got me upset."

"Some of them don't even show their face," Cassy said. "They just send it to you like, Hey, look at *this*."

"But, honestly, there are girls who do the same kinds of things," Julie said. She told of how, the day before, a friend had come over to her house after school and wanted to video chat with some boys on FaceTime—naked. "She came out of my closet naked, ready to answer the call, and I was like, What are you doing? She wanted to be naked in front of the boys. And I said, This is really not okay, you're thirteen years old and you're acting like a twenty-year-old girl."

"What would have happened if the boys had screenshotted her?" I asked.

"That's what they do!" exclaimed the girls.

"They think it's cool to try and trick you," said Cassy.

In porn, the tricking of women into doing something sexual is a common theme. On Pornhub, XVideos, and other sites, you can find videos with titles such as "Tricked Into Sex." "Naive Teen Tricked" is a link on a site called PussySpace, "Dumb Teen Gets Tricked Into 3Some" on Pornhub, and "Hypnotized girl tricked into sex" on XVideos.

The Boca girls said there were "nice boys" in their school—"I have a guy best friend and he's so nice and he would never screenshot a girl," Julie declared—but that there was also a popular "style" for boys, which they called "savage," meaning sexually overt, crass, and disrespectful.

"When boys say it, it's a compliment," Cassy said. "They make their Instagram names like 'Savage Young Boy.'"

"They try and be gangster," Maggie said. "So many thirteen-year-old boys are smoking weed. They'll go on Snapchat and Instagram and post pictures of them smoking."

"They have house parties and they post like, 'Bring the alcohol, bring the weed, don't come if you're a prude,'" said Cassy.

"One of my sister's friends, she was having a hard time," Julie said. "She was acting out. She's a senior in high school and she was caught giving head to a boy—it was at a party and somebody walked in and took a picture and it went all over social media. And so many people were hating on her in the school and she literally had no friends left except my sister. She was being called a slut and it got to her really badly, 'cause she suffers from anxiety and depression, and she wanted to kill herself. But luckily she gave hints to my sister and my sister drove over to her house when she was about to take pills."

I asked what happened to the guy in the picture, the one who had gotten the blowjob.

"Nothing happened to him," Julie said.

"He's a player," Cassy said with a frown.

"A guy will ask you to do it," or give oral sex, Maggie said, "and if you say no, then you're a prude, but then when you actually do it you're a slut."

I asked what effect they thought all this was having on girls—the hypersexualization of girls, and boys, and the double standard which seemed exacerbated by the public nature of social media.

"It stresses me out, honestly," Julie said. "I suffer from anxiety. I've been suffering for so long now. I go to a therapist and I do take medicine for it. It started in my fourth-grade class. I was with a mean group of girls and they all, like, went off on everybody and would tell them their flaws."

"Yeah, they did that at our school, too," Cassy sympathized.

"I think social media made it worse," Julie said. "All people are caring about now is, How do I look on social media?"

"It makes girls feel like they have to try so hard constantly to get people to like them," Cassy said. "And some people feel bad if they don't get enough likes and comments."

"We know a girl whose mom buys her followers!" Julie exclaimed. She was referring to companies, accessible online, from which you could buy fake followers for social media accounts.

"And because of social media you can edit yourself, like how you *want* to be, with Photoshop and apps," Maggie said. "Like I want to be like *her,* I'm gonna make myself look like *her.*"

Like who? I asked.

"Kylie Jenner!" they all said at once, referring to the eighteen-year-old sister of Kim Kardashian.

"And all the Kardashians," said Cassy.

"Everybody wants to take a selfie as good as the Kardashians," Maggie said. "Some girls do their makeup just to take a selfie. They spend *hours*."

"Everyone wants everyone to like them," Julie said. "And everyone wants to be perfect. But to be perfectly honest, it's not possible to be perfect. Everyone's gonna have something wrong. But I just wish everyone could just look past that and look at the personality and the person on the inside rather than the outside."

"What do you think the answer is?" I asked.

"I think the parents literally need to knock some sense into their kids and watch what their kids are doing," Julie said, " 'cause I feel like a lot of kids are sneaking it behind their parents' backs."

"They don't want their parents to know what's really going on," said Cassy, " 'cause they're afraid they'll take away their phones."

Montclair, New Jersey

Valley Road runs through the center of Upper Montclair, the tonier section of town. The buildings there are quaint and small, many of them in the Tudor style familiar to suburbs of New York. The Dunkin' Donuts is like any other in the chain, with a logoed pink-and-orange sign showing a steaming cup of coffee. Through the window, on a Friday afternoon, you could see the place was teeming with middle-school-age kids, some standing on a couch by the window, bouncing and gesticulating.

Riley, Sophia, and Victoria approached the doughnut store tentatively.

"I'm not going in, I can't go in," Riley said, moving against the wall of the building so she would not be seen by anyone inside.

"Really?" said Sophia. "It's okay. It's all dying down."

"No, it isn't," Riley said. She was suddenly breathing rapidly. "I feel like I'm having an anxiety attack. Is this an anxiety attack?" she asked, her voice becoming high and thin.

Sophia and Victoria stared at her with concern, not knowing what to do.

"I know someone who gets them," Sophia said helpfully. "She takes medicine."

Later Riley's mother told me Riley suffered from an anxiety disorder and was being treated with medication. "Sometimes I wonder whether that is why they attack her," her mother said, "because they know she's fragile."

"You go in first," Riley said. "What if Danny's in there? What if Zack's in there? What if they take pictures of me?" And then: "Get me a strawberry doughnut with sprinkles."

Sophia and Victoria ventured inside the store. They didn't often go in the Dunkin' Donuts on a Friday afternoon. That was when the popular kids—"the cliquey kids and thotty," or slutty, "girls in the shortest shorts"—congregated to "try and act cool," said Sophia.

Victoria and Sophia were not part of this crowd, as Riley was, or perhaps once had been. In fact, Sophia said that Riley had "shunned" her at times during that school year. "She gets influenced by other kids," Sophia said. "But she's my friend, so I'm going to stick by her. With social media it's really hard to know who your true friends are, and this is how you know, how someone treats you when everyone hates you."

Inside the store, there were around twenty kids, and all of them seemed to be screaming. They sat on the brown-and-orange vinyl booths in front of half-empty boxes of doughnuts; they stood in clusters in the aisles, talking close up in one another's faces. There were boys in sweatpants and T-shirts, long shorts and sports jerseys, powdered sugar on their cheeks and lips; there were girls in short shorts and tank tops and crop tops, hands on hips.

There were three girls taking a selfie together, all doing the duck-face, smizing—a word coined by former Victoria's Secret supermodel Tyra Banks for "smiling with your eyes."

They vamped for the camera, then peered into the screen, checking the photo.

"Oh, we look hot!" one of them exclaimed. "Post it!"

Kids were talking, yelling:

"Oh my God, she's so fake."

"*So* fake."

"I love your Instagram. You have good feed."

"I know."

"She gets like three hundred likes on every picture. I'm like, Stop it."

"Did you see Kim Kardashian's selfie book?"

"Oh my God. Who would buy a book of selfies?"

"My mom has it."

Giggles.

"Kim is only famous because she did a sex tape."

"I know. The only one I like is Kendall." That was Kendall Jenner, the twenty-year-old sister of Kim, a model. She has more than 42 million followers on Instagram.

"Seriously, Kendall is my lover."

"I like Kylie the best."

"Kylie looks gorgeous in pictures, but she's ugly in person." Kylie Jenner has 35 million Instagram followers.

"Totally. Her head is square."

"This girl at Renaissance [Middle School] did the Kylie Jenner Challenge"—a trend where girls were sucking on the inside of shot glasses in order to create a bee-stung lip effect similar to Kylie Jenner's exaggerated lip fillers look—"and she had a hickey around her mouth for like a week."

"*Hahahahaha.*"

"Oh my God, I did that, too." Embarrassed laugh. "I looked so ratchet."

"What's in the book?"

"It's just, like, pictures of selfies. And her boobs and butt."

"I like the boobs. I like the butt," said a boy in a snapback hat. "I like 'em big."

"Her booty is *too* big," said another boy, who wore a Bob Marley T-shirt.

"Faggot," said the boy with the snapback hat.

"I can't believe you just said that," said a girl.

"Your mom's a faggot," said the boy in the Bob Marley shirt. "You're a one-inch wonder."

A young man in a Dunkin' Donuts uniform working behind the counter looked over at the kids and shook his head.

"Shut up," said the boy in the snapback hat. "I'll take a BJ from all the Kardashians. Except for Khloé. Khloé is the ugly one."

Khloé Kardashian has more than 36 million followers on Instagram.

"Scott definitely cheats on Khloé," the other boy agreed.

The boys laughed, high-fived.

"Totally, bro. She looks like she's thirty," the first boy said.

"Scott is married to *Kourtney*," a girl informed the boy.

Kourtney Kardashian, then the partner of former model Scott Disick (they have since separated), has more than 29 million followers on Instagram.

"And seriously, like Kim Kardashian would give you a blowjob."

"What, are you on your period?" said the boy in the snapback hat.

"Kim is *married*," said the girl.

"To Kanye. So?" said the boy. "Kanye is gay."

"You're gay," said the second boy.

"Your mom is gay," the first boy said, laughing. And, rubbing his chest: "I'm a sexy beast, yo."

"You're a savage," said the girl. "You're a fuckboy!"

"Hahahahaha."

"Oooh."

The boy leaned into the girl, whispering something in her ear.

"This afternoon?" said the girl, shoving him away. "Who else is coming?"

Sophia and Victoria bought some doughnuts and hurried out of the store. No one spoke to them.

YouTube

"Savages" and "fuckboys," two words in use among American girls, describe a strain of boys who seem to have reared their snapback-hat-wearing heads a lot in recent years. "Fuckboy" is generally believed to have first appeared in a 2002 Cam'ron song, "Boy, Boy"; in hip-hop, it came to be a put-down for a kind of loser. Some black writers have argued that using the word in any other context is appropriating and disrespectful. But words are like fuckboys—they get around—and sometimes their meanings expand. To understand the life of American girls, it's useful to know what they mean when they utter this slur.

It was in 2015 that "fuckboy" became a topic of discussion on websites and blogs, having gained attention from its prevalence in posts on social media. There were #fuckboy hashtags on Twitter and Instagram and other sites, with girls of all races using it. "Ladies please don't ever feel the need to lower your standards for a fuckboy," tweeted @ZuleymaaSerrato. "Don't let a fuck boy stress you out," tweeted @dxmnjocelyn. "Don't settle for a fuckboy just 'cause you lonely baby girl. Know your worth," tweeted @RainaRushil. "When you meet a fuckboy," girls posted again and again, with pictures of girls doing the "Resting Bitch Face" and Kendall Jenner giving the symbol for "peace out."

In 2015, *The Huffington Post* defined the term as "something akin to the 'man whore' label" with "a light-to-heavy sprinkling of misogyny." "Primarily, fuckboys do not respect women," *Bustle* said, while the Urban Dictionary posted a new definition: "A player. A guy who will lie to a girl to make them hook up with them or send pics."

Dozens of "What's a fuckboy?" YouTube videos appeared in 2015, many by young women decrying the behavior of fuckboys, and others by young men warning how to spot them. One of my favorites was by the unself-consciously feminist YouTuber Damian Alonso, also known as WorldDamian, a teenage boy in Hawaii.

Alonso, who has big brown eyes and wears a T-shirt with a scene of the sun rising over waves, jumps around breathlessly as he educates viewers in his fast-paced patter: "Fuckboys are mostly heterosexual young men who use sexist language, throw around homophobic slurs, think all girls are either sluts or objects . . . and embody ignorance on every level . . . Girls, if a fuckboy asks you out and you reject him, he'll then call you a slut but still tell all his friends that he banged you . . .

"Fuckboys only communicate through text messaging or through Kik," he says. Mimicking a fuckboy texting a girl, Alonso says with a sly look: " 'Wanna play truth or dare? Only *dare* though.'

" 'Smash or pass,' " he says, pretending to check out pictures of girls on his phone. " 'Look, I *know* I said I loved you yesterday,' " he whines satirically, " 'but once I found out you wouldn't put out . . . I'm not ready for a *relationship*' . . . 'Do you send nudes?' . . .

" 'Surprise dick pic!' " he says, pointing his phone camera toward his groin. " 'What size are your boobs?' . . . 'Dude, I totally *banged* her.'

"Fuckboys have been around for years," Alonso concludes, jokingly putting a knife to his throat. Which is true; there have always been sexist and homophobic men and boys. But new words, or new spins on existing words, rarely arise unless there's something that speakers feel a pressing need to express.

What's different about this variation on "womanizer," "ladykiller," and "philanderer" is that it refers to a type of caddish male who has access to social media. A "fuckboy" is a boy or man who uses social media to mistreat and degrade girls and women. All the definitions of "fuckboy" that have appeared in pop culture mention the fuckboy's behavior online: "He sends you unsolicited dick pics," said *Bustle*. "He's constantly begging for nudes," Thought Catalog said. "He blows off your plans to hang but slides into your DMs"—known as a way of hitting up a girl for sex without asking her out on an actual date.

A fuckboy is a "sexist pig" for the age of social media. The word isn't really equivalent to "slut." For the problem with the fuckboy isn't that he has sex; it's how he treats the people he has sex with. And the word is being used by girls as a kind of feminism.

Montclair, New Jersey

"He'll probably send rumors," Riley said as the girls walked to Victoria's house after leaving the Dunkin' Donuts.

"Yeah," Sophia said, "but after Danny, what can he really say?"

"He could say a lot. He could say whatever he wants," Riley said mournfully.

The streets of Montclair were lined with shady oaks and silverbell and dogwood trees. There was the buzzing of a lawn mower off in the distance. The girls were discussing what Zack, the boy who had asked Riley for nudes, would do if she didn't send them.

In a regular case, where there was no "situation" like Riley currently had with Danny, a boy who asked for nudes could be handled with humor, they said. It must be humor, never anger, said Sophia: "If you get mad they'll think that you have no chill. They'll be like, Oh my God, like *chill*, I was just asking. But if you say no and laugh, they'll think you have chill. They judge you if you don't send nudes, like you're a prude. But if you just laugh, then they'll be aggravated, but they won't do anything bad to you."

Such as what? I asked.

"Start rumors. Pretend like you sent them a naked picture they got off the Internet and it's not even you," Sophia said. "Sometimes it's girls that send nudes first. Some girls do it 'cause they're thirsty"—a disparaging word for someone who seems desperate for sexual attention—"and some girls do it 'cause they have a good body and they want to show boys."

I asked them if they knew if any kids in their school watched porn.

"Oh, yeah," Sophia said. "Boys talk about it in my school."

"They watch it on their phones," said Riley. "Danny watches Pornhub."

At Victoria's house, a white clapboard Colonial house, the girls were joined by another friend, Melinda, age thirteen; she was a girl from their school, white, with streaked blond hair, wearing shorts, a blue button-down, and Converse. Her mother was a university professor and her father a film editor. "I am so excited to be talking about this, because we never talk about social media, we just live on it," she said.

The girls sat around the dining room table eating their doughnuts and the brownies Victoria's mother had left for them on a plate. Victoria's mother was picking up her little sister at soccer practice. The dining room was lined with windows looking out on a deep backyard where you could see round-breasted robins hopping in the grass.

The girls filled Melinda in on Riley's difficulty outside the Dunkin' Donuts.

"I can't believe I had an anxiety attack over this," Riley moaned. "I got afraid someone would post something about me if I went in there. That's what social media is doing. It's anxiety-causing and depressing."

"It causes so much drama," Sophia agreed, her mouth full of brownie. "You don't know how much drama I have over my phone."

"With girls our age, so much drama happens over social networking," Melinda told me. "Probably more stuff happens on my phone than in real life."

"I feel like we're living in a second world," Riley said. "There's a real world and a second world," on social media.

As they started talking about all this, they became urgent and intense, just as the girls in Boca had become when they were talking about social media. They began talking fast, raising their voices, interrupting and overlapping one another.

"All we talk about all day is what's happening on our phones, but we never talk about how *weird* that is," Sophia said.

"I spend so much time on Instagram looking at people's pictures and sometimes I'll be like, Why am I spending my time on this? And yet I keep doing it," said Melinda.

"If I go on my phone to look at Snapchat," Riley said, "I go on it for like an hour, like a really long time, I lose track."

"The minute I start my homework I have to have my phone by me," Sophia said, "to see what my friends are texting or if they're sending me texts, and then I'm automatically in a conversation. It's like someone is constantly tapping you on the shoulder, and you have to look. It's distracting."

All of them said they were in one or more group chats of four to eight friends and that they sent or received "hundreds" of texts a day. "Oh my God, at least three hundred," Sophia said. "I get a text, and it's like, *Oooooh*, I have to check that, like, Oh my God, what are they saying? I don't want to miss anything. I'll be like, Mom, it's really important drama, I have to solve it! But sometimes it'll be like nothing, like what kind of chips you eat.

"But I *need* my phone," Sophia added, "I can't survive without it. I stay up all night looking at my phone."

"Two weeks ago I really annoyed my parents by going on my phone too much, so my punishment was I had to delete my Instagram app on my phone for a week," Melinda said. "By the end of the week I was stressing, like, What if I am losing followers?"

"I've always wanted to delete my Instagram," Sophia said, "but then I think, I look so good in all my photos."

She logged on to her Instagram account to show me her page: it was picture after picture of her face, all with the same mysterious, come-hither expression.

"The classic Sophia selfie, bite-tongue smile," she said with a laugh. "It's my brand."

All of them said they had Photoshopped their pictures and edited them with special filters and apps—especially their selfies. "I've darkened my lips and made my eyebrows on fleek," meaning on point, Sophia said. "I never post the first selfie I take. Sometimes it takes like seventy tries.

"Every time I post a selfie," she went on, "I need to check who's commenting—like, Oh my God, I'm getting so many comments. People are like, 'Oh my God gorgeous,' and you feel good about yourself. I'm so happy when I get likes. We're all obsessed with how many likes we get. Everyone says, I get no likes, I get no likes, but everyone says that even if they *get* likes—it never feels like enough. I feel like I'm brainwashed into wanting likes."

What was striking in hearing them talk about this was how conscious they were of what they were doing, their awareness of the inauthenticity of the self they presented on social media.

"It's funny it's called a 'selfie,'" Riley said, "because half the time it doesn't even look like you. So you're getting people to like this picture of you that isn't even real."

The acquiring of likes has become a major theme in corporate marketing, of course; companies invest serious money in studying how to get social media users to like and tweet and post about their products. Social media users have become the most powerful of advertisers, taking word of mouth to a whole new level. For a *Frontline* segment in 2014, "Generation Like," technology writer Douglas Rushkoff went to Montclair to talk to teenagers about their role in building brands. "When a kid likes something online," Rushkoff said on-air, "a product or a brand or a celebrity, it becomes part of the identity that they broadcast to the world, the way a T-shirt or a bedroom poster defined me when I was a teen. For kids today, you are what you like . . . And guess what? Getting people to be 'all about' something is big business." Including the business of social media itself—the more active users are, the more data about them social media companies can collect, and the higher they are valued, as they can then sell the data to other companies. "That's why companies need kids to stay online, clicking and liking and tweeting," Rushkoff told a group of Montclair high school students.

But the *Frontline* segment didn't touch upon why kids seek likes for themselves—or how their methods often mirror the very techniques

companies use to market brands. The girls in Montclair said, for example, that they planned what time of day they posted, trying to hit prime
times for getting likes—another central tenet of social media marketing. On the *Frontline* segment, *New York Times* writer Brooks Barnes
talked about the "day by day, hour by hour" social media marketing
strategy he witnessed in covering the marketing of *The Hunger Games*
in 2012: "The goal is to create a controlled brushfire online."

"I always find a good time to post," Melinda said. "You don't want to
post in the middle of the night when no one sees it. I was on vacation
and there was a time difference, so I would literally stay up to two in the
morning so I could post pictures at a certain time so more people here
would like them. My mom was like, What are you doing?"

Melinda and Victoria told of how they had gone to a Katy Perry
concert together and posted on Instagram almost identical pictures
of Perry performing onstage, but Melinda's pictures had gotten more
likes, because she had posted them at a more desirable time.

"I thought it meant people liked Melinda better," Victoria said.

"Oh, no, it's just because of when I posted," Melinda reassured her.
"I'm obsessed with getting more likes than other people—I'm always
comparing myself to see how many likes my photo got. I'll post a picture on Instagram and immediately start checking."

The captions that went with their posts were also a source of fore-
thought, sometimes requiring a groupthink, like a brainstorming
session on *Mad Men*—how to make them sound witty and clever?

"I work so hard on my captions," Riley said. "Everyone has that one
group chat where they're like, Oh my God, help me with my captions,
what should my caption be?"

The location of their photos was a crucial consideration as well. "I go
to the woods to get really artsy lighting and stuff," said Sophia.

"You'll ask the people in your group chat, Should this be my location? What should I do?" said Riley.

"You get more likes if you're someplace cool," Melinda explained.

"It's called 'good feed,' " Sophia said, "if you take good photos and
use filters and a VSCO Cam," a spiffy camera and editing app, "and
like, have like really good captions."

They said the most admired style of feed among their friends was the one they called "artsy" or "aesthetic." The "aesthetic" aesthetic evolved in the late 2000s with the 2007 advent of Tumblr and other sites devoted to the posting of one's own art, as well as aggregated images of art and fashion and photography. It's used to describe a sense that social media posting *is* art—or can be art, if it's "aesthetic" enough. (Not to be confused with, although perhaps related to, the "New Aesthetic" concept introduced by British artist and writer James Bridle in 2011 to describe the response to technology by artists working in the digital age.)

"You can, like, post a picture of your cereal," Sophia said, "but you have to make it aesthetic."

"Aesthetic" looks, aesthetically, like a manifestation of hipster style, as exemplified by Sofia Coppola's *The Virgin Suicides,* with a dose of *Rookie* and *Real Simple* magazines. "Aesthetic" Instagrams show pictures of filtered pastel skies, girls with expressions bathed in ennui, vintage-looking buildings in black-and-white, and minimalistic bowls of steel-cut oats.

"People say, 'That's so my aesthetic,'" Sophia said. "And it means literally anything that they like. Like, you could say, 'Cheerios are so my aesthetic.'"

By 2015 "aesthetic" so dominated online culture it was already being satirized. *"Is it aesthetic? Is it aesthetic?"* asked teenage singer Ben J. Pierce (KidPOV) in his satirical "The Aesthetic Song" on YouTube. *"Put a bagel on a blanket—is it aesthetic?"*

"It's so much pressure to make your Instagram aesthetic," Victoria said with a groan. "You can't really do anything *wrong.* And if you do, people could laugh at you, like, Oh, look at her Instagram, it's so not aesthetic—it's so *basic.*"

("Basic" was another thing entirely—basically the opposite of "aesthetic," referring to girls who were behind the trends, the purchasers of too-obvious brands, from Gap to Gucci.)

They talked about how there were girls who used the "aesthetic" style as a way of justifying posting sexualized photos of themselves. "They try to be like Lily-Rose Depp," Sophia said, rolling her eyes. She was referring to the sixteen-year-old model-actress daughter of actor Johnny Depp and French singer-actress Vanessa Paradis, who had recently become a social media "It" girl. Lily-Rose's Instagram page, which had more than a million followers, was filled with shots of her beautiful face looking magnificently bored, along with artsy shots in coquettish poses—a "leg shot" on a bed strewn with rose petals. In a video on Instagram, we see her smiling seductively and lip-syncing a line from the Miley Cyrus song "Fweaky (Freaky)": *"Everything you do just turns me on / So let's go in my room and 'na, na . . .'"*

"This photo makes me suicidal she's so fucking gorgeous," a girl commented on a picture Lily-Rose had posted of herself posing on a runway for Chanel with a horde of paparazzi snapping her.

In an interview in Germany's *Gala* magazine, Johnny Depp reportedly expressed concern for his daughter. "To be honest, I'm quite worried," Depp reportedly said. "What's happening with Lily-Rose right now isn't what I expected. Definitely not at this age. But these are her passions and she's having fun."

"Girls will post, like, pictures of their butt and say, 'It's art,'" said Melinda, giggling. "But really it's just their butt."

"Right now it's considered cool for older girls to dress up in, like, baby-doll dresses with knee socks and do a caption like, 'Babysit Me,' *'Virgin,'*" said Sophia, sounding disgusted.

At a time when the number one search on the Internet's biggest porn site was for "Teen," it was disturbing to learn that it had simultaneously become a trend among some teenage girls to style themselves to look even younger than they were as a way of appearing "hot." The "barely legal" aesthetic is a sort of subset of "aesthetic." There are posts on Tumblr, Instagram, and other sites with hashtags such as #Baby Doll, #LittleGirl, and #DaddysGirl, tagged to images of girls and young women (whose ages can't always be determined) in photos where they seem to appear as sexualized little girls. Often such images include an older-looking man engaging in some kind of rough sex play with the girls. "I think it's weird," said Sophia.

Some young feminists have argued that such photos, or any photos by girls of themselves in sexual poses, are a valid expression of female sexuality, and justifiable as the girls' own choice. "Choice feminism" maintains that whatever a woman chooses is inherently a feminist act. Twenty-three-year-old Canadian photographer Petra Collins became celebrated by the fashion industry for her provocative photos of teenage girls, some of them nudes. "I think people aren't comfortable with feminine sexuality," Collins told *Oyster* magazine in 2012, when she was nineteen. "I find people are uncomfortable when a woman is expressing her sexuality instead of repressing it. In our society, nude or sexually suggestive images of women are automatically seen as negative and objectifying . . . We need to make room for the female view of sex and accept it. Until then we are going to be uncomfortable with photos like mine." Interestingly, Collins speaks of "women" here, not girls. She doesn't address questions of exploitation surrounding images of girls who are underage; and then there is the question of who or what exactly defines "the female view of sex."

And again, the question of what constitutes child porn necessarily presents itself. When kids have easy access to porn and are watching porn, it's not all that surprising that they are also posting what might be identified as porn, child porn. In 2014, The Daily Dot reported that Vine, the video-sharing service on which users share six-second looping clips, banned "sexually explicit material" after reports that children were posting sexually charged videos of themselves on the site.

"One user," The Daily Dot said, "identified as an 11-year-old girl, posted a series of nude videos in which she performs sexual acts alone. Another, who appeared to be between 9- and 12-years-old, repeatedly exposed herself while describing sexual intercourse in exchanges with someone identifying himself as a 32-year-old male. Another profile, dedicated to aggregating sexual and nonsexual videos of children, contained over 1,700 Vines and was followed by 964 users. The comments sections for the videos were equally troubling, loaded with explicit sexual language and frequented by Vine users who were clearly adults. Many attempted to lure the minors off Vine and into private chat rooms."

In a horrifying twist, it's the justification of some pedophiles and child pornographers that their victims "want" to perform sexually in front of cameras. In 2015, sixty-six-year-old Ian Wraith was arrested in Fareham, Hants, England, for running a pedophile website with more than 1.6 million pictures and videos of children with "every single indecent image possibly in existence," he reportedly boasted to investigators. According to the *Daily Mirror*, "He even claimed he didn't believe all of them were indecent—instead saying the abused children were happy to be in front of the camera. During an interview he attempted to defend his actions, telling cops: 'You wouldn't believe what these kids get up to when they're on their own with a camera.' "

"Girls think it's cool" to present an underage aesthetic " 'cause it's supposed to be, like, shocking," Sophia said.

The girls said they didn't think most girls who posted provocative photos in this style were trying to elicit sexual encounters with adults or even boys.

"They're just trying to get more likes," Sophia explained. "It's like a cool girl's way of being like the Kardashians."

It was another essential principle of marketing: sex sells. And so if building a social media presence is similar to building a brand, then it makes a warped kind of sense that girls—exposed from the earliest age to sexualized images of women and girls—are promoting their online selves with sex, following the example of the most successful social media celebrities.

"Some people in our grade post pictures of their butt and boobs in a bikini and you see everything. It's totally common," Victoria said. She thumbed through her Instagram account, pulling up pictures of girls they knew posing in bikinis, lounging next to pools, Kim Kardashian–style. "This is a girl in seventh grade—she's like twelve," she added.

"Sixth-graders have more mature Instagrams than we did in sixth grade," Riley said. "Sixth-graders are posing sexy now—it evolved, it's getting younger."

"This girl, she's really popular," said Sophia, pulling up another girl's Instagram page. "See how her butt is all perfect? It's all editing. People edit their butts on Instagram and do all these thot," or slut, "poses. There's a butt app, a skinny app, a face app—"

"She *obviously* edits herself so her side looks way skinnier," Melinda said. "And her pictures are . . . well. I don't even *know* her—she seems like a *perfectly* nice person—but what I notice about her is that she posts selfies of her butt."

"But sometimes I think girls post those kind of pictures because they're proud of their bodies," Victoria countered. "Body-shaming is a big issue. A lot of people will do, like, the 'confident body challenge.' "

"Body-shaming" refers to the way the bodies of girls and women, especially, are judged for not conforming to an ideal, usually a thin ideal; but women seen as overly thin don't escape body-shaming, either. The fact that famous women's bodies are scrutinized so intensely in the media and on social media has been much discussed in the media and online. Celebrities such as Selena Gomez, Lena Dunham, and Demi Lovato have all spoken out against body-shaming.

And it has been a central theme in the new wave of feminism that has ignited among girls and young women. Rejecting the pressure to be unrealistically thin and the demands of "thigh gap"—a trend which says that in order to be considered attractive you have to have a space between your thighs; and now there is "thighbrow," which judges the amount of definition a woman has in the crease that appears at her leg and hipbone when she sits, kneels, or squats—they've been drawn to the "body positive" movement which arose in the 2010s and is committed to redefining standards of beauty and physical worthiness in response to a rigid, Western ideal of a white, thin body type. (It's a grandchild of the similar, albeit clumsily named, "fat acceptance movement" of the 1960s.)

The "body confidence challenge," a social media "challenge" which appeared in the 2010s, encourages girls and women to post pictures of themselves which show off their bodies as a way of expressing their confidence and pride in their size and shape. #fatkini became a hashtag for photos of curvy girls posting pictures of themselves in bikinis.

"I remember one picture where people were a little bit alarmed by it," Victoria said. "It was a girl we know on Instagram, she had a bra on but she wasn't wearing a shirt. She wrote in her caption how she was beginning to feel more confident about her body and learning to not care about what people think. I guess I did like the message. I'm happy she's accepting herself—and she should, she's pretty; and even if she isn't pretty, she should still feel confident about herself. I don't think anyone should feel ashamed of their body or posting a picture."

Sophia scoffed. "Girls post pictures of their bodies and say they're body positive and everyone's like, You're so beautiful," she said. "But they're *not* body confident—they're Photoshopping their bodies and editing their pictures. They *say* they're confident in their bodies, which is totally ironic—if you have to post a picture of yourself on Instagram to feel confident, then you're *not*."

Victoria considered that a moment. "Well, it's supposed to show you're confident," she said. And then: "But actually it makes me feel less confident when I see those girls. I'm like, Oh, I'm not as skinny as that, oh my God, she's so pretty. It makes me compare myself sometimes if it's a really skinny girl. I wish I looked like her."

"It's like, Oh, look at me, I love food, I'm body confident," Riley said, "and here I am eating this hamburger and I look really skinny doing it."

They laughed.

"I think it's just so *boys* can look at it—it's all for boys," Sophia said.

"I don't think it's always *consciously* for guys," said Riley. "But if guys weren't on Instagram I don't think I'd care that much about it. A like from a guy is definitely bigger than a like from a girl."

"How you look is all anybody cares about anymore," Sophia insisted, becoming a bit agitated. "Being beautiful nowadays is seen as way better than being smart. It's terrible. Like if you're a supermodel on Instagram, everyone loves you. Like I do this, too, so I can't judge: if I find a supermodel on Instagram, I'll comment like, I love you so much. Even though they haven't done anything to help the world and they're literally just standing there looking pretty. People love them just 'cause they're beautiful. And like, being smart—no one cares about that. If people aren't pretty nowadays, they're done with their life. Like, Oh my God, I'm not pretty, I can't live life.

"The new word is 'goals,'" Sophia went on. "Everyone says 'goals.' You find a really pretty girl on Instagram and you're like, *'Goals.'* Goals to have my eyebrows like hers, goals to have my lips like hers, goals to have my hair like hers. You'll see on Instagram comments like, 'My goal is to look like her.' Think about it. That's a *goal*? No one cares about being smart anymore. If you're beautiful everyone will love you."

The other girls had stopped eating the brownies.

"But it's fun to post really hot pictures of yourself even though you don't look like that in real life," Sophia said with a toss of her head. "'Cause when I take a really pretty selfie, people will be like, Oh, gorgeous."

Vancouver, Canada; Cambridge, Massachusetts;
and Santa Clarita, California

"I think, before the digital age," says Michael Harris, the author of *The End of Absence: Reclaiming What We've Lost in a World of Constant Connection*, "girls had more opportunities to develop a rich interior life. At some point they were experiencing solitude. They had time to daydream or write in diaries or just think. Now, they're online most of the time and a lot of what they're doing there is comparing themselves or being compared. Online life is a toxic enabler of the desire to compare.

"And girls are asked to compare themselves in a way boys just aren't," Harris says. "They compare the way they look, they compare who has more likes and followers. Teen girls that I talked to," while doing research for his book in Toronto, "they were often obsessed with whether someone had followed them back on Facebook or Twitter, whereas boys could not care less."

"The idea that girls are putting pictures of themselves up on Instagram, Photoshopping and comparing themselves to celebrities and models and other idealized images of women, is very sad to me," says the writer and filmmaker Jean Kilbourne. "This was something I was talking about in 1979 with *Killing Us Softly*, but social media has only helped make it worse than it was forty years ago." *Killing Us Softly*, Kilbourne's groundbreaking documentary series, explored how media and advertising establish standards of beauty to which women feel pressured into conforming.

"Social media creates a heightened sense of competition and inferiority," Kilbourne says. "Girls are bombarded with images all day long and end up feeling, I'm never going to look like that. I think that now girls end up comparing themselves to idealized images of their peers as well. If it's your peers, then there's an even bigger sense of shame of not being able to look like that girl I actually know—even if it's a Photoshopped version of that girl.

"The biggest problem is that girls are only being given one way of thinking about what is beautiful and sexy and it's a very porn-star, clichéd way," Kilbourne says. "There's a much wider, broader variety of choices of how to be sexy than the Victoria's Secret way. To say 'I'm lib-

erated, I'm empowered'—but not really if it's simply following a stereo-
typical conception of sexiness. It's hardly an authentic choice. I think
a lot of it has to do with porn," she adds. "The Internet has brought us
ready access to pornography—very brutal, misogynistic, violent porn is
a lot of girls' main form of sex education."

"Sex is everywhere. Everything is sexualized," says Kim Goldman,
the director of the Santa Clarita Valley Youth Project, a counseling service for teens that reaches about 23,000 kids in fourteen schools in
its district. "Of course girls want to emulate this stuff. Girls talk about
feeling like they have to be like what they see on TV. They talk about
body-image issues and not having any role models. They all want to be
like the Kardashians. Kendall Jenner posts bikini shots when she's sixteen and gets ten thousand likes, and girls see that's what you do to get
attention. We're seeing depression, anxiety, feelings of isolation.

"We had girls selling oral sex for ten and fifteen dollars in the bathroom at a school," Goldman says. "We have kids who've had sex with
people they meet on Chatroulette," an online site where users can video
chat with strangers. "At one of the junior highs we work with, we found
out there were a few kids having an online orgy. They all signed in to a
video chat room." One of their parents walked in on it.

Montclair, New Jersey

On another spring day in Montclair, kids from the middle schools were
walking along Valley Road on their way home. There were girls and
boys, clusters of friends talking and laughing, phones in hands, some
looking at their screens. There was a group of boys who started laughing raucously as they catcalled some passing girls:

"Hey, girl, you look good."

"Yo, you're fine! Let's hang out sometime."

"Why you not smiling, hottie?"

The girls mostly ignored the boys, some giggling or ducking their
heads.

"Oh, she got a *big* booty," a boy said, loud, stopping in his tracks for
effect.

I met Riley, Victoria, and Sophia at Java Love on Bellevue Avenue (Melinda was home sick that day). The coffee shop's in a Tudor-style building not far from the Upper Montclair train station. There were benches outside where you could sit in the shade. The girls got scones and cookies inside the store and joined me there. I told them about the catcalling I'd just seen and asked if they'd ever seen that before.

"It's mostly the popular boys that are like that," Sophia said, chewing her chocolate-chip cookie.

"It's Danny and the popular guys," said Riley, breaking apart a scone. "They think they have control over everyone—like, they're powerful, they're attractive."

"They smoke weed and go to parties," Sophia said, further describing this type of boy. "They hook up and put pictures of themselves drinking and smoking on Instagram." She scrolled through the app on her phone and held up photos of boys holding bongs, smoke coming out of their mouths; boys grinning, holding bags of weed; boys standing with their shorts down around their "V-line," or lower abdominal muscles.

"They call each other 'faggot' and 'gay,'" Riley said. "This guy group, they have a group chat, and they call each other 'gay' if they don't respond to texts. One of my really close friends, he feels stuck in this friend group with all these guys. He doesn't know how to get out of it 'cause then they'll call him 'faggot.'"

In the year when same-sex marriage was legalized, it was disheartening to hear that some boys were still using homophobic slurs. But apparently it wasn't uncommon. In *Dude, You're a Fag*, published in 2007, C. J. Pascoe wrote of the persistent homophobia she saw in a racially diverse, working-class high school—a problem, she said, in her 2012 preface, which only intensified when the behavior moved online, with the proliferation of social media and the "rapidity and replicability of . . . the fag discourse."

"What they do to boys is exactly what they do to girls," Sophia observed. "They put them down for their *sex*. Like they think they're the best 'cause they're the powerful boys and everybody else is, like, lower than them."

"Some boys are nice," Victoria said, sipping on a water bottle.

"They'll talk to you just normally. But then if you act like you actually want to know them and be friends, they might tell everyone you're thirsty."

"If a girl is constantly talking to them, they'll be like, Hop off my dick, stop sucking me," Sophia said.

"That's like *really* disrespectful," Victoria said. "It's not that we wanna suck your *dicks,* we really just want to talk to you—we just want to be friends."

They discussed how some girls they knew seemed to play up to boys. "Girls our age feel really strongly about being strong and not caving in to peer pressure from boys," Victoria said, "but you'll see that girl who will literally change her personality for one boy, or, like, try to look better for a boy."

The other girls nodded.

It was perplexing to hear that, more than two decades since the "girl power" movement, some American girls still felt this anxious need for male approval. What they were describing was startlingly similar to how girls were advised to ingratiate themselves to boys by a column in the *Ladies' Home Journal* in the 1930s. The column, "designed to teach respectable girls the rules of proper socializing," wrote Grace Palladino in *Teenagers: An American History,* urged girls "to remember that 'boys love to run the show and be it.' In fact, if a girl had brains . . . she would figure out just what a boy liked in a date and adjust her personality accordingly!"

"Completely smart people will act dumb around guys," Victoria said. "Girls think boys like it when they act dumb. I think they get it from movies and TV. Like when I was eight, I really liked *Wizards of Waverly Place,*" a Disney Channel show which aired from 2007 to 2012. "I thought Selena Gomez"—who starred as a wise-cracking wizard girl who lives in the suburbs—"was perfect and I would just look at a cover of a magazine and think, That's how I should look. And then when I got older I realized Selena Gomez's character was the dumb one and her brother Justin was the smart one. It was so annoying. They were always making fun of her for doing badly in school. Even her dad. But like she had all these cute boyfriends and she wore cute clothes, so I thought she was perfect."

"Hannah Montana acted really dumb, too," Sophia said. "But now I like Miley. She rebelled from her good-girl role and turned amazing."

"There's this girl in our school," Riley said with a smile, "she dyed her hair for a guy." Pastel hair dye was a popular trend. "He said he thought it was cool, so she dyed her hair blue." They laughed.

"Sometimes I feel like all the posting" on social media "is just for guys and it's so dumb to do something just to impress a guy," Riley said. "Like showing who you're with in your photos—you just post that so the guys will think you're friends with certain people, like pretty girls or guys *they're* friends with."

"And girls post pictures of themselves kissing other girls even though they're straight," Sophia said. Why? "They do it because it's hot for guys."

I asked them why girls cared so much about what boys thought.

"Because everybody wants a boyfriend," Riley said. "It makes you popular. You're more popular if you even have guys as *friends*."

"Girls think a lot about boys, to be honest," Sophia said. "A lot of girls consider having a boyfriend a really important part of teenagers' lives. I don't want to be the only person without a boyfriend," she added. "I wanna have my first kiss. It's what a lot of people are thinking about around this time. First kiss is a big, big deal."

"Everyone wants their first kiss over with so they're not considered, like, a prude," Riley said. "You have to have your first kiss over by high school or you're a prude."

"Apparently," said Sophia. "That's what everyone aims for, is to kiss or hook up. The new thing is, like, having 'a thing.' You don't say, Me and John are dating—that sounds thirsty. It's, Me and John, we have a thing. It means you go to other people's houses and hook up and post stuff together on social media."

I asked them if boys and girls ever went out on dates, like to a movie. They laughed. "Nooooo."

"That's too awkward," Victoria said.

"Dating is just for other people to *know* that you're dating," said Sophia. "People post about it all the time. Like kissing photos."

"People put pictures of themselves with their boyfriend on Snapchat," Riley said.

"Pictures of, like, a couple kissing, hugging, posing with each other on Instagram," said Sophia. "And other people will comment, like, 'relationships goals!' and 'OTP' "—meaning "one true pairing," or an idolized couple.

"Dating now is just to hook up and take selfies," said Riley.

I asked Riley if her relationship with Danny had been like that.

"Yeah, kind of," she said. "And we hung out. We went over to each other's houses. I had sleepovers at Danny's house," she added with a shy smile. "His parents made us breakfast and brought it up to his room."

The other girls were silent.

Riley laughed, embarrassed.

"I heard some moms at a bat mitzvah talking about their kids having a boy-girl sleepover," Victoria said. "And they were acting like it was so cute. My mom and dad would never let me. Not that I am dating anyone," she added. The girls all said they had heard of parents who allowed their daughters to have a sleepover with a boyfriend.

"It's the parents that say they 'trust' their daughters to 'make their own decisions,' " Sophia said, doing lots of air quotes. "They say it's being 'feminist.' They think their kids will think they're cool. But a lot of parents don't get that it's putting a lot of pressure on their children. It's like a lot of pressure to be allowed to make all your own decisions, you know? And we're just kids, and we don't always know what's the right thing to do."

Riley was silent.

I asked her if she had decided how to respond to the boy who had asked for nudes.

"I don't know," she said, shrugging. "I just don't want him to think he won."

Sophia made a face. "No, you really don't."

The girls went off together, smiling and chatting, down Valley Road.

Chapter Two

14

Huntington Beach, California

She felt the most real when she was being filmed. Alone in her bedroom, sitting in front of the camera, talking to her fans, this was when she became the real Amanda. "People like it when you're real and raw," she said, perched on a kitchen stool at her family's house in Huntington Beach. Raw, she said, like in her "TMI" video when she admitted to never having had a boyfriend, and revealed that her OTP was Chuck and Blair from *Gossip Girl*, and she confessed to being afraid of death and spiders; but she would never reveal her weight. "It's amazing how u don't answer the 'how much you weight' question," commented one of her YouTube fans; "it's really respectful to the over-weighted people. She doesn't want anyone to feel insecure." "Yeah I agree," another commenter said, "she's just so considerate and sweet."

Her fans knew who she really was. "Amanda is my idol!" said one of her 1.5 million YouTube followers. "AMANDA IS MY QUEEN," said one of her 1 million followers on Instagram. "AND THERE'S NOTHING YOU CAN DO TO STOP IT." The people on the other side of the screen saw the true Amanda Steele (her real name, which I use with permission), the fourteen-year-old beauty guru behind Makeup byMandy24. When she traveled from this side of the lens to the other, it was as if through palace doors, to a place where she was no longer a child, but a queen. "SHE IS EVERYTHING." From here, where things could be drab and dull and tedious, to there, where it was permanently bright and as colorful as the set of a Disney show, she became the girl she always wanted to be—that everybody wanted to be—that cute and upbeat, bouncy, sassy, little bit awkward, little bit goofy girl, always meticulously groomed and stylish and funny and sweet, and thin; but not *too* funny, not in an off-putting way. She was the "perfect" American girl, at least in one version embodied by the stars of social media.

"Be yourself," Amanda answered a fan who asked about her favorite quote.

It wasn't an easy journey, crossing over into the LED-lit Promised Land on the other side of the lens. It was every bit as grueling as a trek into outer space—becoming famous, Internet famous, just for being "you." It required preparation and planning and hours of practice and implementation—the perfection of the art of selfies, among other things—and something else; something a little bit special, something even she couldn't understand, and didn't want to analyze, lest it slip away. "I don't even like to call it fame," she said. "I just like to upload cool pictures. I'm just, like, a normal girl."

Behind the Lens

Kids started having their own cameras, en masse, in the 1960s. Kodak Instamatics, which came out in 1963, were inexpensive ($16) and easy to use, durable and small, the perfect size to fit in a child's pocket or the upper tray of a footlocker on its way to summer camp. The Instagram logo, in a conscious nod, echoes the look of the early Instamatics—a dark stripe on top, metallic on the bottom, with a round flat lens and viewfinder in the middle. The logo was nostalgic, also a confident announcement of how this new mobile app would continue to popularize photography as successfully as its symbolic predecessor. More than 50 million Instamatics were sold between 1963 and 1970, making it then the best-selling camera of all time. Between its launch in 2010, by two male Silicon Valley software engineers who met at Stanford, and 2015, Instagram gained over 400 million active users worldwide, more people than live in America, according to its own statistics.

Instamatics were also one of the first cameras marketed directly to girls. In 1932, Kodak had come out with a camera for boys, its Boy Scout

Brownie (a variation on its popular Brownie camera, introduced in 1900), appealing to male youths who fancied themselves living adventurous lives as campers and explorers, near heroic lives which deserved documentation. With the Instamatic, Kodak realized it had a vast new demographic to target: teen girls. But the pitch was very different. It said that girls could use cameras to become popular.

Teenagers of both sexes were experiencing the rapid cultural changes under way in the '60s, but the lives of girls especially were transforming. They were more sexually liberated than girls in the past, as well as more sexualized by the media and advertising, and they were more independent. More of them either worked part-time or had access to their parents' disposable incomes in a strong economy—they had money to spend, with which they were buying more of the clothes and makeup that were relentlessly marketed to them. You can almost hear the unrepentant sexist Don Draper, of *Mad Men,* working up the Kodak pitch: "Why do girls want cameras? They're sentimental, they're vain, they want to be popular, they want to show off their pretty clothes and who they're friends with. They want to make memories. And they want to look good in those memories."

Kodak sold its Instamatics to girls in ads infused with an aura of nostalgia (which Draper once described as "delicate, but potent"). An ad in *Seventeen* in 1968 urged girls to buy Instamatics before they returned to high school after summer vacation: *"What you're going back to deserves a great camera,"* said the tagline. "You can just imagine what's coming up," read the copy. "Homecoming parade. Games. Dances. Old friends and new faces. It makes sense to have a great camera. And it makes sense for it to be one of our Kodak Instamatic cameras . . . It's one back-to-school outfit you really ought to have." It was as if a girl could relate to a technological device only if it offered the same advantages as a miniskirt.

The layout for the ad was accompanied by two candid-looking shots, one of a pretty blond girl dressed as a cheerleader; she's surrounded by five basketball-player boys after a championship game. Their proud coach wields a trophy; they won. The girl is kissing one of the boys on the cheek; he seems to be the team's cute captain. The other photo shows the girl with this same boy; now it's prom night and she's wearing a virginal white dress and gloves. Her hair is in ringlets, a corsage is pinned to the strap of her gown; she's beaming. The boy, standing beside her, is looking suave in a white tux.

The message: cameras were tools for creating an idealized self, and pictures were a kind of self-promotion. And the ideal girl (in Kodak's view, a pretty, blond white girl) would have the attention of boys. If only everybody could see how popular she was.

Instagram gave girls that opportunity. The way many girls use the app is not so different from how girls have been taught to use photography for decades. The difference now lies in the chance to show the whole world one's beauty, boyfriends, special moments, and clothes, not just the other kids in school. And with that broadcasting power comes an enormous thrill: the chance to become not just popular, but actually famous. Famous for just being you.

"I think it's more of a challenge for you to go on a reality show and get people to fall in love with you for being you," Kim Kardashian told Barbara Walters on her *10 Most Fascinating People* special. Walters didn't point out that reality shows are actually scripted entertainment, and Kim didn't mention it, either.

Huntington Beach, California

In the year between when I met Amanda Steele in Huntington Beach and when I sat down to write about her, she had become a bona fide social media star. When I spoke to her in 2014, she had a solid online following as a YouTube beauty guru and up-and-coming Instagram "It" girl; cosmetic and clothing companies were asking her to do endorsements on her YouTube channel. A year later, she was walking the red carpet at the 2015 MTV Video Music Awards in the company of Miley Cyrus, Kim Kardashian, and Nicki Minaj. Amanda was there as the "social media correspondent" for CoverGirl makeup.

It was in 2014 that the mainstream media seemed to catch up to the fact that teenagers were creating their own celebrities, and no longer looking solely to Hollywood or the music industry for people to admire and emulate; they were finding them in their phones. In 2014, *Vari-*

ety ran an eye-opening headline: "Survey: YouTube Stars More Popular Than Mainstream Celebs Among U.S. Teens." The top five most influential figures in the survey among American teenagers, ages thirteen to eighteen, did not include Jennifer Lawrence or Taylor Swift or, for that matter, Hillary Clinton or Barack Obama, but were YouTubers.

Teenagers surveyed cited the relatability and accessibility of social media personalities as the main reason for their appeal, as well as their lack of filter. "You feel like you know them," said Sophia, the Montclair girl, "'cause they're doing the same thing we're doing"—that is, using social media in a way that adults and most celebrities did not: like teenagers. "Celebrities are on their own little pedestal," said Victoria, her friend. "They're not taking a vlogging camera and being like, Hi, guys, I'm gonna get a smoothie." When I told them I had interviewed Amanda Steele, Sophia became giddy: "She's my *idol*."

It became clear it was not only clueless but rather dangerous for the media to dismiss the relevance of these new teen idols, in 2015, when an editor for Eonline.com, Seija Rankin, posted a story in which she joked about how she had never heard of many of the nominees at that year's Teen Choice Awards, all Internet celebrities. "Eva Gutowski? Lele Pans? Joey Graceffa? Felix Kjellberg? Are those even real people?" Rankin wrote (unfortunately spelling Vine star Lele Pons's name incorrectly).

The reaction on social media was swift and fierce. "If this 'article' is representative of @eonline, I fear for the brand's future," tweeted Tyler Oakley, YouTuber, LGBTQ rights activist, and unofficial grand poohbah of all things teen social media. "Hi @eonline! My name is Joey Graceffa, YouTube creator and *New York Times* best-selling author, so nice to meet you!" tweeted Graceffa, whose 2015 memoir, *In Real Life: My Journey to a Pixelated World,* told of his journey from bullying victim to social media celebrity (a recurring theme among Internet stars). And then there were the fans who came out in droves in support of their online gods, with all the acerbity teenagers can summon. "@seijawrites [Rankin's Twitter handle] I doubt anyone actually knows and likes you? These YouTubers have millions of subscribers and you have 486 followers," tweeted @likelionz.

I'd heard from girls how important social media personalities were in their world, so I wanted to meet one and ask her how she had pulled off this coveted feat, and why: What had inspired her to try for Internet fame, and what effect was it having on her young life? I contacted Amanda Steele after seeing her on Instagram, and one summer day found myself driving to her house in Huntington Beach.

Huntington Beach is a town of some 200,000 people, about thirty-five miles south of Los Angeles. It sits on a magnificent 9.5-mile stretch of beach against which the waves of the Pacific ceaselessly beat, famously making it a great place to surf. The town, which trademarked the moniker "Surf City USA," hosts the annual U.S. Open of Surfing, the largest surfing competition in the world. People in Huntington Beach wear flip-flops year-round; it has a laid-back beach town feel.

The neighborhood where Amanda lived was full of streets lined with tall, skinny palms and modest homes with dry, dry lawns, casualties of the California drought. There were boats in the driveways and more American flags flying than you see at a Republican fund-raiser. Overhead the air was crisscrossed with telephone wires. It was surprising to learn that this was where she lived, when her Instagram pictures seemed to depict something more glamorous. She often appeared beside a backyard pool, dressed in the latest fashions, wearing cool sunglasses. "We're failing at life," lamented a commenter under one such picture, full of FOMO (Fear of Missing Out). "MY OBSESSION WITH HER IS SO UNHEALTHY HELP ME," said another. "House tour!" begged others.

Amanda lived in a white one-story house with an interior which resembled the homes on sitcoms like *Everybody Loves Raymond;* it was a comfortable American home in a lot of brown and beige, with a tiny round swimming pool on the bright back patio. Her father, Gerry Steele, answered the door. He was barefoot, wearing a T-shirt and cargo shorts. He looked like Mark Harmon, the actor who played the befuddled stepfather in *Freaky Friday* (the 2003 version, starring Lindsay Lohan). He was a high school history teacher, he said, and Amanda's mother, who was at work, was an attorney.

"She's always had that drive," he said of Amanda, "even when she was a little girl." He took from the wall a framed photograph of Amanda at about age eight, proudly showing it off; she was wearing a team uniform and hurling a softball, her face full of determination, grease streaks under her eyes. "This is my favorite picture of her," said her father.

"Now," he said, carefully putting the picture back, "I mean, you have no idea of the extent of her empire. Everything she touches turns to gold. I tell you, her fans even recognize *me*. They want *my* autograph. They'll say, 'There goes Amanda's dad.'" He chuckled.

Amanda was waiting for her father to finish talking. She wore a curling smile. She was a slender girl with shiny, shoulder-length dark hair and pale blue eyes. She wore short black shorts, a black crop top, and a dark, patterned kimono, like butterfly wings. Her nails were long and cobalt blue. She had creamy white skin ("Here's How to Get Flawless Skin Like Amanda Steele," said a post on MTV.com) and was wearing a lot of makeup. She had none of the bounciness seen in her YouTube videos; she seemed preternaturally poised.

"Disney," her father went on, "paid her *significantly* more to upload her interstitial," a kind of ad, "onto her YouTube channel than to play it on TV—which shows you that they feel they get more bang for the buck on social media. You know, there are TV-star kids out there that are trying to break into social media. I see a whole paradigm shift—*everything's* moving toward social media," he said. He spoke with the enthusiasm of someone who was excited by the vicissitudes of history.

"When you're a YouTuber," Amanda said, trying to break in, "it's a different kind of connection with the fans—"

"It's interactive," her father interjected, "'cause they can *comment*—"

"They also feel like they're your best friend," Amanda explained. "I think that's why so many people come to the meet-ups"—meaning events where fans can come to meet online stars, typically at shopping malls. "They feel like they know me."

I asked her when it all took off.

"A little bit over a year ago," she said. "I signed with Big Frame, my network," a multichannel YouTube network which brings together You-Tubers and advertisers for mutual business opportunities; in 2014 it was acquired by the digital media division of DreamWorks Animation. Big Frame manages Tyler Oakley and other online megacelebrities.

Amanda said, "I have a manager there—"

"Here's what happened," said her father, interrupting. "When she started with this agency about a year ago, she had about a hundred thousand YouTube subscribers—now she has one-point-five million." By the end of 2015, she would have 2.7 million. "That's all hers. All the other deals—the Invisalign, the Disney, Kohl's—the agency gets a percentage. There are agents now just for YouTube stuff. I think her success comes from a multifaceted thing—she's very smart, she's pretty, and she comes off very good in front of the camera. Her timing was good—the stars just aligned for her. You know, girls her age can be very *nasty,* but for the most part she's well liked. She knows what to say and what not to say. And it just snowballed—this thing is growing *exponentially.*"

Gerry showed me a video on his phone of a throng of girls standing in line at a California shopping mall, all waiting to meet Amanda. He watched it with an excited yet puzzled expression.

"All the advertisers want a piece of her," he said. "We get two or three boxes of stuff a *day*—companies sending her stuff, hoping she'll mention it in one of her videos or on her Instagram. I always say she has every teenage girl's dream, all the clothes and makeup you could want . . ."

Amanda pursed her lips. Her father kept talking.

"Can you come here?" she said, beckoning for him to come outside.

Her voice through the door: "You don't even know what you're talking about. You're not a part of this . . . Can you stop talking?"

YouTube

What is a beauty guru? A beauty guru is typically a girl or young woman who shows other girls and young women how to put on makeup. She advises them on fashion trends and shows them how to style their hair. She suggests beauty products, often ones she's paid for endorsing. She sometimes shares details of her life and talks about her insecurities concerning her own appearance. She even discusses how the pressure to be beautiful lowers her self-esteem. And her answer to this problem is always: look better, look beautiful, because that will raise your confidence and make you feel better about yourself.

In the culture of beauty, this notion has a name: "beauty therapy." A beauty guru is a kind of beauty therapist who lives in a computer; she's like a beauty-savvy big sister or friend, and she's always relentlessly cheerful. "They seem really nice and helpful," said Victoria, the Montclair girl. And they're always beautiful.

Beauty gurus are popular with American girls. In 2015, there were more than 180,000 of them on YouTube, along with their millions of beauty "tutorials"; the most successful have millions of subscribers to their channels. They're like a living, breathing version of the "how-to" pages which have appeared in women's magazines for more than a century (in the 1850s, *The Englishwoman's Domestic Magazine* guided women on how to be fashionable). Beauty gurus have more of a presence on YouTube—one of the most wide-reaching media outlets of the modern era, exceeding a billion users—than any of the other popular female YouTubers in a specific role. There are female comedians, singers, actors, activists, feminists, and others who upload content to the site, but beauty gurus eclipse them all in sheer numbers and total numbers of views.

Beauty gurus started appearing soon after the launch of YouTube in 2005. One of the first to acquire a following was Michelle Phan, a then twenty-year-old Tampa girl who, in 2007, uploaded a seven-minute "Natural Looking Makeup Tutorial." In it, she stared alluringly into the camera as she demonstrated how to apply concealer and foundation as tinkling beauty salon–style music played. Today, Phan has had more than a billion lifetime views on YouTube and has achieved the kind of outsized fame and fortune which are the promise of the new American dream via social media: she has her own L'Oréal cosmetics line (em), a beauty products sampling company (ipsy, which had expected sales of $120 million in 2015), and a social media talent network of her own (Icon). In 2015, *Forbes* put her on its list of "30 Under 30—Art & Style," recognizing those who are "creating and designing the future, from the street to the runway."

But is Phan a feminist? In a cultural moment in which it seemed that every female celebrity's feet were put to the fire on this burning question (Taylor Swift, Miley Cyrus, Ellen Page, Shailene Woodley, Meghan Trainor, Kelly Clarkson—yes, yes, yes, and no, no, no), Phan said no. "I don't believe in bringing any politics to an idea like feminism," she said on Cosmopolitan.com in 2015. "I love the idea that women should be celebrated, but I also believe men should be, too."

A post on Seventeen.com argued that while it was "a bummer" that Phan was "perpetuating" the mistaken idea that "being a feminist has anything to do with bringing down men," she was still a source of feminist inspiration because she was a "woman who's found great success following her dreams." In a popular notion of feminism, a woman is a feminist simply if she is successful in her career.

Nowhere in the Seventeen.com post, and rarely anywhere in the current discourse surrounding feminism, is there any question of whether the pursuit of beauty through beauty products is problematic for feminism. Whether a woman who makes her living showing other women how to get "perfect brows" and plump their lips is actually engaging in an antifeminist enterprise does not seem to be a consideration, especially if it makes her rich and famous. Feminists who bemoan the pressures of media standards of beauty also defend the desire of women to try to improve and perfect themselves through the use of makeup, plastic surgery, or whatever means they choose.

This is a change from the early days of the feminist movement, when feminists were more skeptical about beauty as an empowering goal. In 1968, hundreds of feminists traveled on buses to Atlantic City to protest the Miss America pageant, which they saw as ground zero for looks-based sexism. "This was a completely outrageous event and marked a watershed in American history, a watershed virtually ignored in retrospectives of the 1960s in general and 1968 in particular," wrote Susan J. Douglas in *Where the Girls Are: Growing Up Female with the Mass Media*. Women who joined the protest objected to the attitudes pageants promoted—the objectification of women, impossible yet rigid standards of beauty, the Madonna-whore fantasy that women should be both virginal and sexual, and the idea that women are in competition with one another over who is sexier or more beautiful.

Playfully, the protesters set up a "Freedom Trash Can" into which they threw perceived symbols of women's oppression, including high heels, nylons, girdles, corsets, false eyelashes, makeup, and bras (it was from this event that the media myth arose that feminists "burned their bras"). In the PBS documentary *Miss America,* Gloria Steinem reflected on how, for those feminists, the pageant symbolized how marginalized groups in society had to compete for the "favors of the powerful. So what could be a greater example of that than a beauty contest?"

In 1991, Naomi Wolf's *The Beauty Myth: How Images of Beauty Are Used Against Women* amplified this theme. Wolf saw in the increased pressure for women to be beautiful a reaction against feminism. She contended that as women achieved more social and political power, the demands of "beauty" worked to undermine women's empowerment. "The more legal and material hindrances women have broken through, the more strictly and heavily and cruelly images of female beauty have come to weigh upon us," she wrote. "During the past decade, women breached the power structure; meanwhile, eating disorders rose exponentially and cosmetic surgery became the fastest-growing specialty . . . pornography became the main media category . . . and thirty-three thousand American women told researchers that they would rather lose ten to fifteen pounds than achieve any other goal . . . More women have more money and power and scope and legal recognition than we have ever had before; but in terms of how we feel about ourselves physically, we may actually be worse off than our unliberated grandmothers."

Wolf's book was criticized by some women of color for failing to represent their different issues with body image and racism. "The consensus was that Wolf didn't appear to recognize that black women were battling equally tyrannical but very different standards of beauty," says Jeannine Amber, a contributing writer at *Essence*. Many feminists of the 1990s rejected Wolf's thesis as well, though on other grounds. "Lipstick" or "girlie" feminism said that for women, beauty *was* empowerment. Beauty was a form of self-expression; it was liberating, not a sign of internalized oppression—in fact, it could be seen as a symbol of resistance, in that traditional symbols of femininity could be reclaimed by feminists. How a woman dressed or whether she used beauty products was her own choice and not some manifestation of patriarchal control.

This third-wave take on beauty was much in evidence in the attitudes of girls I interviewed at the Miss Houston Teen and Miss Houston beauty pageant in the spring of 2014. When I asked Miss Houston Teen contestants, ages fourteen to eighteen, why they did pageants, almost all of them said that it "empowered" them. They talked about the "empowering" effects of pageantry in a kind of mantra: "Onstage I felt empowered." "I felt like nothing till I started doing pageants." "Pageants saved me." Bri (her real name, which I use with her permission, as with all the pageant contestants quoted here), then age sixteen, said, "Growing up, I've always felt, like, fat. I've always felt, like, not pretty enough, and . . . [doing pageants] helps me. They're a confidence-booster. You feel like a princess up onstage." Taylor, then seventeen, another Miss Houston Teen contestant, said that she had been bullied and cyberbullied in middle school. It was competing in pageants that had given her "confidence." "They told me my head was too big for my body so they called me a Bratz doll," Taylor said with a laugh. "One time on Facebook I got a huge message just saying how I'm ugly, how I have a gap between my teeth, how I was never going to amount to anything in my life, how I wasn't good enough for anybody." Almost every pageant contestant I spoke to had suffered some traumatic event in her past (including a young woman, twenty-one, who said she had been beaten by a boyfriend) which only being "beautiful" and "looking like a princess" onstage had helped her to overcome.

The idea of beauty as empowerment has actually been part of the marketing strategy of the beauty pageant industry for decades. As a result of the feminist critique of the 1960s, it seemed that beauty pageants were forced to repackage their brand. Pageants are sexist? No, they're not, they're just the opposite of sexist, they're empowering, said the rebranding. The current motto of the Miss America pageant is "Style, Service, Scholarship, and Success." Its literature stresses the idea that competing in pageants actually prepares girls and young women for the business world. "Some call her a beauty queen, we call her a scholar," says its familiar fund-raising ad.

The bigger picture is the way in which things once considered sexist have been reinterpreted by and for girls as "empowering"—beauty pageants, stripping, even porn. Girls Gone Wild founder Joe Francis often argued in interviews that it was the "choice" of the teenage girls and young women who appeared in his infomercial-marketed soft-porn videos, a symbol of their "freedom" that they flashed their breasts for his cameras. "I'm ready and willing, and I'm a dirty slut," said a girl in a typical Girls Gone Wild moment from 2005. But whether or not the girls in Girls Gone Wild videos acted out of choice, some experienced unwelcome consequences. Lindsey Boyd was fourteen when she says she accepted beads in exchange for exposing her breasts to a Girls Gone Wild camera crew while she was on spring break in Florida; her face wound up on the cover of a Girls Gone Wild video box. "Teachers knew about it, coaches knew about it. It was devastating. It was so embarrassing," Boyd told ABC News in 2012. "A stupid split-second decision you make could follow you for the rest of your life." Four young women in a 2008 Florida lawsuit said they suffered emotional distress and had to leave their schools after appearing in Girls Gone Wild videos, which were shot when they were thirteen, fifteen, sixteen, and seventeen. In 2011, an all-female jury denied their claim, deciding that Francis had shown no intent to cause them emotional damage.

"I think what happened in the nineties," says Susan J. Douglas, the author and a professor of communication studies at the University of Michigan, "was that various advertisers in corporate America picked up on the whole third-wave 'girl power' moment and they ran with it. They took this desire among girls and young women to have the same sexual agency as boys and young men and they exploited it. They started taking this idea of 'sexuality as power' and turning it around to young women, telling them they were more powerful if they were more sexualized. There was a lot more sexual display by women in television, advertising, and music videos, and this started getting sold back to girls as empowerment." In her book *The Rise of Enlightened Sexism: How Pop Culture Took Us from Girl Power to Girls Gone Wild,* Douglas expands on how advertisers, beginning in the 1990s, co-opted the third-wave feminist celebration of female sexualization to market everything from media to clothing to beauty products.

The idea that sexualized fashion is an expression of feminist power can also be found in the controversy over dress codes in American schools. Two thousand fourteen was a battleground year for the issue of dress codes all over the country; in Illinois, Iowa, New York, California, Utah, Texas, and other states, high school and middle school girls held protests over the installing of dress codes banning clothing items such as crop tops, tank tops, yoga pants, and booty shorts, restrictions the girls called sexist. The issue had its own hashtag, #iammorethana distraction, with which girls were tweeting their indignation over being told what to wear, especially when similar limitations on boys' attire were not being imposed. The hashtag was a reference to how some schools had been alleging that girls' fashions were "distracting" to boys, as if boys' rights rather than girls' were of primary concern.

A middle-schooler in Montclair, Beatriz Bellido-Guevara, wrote a letter to *The Montclair Times* denouncing the "sexualizing" of girls she believed dress codes promote. "Why don't schools do something to stop this rape culture and sexism, instead of slut-shaming females for their bodies?" she asked. It was a powerful point, as well as an example of the complicated terrain for discussions about feminism which a general atmosphere of hypersexualization has created. Girls agree that they are sexualized and objectified by a sexist culture; but when they self-sexualize and self-objectify, some call it feminist; or they reject the notion that there is any self-sexualization or self-objectification going on in their choices, and to suggest as much is called slut-shaming and an example of rape culture. It's a sticky wicket. A 2014 article in *The Nation* on the protest movement over dress codes cited the APA's seminal 2007 report on the sexualization of girls in support of the idea that dress codes themselves are sexualizing, quoting the report as saying, " 'Sexualization occurs when a person's value comes only from his or her sexual appeal or behavior, to the exclusion of other characteristics.' "

You could use the same passage, however, to argue the opposite case—to ask whether girls placing so much importance on what they wear is itself another aspect of sexualization. The APA report also says that "girls sexualize themselves when they think of themselves mostly or exclusively in sexual terms and when they equate their sexiness with a narrow standard of physical attractiveness," which it suggests that a hypersexual culture influences them to do.

The nuances of this debate often seem to go unexplored by parents, especially mothers who support the idea that their daughters should be allowed to wear whatever they want as an expression of their rights as young feminists. A woman who is the mother of a fourteen-year-old girl in Brooklyn told me, "In our middle school there was a meeting with parents about dress codes and one mother said, You are sexualizing these girls. The school said, Look, some girls are coming to school in a shirt and tights—not leggings, tights—where you can see their underwear. Can we really call that a good choice for them?" And on the subject of distraction, the APA report also cites studies which have found that sexualized fashions can become a distraction to the girls who are wearing them, even impeding their cognitive function: "Perhaps the most insidious consequence of self-objectification is that it fragments consciousness."

And not every girl is comfortable with the revealing clothing some girls wear to school; at issue is also these girls' comfort level, which often goes unacknowledged. "It makes me really uncomfortable," said a fifteen-year-old girl in New York, "when you walk up the stairs in school and all you see is butts. You can see everything coming out of their shorts. Boys like it. But if you say that, then they say you're slut-shaming and they might gossip about you or post something about how you're not feminist" on social media.

It's true that the policing of women's fashions has long been a source of patriarchal control, from whalebone corsets that left women little room to breathe to, some would argue, burqas; and it's also true that some teachers and administrators around the country have abused their authority over girls and have disciplined and shamed them for how they dress in ways that are unacceptable and sexist. There have been reports of administrators taking girls out of class and sending them home, even suspending them for what they wear, as well as making inappropriate comments about their bodies and appearance. You don't need to look any further than the case of the middle school girl in Batavia, Ohio, whose "Feminist" T-shirt was Photoshopped out of her official class photo in the school yearbook to get an idea of what is lurking behind the dress code enforcement in some schools (after the girl and her mother complained to the school, the principal apologized). It's admirable when girls react to such outrages with protest. (The girl with the "Feminist" shirt, Sophie Thomas, started a Twitter campaign.) But the fact that it is dress codes which have become the focus of the feminist activism of many girls seems strange at a time when there are so many other issues facing them.

"Girls want to talk about dress codes everywhere I go," says Soraya Chemaly, who often speaks at schools. "What I tell them is that this is the icing on the cake. It's fine to confront administrations and try and create new norms. But if you have a highly gendered dress code that is rigidly enforced, that probably means other things are going on in your school that are much more important. Dress codes are unfair and there are double standards, but they may be a symptom of other things going on in your school community."

And these may be things girls feel hesitant to speak out against or protest because the danger of condemnation for doing so is much greater, the risks much higher: for example, slut pages in their schools, sexual harassment in their schools, and offensive behavior by both boys and girls on social media—including slut-shaming. Dress codes are a weirdly safe subject for girls' expression of their feminism. To protest them is to be in sync with a culture that places a premium on being "hot" and promotes the idea that one can be seen as sexually liberated by means of provocative fashions. And it doesn't criticize boys.

"I gave them this example," Chemaly says, "of girls who were told by their principal that he was afraid they would be mistaken for 'prostitutes' if they wore short shorts on a class trip. I said, Well, what did you do to get the boys involved? The boys could have all worn short shorts with you in solidarity. The problem is that boys, while they weren't to blame for the policy, they were privileged by the policy. But none of the girls talked about whether the boys were responsible for what was happening with them, their peers. The girls felt these problems had nothing to do with boys, and that is not true."

And the sexualization of girls doesn't come from dress codes alone. As detailed in the APA report, it's found in the fashion and beauty industries, in the media, advertising, and the Internet, among other sources, to which I think you could add porn. It comes from the attitudes of parents—who, according to the APA, "routinely" engage in "fat talk" around their daughters and surround them with "excessive concerns" about their physical appearance. It comes from teachers and other adults, as well as, sometimes, peers.

Meanwhile, the adverse effects of sexualization continue to plague huge numbers of girls. Eating disorders have been on the rise since the 1950s and are now seen across racial lines. Forty to 60 percent of girls ages six to twelve are worried about their current weight or about becoming too heavy, a concern which persists throughout their lives as women, according to the National Eating Disorders Association. More than half of teenage girls use unhealthy dieting methods such as skipping meals, vomiting, taking laxatives, and fasting. A 2014 study by researchers at Florida State University found a link between college-age women's risk of developing eating disorders and their time spent on Facebook, where contributing factors such as the influence of media and pressure from peers are merged.

There's been an increase in anxiety and depression among teen girls that has been linked to sexualization and social media use as well. According to a 2014 review of nineteen studies from twelve industrialized countries, adolescent girls around the world are now experiencing more depression and anxiety attributed to "high expectation on girls in terms of appearance and weight," among other factors. "What is very clear is that girls have almost double the anxiety and worries as boys," said child psychiatrist William Bor of the University of Queensland, the study's leader. A 2015 study at University College London found a possible link between anxiety in girls ages eleven to thirteen and seeing images of women being sexually objectified on social media. Girls this age were significantly more likely to feel nervous or show a lack of confidence than they were just five years ago, according to the study. "We were surprised to see such a sharp spike in emotional problems among girls" in "a relatively short period of time," said psychologist Elian Fink, the study's lead author. It seems relevant that it is in about the last five years that the majority of girls have gotten smartphones.

The constant seeking of likes and attention on social media seems for many girls to feel like being a contestant in a never-ending beauty pageant in which they're forever performing to please the judges— judges who have become more and more exacting. For it's no longer enough for girls and women to be just pretty—even beautiful is not enough; now the goal is to be "perfect," "flawless." In the 2000s, beauty companies started promoting products that promised to make women "flawless" and "perfect." Max Factor, Laura Mercier, bareMinerals, Avon, Pond's, and dozens of other beauty brands now sell products with "perfect" and "flawless" in their names, a trend in marketing with reverberations in the world of girls. Telling a girl she looks "flawless" has become a social gesture, a kind of ultimate compliment, girl to girl; "#flawless," girls write on each other's selfies. "If I had a dollar for every time someone comments 'you're flawless' on one of Kendall Jenner / Shay Mitchell / Selena Gomez's Instagram selfies, I'd be able to afford a Birkin," joked blogger Zara Husaini on the College Candy website.

The age at which girls wear makeup is getting younger, starting between the ages of eight and thirteen, according to a 2013 survey by Harris Interactive; of the three in five American girls who say they wear makeup, many say they have negative feelings about their looks when they don't wear it, such as feeling unattractive, self-conscious, or as if something is "missing" from their faces. When makeup alone isn't enough to assuage feelings of unattractiveness, some seek plastic surgery. More than 220,000 cosmetic procedures were performed on patients ages thirteen to nineteen in 2013, and in that year plastic surgeons were noting that teenagers were saying they wanted to have "something done" for a new reason—to look good in selfies. The American Academy of Facial Plastic and Reconstructive Surgery (AAFPRS) in 2013 reported an increase in plastic surgery requests from teenagers resulting from patients becoming more focused on their appearance on social media. "Social platforms like Instagram, Snapchat, and the iPhone app Selfie.im, which are solely image-based, force patients to hold a microscope up to their own image and often look at it with a more self-critical eye than ever before," said Edward Farrior, president of the AAFPRS.

To learn how to become "flawless" and "perfect," some girls turn to beauty gurus. A search of some of the top beauty tutorials finds: "Flawless First Date Look with Lancôme and Michelle Phan." "Flawless Full Coverage: 5 Makeup Steps by MakeupByMandy24 | COVERGIRL" with Amanda Steele. And "Perfect Back to School Hair, Makeup and Outfit!" with Bethany Mota.

The Bronx, New York

"Hey, guys!" said bubbly Bethany Mota, also known as Macbarbie07. "So right now I'm going to be doing another episode of 'Back to School with Beth' in my back-to-school series, and today's video is all about the perfect hair, makeup, and outfit for back to school."

"I love Bethany Mota," said Jasmine, age fourteen.

We were sitting on her bed in Crotona Park East, her neighborhood in the South Bronx, watching Bethany do her thing.

"I'm wearing this amazing makeup look that I'm honestly obsessed with," Bethany said, wriggling with delight, "and I'm probably gonna wear it every day . . . It's really pretty and I like it. It makes me feel fab."

"I love everything about her," said Jasmine in her soft New York accent.

This tutorial by Mota, posted in 2013, had gotten more than 3 million views. In it she showed girls how to get her back-to-school makeup look, which included products by Almay, Maybelline, CoverGirl, and L'Oréal. "Of course we need some powder," Mota said, swirling a brush around her cheeks. "We do not want to go to school with an oily face . . ."

"I follow her on Instagram," said Jasmine. "I like to watch all her tutorials."

Jasmine was a Latina girl with long straight dark hair and over-sized black glasses. She wore a pair of fashionable ripped jeans, a pink sweater, and a headband with cat ears she said she had bought online after seeing Taylor Swift wearing one like it in a music video. She confessed to being a "girlie girl" like Mota; her pink-themed bedroom was decorated with Hello Kitty dolls, not unlike the girlie bedroom from which Mota did her tutorials.   .

"I like her 'cause you don't hear bad stuff about her," Jasmine said. "She's a good role model. She's nice, she's cute. Like, I would love to meet her."

Being nice and cute is at the core of Mota's brand. In her videos she often praises things she likes—whether tennis shoes or nail polish or hair bows, which she admits to being "obsessed" with—for being "cute" and "girlie" and "adorable."

Jasmine said, "She's, like, not ghetto."

Jasmine told me that, more than anything, she wanted to escape her neighborhood someday. "Basically I'm like a prisoner," she said, "'cause my mom won't let me go anywhere 'cause it's too dangerous." After a visit to Crotona Park East in 1977, President Jimmy Carter somberly called it "America's worst slum." The neighborhood had been ravaged by the violent crime and arson epidemics of the 1970s; and then, in the '80s, there was crack. With its burned-out buildings and vacant lots, Crotona became a symbol of urban blight. It was overrun with gangs, dangerous and poor. It was also a hotbed of creativity, a place where graffiti art and hip-hop music and culture flourished.

Today, Crotona has been largely rebuilt. People say it has "calmed down," partly due to the constant and, according to some residents, unwelcome presence of the police. Blue-and-white cop cars creep up and down the blocks. The cleaned-up streets look beautiful again, with their grand art deco apartment buildings and cozy ranch-style homes. But appearances can be deceiving. In 2013, the Citizens' Committee for Children, a children's advocacy group, called the South Bronx one of the hardest places in New York City to be a child. In 2010, it was the poorest district in the country, with a quarter of a million people living in poverty. Forty-nine percent of children in the South Bronx were living in poverty that year, according to the U.S. Census.

When Mota finished putting on her makeup, she looked as if she were ready to walk the red carpet on Emmy night, forget about the halls of school. Then she demonstrated how to use more products and a curling iron to get her wavy locks. "It looks so adorable," she said of her own hairstyle, gazing in the mirror.

"I can't really get my hair like that," said Jasmine, touching hers. "It's too thick."

Mota, a Latina girl from Los Banos, California, became YouTube's number one producer of beauty content in 2015, surpassing former reigning beauty queen Michelle Phan. At nineteen, she now had 9 million followers and 25 million views a month. *The Wall Street Journal* attributed Mota's appeal to how her "videos often focus on encouraging her teen fans to build up their self-confidence." Buzzfeed called her "the quintessential girl next door." *Time* put her on its list of the "Most Influential Teens of 2014." In 2015, she took a selfie with President Obama at the White House, where she had been invited with a group of other social media stars.

"One day I will get there," Jasmine said. "I am going to be famous. Maybe from a reality show." She said she also might want to be a fashion designer. "I think my style is cool."

Mota got dressed, putting on a floral, short "cute dress" from Brandy Melville, an Italian-based clothing company, trendy among girls; the line has been accused by some media outlets and blogs of encouraging "body dysmorphia" with its "one-size-fits-all" sizing, which has been found to fit skinny girls most comfortably.

Mota called her oversized Brandy Melville cardigan "perfection . . . I love it so much."

"I love that, too," Jasmine said. "I'd wear it. And it would fit me."

Mota started vlogging in 2009, when she was thirteen, as an escape from cyberbullying; she has said that the likes she got on her videos made her feel better about herself. Her early videos were "hauls," videos where mostly girls and young women who've returned home from shopping trips show off what they've bought, usually makeup and clothes. "I think that this is so adorable!" Mota says in a haul from 2014, holding up a sunflower-patterned dress from Forever 21. "I love sunflowers, they're one of my favorite flowers, and when I saw this I was just like, That is *adorable*."

Haul videos started appearing on YouTube as early as 2007; by 2010 more than 250,000 had flooded the site. At a time when the media is full of images of conspicuous consumption and unattainable luxury brands, a study found that YouTube viewers liked watching hauls because the products featured were affordable, "low- to mid-range fashion and beauty" items rather than the more high-end items displayed in fashion magazines such as *Teen Vogue*.

"I shop online," Jasmine said. "That's where you can find everything for bargains." She lived with her single mom. Her dad, a mailman, lived in Brooklyn.

After gaining a following with her hauls, Mota started doing beauty and fashion tutorials. Her signature style is her girlie self-deprecation, which involves making faces, crossing her eyes, and drawing attention to her own "awkwardness." She's like a teen version of the adorable actresses you see in rom-coms who are always falling down for no clear reason. Mota's accessible and nonthreatening girlie-girl persona has proven attractive to corporate sponsors. She makes an estimated $500,000 to $750,000 in annual ad revenue. She also has her own clothing line with Aéropostale.

I asked Jasmine if she knew any girls who acted like Mota in real life, in the unfalteringly upbeat mode of beauty gurus. She laughed and said no. "You couldn't act like that in this neighborhood," she said. "People would think you were corny." In her neighborhood, she said, you had to be tough. "You have to show people they can't mess with you."

"It's so much people getting killed, in jail, drug dealing and all that stuff," Jasmine said. "There's a lot of gang activity. In my grandmother's building there's people doing nasty things in the hallways. There's people passed out with needles in their arms. I'm not allowed to go in that building. I don't feel safe walking around in this neighborhood by myself as a girl. I get scared. I have never experienced walking by myself around here."

On her computer screen, Bethany Mota was breezing into a high school building, outfitted in her "perfect" back-to-school look.

Watching Mota's video with Jasmine brought home to me that, for girls who are poor, the omnipresence of images on social media stressing the importance of "beauty" had a whole other layer, an added set of pressures. Beauty costs money. When Jasmine compared herself with Mota, and Mota's ability to "flawlessly" execute some look, she was not only challenged to wonder how she might measure up physically, but also reminded of the difficulty she might have in purchasing the things she needed to pull the look off. No matter how relatable Mota tried to be with her trips to Forever 21, Brandy Melville was an expensive brand. And then there was the issue of race. There are many successful beauty gurus who are girls of color, and Mota herself was Latina. But Mota's "cute" persona read culturally, for Jasmine, as "not ghetto," and therefore in some way aspirational. Jasmine wanted to be like her. But when she couldn't be like her—when she couldn't get her hair like hers, for example, because it was "too thick"—it was another reminder for her of a racist discourse which says that girls of color are "too" this or "not enough" that physically.

"You want to watch another one?" Jasmine asked.

Ithaca, New York; Salem, Massachusetts; and New York, New York

"It's not an organic thing that happens to girls, this desire for a perfect image," says Joan Jacobs Brumberg, author of *The Body Project:*

An Intimate History of American Girls. "It's foisted on them. The obsession with the perfection of looks and of the body has happened because of advances in technology and the spread of commercial culture and articulations of the beauty industry."

"Girls start out life now being immersed in princess culture," says Rebecca Hains, author of *The Princess Problem: Guiding Our Girls Through the Princess-Obsessed Years,* referring to the obsession with princesses seen in little girls since the launch of Disney's multibillion-dollar line of princesses and princess toys in 2000. "I think princess culture is part of the overall backlash against feminism," says Hains. "This obsession with princesses is concurrent with a cultural pendulum swing that happened when the Republicans got back power in the 2000s and [in the 2010s] launched the War on Women," meaning efforts to roll back reproductive rights and restrict women's rights in other areas. "What became appropriate for girls again was to be pretty, sweet, passive—clearly this is part of a culture shift in our political landscape," Hains says. "What girls learn from princess culture is that how they look is very, very important. If you're hooked on external validation at age four, that plays into self-objectification and self-sexualization."

"When girls say, 'I want to be a model,' they're putting beauty over any other value, like brains," says Jennifer Sky, an actress and former model who is now a vocal critic of the fashion industry's treatment of teenage models. "Not that one is exclusive over another. But being a fashion model, you're a commodity, your body is turned into an object; you're a salesperson to sell somebody else's products. You are not a person with a mind or a voice. I think it's interesting that when women got the right to vote in America is when some men got together and created the first Miss America pageant," in Atlantic City in 1921.

Garden City, Long Island

It was the day of the night of Lily's first date, and she was worried about the eyeliner she ordered arriving from Amazon on time. It wasn't exactly her *first* date, she said—she had been on dates, of sorts, since seventh grade, but this was the first one where she "really liked" the boy. He was "really smart, really funny, really athletic, really tall," she said, eating chips at the long wooden table in the kitchen of her home, an eight-bedroom house on a leafy street in Garden City. "And he's been my friend for a while"—since the previous summer, when they went to science camp together at an Ivy League university ("it sounds really nerdy, I know, and it *is,* but honestly it's fun")—"and I really like him and he really likes me so I think it's . . . yeah." She nervously rearranged her hair.

Lily said she wanted the date to be "perfect," so she really wanted this certain Lancôme eyeliner to come before she had to start getting ready to go out. "It goes on the best and you can make wings like Audrey Hepburn's. I saw it on a beauty tutorial. I watch *tons* of them 'cause they give you really good information."

She had ordered the eyeliner on Amazon the night before for next-day delivery. "My mom's credit card is on there," she said, "so we can just, like, get whatever we want. She never notices."

The doorbell rang and some packages came—the UPS man had two: some squishy neon-colored balls for Lily's younger sister, Olivia, ten, and Lily's eyeliner. "Oh, thank you!" Lily told the UPS man, signing for them.

"Don't tell Mom," she told Olivia, the package under her arm. "Where is Mom?"

"She took Henry to the Apple store," Olivia said, tearing open her box of squishy balls. Henry was her brother, age twelve.

"Why?" Lily asked.

"To buy him a new iPhone," Olivia said. "He broke his. He threw it at the wall when he got mad at the game he was playing. He threw it twice."

Lily was glad Henry wouldn't be in the house while she was getting ready to go on her date; he was always saying things to try to make her doubt herself, always comparing himself with her, saying he was better at sports and she was "dumb" for caring about things like clothes and makeup. "Little brothers, you know?" She shrugged. "He's a pain. He's just jealous because I'm older and he's immature. He has ADHD; he never wants to do his homework. And sometimes he smells." Lily had ADHD, too, she said, but the prescription drugs she took controlled it and she could concentrate. "And I'm just, like, very driven," she added. She said she also suffered from anxiety and took medication for that.

She was one of the top students in her grade at a competitive Manhattan private school. She was also an athlete, good at many sports. "My whole family's good at sports," she said breezily. "That's one of the reasons we moved out here to Garden City, so my brother could play soccer."

Garden City is a village of some 22,000 people, about an hour's drive from Manhattan, an affluent community with many beautiful churches, a place centered on raising kids, raising them to be successes. An estimated 99 percent of Garden City High School graduates go on to college, many of them high-ranking. The school district is known for its strength in sports; in the afternoons, the playing fields are dotted with kids in team uniforms, running up and down. "Garden City kids are sick at sports," said Matt, a seventeen-year-old boy at Roosevelt Field, a mall in East Garden City, the tenth-largest mall in America; it used to be an airfield.

"You work hard, you excel at sports," Matt said, "you get into an Ivy League school, or even like an NYU or a Boston College, you make your parents look good, and they, like, pay you for your time. They see everything in terms of money so that's how they show their love—through money." "But a lot of kids who are fuck-ups get whatever they want, too," his friend Roxanne, sixteen, observed.

During the financial crisis of 2008, *The New York Times* ran a story about how the residents of Garden City were coping; one resident, a wealth manager, told the paper, "Someone from Des Moines might not feel bad about well-off people like this losing their money, but people get used to an income level." The number of Garden City residents who work in finance and real estate has been estimated at 20 percent.

Lily's father was a lawyer who worked in Manhattan and her mother was a stay-at-home mom. As the oldest of five, Lily said she never felt she had her parents' full attention; the littler kids took up so much of her mother's time and "my dad is, like, never home." Her mother did pay her attention, she said, but she was "always, like, managing me and making sure I'm doing everything right." So now it was nice—"so nice," she said—to have someone in her life like Josh, her date, who would just talk to her and listen to her, and tell her she was pretty, "Oh my God, like all the time."

They hadn't actually seen each other in person for about a year. After camp, they started gradually making contact through Facebook messaging, occasional texting, favoriting each other's tweets, and liking each other's pictures on Instagram. "I just thought of him as a friend after camp until a month or two ago," Lily said. And then something happened when they Skyped. "We just talked and talked for like four hours and he really liked talking to me and I really liked talking to him so . . . yeah." Again she nervously rearranged her hair.

Ever since then, she said, she and Josh had been Skyping most nights for about an hour, and then for three- or four-hour stretches every weekend, only stopping "when we have to, like, go to the bathroom or take a shower." Now they were texting all day, every day, even during school ("We just talk about whatever we're doing, or we'll say like, Hey, what's up, hi, bye"). He was the last person she talked to at night before she went to sleep and the first person she talked to in the morning, "when I open my eyes.

"He kept asking me out," she said, "but I said no, because there's just so much going on in my life right now and I just didn't feel like I had the time. My school is a lot of pressure, a lot of stress. We have hours and hours of homework a night, and it's a lot to deal with, all the work. It's partly the pressure I'm putting on myself and partly the pressure that my parents put on me to do well—all this pressure combined, to take this education and do something great with it, it can all make you feel really overwhelmed. Of course I want to amount to great things," she said, "but when everyone's telling you and constantly badgering you about it, it can be really stressful. At the school I go to, one bad grade can, like, crush a person."

And so she wasn't sure whether she could fit "a relationship" into her jam-packed schedule. Josh lived on Long Island, too, in a town nearby, but through all of this texting and Skyping and favoriting and liking, they had never managed to actually see each other in person. "And that's why I wanted it to be a *movie* date," Lily said, rambling along in her restless way, "a *double* date, because if it's weird to see each other again there will be other people there."

She had enlisted the help of her best friend, Priya, to come along that night "in case it gets awkward," and Josh was bringing another boy as Priya's date. They were going to see *22 Jump Street*, rated R. "My dad will buy the tickets and sit in the car or something while we watch the movie. My dad is *crazy*—he has to, like, thoroughly check out the guy."

So tonight was "kind of a big thing," Lily said. "Well, not really a *big* thing, I mean, I'm just seeing if I really like him in real life, right?" Still, she was glad that the eyeliner had come—"thank *God*." There was a five-tier makeup tray in her bedroom, overflowing with shiny, colorful cosmetics.

Now that she had the eyeliner, the next thing was to figure out what to wear. She searched in her closet and among the heaps of clothes strewn everywhere. Her room was messy, crammed with things: a bed, a desk, a chair, clothes, books, shoes, discarded toys, and an elliptical exercise machine she used to "stay in shape." "Sometimes when I'm stressed out I just go on it for like an hour and it takes the stress away."

She began piecing together an outfit. "I have a pretty good fashion sense," she said. "I modeled for like two years, but then I gave up because I fell down on the runway," in a practice show, "and I didn't like it anymore. I modeled from like eleven to thirteen—I was in a modeling agency. It was cool, it was fun, but it got to be too much, so I quit." When I talked to Lily's mother, later, she said that Lily "could be" a model, if she were only taller. "The lady at the agency would do our makeup and we would practice doing fake photo shoots and we would practice the catwalk in high heels," said Lily. "It was fun to feel like everyone was watching you and it was cool to be able to say, like, I'm part of a modeling agency."

I asked what had made her want to model. She thought a moment. "I guess I wanted to do it from seeing models on TV and in magazines—it was like, Oh, if I can be a model, girls will look up to me like I look up to these girls. Whenever I'd see models in magazines, it was like, Wow, she's really pretty, and if I can be a model girls will be like, Wow, she's really pretty, too. I love *America's Next Top Model*. It's cool to watch what that life would be like. It's such a glamorous life."

America's Next Top Model, hosted by Tyra Banks, was one of the most popular shows for American girls for more than a decade. Between its premiere in 2003 and cancellation in 2015, it aired in more than 146 countries. The reality show involves a competition among a handful of aspiring young models with Tyra as their mentor and judge; and Tyra's judgments can be harsh, not just about the contestants' appearance, but their character and motivation—how much they appear to "want it." Sometimes Tyra makes fun of the would-be models on the show with a corrective zeal; in an infamous episode, the subject of a viral meme, she shouts hysterically at a girl she feels has not exhibited the appropriate level of commitment, making her weep. ("I was rooting for you! We were all rooting for you! How dare you!" Tyra chastises.)

When I interviewed Tyra in 2007, she told me that, growing up in L.A., "I used to be a mean girl. Mean as hell. I was a bully." *America's Next Top Model* thrives on scenes of meanness between the girls. (A typical catty comment: "She eats candy all the time.") The contestants are often depicted as shallow and not that bright. It was a favorite show of many of the beauty pageant contestants I interviewed in Houston. "I watch it all the time," said Bailey, seventeen. "I decided I want to be a model from that." Livia, sixteen, said, "I'm obsessed with *America's Next Top Model*."

As for Lily, she said she knew she was being influenced by the media even as it was influencing her—they talked about it a lot in her school; there were speakers who came to educate the girls and group sessions where girls expressed their feelings about media pressure.

"Oh, yeah, it's a big deal," she said. "We talk about it all the time. Pop culture and the media really influence girls my age—we're growing up, finding out who we are and what we want to be. We're becoming comfortable or uncomfortable with our own bodies, and it definitely plays a role in how we feel about ourselves.

"I'm confident with *my* body," she went on, "I'm confident with how *I* look, I'm not worried about *that*. But for so many other girls my age it's a really big problem. You have all this anorexia and bulimia from girls seeing girls on TV and in magazines and Instagram and wanting to look like them. It's difficult for girls who *aren't* confident with their bodies because they can develop these terrible things like eating disorders that affect them their whole lives until they're adults." She said there was a girl in her school whom she "literally had not seen eat in three years."

I asked her why she thought girls were still influenced by the media, even when they were aware of its pressures. "I don't know," she said. "It's weird. Sometimes I wonder if it's the parents," she mused after a moment. "Like I wonder why our parents let us do grown-up things. Like why do they let us go to these parties?" She talked about bat mitzvahs and birthday parties where there were "mocktails," or faux alcoholic drinks in cocktail glasses. "It looks just like alcohol," she said. "There's so much adult stuff at these things. We go to these parties with high heels and fancy dresses and we're like twelve and thirteen and we party till one o'clock in the morning. But by the time we're in college, we'll already know what that feels like to party till one in the morning. So what will we do for fun then?"

She talked about a party where there was a "runway show," and girls could "pick a designer dress and put it on and wear it on the runway, and there was a paparazzi taking pictures so we could pretend like we were famous.

"The way girls dress now is just *ridiculous*," Lily said.

She was deciding between two outfits to wear that night on her date: it was either going to be a black minidress from Brandy Melville or a short white skirt and black tank top from Urban Outfitters. She was hanging the outfits on her bedroom door so she could get a better look, standing back, evaluating them.

"Like, there was a party for the private schools on a boat and all these girls were wearing cutout dresses, dresses with random cutouts," she went on, "like a belly cutout to show your belly button; you'll even see, like, twelve-year-olds wearing these things. They were wearing, like, the shortest skirts. Like, why do their moms let them go out like that?"

She decided that in order to make a decision about which outfit to wear she would have to put on both and text pictures of herself in them to Priya, to get a second opinion. She went into her bathroom and came out wearing the short white skirt and black tank top. "How's this?" she asked, turning around to look at herself in her bedroom mirror. "Do you think this is like a *date* outfit, or do you think it looks too casual?"

I asked her if she thought this could be an example of the very thing she was just talking about, clothing that was sexualizing.

"Well, I don't feel compelled to go out *naked*," she said, "but when you see every girl dressing sexy, you do feel compelled to do it, too.

The media, like, completely oversexualizes everyone now—in every magazine you see everyone in some sexy outfit. That's just what we're shown, and what we're shown is what we *do*. A lot of girls my age look up to these older girls in the media who wear all these sexy things— basically anyone you see in a magazine, all the big movie stars. Everyone loves Mila Kunis. Rihanna. I mean, I would say Miley Cyrus, but it's kind of controversial. A bunch of people are like, Go Miley, and a bunch of people are like, *No*, Miley." She laughed.

"The people who support Miley love her because she's being her own person now, and good for Miley for that. But Miley's own person is not what some people would *like* her to be—and some people consider her a role model. So the people who are saying No, Miley are saying that because she wears these revealing bathing suits onstage and twerks with teddy bears," a reference to Cyrus's controversial 2013 performance at the MTV Video Music Awards, "which is weird. She's expressing herself, but not in the way that we want our kids to see."

There was a *Hannah Montana* DVD on her shelf, a relic of yesteryear. A One Direction pillow on her bed. "I know, embarrassing," she said.

Lily took pictures of herself in the white skirt and tank top and texted them to her friend Priya. "She'll tell me what she thinks," she said. "She's *very* blunt." Then she went in the bathroom again and changed into the black minidress. She took more pictures and sent them. Priya texted: "The black kinda looks like what a mom would wear to a wedding." "So I guess that settles *that*," Lily said with a laugh. She texted Priya emojis of a face laughing so hard there were tears running down its cheeks.

She said that the "pressure" about how to look and what to wear came from other girls, too. "If you don't wear the right thing, they just *look* at you and you can get ostracized," she said. "Boys are a lot less *cattier* than girls and they're a lot more laid-back, so that's why I like to hang out with them. I'm kind of a *guy's* girl, not a girl's girl. I have a lot of guy friends."

Did the "pressure" ever come from boys, too? I asked.

"Oh, definitely," Lily said. "When I'm in school with boys, I definitely do feel inclined to wear makeup and dress up, 'cause if there's a boy you like there's all these other girls around and *they're* wearing makeup and fancy clothes and looking really nice and you can't kind of just slack off. You feel like you have to do it; it's definitely an additional pressure; you want to look nice, you want all the boys to think you're pretty, and so you feel like you need to wear makeup. But I'm pretty sure you don't . . . ," she added, her voice trailing off.

"It *is* distracting," she said, "especially if the boy likes you back, you'll be, like, looking at each other and you don't really focus—it does distract you if you like a boy and you're in his class. You're like, How can I talk to him? How can I make him notice me? I'm pretty sure most girls do that."

Lily said that she first started "dating" boys in seventh grade. "I had my first boyfriend then. I think I would have little crushes, like cute little crushes from fourth grade, but I wouldn't go on dates. I don't have serious relationships now, because what's the point, what's the rush? You can be young and have your fun. But a lot of girls my age have serious boyfriends, serious dates. They'll go to fancy restaurants together in the city, go to parties together. It's crazy. They have, like, serious plans for the future, like what they'll do when they go off to college or something, and I'm like, How can you even *think* of that at this moment?

"Girls in my school and girls on Long Island where I live," she went on, "they do the same thing. There will be pictures on Facebook of girls my age out at these fancy places in fancy dresses, like they're going to get married next week or something. They put pictures on social media—it's a huge thing, boyfriends and social media. Girls that have boyfriends show them off on Facebook and Instagram. It's not like they're *maliciously* wanting people to think, Oh, look at my boyfriend, he's so much hotter than your boyfriend, it's just they want to show off what they're doing, and the boys want to show off what they're doing, too; so you'll see all these photos on Facebook and Instagram and Twitter, status updates twenty-four/seven—maybe to, like, even make people jealous.

"In seventh grade, that's when it picks up," she said. "They would have these little dances in seventh grade for private schools; I met my first boyfriend at one of those. It was cute, a little kiss on the cheek and stuff; sometimes we'd go out for ice cream. And seventh grade is when things really heat up on social media. That's when boys start liking all your posts to get your attention. If a boy likes a lot of your posts, then he likes you. Especially if he likes your profile picture, 'cause that's how you're represented online—if he likes your profile picture, that's how you *know*.

"Social media is ninety-five percent of what happens in all relationships now," she said. "How we talk is on social media. A lot of people don't even meet; they just have boyfriends online. Girls meet their boyfriends online. That's really scary to me; like, I have a friend who just recently met a guy on social media—she never met him before in her life—and they were dating, and, like, that freaks me out, because what if he were a serial killer or something? I mean, good for her for having a boyfriend at all, but, I mean, she never even really met this guy, she met him on iFunny—it's this place where you share pictures and stuff, you make funny captions for pictures; they opened up a chat room and started to chat and Snapchat. It's creepy to me to think, Well, what if he's a *rapist*?"

Concerns about kids being approached by predators online have existed since children started going online. Over the years such fears have been stoked by dramatic cases in the news, such as that of Kirsten Ostrenga, famous on Myspace as "Kiki Kannibal." Ostrenga was the fourteen-year-old Florida girl who was raped by an eighteen-year-old boy she met on Myspace in 2006. After the boy, Danny Cespedes, killed himself at the scene of his arrest, the story became a sort of Internet legend. And yet such stories have become increasingly routine and pass without much comment. In 2011, Michael Downs, a twenty-year-old from Santa Clarita, California, was sentenced to fifteen years in prison for sexually assaulting fifteen underage girls (one a twelve-year-old), many of whom he met on Facebook. In 2015, twenty-year-old Cody Lee Jackson, of Blue Ash, Ohio, abducted a fourteen-year-old girl he met on Facebook, then repeatedly raped, sexually abused, and later impregnated her, all while under charges he had kidnapped two other teen girls, according to authorities. These cases received scant attention.

In her book *It's Complicated: The Social Lives of Networked Teens*, danah boyd (who uses no capital letters in her name), a principal re-

searcher at Microsoft and visiting professor in the Interactive Telecom-
munications Program at New York University, likened the fear of online
predators to the "moral panics" surrounding teens' engagement with
other "new genres of media" such as novels in the eighteenth century
and comic books in the 1930s. "American society despises any situation that requires addressing teen sexuality," wrote boyd, "let alone
platforms that provide a conduit for teens to explore their desires."
Similarly, in *Kids Gone Wild: From Rainbow Parties to Sexting, Understanding the Hype over Teen Sex,* coauthors Joel Best and Kathleen A.
Bogle wrote, "The 1950s witnessed warnings about the new practice of
going steady . . . Each generation's critics have managed to warn about a
revolution in sexual manners, even as they often failed to acknowledge
the longer history of concern about youthful sexual play."

What this point of view fails to acknowledge, however, are the ways
in which the sexual behavior of teenagers actually is being changed and
shaped by thoroughly new technology, smartphones and social media,
not to mention the influence of online porn. What's being avoided are
the hard questions about whether these behaviors are in fact healthy or
abusive or even legal, from the perspective of the age of consent. And
one reason for this may not in fact be "discomfort with teenage sexuality," as boyd suggests, but the fear of seeming less than "sex-positive"
or raising a moral panic. boyd claims a connection between anxiety over
teens being sexual on social media and an uneasiness with teenage
sexuality in general. But this is a type of analysis and even a moral judgment of its own, which also has a history, going back at least as far as
the 1960s, when parents who didn't "get" the new sexual mores of their
hippie children were deemed "squares." It's a thesis which ignores the
interactive nature of social media and dismisses the salient question of
whether the person on the other end of the interaction, sometimes in
fact a stranger, is an emotionally and sexually healthy person—a person
who respects boundaries, and who is aware of the law, which varies
from state to state, but does set limits on who is sexually available in
order to protect children from being abused and exploited.

In 2014, researchers at the Crimes Against Children Research Center at the University of New Hampshire found that one in eleven young
people said they had experienced an unwanted sexual solicitation online

within the previous year. An earlier study by the same group found the number to be higher, one in seven. "Internet sex crimes involving adults and juveniles," said this earlier study, "more often fit into a model of statutory rape—adult offenders who meet, develop relationships with, and openly seduce underage teenagers—than a model of forcible sexual assault or pedophilic child molesting." In other words, it isn't the classic, horrific scene of a "dirty old man" jumping out from behind some bushes that kids are most commonly experiencing; it's interactions between themselves and adults, sometimes young adults, whom they may not view as predatory because they have "relationships" with them on social media. This begs the question of whether some kids would even see overtures by potential predators as "predatory," if asked, since it is part of the culture of social media to seek out and develop relationships with strangers.

This all becomes very complicated in an atmosphere of heightened sexual display, in which sexting and the sending of dick pics and nudes have become normalized. Much of the new normal would have been considered predatory or unhealthy in the past. For example, many girls have come to feel that the acquiring of likes and congratulatory comments on sexualized pictures of themselves is an achievement, a sign of self-worth—even when the likes and comments come from strangers. The comments about their bodies and beauty they receive from boys and men they know, but also some they don't, are very often valued, not disparaged. Many girls show an appreciation for comments which, if delivered on the street, would be regarded as catcalling or harassment. But in the culture of social media, a girl will most often respond to such comments acceptingly, with grace: "Aw, thank you," with emojis of kisses being blown, for example. It's not social media etiquette to resist such comments, to be that girl with no "chill" who objects, or who fights back.

"It's happened to me, too," Lily said, "that guys I don't even know will approach me online and ask me out. This guy who has maybe a few mutual friends with me will start asking me out and saying, Hi, you're really pretty, will you go out with me? Stuff like that; and it's really creepy because I don't know him—it's like, Why are you talking to me? Ew." She confessed that another boy had once asked her for nudes.

"Just some boy my age, I hardly knew him," she said. "And I was like, shocked, 'cause like why would you think I would send naked pictures of myself to you when I don't even know you?

"I didn't tell anybody except my friends, and some of them were like, Yeah, that's happened to me, too," she said. "I didn't tell my mom because my parents would freak out and like call the police or something. This one friend of mine she said I should send him a picture of myself nude with my head cut off so nobody would know who I was, but, I mean, I would never do *that* . . .

"I guess it's my fault for friending him back in the first place," she went on, "and of course I defriended him immediately after he got creepy. I've heard worse things—like this girl in my school, she was on Kik and this older guy who said he was sixteen asked her for naked pictures, and he knew she was fourteen. And like how does she even know he's sixteen? He could be like some forty-year-old man with a big belly.

"I had another situation once," she said. "There was this really attractive guy who friended me on Facebook and he was really cute, and he said hi to me so I said hi back and we were talking and he was like, How old are you? And I was like, That's a weird question to ask. How old are *you?* And he was like, Well, I'm twenty-three and I live in France and I think you're really pretty. And I was like, Nooooo, I'm fourteen, no. There are guys who friend you who are so much older. I mean, that just can't happen. It's *illegal.*

"It's so easy for older predators to go online and just find a girl; it's so easy for them to do, because girls want the most friends and they want the most followers and likes, so if someone tries to friend them they'll just friend them back right away without even knowing who they are. So even if it's a serial killer, they still friend them back and maybe even start talking to them. It's scary. Especially since a lot of girls will post pictures of themselves like in their bras and bathing suits, and the people they friend back can see those pictures.

"*I* don't do that," she added. "I know that colleges can see that— anyone can see that; that's one of the good things about going to a school that educates you about all this stuff, they tell you what everyone can see and what's appropriate to put online. But some girls don't know about that and they just put it all out there and they're not educated enough to know that everyone can see that and anyone can get the wrong idea and just *stalk* you. Especially with, like, Twitter or Instagram or Facebook, where you, like, tag your location, people can see where you are; and girls tweet out exactly where they are on Twitter, people just see that and they can go and find them."

Lily's Facebook and Instagram pictures were mostly selfies; there were many glamour shots of her doing the duckface and "the sparrow," the name for another selfie expression where the lips are more tightly pursed. There were pictures of her playfully sticking out her tongue to the side, Miley Cyrus–style, and others where she was modestly exposing her cleavage or posing in short shorts. It was as if she were trying to present a sexualized self within the limits of what she knew would be seen as acceptable to parents, colleges.

I asked her why she thought girls posted so many provocative pictures of themselves.

"I think it's just to get attention," she said, "to get the likes, everything's about the likes.

"Everyone wants to be famous," she said with a sigh. "It takes a certain kind of person to want to be famous. I don't think I could handle the attention and the cameras."

Huntington Beach, California

Amanda was ten when she made her first video. Sixth grade. She was a little girl who loved fashion. She wanted to be a designer. "I used to design my own clothes," she said. And then one day, searching YouTube for a video on how to sew, she stumbled on a brightly colored, sparkly world where grown-up girls taught you how to put on makeup and shop and dress. She was fascinated, watching all these pretty girls applying foundation and eye shadow, swirling their brushes around their faces, and speaking so confidently into the camera. She saw how tens and hundreds of thousands of viewers clicked to watch them talk about beauty products and how to make yourself look beautiful. She was particularly taken with Blair Fowler, also known as JuicyStar07, one of the reigning queens of beauty gurudom, who, as of 2014, had more than 251 million views on YouTube and nearly 2 million subscribers. JuicyStar07 became a "role model" for her.

"Watching her," said Amanda, sitting on a kitchen stool in her family's house, "inspired me and made me want to do my own." She set up a camera in her bedroom and made a video on how to do "a brown smoky eye." She had already practiced a lot with makeup, she said. "I had more makeup than my mom . . . I was still only ten, so the video wasn't that great. I got, like, a lot of hate. I stopped making videos for a while after that just because people were kinda mean."

Commenters on her early videos wondered why such a little girl was wearing makeup at all: "Lol I'm 11 and I'm only allowed to wear lip gloss or babylips and CLEAR mascara . . . but some girls are like 8 and go to school with dark eyeshadow and eyeliner and foundation and red lipstick and there I am just like 'Wahh.'" And how did Amanda have so much "high-end makeup"? some asked: "When I was 10 I had no idea what Mac was!"

Still, there were girls who seemed to like seeing someone their own age talking to them from the intimacy of their screens. Reading these girls' comments, Amanda felt emboldened. "When I first started doing this," she said, "there was no one my age on YouTube. I think that's why they related to me more . . . they were like, Oh, wow, this girl's just like me.

"I also just kind of got lucky," she added. "When you searched 'Middle School Makeup Tutorial,' mine was one of the first ones that popped up, so that really helped. A lot of people watched that video"—well over a million. Amanda's mother was all for her new hobby. "She was like, Yeah, you should do it." And Amanda was off and running, making videos every week.

Her early videos show a calm and confident little girl, very natural in front of the camera, curling her eyelashes and talking about covering up pimples with foundation—not that she ever got pimples, she was quick to mention. In real life, she had always been popular, was a cheerleader and a softball star—her jersey number was 24, hence the name she chose as her handle: MakeupbyMandy24. After that first video came hundreds of others. She went from makeup tutorials to fashion tutorials to hauls. She said, "I love watching hauls."

And then came what she describes as the "lifestyle" videos that were just about herself, Amanda, "real and raw." There was "My Summer Morning Routine" from 2014, where she eats her breakfast and brushes her teeth; it got more than a million views. "When I wake up, I grab my phone and go on Twitter, Instagram," Amanda says on-screen, "and realize I should get out of bed and actually do something with my day." Then she gets out of bed and puts on her makeup.

"People like it when you're just, like, being yourself," Amanda said. "I think that's what my channel is mostly like. Some people spend a lot of time editing or filming their videos to make them really professional. I don't do that as much"—although she does use a professional video editing program, Final Cut Pro. "I think people watch my videos more for my personality," she said.

"It's totally crazy how more and more people are coming onto social media," to find their favorite stars, "and so many people can get"—air quotes—" 'famous' off it now, like with all the platforms," she said. "It's just, like, gotten so much bigger, and people are just realizing how cool it is, being more into someone you can actually relate to rather than a TV character."

For example, there was Amanda's "A Day in My Life" video from 2014, where she filmed herself going to a shopping mall with a friend who "just got her eyebrows done." "And I am super lazy," Amanda says on-screen, now lying on a couch with her computer. "So I'm just chilling on Netflix. Netflix is my life. Netflix is my bae"—meaning friend or boyfriend, crush. "I'm watching *Desperate Housewives* right now," she says, referring to the 2000s dramedy about rich women who are frenemies. This video of her essentially just watching a television show got more than a million views.

"My whole YouTube/social media thing is all around what people want from me," Amanda explained. "At the end of my videos I'll always ask, 'What do you want to see next?' 'Cause they're everything to me," meaning her followers and fans. "They're all my views . . . so I definitely want to do what they want . . . You have to understand what the audience wants, what attracts them," to be successful on YouTube, she said.

"I think there's a lot more to it than people think," she said. "You're really all about pleasing the audience, but sometimes people will also judge you no matter what you do; so it's always, like, an inner thing, like, Should I put myself out there, being totally myself? Or should I kinda lean toward what people want to see more? So it's hard work," she said—that is, figuring out if people will like who you really are, or if you need to be who they want you to be in order to get their attention and likes.

"And now it's this huge thing," she said brightly, meaning herself and her success. She smiled. "YouTube has taken over my whole life . . . Everything about my life now is from the Internet."

As Amanda's following grew, her on-screen persona began to change; the cool and collected, matter-of-fact little girl gave way to the perky "personality," a girl whose flirtatiously awkward style was reminiscent of the legendary YouTube beauty gurus who had come before her. She took on the smiley sunniness of a daytime talk show host—in fact, she became the host of her own online talk show, *The Meetup*. On-screen, she transformed into a charmingly flibbertigibbet girlie girl, the granddaughter of Sally Field's Gidget and Annie Hall.

Her fans seemed to like this new Amanda, as they did the girl on Amanda's Instagram, who seemed to be a still different girl. On Instagram she was "aesthetic" Amanda, a fashionista and glamour girl who could make an unabashed duckface look good. She was an edgier girl— now with dyed platinum hair—who might show off a suggestive knee in ripped jeans, or her torso in a bathing suit top. ("You're 15 . . . 15 . . . calm tf [the fuck] down," one follower commented.) She was a girl we'd see spending a night out dining at Nobu in Malibu, or partying at what looked to be a nightclub; there she was posing with other pretty girls; there she was on red carpets, having an awesome, FOMO-inspiring time. "I wanna be her wtf [what the fuck] this isn't fair," someone commented.

"Shopping is my cardio," Amanda wrote on an Instagram picture of herself looking dead-eyed in a high-end store. Her Instagram suggests the lifestyle of girls growing up in Beverly Hills, girls who shop on Rodeo Drive and will grow up to be Desperate Housewives.

"She's trying to be Kylie Jenner," commented a persnickety fan.

"It's hard being my age and having girls attack you all the time,"

Amanda said, "but you have to learn from it—I've become more confident, it makes me stronger; if I didn't have all this, and I hadn't been through it, I don't know what I would be like. It definitely makes you grow up."

She still couldn't completely understand why girls did like her, she said, because she was so "normal." "When I have a meet-up or I go to an event where there are people waiting for me, I'm still so amazed. I don't get it, it's crazy. I'm so, like, normal—I'm literally just like you. Like, I could be best friends with all of these girls that are coming up to me, but they still, like, *fangirl* over me"—she did jazz hands, depicting fangirling—"and I'm like, What?" She smiled again. In 2015, she would have more than 2 million followers on Instagram and nearly 800,000 on Twitter.

She added that she wasn't actually friends with any of her fans, although every now and then she would follow one of them on social media or like one of their tweets or posts. "It's exciting for them," she said. She said that she wasn't really friends with anyone anymore except for other kids who were Internet famous. "All my friends now are from the Internet and it's really awesome," she said, "'cause we all relate to each other . . . and we all get along so well, 'cause we all just *get* it . . . We get what it feels like" to be Internet celebrities.

"A lot of them are YouTubers or on Vine or other social media," Amanda explained. "We meet at conventions and meet-ups all over the country. There's conventions all over—in L.A. there's VidCon," a gathering of online celebrities from many platforms, established in 2010. "That one's huge. There's like twenty thousand people and stages for people who perform on social media. There are YouTube personalities and the Magcon guys," a fraternity of Vine star boys who then were touring together and hosting their own conventions. Amanda was now part of a coveted circle of about 100 young people, all social media stars; each had no less than about 500,000 subscribers on his or her YouTube channel—it was the unspoken minimum number required for admission to the group, she said.

"It's like this amazing thing and it's so awesome to be a part of it," Amanda said. "I like being friends with so many people that are in the same position as me . . . They come from all different states but now they're all moving to L.A. to pursue their careers." She said she envisioned a career for herself that would capitalize on everything she was doing now; she wanted to go into modeling or acting, have her own clothing line. "I wanna try everything. I wanna have a brand someday.

"So I do online school now," she said. "I had to leave my other high school. I was just traveling too much and working too much to be there. It would be cool to just be a normal girl going to high school, but I really like how my life is now."

"She can't go to school," said Amanda's sister, Lauren. Lauren had joined us. She was home from college for the summer. She had long dark hair and a nose ring and wore a ripped rock 'n' roll T-shirt over a black bra. Lauren often appeared in Amanda's Instagram pictures as her edgy-older-sister sidekick. "People are intimidated by her," Lauren said. "Meanwhile, she's the shyest person. Most fourteen- or fifteen-year-old girls dress sloppy and she's so clean and well put together. She can't be friends with kids at school. She presents herself better. They're jealous of her."

Amanda said nothing, listening.

Later that afternoon Amanda went out back and filmed herself by the pool. She set up her Canon DSLR with the fluffy mic on a tripod and did a fashion shoot, showing off her look. "Hey, guys, it's Amanda," she said, waving to the camera with a smile. "So today I'm going to be doing my outfits of the week . . ." She modeled her shorts, her nails, her shoes, her wrap. She wriggled and bounced. She acted a little seductive, blowing a kiss to the camera. When she was done filming, she sat down on the living room couch and took some selfies. She stuck out her tongue and pursed her lips and smiled and winked at her image in her iPhone screen.

Vine

When I asked girls around the country why they thought some boys acted like "savages" and "fuckboys," many of them said: "Vine." "Vine stars." "They wanna be like Nash Grier and all those guys that are big on Vine."

Vine, which was founded in 2012 by three male Web developers based in New York and acquired by Twitter just before its launch, has become one of the most popular online services, with 200 million monthly active users in 2015 and 1.5 billion Vines played daily, according to the company. It's an unending stream of ordinary moments: people talking, shopping, driving, eating, walking, playing with their babies and dogs, existing, often trying to make viewers laugh. When they can make them laugh a lot, they can become famous. They can become "Viners."

The biggest Vine stars are mainly men and boys. In 2015, *Business Insider* posted a list of the thirty most popular Viners based on numbers of followers; only five were female. The most beloved Viners are comedians and pranksters, exuberant American boys who do rambunctious stunts and make irreverent jokes. They have a certain swagger. They're cute and silly, and millions of girls love them in the way girls once loved John, Paul, George, and Ringo—in fact, many of their Vines owe a debt to the high-spirited style of the Beatles movie *A Hard Day's Night* (minus the genius filmmaking). Most of their antics are innocuous enough: they slide around on snowboards, ride on shopping carts, dance in their living rooms to rap songs, and generally cut up.

However, there's a pernicious strain in male Vine culture that often goes unremarked in the increasingly glamorizing media profiles of Vine boys that have appeared as their online popularity has translated into offline celebrity, with the inevitable clothing lines, and movie and TV deals. There's almost a genre of Vines in which Vine boys make fun of girls—the way girls talk, dress, act, dance, and relate to boys. But there's also a sense that this is all in good fun—that "Vine boys will be boys," and don't really mean any harm—and if you object, well, then you might be one of those girls that Vine boys make fun of.

There are Vines where Vine boys are wolfish, "savage," in ways that are plainly offensive. In one of his Vines, Carter Reynolds, a nineteen-year-old boy from North Carolina, is told by a girl that she enjoyed their date, to which he responds, "I can't wait to see those big beautiful nipples, uh, dimples of yours!" Sam Pepper, twenty-six, a British YouTube star and Viner, released a "prank" video in 2014 in which he walked around filming the reactions of unsuspecting women as he groped their behinds. And there have been offline incidents involving Vine stars which are more disturbing. In 2014, Viner Curtis Lepore, now thirty-two, pleaded guilty to felony assault of Jessi Vasquez, now twenty-two, a popular Viner known as Jesse Smiles, who had claimed Lepore had raped her (the rape charge was dismissed). "I don't feel like living on this planet today. Good bye," Smiles tweeted after Lepore's arrest. She seems to be doing better now. As is Lepore himself. "In other news," he tweeted, after he took his plea deal, "I just hit 3.9 million followers on vine. Despite the obvious setbacks I'm still doing just fine." He added an emoji of a hand doing the symbol for "O.K."

Carter Reynolds had more than 4 million followers on Vine in 2015; that same year, he was at the center of a scandal after a video was leaked in which he appeared to be pressuring his then girlfriend for a blowjob. In the video Reynolds is seen with his pants down, his erect penis exposed. His former girlfriend, Instagram star Maggie Lindemann, then sixteen, tells him, "I don't think I can . . . This makes me so uncomfortable." Reynolds tells her to "do it," and "just act like nothing is there," seemingly referring to the camera. She refuses. "Oh my gosh, Maggie," says Reynolds, sounding exasperated.

In the wake of the controversy surrounding the video, some of Reynolds's fans started a hashtag in support of him: #WeLoveYouCarter. He urged them to tweet it, saying, "Couples do stuff like that all the time." When Lindemann wound up in the hospital after an overdose, which she insinuated on Twitter was possibly suicide-related, Reynolds tweeted: "maggie is saying I'm the reason why she's in the hospital . . . lol nah you're just crazy and psychotic." The scandal seems to have had little effect on Reynolds's popularity; since then he has gained Vine followers.

Nash Grier is the second-biggest Viner of all—the self-described "King of Vine," with more than 12 million followers. He was on *Time*'s list of the most influential teens of 2014 and called a "social media prodigy" by ABC News. In 2015, Grier, now eighteen, a blue-eyed North Carolina native, had a higher social media rating than the White House. Like Reynolds, he was a member of the "Magcon family," the Vine-boy frat including Cameron Dallas, Jack Johnson, Jack Gilinsky, Taylor Caniff, Shawn Mendes, Aaron Carpenter, and Matt Espinosa (the group broke up in 2014). "Don't worry, the boys' parents come along to make sure the boys aren't doing anything they aren't supposed to," says a post on a Magcon website. "You may think that these boys are selfish, self-centered, immature boys looking for attention and money. Well, they aren't. Many girls have tweeted, commented, or told them in person that they have saves [*sic*] their life. These teenage boys have convinced many teenage girls that they are worth it and life is worth fighting for. They helped save many teenage girl's lives."

Grier's popularity seemed as Teflon-coated as Reynolds's in the wake of a 2014 scandal in which he was called out by YouTube king Tyler Oakley for posting a Vine in which he screamed the word "fag." (Grier apologized for the video, saying he was "in a bad place," and took it down.) It was then revealed that Grier had used the word—as well as the words "queer" and "gay," in a seemingly pejorative manner—many other times on Twitter. He had also posted a Vine in which he mocked Asians.

But most puzzling is how Grier has continued to attract fans after a 2013 YouTube video, "What Guys Look for in Girls," caused an outcry online for its sexist content. In a nine-minute conversation, Grier and two friends, nineteen-year-old Vine star Cameron Dallas and twenty-one-year-old YouTube star Jc Caylen, talk about "what we find attractive in girls," which does not include good character or intelligence. Grier does say he likes a girl who has her "own ambitions and goals," but laments how "so many girls these days don't do anything, they're just like a glorified, like . . . yeah, I'm gonna marry a rich guy." To be attractive, Grier says, a girl "[has] to be entertaining . . . Entertain me." "I hate it when girls are obnoxious and loud and crazy, like, calm down," he says. He offers this tip for how girls should behave with guys when texting: "If you play too hard to get, then it's just like, Oh, she doesn't even like me, but if you play easy, then it's just like, Oh, she's a whore. Find a balance." Grier also offers suggestions for girls' attire and hygiene, urging them to remove their facial and body hair: "When you have peach stuff and we're making out, no," he says. "Wax, shave . . . Take the hair off." The video was up for several days and then taken down, but it continues to be seen in repostings.

"That [video] was a big deal," said Sophia in Montclair. "Everybody saw it. But on YouTube there's a million videos like that." In fact, a search for "how to get a guy" on YouTube turns up more than 26 million results. "Like, '10 Ways to Get a Guy,' 'How to Get a Guy to Like You,' '10 Ways a Guy *Won't* Like You,' stuff like that," Sophia said. "Boys always post videos on YouTube telling girls how to impress boys—it's all over YouTube, they get millions of views. I always watch them. I wanna know what boys think about me—like, Oh wait, should I flip my hair more, or should I bite my lip more?"

Brooklyn, New York

From the subway to the street to the block to her building, Edie listened to the song. Running up the stairs to Grand Army Plaza, she listened; tearing down Seventh Avenue, she played it. She was already imagining how it would feel, to become this other, secret self that no one knew was there; she was readying herself for what she was about to do—and the relief, the release from everything that had happened that day, and was happening every day, at school.

"I'm so fancy / You already knooooow—"

She slammed the front door and ran into her room, threw her backpack on the bed; peeled off her clothes and pulled on her shortest shorts, the ones she was not allowed to wear outside and would never even want to wear (she would be too "embarrassed"), and a crop top— ditto—and in her mother's medicine cabinet she found some lipstick, NARS Jungle Red, and, in the back of her mother's closet, the Steve Madden heels that her mother wore on dates.

Earbuds in, iPod on, she caught her breath, standing in front of the mirror hanging on the back of the bedroom door, seeing how incredibly hot she looked, how transformed. She was no longer that boring girl in sweatshirts, sneakers, and jeans. She looked like an Instagram girl, a Tumblr girl.

A star.

In real life, she was not one of the girls the boys called "hot." She was a girl that a boy had put at the top of the list of "The Ugliest Girls." The boys had a rating system of one to ten and Edie had gotten a "zero." But she knew she didn't belong on that list. She could look around her and objectively see that she didn't look so very different from the girls boys said were "hot." But in her eighth-grade class, she said, she was considered "ugly" because she was not white. "Or I'm not the 'right kind' of black girl," she said, doing air quotes. "I don't fit in with what they expect a black girl should be. I'm an outcast."

She and Iggy Azalea roamed the halls, laughing at all the girls who couldn't walk with them. She danced.

What Edie didn't understand, she said, was that the "super popular" girls and the "not so popular" girls at her school could dress exactly the same—"like, really slutty"—and yet the super-popular girls would not get called names and the not-so-popular girls would get called "sluts."

It was very confusing.

What she didn't understand was why a girl like Minerva, who wore short shorts and crop tops and got "dress coded" almost every day—that was when you got called into the office and told to change into your gym clothes or even sent home—was called a "thot," or slut, by both girls and boys; but Savannah, who dressed almost exactly the same, in short shorts and halter tops that showed "side boob," was popular and ruled the school and nobody ever called her anything. ("A little side boob never hurt nobody," Kendall Jenner captioned a provocative picture on Instagram in 2014.) Minerva hooked up with boys and took nude pictures of herself and sent them to boys and boys showed them around the school, and everyone said she was a "slut." But Savannah had a boyfriend who stayed over at her house all night sometimes and people thought she was cool.

It didn't seem fair.

Was it because Savannah's dad was famous? He was someone in the news. That probably had something to do with it, Edie thought. "In New York it's like if your mom or dad is someone famous, then everybody thinks you're cool." And it seemed like famous people could do whatever they wanted. Savannah's mom and dad smoked pot with Savannah and didn't care if her boyfriend slept in the same bed with her at night. Savannah's parents said it was Savannah's "choice" to have him over, and they didn't want to "repress" her or "control her sexuality." Or so Savannah claimed. People thought Savannah's parents were "cool." They said Savannah was cool. Edie thought it was weird.

Savannah was so powerful now that her boyfriend, Sam, had group-ies. They were some girls in the sixth grade who called themselves "Sluts for Sam," and they followed Sam around and stalked him on social media. They had even started cutting for him—they said they were "cutting for Sam," cutting themselves like how they heard those girls were "cutting for Bieber." (In 2013, a hoax perpetrated by users of the Internet bulletin board 4Chan claimed that teenage girls were cutting themselves in order to get Justin Bieber to stop smoking marijuana. Fake Twitter accounts posted pictures of bleeding arms and wrists with the hashtag #cuttingforbieber. Despite its being a hoax, there was concern that #cuttingforbieber would inspire copycat behavior.)

Then somebody started a Facebook page called "We Hate the Sluts for Sam" and made death threats against them and said they wanted them to die. But then it turned out that it was the Sluts for Sam themselves who had made the page. They just wanted the attention.

Some girls wanted attention so bad, Edie said, it was like they would do anything for it. Anything for the likes. Minerva would post a picture of herself in a bikini and people would make fun of her and call her names, but she would still get like 100 likes—mostly from boys. Girls would post comments making fun of Savannah and her weight and the shape of her body and stuff like that ("Diet much?"). And then Savannah would post a picture of herself in a bikini lying by her parents' pool in the Hamptons—"Just chillaxing," it would say, or something "stupid" like that—and she would get like 300 likes on that picture. "Literally, like three hundred likes."

Edie and Savannah used to be best friends when they were small. They used to play in Prospect Park. Their nannies were friends. They would swing on swings and run around the playground, push baby dolls in their strollers side by side. They were best friends through fifth and sixth grade . . . and then in seventh grade something had happened. Savannah became cool. And Edie did not become cool. She was a black girl growing up in a mostly white neighborhood—Park Slope—so it wasn't as if no one had ever made her aware of her race. They did, she said, "like, every day." People had always said things to her and her mother—strange things, like, "What are you?" as if Edie were not in fact a human but some other type of being. She had learned early on that she was "light-skinned." "People have asked me if I'm like Spanish or Turkish," she said. "Why do they even need to know?"

But the one person who had never seemed to notice her color or said anything about it one way or the other was Savannah. Edie was always just Edie to her. "You're my Edie," Savannah would tell her, grabbing her and hugging her. They used to pretend they were sisters. And then one day in seventh grade, after Savannah had started getting cool, she suddenly turned to Edie and said, "You don't really act black, you know?"

"What do you mean?" Edie had said, annoyed. Savannah had been doing a lot of things to annoy her around that time, but this "literally made me feel nauseous." "How do 'black people act'?" she asked her.

Savannah had just shrugged in that cool girl way she had been developing. "I don't know," she said, "like, black people are cool."

Edie was aghast. How did Savannah suppose that she had any idea what black people were like—or, for that matter, what was cool? Most of the things that white people called cool *came* from black culture, but that didn't mean that black people stopped being black if they weren't rappers or Samuel L. Jackson. Did Savannah actually think she had the right to tell Edie whether or not she was "black enough"?

Edie wasn't cool. She knew she wasn't cool. She liked things uncool people liked: Taylor Swift and *Doctor Who* and *Drake & Josh*. She didn't like the crude and vulgar media fare that kids her age had started liking as far back as second and third grade—*Spongebob SquarePants, Adventure Time,* and *Family Guy* (cartoons with obnoxious jokes); and then, in the sixth and seventh grades, *Gossip Girl, Pretty Little Liars,* and *Degrassi* (dramas about high schools where kids are mean and sexually active). "It's all so inappropriate," Edie complained. "It should not be for our age." She had very definite ideas about what kids "should" and "should not" see. She guessed she learned it from her mom and her grandmother, who was from the Caribbean and "really strict" and said that kids today were "too grown up."

But the epic, friendship-ending fight Edie and Savannah got into in seventh grade was not about any comment regarding her race, but about the fact that Savannah told some other girls in the school that Edie "liked" a boy named Harrison. Harrison was a boy with lustrous brown hair that wafted above his forehead like an ocean wave. Edie had liked him since the beginning of the year, and when she confided this to Savannah, Savannah just giggled and said, "No way."

Soon the whole school knew—even Harrison. "Like I would ever like you," he said to Edie in the hallway one day, with some girls standing around, suppressing laughter. "You're, like, the ugliest girl in the school," he declared. It stuck. Now Edie was on the top of "the lists."

"They keep lists of, like, who is the hottest and who is the ugliest," she said. "The boys do it."

It became Team Edie and Team Savannah after that. Girls who had been friends with both of them were forced to choose. Savannah easily brought almost everyone over to her side. She had so much more to offer them than Edie did. Now there were parties at Savannah's house where kids played Spin the Bottle and Seven Minutes in Heaven, parties where kids drank and smoked weed. "They would be like, I'm sorry, Edie, we can no longer associate with you. I'll see you later," Edie said. Everyone stopped talking to her, "pretty much." She was alone in the lunchroom. People who had been very close to her all her life, "they were like, Well, I hope you understand."

In exile, she became even more of a target; and somehow now the taunts became tinged with allusions to her race. Kids said that she had "ramen-noodle hair."

After that went on for a while, Edie's mother suggested she get her hair cut off, "just to try a new style"; but Edie knew it was to make the kids stop saying mean things to her, and it hurt her to know her mother had to worry about that. But she did. Edie got a pixie cut and dyed it blond. And after that, kids said she looked like Chris Brown. "Yo, Chris, where Rihanna at?" boys would say—a reference to the troubled relationship of pop stars Chris Brown and Rihanna, which effectively ended in 2009 when Brown was charged with felony assault of Rihanna.

Subsequently, comedians and social media users made light of the abuse. "Chris Brown beating Rihanna jokes" turns up nearly 250,000 results on Google. More than twenty years after the passage of the Violence Against Women Act, which imposed federal penalties for acts of domestic violence, it "continues to be normalized through its comedic portrayal via news outlets, magazines, advertisements, and television shows," according to a 2014 study by researchers at the Chicago School of Professional Psychology; and you could add to that list social media. The average American girl or boy is likely to have seen one of the domestic violence jokes and memes which crop up regularly online, such as the one of a smirking man saying, "WHAT DO YOU DO WHEN YOUR DISHWASHER STOPS WORKING? HIT HER."

Meanwhile, domestic violence continues to be a national problem. The Centers for Disease Control and Prevention (CDC) estimates that about 1.3 million women in the United States experience domestic violence every year. In 2011, the CDC found that nearly 10 percent of high school students reported experiencing some form of physical violence by the person they were dating within the previous year. And now there is a new kind of domestic violence in teenage dating, via cell phone. In a 2007 study by Teenage Research Unlimited, teens identified "digital dating abuse" as a "serious problem." Examples include when abusers try to control their partners through constant texting and phoning, or try to control and intimidate them through texting and posting on social media. Sometimes abusers enlist friends to check on their partners and stalk them with social media and phones. Boys and girls have created fake Facebook accounts in order to check whether their partner would carry on an inappropriate conversation or cheat. "Social media breeds obsession," says Jenna, the nineteen-year-old Hunter College student.

Edie said that one boy in school had laughed and said she was "a ghetto baby" and didn't have a dad. In fact, Edie's mother was a highly successful professional woman who was a single mother by choice.

There was one girl who would still talk to her, one girl who was still nice to her; that is, when no one else was around. "We were in the bathroom," Edie said, "and we were talking about how crazy it was that all this stuff was happening, and she said, Well, if you would wear a little bit of a lower-cut shirt one day, it might help people like you more. And I was like, But why? And she was like, Well, if you just start dressing sexy you'll 'move up in the ranking.' If the boys notice you, it'll affect how the girls act. And I told her, You shouldn't dress for boys.

"The thing is," Edie said, "if you asked most of these girls if they were feminists, they would say yes, because that's a cool thing to be now and so they would say they were. But they're not feminist, because they're objectifying themselves."

Edie tried to go to the school guidance counselor and talk to her about all these things that were happening to her; but there was only one guidance counselor for more than 350 kids and "she seemed over-whelmed. She asked me if I was cutting or anorexic or bulimic or any-thing like that, and when I said no, she didn't seem worried about me anymore. It's like she didn't really have to listen."

One night, Edie called a suicide-prevention hotline.

It was the night she got into a fight on Instagram with some of the girls from Team Savannah. Some girls had posted mean things about Edie, and so Edie then filmed a video of herself saying what she really thought of the girls. "Being mean is *not* cool," she said in her video, which she posted on the app. "Being *mean* is the ugliest thing in the world." It quickly spread. Within minutes, there were no likes on her video, but many "horrible" comments. "They said things about the way I look and how I act."

It was the only time they had made her cry.

Chapter Three

15

New York, New York

The subway ride downtown was thirty-five minutes of "hell." As the train rocketed down the tracks from the Upper West Side, she avoided the looks. "Are you a girl? Are you a boy?" She stared into her phone. She found refuge there. Even if she wasn't really seeing anything on her screen, it protected her from having to face the looks. It was in her phone that she had found relief—"transgender kids on YouTube saved my life; just knowing they were there, hearing them talk and seeing them be strong"—and it was in her phone that she had gazed into "evil." "People will say anything to you on social media. I've been told I'm ugly, a freak, a fake, an 'abomination.' That was a good one. I had to look it up. I've been told to kill myself. I'm amazed sometimes I'm still alive because sometimes you want to die from it."

She knew if she could just hold on she'd make it to a place downtown where she could be herself for a while. But there were always the looks. "It's the eyes." Eyes that telegraphed confusion or disgust. "Or sometimes they just look at you like you're not there—like they're killing you by *not* looking at you." And there were comments. "It can come from anyone. You'd be surprised. I've had old men say stuff to me but also like really young girls. I'm like, But how can you hate me for being like you? For being a girl inside? Don't you know they already look down on us as girls?"

She'd found hope in the thought of Jazz, the famous transgender girl, age fifteen, star of her own YouTube channel and reality show

(*I Am Jazz*). "I'm not like Jazz," Montana said. "I'm not a girlie girl." But she loved Jazz for her honesty and her "realness." Loved it that when Barbara Walters had asked, "What part of being transgender hurts you the most?" Jazz had said, "My genitalia." Montana had laughed out loud at that; and then she had wanted to cry. Because Jazz wasn't blaming anyone, she was just being real; but Jazz had parents who supported her in her decision to be who she wanted to be, and Jazz's parents had money to make that happen.

The subway doors opened up and Montana slid into the sea of people.

Online

The problem of bullying came to national attention in 1999, with the mass shooting at Columbine High School. Media reports alleged that Eric Harris, eighteen, and Dylan Klebold, seventeen, had been the victims of bullying, and that this had contributed to their horrible massacre. After another school shooting at a California high school a year later, Attorney General John Ashcroft bemoaned an "onerous culture of bullying." "Americans were finally paying attention," wrote Emily Bazelon in *Sticks and Stones: Defeating the Culture of Bullying and Rediscovering the Power of Character and Empathy*. With school shootings up nearly 70 percent in the 1990s over the '80s, the Secret Service and the Department of Education conducted an investigation into the causes of thirty-seven attacks since 1974, finding that, "in several cases, individual attackers had experienced bullying and harassment that was longstanding and severe."

In the case of Columbine, however, bullying was not ultimately seen as a contributing factor. A lengthy FBI investigation found that Harris was a classic "psychopath" and Klebold a depressive in his thrall. Since Columbine, school shootings have continued to plague the nation; there were thirty-five with fatalities in 2014, almost all of them committed by teenage boys and young men. Cyberbullying has been increasingly discussed in the news as a possible cause, because of its concurrent rise. But according to research by the Cyberbullying Research Center (CRC), one of the leading research organizations on the subject in the country, there hasn't been a single school shooting in the United States resulting directly from cyberbullying.

Meanwhile, we have seen the emergence of a new and equally disturbing phenomenon—cyberbullicides, which the CRC defines as "suicide indirectly or directly influenced by experiences with online aggression." And many of the victims of cyberbullicide have been girls. There was Megan Meier, the thirteen-year-old Dardenne Prairie, Missouri, girl who hanged herself in her bedroom in 2006 after being catfished on Myspace by her former friend, her friend's mother, Lori Drew, and Drew's teenage employee. There was Rebecca Sedwick, the twelve-year-old Lakeland, Florida, girl who jumped from an industrial tower in 2013 after being cyberbullied by two other girls. "Drink bleach and die," one of the girls allegedly told her—a cruel reference to Amanda Todd, who once attempted suicide this way. Todd was the fifteen-year-old Canadian girl who killed herself in 2012 after being bullied on- and offline; she had shown herself topless via webcam during a video chat, and an older man screenshotted her image and shared it on Facebook.

It's not known just how many cyberbullying-related deaths have occurred; according to the CRC, "empirical research . . . is sparse." The suicide rate of kids ages ten to nineteen dropped between 1990 and 2003, but then started to rise again, according to the CDC. Suicide is still the third leading cause of death in children ages ten to fourteen, and the second leading cause in older teens. In teen suicide, boys are more likely to be successful at committing the act, while girls make more attempts. And cyberbullying victims are nearly twice as likely to have attempted suicide, as well as more likely to have suicidal thoughts, according to the CRC.

Girls are more often the victims of cyberbullying than boys. Studies of how many children and teenagers are cyberbullied vary, but most report more girls than boys being cyberbullied. A 2007 survey by the Pew Research Center found that more than 40 percent of girls ages fifteen to seventeen reported being bullied online, and about 30 percent of boys of the same age. A 2011 report by the CRC found that nearly 25 percent of heterosexual girls had been bullied online, compared with around 16 percent of heterosexual boys. In that same study, more than

38 percent of non-heterosexual girls reported being cyberbullied, and more than 30 percent of non-heterosexual boys. What is similar for all girls, as opposed to heterosexual boys, is that when girls are cyberbullied, they are targeted for their sexuality and sexual behavior.

The cyberbullying of girls "tends to focus on promiscuity or perceived promiscuity," says Sameer Hinduja, codirector of the CRC. "For girls who are cyberbullied there is a double standard; teen girls are not wanting to come across as prudish, but then when they demonstrate a familiarity with sexuality, they are immediately denigrated. They tend to feel that people give them grief no matter what."

In the CRC's 2010 report "Victimization of Adolescent Girls," the results of an online survey of more than 3,000 girls ages eight to seventeen showed 38 percent of girls reporting being cyberbullied. Girls in the survey said that they had been "disrespected" and "ignored" online; they said that they had been threatened physically and called "a host of . . . unpleasant names," including "fat," "ugly," "slut," and "bitch." They reported being teased for "sharing their opinions." They said that they had been sexually harassed by anonymous strangers: "Behaviors mostly involved unsolicited sexual advances ('[I] was online playing a game and a guy asked me if [I] wanted to "suck his ****" '), including requests for the victim to 'cyber' (i.e., engage in cyber sex with) the aggressor." Girls said that cyberbullying made them feel " 'sad,' 'angry,' 'upset,' 'depressed,' 'violated,' 'hated,' 'annoyed,' 'helpless,' 'exploited,' 'stupid and put down' . . . Some girls said the victimization made them feel unsafe: 'It makes me scared. I [sometimes don't] know the person so that makes me wonder if [I] have a stalker, and that gets me pretty scared.' " Some said that they had received death threats. "Adolescent girls do receive online threats," the CDC report concluded, "ranging from vague warnings . . . to threats that are . . . very serious."

Not every girl who is cyberbullied is going to try to kill herself or have suicidal thoughts, of course; in fact, many girls who experience online harassment also "exhibit healthy resilience to this behavior," says the CRC. But millions of girls are still affected by online harassment; and yet there has not been much in the way of studies of its emotional and even physical effects, not to mention the question of its causes, including sexism and misogyny. "I feel like it's understudied," says Hinduja.

One reason for this lack of attention may be that the cyberbullying of girls is often dismissed as "normal" female behavior, due to the
common perception that "girls are mean." "When I give presentations
[about cyberbullying] to parents, schools, and law enforcement," says
Justin Patchin, the other codirector of the CRC, "one reaction I often
hear is 'girls are mean,' as if that means there's nothing we can do
about it. Well, adults are mean. I see more adults being mean than
young people. We make pretty terrible role models when it comes to
interacting online."

Although many states have laws allowing for criminal prosecution
of cyber-harassment, it has been difficult for victims to find any legal
recourse, due to the problem of proving cause and effect in terms of
harm, as well as the strength of the First Amendment and the fact that
the legal system hasn't kept pace with new technology. In 2007, Missouri prosecutors declined to charge Lori Drew, finding that her behavior did not violate any laws, behavior which included engaging Megan
Meier in online conversations that "became sexual for a 13-year-old."
Prosecutors explained that this was in part because the state's harassment laws didn't cover Internet activity. (Drew was later convicted of
three computer fraud misdemeanors, but in 2009 a federal judge
overturned all three guilty verdicts.) In 2013, felony charges of aggravated stalking were dropped for the two girls who allegedly tormented
Rebecca Sedwick after prosecutors found it difficult to make their case
in the absence of evidence. Tricia Norman, Sedwick's mother, alleged
to CNN that when the case made headlines, Rebecca's Ask.fm page,
where she was allegedly harassed, was deleted from the site. (Ask.fm
responded that it cooperates willingly with authorities.)

"The laws haven't caught up with use," Hinduja says. "They're trying to shoehorn cyber cases with traditional laws, and it's not necessarily consistent with our ideas of justice. Tyler Clementi's roommate,"
Dharun Ravi, "served twenty days of a thirty-day sentence."

Clementi was the eighteen-year-old Rutgers University student who
jumped to his death from the George Washington Bridge in 2010 after
Ravi showed a friend a live webcam stream of a kiss Clementi shared
with another young man in their dorm room. After his death, and that
of Jamey Rodemeyer—a fourteen-year-old, openly gay boy from Buffalo,

New York, who hanged himself in 2011 after being harassed online—
President Barack Obama spoke out against cyberbullying. He released
a video, "It Gets Better," which has been one of the most watched and
most heralded videos of his presidency. "Like all of you," the president
said, "I was shocked and saddened by the deaths of several young people who were bullied and taunted for being gay and who ultimately took
their own lives. As a parent of two daughters, it breaks my heart, and
it's something that shouldn't happen in this country." The president
never directly addressed the cyberbullying of girls.

Boca Raton, Florida

On another day at the Town Center mall, three friends had stopped at
a Starbucks to have sweet coffee drinks. They were sitting at the same
table but not talking to one another. They were staring at their phones,
thumbing, scrolling, tapping. When I remarked on the picture they
made, all together, but not together, they laughed.

"I know, it's terrible," Carrie said. "I always feel like I have to check
my phone. It's like I have to deal with responding to all these things and
see who's saying what."

"You don't want to miss out," said Kayla.

"I check on what everyone is doing," Dara said. "You see who sent
you Snapchats and find out what's happening."

She showed me the last Snapchat Story she had viewed, where there
was a picture of a girl wearing a funny face and eating a plate of bacon.
"Bacon," said the caption over the photo. The girls all giggled.

"I know, it's kind of silly," Dara said, "but if you don't show that you
saw it, she'll be like, Why didn't you open my Story?"

"People's Instagram pictures," Kayla remarked. "If you don't like or
comment on them, someone can get offended and it can cause some
drama."

"So much drama," said Carrie.

"It's ridiculous," said Kayla.

The girls were fifteen and knew one another from school, where
they were all in tenth grade. Carrie and Dara were white, and Kayla

was black. They were wearing short shorts and tank tops and flip-flops. Carrie and Dara had long black hair, while Kayla had shoulder-length brown hair. They all had shiny black-and-white shopping bags from Sephora, the cosmetics chain, on the floor beside their chairs. Carrie's mother was a therapist and her father worked in real estate; Kayla's father was a business owner and her mother a school administrator; and Dara's parents were a doctor and a stay-at-home mom. Carrie's parents were divorced and the other girls' were still married.

"Sometimes I feel like I'm not just checking to see what people are saying about whatever—I'm making sure they're not saying anything about *me*," Carrie said with a little laugh.

"And if they do, you have to respond, or it can cause complications," said Kayla.

"So many complications," said Dara. "It's like you spend half your time managing your reputation."

"Social media can cause a lot of drama because of the way you can send it *around*," Carrie said.

They talked about social media "drama" and how it usually began. Often, they said, it was when someone shared someone else's texts without the texter's knowledge, in order to show what was being said in a private conversation.

"That happens to everybody," Dara said.

"And it makes it hard to trust," said Kayla.

"I have terrible trust issues," said Carrie. "Ever since middle school and everybody got their phones. I don't feel like I can trust anyone."

"Certain people will even record someone talking on their phone and let other people hear the recording," Dara said.

"Oh, yeah," said Kayla, "that's a bad one."

"Once you press send, it's over," Carrie said. "Whatever you say over text, people can screenshot it and send it to anyone—that's happened to me a lot."

"And you feel betrayed," said Dara.

"Over and over," said Carrie.

They said there were other ways kids "betrayed" one another and did things that were "mean," such as unliking posts and pictures or blocking.

"It's ridiculous how you'll have some little misunderstanding with a girl," Kayla said, "and then she'll go on all your accounts and unlike everything she ever liked of yours."

"My little sister who's in middle school is doing finstas," Carrie said. The other girls smiled. "Finstas" were fake Instagram accounts that didn't show the user's real name. "They make them so the parents can't see what they're doing on social media," Carrie explained. "Especially if it's like sixth-grade girls posting pictures in their bras. Or like they use them to talk crap about each other."

"The posts are really dramatic," Kayla said. "Girls will be like, Did you *see* that finsta post? Oh my *God*, I can't believe what she *said*."

They laughed.

"But I feel like we do that, too," meaning in the higher grades, said Carrie. "I feel like people will say mean things on social media they wouldn't say in person."

According to studies, she's right. A 2013 review of studies on cyber-bullying in the *Universal Journal of Educational Research* reported that "perceived anonymity online and the safety and security of being behind a computer screen aid in freeing individuals from traditionally constraining pressures of society, conscience, morality, and ethics to behave in a normative manner." In other words, digital communication seems to relieve people of their conscience, enabling them to feel more comfortable behaving unethically. It's a startling conclusion, however obvious it already may be to anyone who has witnessed examples of it online, from the relatively minor rudeness you see in comments on the average Facebook feed to the viciousness of Gamergate—the online harassment campaign waged against women in the video game industry and the cultural critic Anita Sarkeesian in 2014. Threats made against the women included doxing, or the exposure of personal infor-mation on the Internet, as well as rape and death threats. Gamergate supporters were largely anonymous.

And yet despite evidence of how the anonymity of social media can contribute to antisocial behavior, anonymous apps such as Whisper, Secret, Yik Yak, and Sneeky have multiplied in recent years, as has the debate over their ethical standing. On Twitter in 2014, Netscape cofounder and Silicon Valley venture capitalist Marc Andreessen criticized anonymous apps—also known as "bullying apps"—as well as their investors for failing to take responsibility for their negative impact. "As designers, investors, commentators," Andreessen wrote in a series of twelve tweets, "we need to seriously ask ourselves whether some of these systems are legitimate and worthy . . . not from an investment return point of view, but from an ethical and moral point of view." While individual social networking sites have responded with increased monitoring of users' posts and comments, often when under fire for some story in the news involving abusive behavior online, there's been no general reckoning in Silicon Valley about the ways in which its products may be encouraging unethical and harmful behavior. The First Amendment has become the blanket behind which social media companies seem to hide from any questions regarding the online speech and activities of their users.

"There's no such thing as rules" on social media, said Dara.

The girls confessed that they sometimes found themselves engaging in the same online behaviors that had angered or hurt them in the past.

"I've screenshotted someone and showed the texts," Carrie admitted. "I know I shouldn't, but when you're upset about something someone said and you want to show it to someone else, you just do it. I've said things on text I really regret," she went on, "and then I'm not friends with that person anymore. And then I see them at school and it's so awkward because we never actually talked about it face-to-face."

"Friends have a fight on Facebook and it's like a thing that happened but it didn't really happen," said Kayla.

"I feel like saying things over social media is so much easier," Dara said. "But if you say something on Facebook, it hurts the same amount as if the person said it to your face; but that person doesn't think about that because they're just typing it on a computer."

Studies have found that the winnowing away of face-to-face communication in the digital age may be having an effect on the ability of kids to interact in person. A 2014 study at UCLA found that sixth-graders who went just five days without looking at a smartphone, television, or other screen were significantly better at reading human emotions in face-to-face communication than sixth-graders from the same school who continued using their electronic devices. "Kids are spending so much time communicating through technology, they're not developing basic communication skills that humans have used since forever," says psychologist Jim Taylor, author of *Raising Generation Tech: Preparing Your Children for a Media-Fueled World*. "Communication is not just about words. It's about body language, tone of voice, facial expressions, even pheromones, all of which can't be conveyed through social media. Emoticons are very weak substitutes."

And when nonverbal cues are stripped away, it can limit the potential for understanding, arguably the foundation of empathy. When researchers at the University of Michigan reviewed data from seventy-two studies conducted between 1979 and 2009, all focused on monitoring levels of empathy among American college students, they found that students today were scoring about 40 percent lower than their earlier counterparts.

It's something that comes to mind when hearing about "The New Intolerance of Student Activism," as *The Atlantic* described it in a headline in 2015. The article reported on a perceived breakdown of civility among college activists, focusing on a case at Yale in that year in which students demanded the resignation of the master of Silliman College (a residential dorm at Yale), Nicholas Christakis, and his wife, Erika, a lecturer in early childhood education. Erika had written an e-mail encouraging students to consider one another's right to freedom of speech in selecting Halloween costumes, even if it meant tolerating costumes they found offensive.

"Hundreds of Yale students are attacking [the Christakises]," *The Atlantic* reported, "some with hateful insults, shouted epithets, and a campaign of public shaming." In a video of a protest in the courtyard of Silliman, it's striking to hear some of the students addressing Nicholas Christakis with the very same insults one sees online when fights erupt on Facebook and other social media platforms. "You are disgusting! . . . Be quiet!" one young woman shouts at him, as if he is another social media user who can be bullied offline. "You should step down!" she demands, when Christakis doesn't agree with her. "Walk away," another student says, encouraging his fellow students to leave the conversation.

Whatever you think of the students' position on Halloween costumes (and I see their point; insulting Halloween costumes are to be despised), their refusal to engage in dialogue with Christakis is troubling, as is their readiness to attack him when he does seem to be trying to talk to them respectfully. Another young woman at the protest, demanding an apology from Christakis, says, "Are you going to [apologize] or not? 'Cause I can just leave if you're not going to say that." Leave, or log off, or block?

When talking about the rise of "social justice warriors"—the term for the aggressively outraged and rigid type of young activists seen both on- and offline—articles have mentioned as possible influences narcissistic parenting and the increase in narcissism among the young, as well as the fragmenting of discourse allegedly caused by identity politics. A more consistent picture emerges when you consider that this is the first generation of college students to grow up with smartphones and twenty-four/seven access to social media; this is a generation unlike any other before in how it has learned to communicate from behind screens, where the majority have either experienced cyberbullying or witnessed the cyberbullying of their peers. (Almost 90 percent of teens have seen cyberbullying on social media, according to the Pew Research Center in 2011.)

It's unfortunate that the phrase "social justice" has become entangled with "social justice warrior," as social justice is certainly an unmitigated good, something to strive for, and something social justice warriors seem to want to strive for themselves. Some of their methods, however, seem to resemble bullying. In the wake of the Halloween costume controversy, in December 2015, Erika Christakis resigned from her teaching position at Yale; the administration said that she had been a "well-regarded instructor."

The Boca girls all said that they felt kids were "meaner" online than they were in person, and that they themselves had been meaner on social media than they would be if they were talking to someone face-to-face. They said that they, too, had blocked and unfollowed people, gossiped about people, and deliberately not followed or friended someone back in order to send a message that they didn't like that person or were upset with something she had done. According to Pew in 2013, "Unfriending and blocking are equally common among teens of all ages and across all socioeconomic groups."

"Like, I'll follow someone on Instagram, and if they don't follow me i'll immediately think that person is mean or doesn't like me," Carrie said. "So when I don't follow someone back, I know they're going to probably think that same thing about me . . . But then why do I do it?"

"Because it's on your phone, so it doesn't seem real," said Kayla. "But it is real, in a kind of way."

"You assume so many things about people on social media without really knowing the truth of the situation and it makes you think crazy things based on the wrong information," Carrie said.

"I would rather *not* know as many things about people as you know from social media," said Dara. "You watch people and see their insecurities and you find out too much information and you compare yourself to them. It makes me more judgey, I guess."

They all said that they had ignored someone's texts—"oh, yes!"—even when they suspected it would "make them mad." "How long it takes to respond is who has the power," Kayla said wryly.

They said that they had also posted pictures they knew would make someone jealous or upset. "Like if you're mad at somebody and there's some guy you know she likes, you'll post a picture of yourself with him, just hanging out or whatever, 'cause you know she'll see it and get upset," said Carrie.

"You've done that?" said Dara.

"Well, not to you!" said Carrie.

"Social media lets you make a lot of impulsive decisions," said Kayla.

"And the younger you get a phone"—all of them said they had gotten smartphones in the sixth and seventh grades—"the more impulsive your decisions are, and then you get older and you just keep doing the same things from there," said Carrie.

When I talked to Paul Roberts, the author of *The Impulse Society: America in the Age of Instant Gratification,* he spoke of the lowered impulse control teenagers have due to the stage of their brain development. Teenagers have highly reactive limbic systems—the brain's complex set of cortical and subcortical structures that influence emotional response—and so are thought to be more emotional and bigger risk-takers than either adults or children. They're less able to control their actions in regard to their sense of right and wrong, according to studies, especially if it has anything to do with winning the admiration of peers. "They have a kind of future blindness," Roberts said. "It's, What will doing this get me now? Not, What are the consequences?"

But this depiction of teenagers' lack of impulse control could also describe what Roberts believes has happened to American society over-all, as seen in everything from the culture of Wall Street ("short-term performance" focus and collateralized debt obligations) to Washing-ton's failure to take serious action on the threat of global warming. As I read his book, it occurred to me that it's as if we've become a nation of teenagers, from the limbic point of view. And this also could be said to be true of our collective behavior online—for it's not only kids who are mean to each other on social media, not just kids who slight one another and get into fights; uncivil discourse has become a hallmark of online behavior for everyone. Adults, too, are gossiping about one another and stalking and surveilling each other online at a time when gossip drives our media and entertainment news, and our government is openly engaging in mass surveillance.

In an interview on WNYC in 2015, William Arkin, a former U.S. Army intelligence officer, national security expert, and the author of *Unmanned: Drones, Data, and the Illusion of Perfect Warfare,* compared the military's compulsive data-collecting with unmanned drones to our collective addiction to our smartphones. "You just can't stop yourself from checking your e-mail or texting," Arkin said. "And that's the world of drones in a nutshell." Are we using our phones like drones? Com-pulsively checking on one another? And when we don't like what some-one has to say, or perhaps how they look, dropping destructive speech bombs whose after-effects we never have to see in person?

"I really wonder what's going to happen to our generation," Kayla said. "We're not learning how to communicate well or deal with our problems with each other."

Williamsburg, Virginia

I met Janie and her mother at the Williamsburg Indoor Sports Complex on a drizzly gray afternoon. Janie was attending the fifteenth birthday party of a friend. The girls were playing laser tag in a small, darkened arena. The room was swirling with fog and glowing with black lights, techno music blaring. The girls were shrieking, jumping out from behind walls, and firing their lasers, flashing pink and yellow beams. "I got you!" they called. "No, you ain't!"

"Which one is Janie?" I asked her mother, Betty. "She's the one making all the hits!" Betty said. Janie came out of the room when it was over, flushed with excitement, pink-cheeked.

She was an athletic girl with honey-blond hair, which she wore in a ponytail, and liquid brown eyes. She was white. She changed into her street clothes—a purple Adidas sweatshirt, jeans, and sneakers. She had a matching purple Adidas headband.

We drove along the woodsy Colonial Parkway and went and sat in the book-lined library of a nearby hotel. Janie sat on a leather couch next to her mother. Betty, who was in her forties, had puffy shoulder-length hair and glasses. She said she was a stay-at-home mom, and Janie's stepfather was a government official. Betty said she wanted to sit in on our conversation, as the story Janie had to tell was "difficult." Betty looked tired from worry.

Janie was gay, which she had known since sixth grade, she said. "I kind of started figuring it out because I got involved with one of my best friends. Bad idea," she added with a little laugh. Her voice was deep and she had a southern accent. If you closed your eyes, you might think it was a boy talking. She later explained that this was something that had evolved after she started getting bullied, and she pitched her voice lower, to sound tough, as self-protection.

She said she never officially came out at school. "They kind of just figured it out, by how me and the girl I was with at the time interacted. Nobody accepted it," she said. "It was not okay. It was not okay at all. This is a very conservative area."

Virginia legalized same-sex marriage in 2014 following a Supreme Court ruling; but according to opinion polls, only about 50 percent of voters supported it. Virginia is a battleground state, with both Democrats and Republicans winning major elections, and it has its share of right-wing conservatives. In 2012, then governor Bob McDonnell signed into law a controversial bill requiring women to undergo an ultrasound procedure prior to having an abortion (it was repealed in 2014). Pat Robertson's Christian Broadcasting Network is headquartered in Virginia Beach, about an hour down the coast from Williamsburg. Until 2014, there were sodomy laws on Virginia's books.

When people realized Janie was gay, she said, "they just didn't talk to me anymore and they talked about me behind my back." She was twelve at the time. "It was a very country school," meaning intolerant, she said, "and [being gay] was not accepted. So there were comments. Basically all of the country people would make comments about how I had made my preference and that wasn't okay and I wasn't accepted. I had a hard enough time accepting it *myself* at first," she said. "I struggled with it."

She said she came out to her mother and stepfather when she was twelve, and they had a hard time "accepting" it, too; her biological father, whom she saw on the weekends, was still not always "totally accepting." Seeing she was not going to get the support she sought from family and friends, she decided that first she needed to have "acceptance in herself." She worked to become someone "who doesn't need anybody to support her." She developed her tough exterior. She tried her best never to betray her emotions, never to react to comments.

"Everybody would always say that I looked like a very strong, tough person, but on the inside, no," said Janie. "I would keep everything in so I wouldn't show anybody that I was hurt or upset or angry because I didn't want to look weak."

By the seventh grade, the atmosphere in school had become "a little more tolerant," she said, "because I got more friends. I got more people to accept me, just a little bit. The band kids accepted me"—she played the tuba—"and a few of their friends, so it got a little better."

It was that same year that she started dating a girl, a girl who in time, she said, would "ruin my life." They played together on the field hockey team. They stared at each other during practice, noticing each other; and then they started to like each other, and then they were together.

The girl was popular, emotional; "a southern belle," Janie's mother said with a frown. She was sensitive; she cried, and Janie became the shoulder she would cry on. Sometimes the pull of her neediness felt like too much for Janie and she wanted to break away. The girl wanted all her attention. She was always texting, texting, seeking reassurance and wanting to chat. "Sometimes she would text me like a hundred times a day," Janie said. "It was just too much. And if I didn't text her back right away, she would start a fight about it and say I didn't care about her. And she wanted to put everything we did on social media," she added, "and I just didn't want to reveal that much of myself to the public."

Janie didn't always feel that she could live up to the girl's demands, she said. There was so much to do already, with homework, band, and sports. On top of field hockey, Janie played soccer and ran track. She felt she didn't have time to always be texting and going on social media and updating everyone on her relationship. Still, she said, she and the girl managed to stay together for more than a year. "It was pretty serious."

And then at the end of seventh grade, the girl "cheated" on her, "going with" someone else, a boy. "She lied and said she didn't, but I knew it was true," Janie said. She heard about it from friends. It was hard to keep anything a secret at their school. It was gossiped about in texts and talked about on Facebook.

So Janie broke up with the girl. It was a middle school breakup, the kind of thing that has happened since there have been middle-schoolers falling in and out of love—somebody gets jilted, someone's feelings get hurt, someone lies on her bed listening to music and thinking about what was and what might have been. And then it goes away. But with social media, it took a different turn.

When Janie broke up with the girl, "she didn't really like it," she said. "So she decided to go on Instagram and post a picture of me and her"—it was a picture of the two of them standing close together—"and she posted like, I'm glad this is officially over.

"And my friend saw it and she showed it to me and I was like, There's no need for that." Janie confronted the girl; they had words. "And she said, It just needed to go out. And I said, Nobody needs to know about this. And then she started getting really angry with me, and I told her that she just needed to leave me alone. I told her that we were finally over, and then she told me that I could go kill myself and she wouldn't care and she would give me the gun to do it."

For a moment Janie looked as if she was going to cry.

"It kind of made me feel really bad," she said.

Then she regained her composure, her controlled demeanor.

"You could kill yourself & I wouldn't shed a single tear from my eyes," said the girl's text, which Janie's mother sent me later. "Actually that's a good idea ill give you the damn gun to do it with it'd make my damn life easier I'm so glad I moved on because I would be hurt as fuck."

They both were hurt. And when people get hurt, they sometimes turn to social media as a place to vent. In venting, they seek the support of online friends to help them through their emotions; and emotions on social media can be contagious, according to studies. A "massive . . . experiment on Facebook" published in *Proceedings of the National Academy of Sciences* in 2014 found that "emotional states can be transferred to others via emotional contagion, leading people to experience the same emotions without their awareness"; "emotional contagion occurs without direct interaction between people," the study found, "and in the complete absence of nonverbal cues," as on social media.

The girl got "everyone" involved in their problem, Janie said, over the summer and into the next school year—the "entire school," as well as some parents and teachers. The girl ranted about how Janie had hurt her emotionally, portraying Janie's treatment of her as abusive and cruel.

"And then everybody decided to take her side," Janie said. "Even friends that were really close to me decided to take her side and say it was all my fault. She was harassing me and her friends started harassing me and then some of my friends started harassing her and her friends." It was social media war.

"They all went onto social media, onto Instagram, and they followed me on Twitter and Facebook," Janie said. People posted nasty comments. And some of the comments were about Janie being gay.

"They tried to message me and say that they were glad I was finally out of her life and that I was the problem. Two teachers, they would give me nasty looks in the hallway. The teachers got involved and said it was all my fault and that they didn't agree with any of it and they didn't approve of me."

The comments were almost never in person, almost always on social media. "They wouldn't say it if it was in person," Janie said. "They think they're protected by a computer screen.

"Her mom even tried to follow me" on Twitter, she said. "Her mom harassed me and texted me."

There's been debate around the question of whether parents should, or have the right to, monitor their children's activity online; there's less awareness of how parents and other adults sometimes insert themselves into kids' online drama or make comments about children on social media. Over the past few years there's been a steady trickle of news reports; for example, in 2015 a Colorado teacher was fired after posting a picture of a student on her Instagram account with the comment "I don't know him, but I hate him," and the hashtag #pothead. In Montclair, the mother of a middle school girl told me that some other mothers who had been monitoring their daughters' texts became involved in ostracizing one of the girls in their daughters' group chat. "They told their daughters to stay away from this girl, she was bad news. It led to an incident where a girl was saying she was going to punch this girl in the face in Watchung Plaza."

When Janie texted her ex and asked her to stop harassing her, the girl fired back: "I don't think about you I don't feel anything for you, nothing you're a fucking worthless stranger to me you can go to hell . . . Out of my life bitch I never want to see your ugly-ass face again."

The Bronx, New York

Madeline had just had her *quinceañera*, "like a Sweet Sixteen except for fifteen-year-olds," in San Martín Texmelucan de Labastida, the Mexican town where her grandparents lived. She showed me the pictures of the party she kept in an album decorated with ribbons. She'd worn a sea-blue gown, a tiara, and white flowers in her hair; the theme was "Under the Sea." She'd choreographed a reggae dance for the event with a local choreographer. Madeline wanted to be a dancer someday. "It was the best experience of my life," she said. "If only I could live it over again." It was a day when "you felt like a princess, and all your family is around you saying they care about you and now you are a young woman."

Madeline and her friend Breanna, both fifteen, were eating pizza at the kitchen table of a woman I know who lives in Crotona Park East. Madeline was wearing hoop earrings and jeans and an off-the-shoulder blouse; she had a merry, convivial air. She was Latina and Asian. Her mother was a single mom who worked three jobs, one at a delivery service and two at superstores.

Breanna was wearing jeans, a T-shirt and a hoodie, and hoop earrings, too. She was black and Latina, tall, with shoulder-length hair and braces. She seemed thoughtful. She wanted to be a writer, she said, and was part of an online writing club. Her dad worked in computers and her mother at a hospital. The two girls went to different schools. Their parents were friends.

Madeline talked some more about her *quinceañera* and her ex-boyfriend, her first boyfriend, who had been there. They had known each other "since we were babies" in Mexico, she said. At her seventh birthday party, "I was in a really pretty dress. It was a princess theme, so I was dressed up like Belle," from *Beauty and the Beast*. "And somebody asked, Are you guys going out? And he said, Yes," she said, her face softening at the memory. "And after that, we were girlfriend and boyfriend. I go to Mexico every year, so I would see him. We talked on Facebook. We were texting. We'd text all afternoon. We'd text until we fell asleep.

"He was my main escort at my *quinceañera*," she said. "We said we were going to live happily ever after. But we ended up breaking up. My friend in Mexico told me that he cheated on me."

She seemed sad about it.

The girls said that cheating was common in relationships these days. "I think it's social media," Madeline said. "Because on social media he could seem like he loved me. But I couldn't see his face. And he was doing something completely different in real life."

Breanna said that she had also had a boyfriend she found out had been cheating on her on Facebook. "As soon as we broke up I could see him messaging some other girl," she said. "And I was like, Oh, okay. So this must have been happening for a while."

Cheating on social media has become a problem in modern relationships, a factor increasingly cited in American divorce filings. Psychologists point to the ready access people now have to others, friends and strangers, in whom they might have interest or to whom they turn when they're feeling dissatisfied in their relationships. "There's never been another moment in history when we've had instant access to anyone who crosses our minds," Jaclyn Cravens, an assistant professor of community, family, and addiction sciences at Texas Tech University, who specializes in Facebook infidelity, told *Redbook*. Her 2013 study found that even when infidelity is manifested only online, the partner who is cheated on experiences emotions as painful as if it were a physical encounter.

The increased accessibility of potential sex and dating partners has also affected the relationships of teens, who are on social media throughout the day and night, often looking for people to date or sext with or just talk to, out of loneliness or horniness or boredom. "I dated a guy that cheated on me eight different times," said Jill, a nineteen-year-old sophomore at the University of Detroit Mercy. "Everybody cheats," said her friend Mirella, also nineteen. "Everybody thinks that you're *gonna* cheat—like, cheating is a part of how things are now. If you haven't been cheated on it's like, Oh, you haven't? Oh, that's weird." "If your girlfriend-slash-boyfriend asks to check your phone, you could just have deleted everything the night before and she could not see it," said a fourteen-year-old girl in San Diego, California. "It's so easy to just hide everything."

"Like your boyfriend could have been talking to somebody for months behind your back and you'll never find out," Madeline said.

They said it destroyed their sense of trust.

"There is no trust," Madeline said.

"In our generation," Breanna agreed.

"Love is just a word, it has no meaning," Madeline said. "It's very rare you will ever find someone who really likes you for who you are—for yourself, your originality. And it doesn't matter what you look like, if you have a big butt or whatever. Rarely, ever, do you find someone who really cares."

A big butt? I asked. It wasn't the first time I'd heard girls talk about the importance placed on having a "big butt."

"You're supposed to have a big butt, big boobs, and if you don't have both, you're nothing," Madeline said. "You better have a pretty face."

In 2014, *Vogue* announced, "We're Officially in the Era of the Big Booty." With "today's most popular celebrities, the measure of sex appeal is inextricably linked to the prominence of a woman's behind," said the magazine. According to *Vogue*, the "booty movement" had its most "prominent" representative in Kim Kardashian, who used Instagram "to inundate followers with a steady stream of portraits" of her rear end, "slowly redefining the Hollywood body."

Kardashian's behind had actually appeared on screens after more than two decades of hip-hop videos showing beautiful, curvy women of color dancing in hypersexualized scenes. Sir Mix-a-Lot rapped that he *"liked big butts"* back in 1992. But 2014 did seem to be the year when "big booties" went fully mainstream, à la *Vogue* and other media outlets, which finally seemed to acknowledge the existence of an appreciation for bodies shaped more like Beyoncé's than Gwyneth Paltrow's. It was a reversal from the 1980s, when women were advised that they had to mold their butts into compact "buns of steel," and if they had a backside any larger than Jane Fonda's, it was seen as a sign of laziness and even moral decrepitude. In the late '90s, Jennifer Lopez's curvaceous behind became a locus of national fascination. In 1999 I wrote a piece for *New York* wondering if, hoping that, the celebration of a female star with a different body type than the standard ideal heralded a new acceptance of the bodies of many women of color by mainstream pop culture.

In 2014, in a review of Nicki Minaj's "Anaconda" in *Grantland*, Molly Lambert wrote, "Nicki's body is the modern ideal." And while it was great to see that Minaj's voluptuous form was being admired, it was also discouraging to realize that it was just one ideal exchanged for another, and that some women were still being made to feel lesser-than if they didn't resemble the newly imposed standard. "What alarms me," says Jeannine Amber, the writer, "is that there are black women who've hailed this obsession with big asses as a great step forward. They see this as a move toward cultural 'acceptance' of black women's naturally curvy physiques. I can't tell you how many stories I've heard of young black women risking their lives with back-alley butt injections hoping for a Nicki Minaj silhouette." In 2012, *Essence* ran a piece about how "silicone butt injections" had caused one woman to lose limbs, while others had lost their lives.

And why does the size of a woman's behind allegedly matter? Meghan Trainor's 2014 hit, "All About That Bass," is a body-positivity anthem many girls found inspiring; and yet its self-acceptance message seems clouded by how triumphant Trainor is about the power a big booty has over "boys." She exults in the song over having *"that boom boom that all the boys chase."* Her mother, she says, has encouraged her in having this view of her body as beautiful because of how it will be sexually desired by "boys": *"boys like a little more booty to hold at night."* She also voices disdain for *"skinny bitches,"* mocking them: *"I know you think you're fat."*

In 2014, Jennifer Lopez released "Booty," featuring Iggy Azalea, with a video that's basically a four-and-a-half-minute close-up of the two women's behinds undulating and rubbing together. *"Big, big booty,"* Lopez sings. *"It's his birthday / Give him what he asks for,"* suggesting that "booty" is for men. Meanwhile, in 2014, the top gaining search on Pornhub was "big booty," with a 486 percent increase from the previous year, underscoring an impression you can get that there doesn't seem to be anything that happens in the world of women that isn't fetishized in porn.

"Girls put pictures on Facebook in booty shorts sitting in a certain pose where their butt looks big," Madeline said.

"The famous sink shot," said Breanna.

Sink shot? I asked.

They explained that this was "when a girl takes a selfie in the bathroom, like wearing a thong," "with her butt pushed up on the sink to make it look bigger. And you can see all of her butt up on the sink like in the mirror." It was a variation on a genre of selfie popularized by Kim Kardashian, also known as a "belfie," or a selfie of a butt, repeatedly seen in the Instagram shots of the derriere-endowed fitness model Jen Selter.

"You have to have a perfect body and big butt," Breanna said. "For a girl, you have to be that certain way to get the boys' attention. Boys say, I want a bad chick."

"Which is, like, big butt, big boobs," Madeline said.

"A girl who has everything," said Breanna.

"Skinny waist, perfect figure, nice hair, all of that," Madeline said.

"If you go on Facebook, there are pictures of hundreds and thousands of girls that are pretty and have, like, the hourglass figure—big boobs, big butt—and have the blond hair or the red hair with the pretty eyes and the piercings that go with the dimples and everything. And, if you look down, you'll see she has like a thousand likes and hundreds of comments with the boys saying, Oh, she's pretty. Oh, I would want her to be my girlfriend."

Facebook was still the social media site where most kids in their schools interacted, said the girls. It was on Facebook that they talked to their friends and family members who lived far away. "Everyone is on it," said Madeline. "Me, personally, I'm on it every day, school hours, after school. So I'm on it twenty-four/seven."

Facebook was also the place where boys would like a girl's picture and then ask if they could "see more of you."

"They'll message you on Facebook," Madeline said. "They'll be like, Oh, I saw that picture. You're looking really nice."

"And they'll go from there," Breanna said. "They'll play the nice guy, and all of a sudden it's like, Yeah, I'm feeling some type of way," meaning horny. "You want to send me pictures?"

"After a five-minute conversation," Madeline said.

"Some girls will do it! They'll be like, Okay, I'll send you pictures," said Breanna.

"Girls send nudes, to show what they have."

"To be approachable."

"They think that's how they attract the boys' attention."

They talked about a girl they knew who had become "Facebook famous" after posting provocative pictures of herself online; but then her fame had backfired on her.

"She went on Facebook and started posting herself in revealing clothing," Madeline said, "and people started paying more attention to her, and then she thought she was a bad 'b' and wouldn't talk to you anymore. But then she got mad because they created a fake page of her," meaning a slut page. "They used her pictures with posts that had explicit statuses that said things like, Oh, come to my house with thirty bucks and I'll do this and that.

"So she was frustrated about that," Madeline went on. "She told everybody, I would never do something like that. I don't know who this person is," meaning the person who had created the page.

Slut pages on Facebook appeared in their school often, they said.

"People will do it to embarrass a girl, to expose her in some way," said Breanna.

They talked about another girl they knew who "sent a boy a naked picture, like full-on." "He broke up with her the next day," Madeline said. "And then he posted the picture all over Facebook. But she didn't worry about it. She just put up another picture of herself."

"In a thong," Breanna said. "But then the next thing, she went to the hospital. She started cutting herself."

"They say it takes the pain away," Madeline said.

They shook their heads.

But the worst thing about Facebook, said the girls, was that "fights always start on Facebook." Sometimes physical fights between girls. "It starts on a thread," they said, "and they take it to the street."

"Someone will say, Oh, I'll hurt you, I'll hurt someone in your family," Breanna said. "They'll start threatening to hurt your family members just to scare you."

"And then somebody says something about somebody," a rumor or insult, Madeline said, "and then it just escalates and then it's, Okay, I'm going to fight you right now. Meet me tomorrow at this place, wait for me at this spot."

"And then people hear about it and people post about it and they're like, Oh, there's going to be a fight tomorrow. And sometimes they film it," Breanna said.

"And then they put *that* on Facebook," said Madeline.

They shook their heads again at the cyclicality of it.

I asked them what the fights were about.

"Oh, she doesn't know how to dress, she's ugly, she's a ho," Madeline said.

"It will go back and forth," said Breanna. "People call each other thot, slut, whore."

"Boys do not get called that," Madeline said. "If they sleep around, it's like, Oh, yeah, congrats!"

But when girls called one another those words, they said, it could lead to violence.

"Last year, we had like four fights in one day because of gossip on Facebook," Madeline said. "It starts in seventh grade, when girls finally start getting their body, and they start caring about looks and how people think of them."

Girls gossiped about one another on Facebook, they said. " 'She's cheating on her boyfriend,' " Madeline said, as an example.

"Sometimes they just say, like, You stink. They pick on any little thing," said Breanna.

"They go for your insecurity, like what you wear and what shoes you have, what jewelry you have, what kind of hairstyle you have," Madeline said.

"If you don't have Jordans," meaning the sneakers, "good luck," Breanna said. She was wearing a pair herself.

"If you're not wearing the brands in style," said Madeline, "like True Religion and Adidas, they'll be like, Why are you wearing *that*?"

I asked them where they thought all this focus on brands was coming from.

"Celebrities, TV," said Madeline. "I just saw a show, it was like the fifty richest celebrities, and it was all about all the stuff they have. They were talking about the rich people like Beyoncé and Jay Z, and their baby, Blue Ivy, and Kanye West's baby, North West. They were talking about who has the most expensive stuff—which *baby*."

"They said Blue Ivy, Jay Z's baby, had a fifteen-thousand-dollar Swarovski highchair or something like that, all jeweled out, blinged out," said Breanna.

"And it's like, Oh, they grew up like me, but how do I get to that level, that I can have all those nice things?" asked Madeline.

"And people want that; and so that's what you must have," said Breanna.

"You want that life," Madeline said. "TV now is all about competitions. Rivalries. You have all these shows where people are competing against each other for money. And you feel like, if I could fight the best, I could get that money."

I asked them if they had ever been in fights themselves.

"Once," said Madeline.

"I try not to get into fights," Breanna said. "Because of past experiences I've had, I'm always aware of who's around me or what's going on. If someone comes up to me and says they're going to jump me or threaten me, or try and hurt me, I just try and walk away."

In the Media

In 2005, *Newsweek* ran a story headlined "Bad Girls Go Wild," which raised an alarm about an alleged increase in violence among girls. Citing a new study from the FBI, the magazine reported that the number of adolescent girls arrested for aggravated assault had seen a shocking rise over the last twenty years. Though the FBI had given no theories about the reason for this spike in violence, *Newsweek* blamed feminism. "The women's movement," said the magazine, "which explicitly encourages women to assert themselves like men, has unintentionally opened the door to girls' violent behavior."

But when the Justice Department looked into *Newsweek*'s claims, in 2008, it found them to be based on a faulty analysis of data. Girls weren't becoming more violent, but they were being arrested and incarcerated more frequently for lesser offenses. "There is no burgeoning national crisis of increasing serious violence among adolescent girls," said the Justice Department's report. It's worth considering whether the women's movement actually may have opened the door to, not more violent behavior among girls, but more policing of girls' behavior, as a form of backlash.

And yet, in 2008, *People* magazine ran a story titled "Mean Girls," about the alleged rising tide of girl aggression. In 2010, there was another panic about girl violence in the wake of the suicide of Phoebe Prince, a fifteen-year-old South Hadley, Massachusetts, girl who was bullied and harassed by six classmates. Two of these classmates were boys, and both were arrested and charged with statutory rape.

"This panic is a hoax," wrote two experts on juvenile justice, Mike Males and Meda Chesney-Lind, in *The New York Times* in 2010. In their op-ed, "The Myth of Mean Girls," they said, "We examined every major index of crime on which the authorities rely. None show a recent increase in girls' violence; in fact, every reliable measure shows that violence by girls has been plummeting for years . . . Why, in an era when slandering a group of people based on the misdeeds of a few has rightly become taboo, does it remain acceptable to use isolated incidents to berate modern teenagers, particularly girls, as 'mean' and 'violent' and 'bullies'? That is, why are we bullying girls?"

Good question. Nowhere in this op-ed did the words "sexism" or "misogyny" appear, but perhaps they were implicit. People seem to like to see girls fight. At least one would think so from the profusion of reality TV shows which center around girl-on-girl aggression. Unfortunately, these are some of the most popular shows among girls themselves. Shows such as *Dance Moms, America's Next Top Model, Jersey Shore,* and *The Hills* all depict women in conflict with one another, gossiping and backstabbing. They rely on those dramatic moments when the women's animosity toward each other erupts in some sort of showdown, the vicious "catfight." When I asked girls in the Bronx about the favorite shows among girls in their schools, all brought up *Bad Girls Club,* a reality show in which the main draw is scenes of women physically assaulting one another, sometimes hurting each other badly. What's perhaps most disturbing is that these scenes are played partially for comic effect; we are meant to laugh at the women's outrageous inability to control themselves; but many girls also see it as a display of badass power.

Several studies have shown a potential connection among violent behavior, bullying and cyberbullying, and reality TV. A 2011 national survey by the Girl Scout Research Institute on reality TV shows found that girls ages eleven to seventeen were heavily influenced by their viewing of such programs. Seventy-five percent of girls surveyed believed that reality competition shows were "real," as opposed to scripted. Girls who watched reality shows expected girls in real life to be more aggressive and mean than did girls who didn't view them. An overwhelming majority of young female reality TV viewers believed that gossiping is a "normal part of a relationship," that "it's in the nature of girls to be catty and competitive," and that "it's hard to trust other girls." And 37 percent believed that "being mean earns you more respect than being nice."

Jeannine Amber says that when she did an investigation for *Essence* on the impact reality TV has on girls, she found that "there is an expected agreement going in with the characters [on the shows] and the producers that there will be a physical altercation at some point because that is going to cause a spike in the ratings. Kids watching it think it's real—they think this is how people behave. If they are low-income kids and their parents are working all the time, the TV is the babysitter; this is their role model."

There is girl-on-girl violence in and out of schools, and it tends to start on social media. When girls fight, it's often because of some affront online, as the Bronx girls described, and then it turns into a physical confrontation—which in turn is sometimes filmed on cell phones and posted on social media. A search on YouTube for "girl fight at school" turns up more than 20 million results. The videos show girls tearing into each other as crowds of kids watch and cheer them on. On Twitter, Facebook, Vine, and other sites you can find such videos, which typically get lots of views. It's often boys who post them, and their running commentary often sounds amused.

But girls aren't fighting because they're mean or violent by nature. When researchers at the Justice Department examined the social and cultural reasons behind girl violence in 2008, they found them to include poverty, domestic violence, and growing up in "disorganized communities" with "parents who are themselves coping with structurally disadvantaged neighborhoods and poverty."

In *Violence by Teenage Girls: Trends and Context,* the Justice Department reported that "another factor in girls' violence against other girls involves the contradictory messages girls receive regarding sexuality. For most girls, models and images of healthy sexual desire are rare or nonexistent . . . Rigid imagery about 'appropriate' behavior for girls can emphasize being attractive to and desired by boys and at the same time send girls messages that they are valued for abstaining from sexual behavior.

"Girls at risk for engaging in same-sex peer violence," the report went on, "did not have any sense of themselves or other girls as having their own legitimate sexual desires or being valued. They understood their own sexual value only in relation to how they satisfied males and lived up to idealized standards of femininity. Thus, these girls were quick to strike out at other girls who threatened their view of self or their relationships with valued males."

New York, New York

It was Saturday, and the three girls had decided to take in the new movie based on a John Green novel, *Paper Towns*. Afterward, they went to a pizza restaurant near the theater to get slices. They were Alex, Hannah, and Zora, friends from an Upper East Side private school. They were white girls with long straight hair in varying shades of blond; they wore sundresses and leggings and dangly necklaces and ankle boots.

Alex carried a Fendi bag, from which she withdrew the money to buy her friends lunch. "I'll be the mom," she said jokingly, bringing the slices to the table.

Alex was a "Park Avenue princess" by her own description, tall and broad-shouldered, with a commanding presence. Her friends called her a "diva." She revered the British monarchy and said that she would like to marry Prince Harry someday—"he's only like thirty so it's not impossible"—"or be the editor of *Vogue*, or the CEO of Disney."

Hannah, who was also tall, with a wide, open face and pea-green eyes, lived in a brownstone in Brooklyn with her parents, both men, and said she wanted to be a doctor so she could join Doctors Without Borders and "help people in wars." And Zora, a scholarship student who lived on the Lower East Side, was sometimes called "Rory," for Rory on *Gilmore Girls*, because she was quiet and bookish and had a kooky single mom. She had a book sticking out of her bag, *Romeo and Juliet*.

"It's so funny that you brought that," Alex said.

"I read it on the subway," said Zora.

"We don't have to read it for like two months," Alex said with a smirk.

"I already read it," Hannah said. "My dads make me read all of Shakespeare."

Alex sniffed. "I *want* Cara Delevingne's eyebrows," she suddenly exclaimed. "She has such good eyebrow game."

Delevingne was the twenty-three-year-old British model and actress who had starred in *Paper Towns*. She was known for being part of Taylor Swift's girl squad and for her dry responses to chirpy TV talk show interviewers.

"Have you seen her Instagram?" Hannah asked with a smile.

"Of course I've seen her Instagram," Alex said. "I live for her Insta-gram. I am literally sustained by it." She folded up her pizza and took a bite, New Yorker–style.

Delevingne's Instagram featured shots of her standing around top-less with other models; in one, she's touching herself while wearing a pair of Superman underwear. "Don't have sex," she warns in a joke video, her voice overlaid with the ominous voice of Coach Carr from *Mean Girls.*

"Her Instagram is literally perfect," Hannah agreed.

"I think it's so cute the way Taylor Swift has BFFed Cara," Alex said. "Like she's trying to make us think she can *be* a Cara. Oh, Taylor, you'll never be La Delevingne."

"I like Taylor Swift," said Zora.

"I guess she is a good role model," Alex said, smirking again.

A couple of boys about their age came into the pizza place. They stood at the counter and ordered slices. They were nice-looking boys in T-shirts and jeans.

Alex snatched up her phone and started texting.

A moment later, Hannah's phone buzzed on the table. "Oh!" said Hannah. Alex had sent her a text with the names of the two boys and where they went to school. Alex knew them. "Of course, they come with their parents to my parents' Christmas party," she said offhandedly. "My father plays squash with Dylan's dad."

But they didn't speak to or even acknowledge each other.

"Alexandra knows everyone," Hannah said, low. "She's Gossip Girl."

"Not *that* Gossip Girl," Alex said pointedly.

Hannah said, "Slug word: Nell."

In whispers they relayed that Nell was a girl who, the previous year, had posed as "Gossip Girl" on Ask.fm and "told people's secrets and said *awful* things—mostly about the really popular girls," Alex said. "Like the top girls in the private schools, the type of girls who have like seven hundred followers on Instagram.

"It was all very thinly veiled," she went on, "so you knew exactly who the people were. She would say things implying that the girls were sluts and had multiple boyfriends at one time. It was outrageous the way she posted it, but personally I know that every word of it was accurate."

"She gossiped about this girl who got kicked out of school for sending around a video of herself masturbating—in eighth grade," Hannah said.

"Well, we all saw that," said Alex, shuddering for effect.

"Nell's parents sent her to a wilderness school," Hannah sighed. That was a type of boarding school/rehab facility, usually set in a remote, rural location. Such schools, also known as "therapeutic boarding schools," have been a burgeoning business since the '80s, notorious as places where wealthy parents send their troubled children.

"There's a rumor that she bought a phone for a boy with her parents' credit card," Hannah said. The girls tsk-tskd. "She was having substance abuse issues."

"Her mother had serious Botox issues," Alex said.

They started talking about how some girls' mothers had "issues" and were "mean." "Like some of them are really mean"—"not *mine*"—"no, not mine, either, but like some girls' moms seem like they're mad at their daughters"—"like totally, they're in competition with them and they put pictures of themselves on Facebook in bathing suits and it's so embarrassing"—"oh, I know, I feel so sorry for their daughters"—"like, Please put on some clothes, you're not a teenager—"

"You need your mom to be your best friend," Zora said earnestly. "So what would you do if you didn't have her as your best friend?"

"I wouldn't know," Alex said dryly. "My mother's best friends are the girls in her bridge club."

They brought up the name of another girl they knew and said, "Her mother swears at her," "I think she takes pills," "I know, and it's just sad for her—the *mom*—because her daughter hates her and she can, like, never get these years back—"

"I think the reason Nell was the way she was, it was because she was lonely," said Zora.

"She watched too much *Gossip Girl*," Hannah said. "I think *Gossip Girl* had a huge influence on our grade. It was a big deal at one point, remember?"

Gossip Girl, which aired from 2007 to 2012, was about students at the fictional Constance Billard School for Girls, Park Avenue princesses with limitless shopping power at the height of the Great Recession. They shopped, and they fought and backstabbed one another, all while dressed in an endless selection of dazzling luxury brands, often micro-minis, cutout dresses, and blouses with plunging necklines. The girls on the show, based on the best-selling book series by Cecily von Zie-gesar, were as mean to one another as they were sexualized. And their sex lives—all the subject of a scandalous blog by an anonymous mean girl in their midst who called herself "Gossip Girl," and was voiced by actress Kristen Bell—were as active as their adult counterparts on *Sex and the City*.

But the girls on *Gossip Girl* didn't just have a lot of sex, they used sex as a weapon, to manipulate or take revenge. As on *Sex and the City*, there was a lot of drinking, although the girls were underage. The Parents Television Council repeatedly warned against the potentially damaging effects of this material on young viewers, admonitions which were depicted as hopelessly unhip by the makers of *Gossip Girl*, who included these criticisms and others—"Mind-Blowingly Inappropriate," "Every Parent's Nightmare," "A Nasty Piece of Work"—in their 2008 "OMFG" ad campaign. *New York* magazine called *Gossip Girl* "The Greatest Teen Drama of All Time." "All girls love *Gossip Girl*," a New York girl, age fifteen, told me.

"I *lived* for *Gossip Girl*," Alex said. "When it went off the air, I had a wake—just for the shoes."

" 'X-O-X-O Gossip Girl,' " Hannah said, quoting the show's tagline.

Alex's phone buzzed. A text.

Alex's eyes grew wide. It was from one of the boys who had come into the pizza place. The boys were sitting at another table. Everyone looked over at them. They were both on their phones, neither giving any indication that he was texting Alex.

"What'd he say?" Hannah asked.

"Oh," Alex said dismissively, dropping her phone on the table, "he just wants to know when my brother's coming back from Spain. I hate boys."

"Um, I didn't really know how to say this," Hannah began after a moment. "So I guess I should just say it—I have a boyfriend!"

She looked gleeful and expectant.

Alex and Zora stared.

"Oh, Hannah, that's so great!" said Zora.

"You have a *boyfriend*?" Alex said. "How'd you get a boyfriend?"

"What do you mean?" said Hannah. "That doesn't sound very nice."

"I just mean—well, what school does he go to?" Alex demanded.

Hannah said, "He goes to public school in Brooklyn. I met him in Prospect Park. He's Mexican."

"He's *Mexican*? Can he talk right?" Alex said.

Hannah's mouth opened.

Zora said, *"Alex."*

"Oh—I didn't mean it like *that*," Alex recovered. "I just wanted to know if you meant he was an immigrant."

"No, he's American," Hannah said firmly.

"Alex," said Zora.

"I just meant—I mean," Alex said, flustered. And then her tone became outraged. "Well, why didn't you tell me about this before? I thought I was your friend. This is not girl code. You have to tell your friends about your boyfriend. You have to tell your friends about all the gossip and the drama going on in your life."

"Well, I wasn't really sure if he *was* my boyfriend until yesterday," Hannah said. "It just happened yesterday. We were at his house—"

"At his house? You go to his house?" Alex asked.

Hannah said, "Yes."

"Are there other Mexican people there?" Alex asked.

"Alex," Zora said, "you're actually being horrible."

"Well, this isn't the first time she's done something like this," Alex said, looking wounded.

"What? What have I done to you?" Hannah asked.

Alex launched into a litany of alleged offenses, including accusations that Hannah did not pay proper attention to Alex's activity on social media: "You never like my pictures or make any comments on my pictures."

"Yes, I do!" said Hannah.

"You don't even follow me on Tumblr," Alex said.

"I didn't even know you had a Tumblr!" said Hannah.

"I do," Alex said. "I post pictures of handbags I like. I post pictures of beautiful Birkins."

Hannah and Zora gave each other a look.

"Are you going to change your status on Facebook?" Alex said in a mocking tone.

"I don't *know*," said Hannah. "He hardly ever goes on Facebook."

"Well, duh, no boys go on Facebook unless they want to hit on you," Alex said.

"Which you know 'cause that happens to you all the time," said Hannah.

Zora blanched.

"Oh," said Alex, shaken, "now you're being mean. That was really uncalled-for."

"Well, you were being racist!" Hannah exclaimed.

"I was not!" said Alex. "Mexican is not a race!"

"I think we need to dial this down," Zora said. "We're friends—"

"You're right," Alex said. And to Hannah: "I'm sorry. I just was shocked, that's all. I'm sorry."

Hannah shrugged. "It's okay."

"Can we see a picture of him?" Alex asked.

Hannah picked up her phone and eagerly started thumbing and scrolling. "Well, I haven't taken any pictures *with* him," she said, "because I didn't want him to think I was rushing things, like doing selfies together, you know? But here's his Facebook." She held it up, proud. It showed a Facebook profile picture of a smiling dark-haired boy in a green soccer jersey.

"Oh my God, he's so cute!" said Zora.

"He is really cute," Alex said, examining the photo like a coroner poring over a dead body.

Hannah smiled. "I know."

"Well, why does he like you?" Alex said.

"*Alex*," Zora said.

"I just mean, like, how did you two get together?" said Alex, putting her face on her folded hands and fluttering her eyes.

Hannah started telling the story: she was walking her dog along Prospect Park one day when the boy had come out of the park with a soccer ball. They started walking together, talking together, and now they were talking all the time. "It's just so easy to talk to him," she said breathlessly, "it's like we've known each other forever. He's just so—

oh, he's just so sweet and I love the way he does all these stupid things to try and make me laugh, like he sends me funny texts and funny emojis . . ."

Zora listened, eyes shining.

Alex was scrolling through Facebook on her phone. She had found the boy's page. "I'm going to friend him," she said.

Hannah started up from her seat. "Alex, no! You can't friend him! Then he'll know I've been talking about him!"

"Don't you want to know what he says about you?" Alex grinned.

Hannah said, "No!"

Zora said, "Alex, no!"

"I'm going to tell him I think he's hot," Alex said, fingers poised over her phone.

"Alex!" Hannah whimpered.

"Oh my God, I'm just kidding," Alex said, putting down her phone. "I would never do that."

Hannah tossed her head. Her face was flushed. "I shouldn't have told you anything," she said, grabbing her bag off her chair. "I knew I shouldn't have told you." She stormed out of the pizza place.

"What an overreaction," Alex said. "I was just kidding. Anyway, I bet she's lying. He's not her boyfriend."

"Alex, if you're going to act like a bitch, then you have to expect to be treated like one," said Zora, standing up and leaving the restaurant.

In the Media

According to popular opinion, "girls are mean." Over the two and a half years I spent reporting on girls, people often asked me, "Why are girls so mean?" A Google search for "girls are mean" results in more than 295 million links: "Why mean girls are mean." "Little girls can be mean." "Are mean girls getting meaner?"

It's a fairly recent trope, and one which bears examining at a time when cyberbullying is such a big issue in the lives of girls, and one often dismissed as "normal," if regrettable, girl behavior. There has always been the suspicion that women harbor evil within their breasts, beginning with Eve. Western culture has long trafficked in Madonna-whore-based stereotypes of women who are either pristinely good or sinfully bad. But the idea that "girls are mean" arose at the beginning of the twenty-first century in America with the publication of a couple of books making this claim with virtually nothing substantive in the way of evidence. It's interesting to look at the trends at work when this all came about, and to ask why this myth was so embraced by the media and popular culture.

The notable book about girls just prior to the "mean girls" craze made a good case that girls were, in fact, under attack. It was 1994's *Reviving Ophelia: Saving the Selves of Adolescent Girls* by Mary Pipher. Pipher, a clinical psychologist based in Lincoln, Nebraska, had become concerned about the rise in self-destructive behaviors she saw in her practice through the 1980s and '90s—problems still very much plaguing girls today—including body dysmorphia, eating disorders, self-mutilation, drug and alcohol abuse, suicide attempts, and suicidal ideation. Based on her conversations with hundreds of girls, Pipher came to believe that these problems could be traced to girls' experiences of sexism and sexual violence. She posited that at the onset of adolescence, girls' confidence levels drop as they begin to become aware of their own objectification and sexualization in the wider world. "They lose their resiliency and optimism and become less curious and inclined to take risks," Pipher wrote. "They lose their assertive, energetic and 'tomboyish' personalities and become more deferential, self-critical and depressed. They report great unhappiness with their own bodies."

Reviving Ophelia became a subject of national discussion in an atmosphere of renewed interest in feminism in the early '90s. In 1991, women throughout the country had become incensed at Anita Hill's treatment by a panel of all white male senators when she testified in the Clarence Thomas confirmation hearings. Nineteen-ninety-two was deemed the Year of the Woman after the election of four women to the Senate. Susan Faludi's *Backlash: The Undeclared War Against American Women* was a best seller in 1991, raising awareness of how the women's movement had met with opposition in almost every sector of the American media and politics, virtually since its inception.

Third-wave feminism was emerging and broadening the focus of feminism to include an understanding of the connections among race, class, and gender. In the Pacific Northwest, Riot Grrrl, the feminist hard-core punk rock movement, was having a wide-ranging influence. In pop culture, there was Madonna, challenging accepted notions of female sexuality. And *Thelma and Louise* (1991), a movie about two women who flee the law after one kills a man who has attempted to rape the other, was provoking "table-pounding discussions between men and women," said *Time*.

The early '90s also saw a number of studies contending that American public education was disadvantaging girls. In 1991, the American Association of University Women published a nationwide study reporting that girls ages nine to fifteen suffered lower self-esteem, were less willing to voice their ideas, and had lower interest in math and science than boys as a result of how they were treated in classrooms—for example, by being called upon less and encouraged less than male students. In 1994, American University professors Myra Sadker and David Sadker echoed these findings in a report based on a three-year national study, *Failing at Fairness: How America's Schools Cheat Girls*.

The "girl power" movement of the '90s was in part a response to a growing awareness of an emotional and educational crisis among girls. There were multi-agency government initiatives addressing the inequity in girls' education, as mandated by Title IX in 1972 and the Women's Educational Equity Act of 1974. In pop culture, *Sassy* magazine gave girls a feminist alternative to *Seventeen*. The entertainment industry responded with an avalanche of TV shows featuring strong female characters: *Buffy the Vampire Slayer*, *Xena: Warrior Princess*, *My So-Called Life*, *Moesha*, and more.

But as Susan Faludi noted in *Backlash*, feminist movements and moments are typically met with resistance. The backlash to "girl power" was a media wave announcing "girls are mean." Rachel Simmons's best-selling *Odd Girl Out: The Hidden Culture of Aggression in Girls*, published in 2002, declared it was time to expose the "hidden culture of girls' aggression in which bullying is epidemic, distinctive, and destructive." In the world of girls, Simmons wrote, "friendship is a weapon, and the sting of a shout pales in comparison to a day of someone's silence. There is no gesture more devastating than the back turning away." It was a serious claim for a book about girls which never mentioned the sexual harassment of girls by boys or men, and devoted less than a full-page to girls' experiences of sexual abuse or sexual violence.

Simmons, who began her book with an account of her own experience being bullied by another girl when she was eight—and in it later confessed, "I count myself among the many women and girls who have demonized the girl bullies in their lives"—presented scads of anecdotal examples of girls being pitilessly bullied by other girls; she gave little indication of girls having negative interactions with boys or men. She didn't go into the influence of the media, advertising, or other cultural forces on girls' behavior. In a book about children and meanness, you might have expected at least a mention of the much-remarked-upon increase in meanness in American public life in the 1980s and '90s, as seen in the cultures of Wall Street and Washington and in the rising violence of popular entertainment, and discussed, for example, in 1997's *The Triumph of Meanness: America's War Against Its Better Self,* by Nicolaus Mills.

The underpinning of Simmons's thesis lay in studies done in the early '90s on "relational aggression," a term used by researchers led by a Finnish professor, Kaj Björkqvist, to describe aggression that is covert rather than overt and targets a person's reputation or social status. What the Finnish findings actually said was that girls are equally as aggressive as boys, but in different ways, not more aggressive. Recent research suggests, however, that "contrary to popular perceptions, higher levels of relational aggression [are] more common among boys than girls." This is according to StopBullying.gov—a website with content on bullying and cyberbullying provided by the Justice Department, the CDC, and other government agencies, and which in 2015 published an article titled "The Myth of 'Mean Girls.'"

"In the past two decades," the article says, "relational aggression has received an abundance of media attention. Books, movies, and websites have portrayed girls as being cruel to one another, thus creating and reinforcing the stereotype of 'mean girls.' However, this popular perception of girls being meaner than boys is not always supported by research . . . Several large cross-cultural studies and meta-analyses have found no gender differences in relational aggression." But one 2014 study did. The Healthy Teens Longitudinal Study by researchers at the University of Georgia, which followed a group of adolescents for seven years in the 2000s, found "significantly more" relational aggression in boys than in girls in middle school.

In 2002, however, "relational aggression" was a media buzzword and "mean girls" were a hot topic. "Girls Just Want to Be Mean," said a cover story in *The New York Times Magazine*. Rachel Simmons and Rosalind Wiseman appeared on *The Oprah Winfrey Show* to discuss it. Wiseman is the author of 2002's best-selling *Queen Bees and Wannabes: Helping Your Daughter Survive Cliques, Gossip, Boyfriends, and the New Realities of Girl World*, the other book at the center of the "mean girls" media blitz; her book described a rigid hierarchy and pecking order in a place she called "Girl World," in which girls are constantly at odds with one another, jockeying for position and generally being mean.

There's even less in Wiseman's book in the way of evidence from psychologists, sociologists, or other researchers; there's none. Wiseman doesn't say how many girls she interviewed or where. Her book isn't really an investigation but rather a parenting guide. Prior to writing it, she taught self-defense to girls and young women. Her book became the basis for the hit movie *Mean Girls*, which came out in 2004, further popularizing this new idea of "mean girls."

Mean Girls, one of the most beloved films for girls of the last decade, written by Tina Fey and starring Lindsay Lohan, is ostensibly a critique of meanness—Tina Fey's character, a high school teacher, tells the girls in her school, "You have got to stop calling each other sluts and whores." But the movie arguably does just that, making fun of the sluttiness of the girls, and offering such a glamorous vision of their sluttiness and meanness, a girl just might wannabe them. In the movie, the girls of the Plastics clique, all age sixteen, move down the halls of school in short-short skirts and heels, breasts bouncing in slow-mo. "Being with the Plastics was like being famous," Lindsay Lohan's character says dreamily in voice-over. The Plastics do a burlesque-ish rendition of "Jingle Bell Rock" wearing sexy Santa suits. In *Mean Girls*, meanness is sexualized. "A movie you masturbate to," says an entry about the film on Urban Dictionary.

The ten-plus years since *Mean Girls* premiered have seen a deluge of mean girl–themed TV shows—*Gossip Girl, Bad Girls Club, Pretty Little Liars, America's Next Top Model,* and more. "But it's all a stereotype," said a fourteen-year-old girl in New York. "Stereotypes on TV always show girls being mean. You never see a girl who's nice and smart—she's either bitchy and mean, or smart and a nerd." "That's true," said her friend, another fourteen-year-old girl. "Those are the two archetypes—the really mean pretty girl and the ugly serious girl. Oh, and the slut. You never see a girl who's normal and nice and, like, gets B-pluses."

And while America was watching girls being mean on their screens, the media, in 2006, was awash in reports of how it was actually boys who were "in crisis." In 2004, the U.S. Department of Education had published research suggesting that girls and women had closed some existing gender gaps and even surpassed boys and men in many markers of academic achievement. As this information filtered into the media, op-eds and articles started to sound the alarm that boys were allegedly falling behind because of their mistreatment by the American education system. *The New Republic* and *Esquire* ran features, and *Newsweek* did an explosive cover story, "The Boy Crisis," which charged that "by almost every benchmark, boys across the nation and in every demographic group are falling behind." Once again, *Newsweek* blamed feminism.

"Some scholars," said the magazine, "notably Christina Hoff Sommers, a fellow at the American Enterprise Institute, charge that misguided feminism is what's been hurting boys. In the 1990s, she says . . . feminist educators portrayed [girls] as disadvantaged and lavished them with support and attention. Boys, meanwhile, whose rates of achievement had begun to falter, were ignored and their problems allowed to fester." *Newsweek* didn't let its readers know that Sommers was the author of the antifeminist polemic *The War Against Boys: How Misguided Feminism Is Harming Our Young Men,* published in 2000; her best-selling book had also alleged that it was boys who were in crisis, not girls, and all because of the successes of feminism.

"There have always been societies that favored boys over girls," Sommers wrote. "Ours may be the first to deliberately throw the gender switch. If we continue on our present course, boys will, indeed, be tomorrow's second sex"—an outlandish appropriation of the thesis of Simone de Beauvoir's feminist manifesto *The Second Sex*.

But the so-called boy crisis turns out to be a myth as well. The idea has become so deeply rooted in the national consciousness that it's rarely questioned. A 2015 op-ed in *The New York Times* on men's shrinking job opportunities said, "The male malaise starts in the classroom," without a reference to any data. "Girls have overtaken boys at every stage of education," the op-ed went on, "with higher grades from the early years through high school and college."

This appears to be only partially correct; it is true that some girls are getting better grades than boys, but they've hardly "overtaken" them "at every stage of education." In 2006, the Education Sector, an independent education think tank, now a part of the American Institute for Research, published a report titled *The Evidence Suggests Otherwise: The Truth About Boys and Girls*. When the author, analyst Sara Mead, reviewed the Department of Education's own National Assessment of Education Progress reports since the 1970s, she found that this data "[did] not support the notion that boys' academic achievement is falling." Instead, these national report cards showed that there hadn't been any dramatic change in boys' academic performance. Meanwhile, "men are actually enrolling in college in greater numbers than ever before and at historically high rates," Mead wrote. "But girls have just improved their performance on some measures even faster. As a result, girls have narrowed or even closed some academic gaps that previously favored boys, while other long-standing gaps that favored girls have widened, leading to the belief that boys are falling behind."

The Education Sector report tried to put things in perspective: "While most of society has finally embraced the idea of equality for women, the idea that women might actually surpass men in some areas (even as they remain behind in others) seems hard for many people to swallow. Thus, boys are routinely characterized as 'falling behind' even as they improve in absolute terms . . . Some blame 'misguided feminism' for boys' difficulties, while others argue that 'myths' of masculinity have a crippling impact on boys . . . But the evidence suggests that many of these ideas come up short." The report also noted that "Hispanic and black boys and boys from low-income homes" continued to be disadvantaged, but "closing racial and economic gaps would help poor and minority boys more than closing gender gaps."

In June 2012, the Department of Education's Office for Civil Rights published a survey on "Gender Equity in Education," reporting that the gender gap between boys and girls in American schools still had not been closed: "Despite the enormous progress made in ensuring equal education opportunities since the passage of Title IX in 1972 . . . much work remains if we are to achieve full gender equality among our nation's students."

London, England

"It's become a way for people to dismiss sexism," says Laura Bates, talking about the evolution of the notion that "girls are mean." Bates heads the Everyday Sexism Project, a feminist website she founded in 2012, at the age of twenty-six. In 2015, she was awarded the British Empire Medal for services to gender equality.

"When I start talking about sexism in schools," she says, "people interrupt and say, Well, but girls can be mean to each other. Oh, but women are their own worst enemies. I don't believe it. Of course there are instances of meanness in everyone, but we have bought into wholesale this idea of the bitchy, competitive woman who can't bear other women's success. Competitiveness is a difficult human trait. Bullying comes from all kinds of people. I don't believe it's some ingrained genetic trait in women or girls.

"So many of these instances where there is this kind of competitiveness and girls being mean to other girls," Bates says, "it's being driven by societal messages of who they are and how they're supposed to be. It's *caused* by sexism—but then people try to turn it back on women and use it as a reason to not support feminism. In a world where there is such sexualization of women and oppression of women, it just feels like it's too easy to blame girls for meanness. And it's such a clever attempt to create a diversion. Why is it that everybody loves to talk about 'mean girls'? It's another attempt to stymie the feminist movement."

Jamestown, Virginia

Sierra had tried to kill herself more than once with pills she found in the bathroom cabinets at home. She said, "I'm not even sure what they were." Something "bad" would happen and she would feel that she just wanted to "stop it," and so she would gather up all the pills she could find and, as she had seen people do in the movies, swallow a handful.

Most of the time she would "just wake up" with a terrible headache and a queasy feeling in her stomach. She would throw up. Once, she had to go to the hospital and have her stomach pumped. She had tried to kill herself another time by jumping in front of an oncoming car when she was walking home from school, but a friend had grabbed her by the arm and pulled her back.

She had scars on her wrists and the insides of her arms from cutting herself. "I had to get on depression pills to stop" the cutting, she said. But the pills weren't really helping her, so she had started cutting again. There were hatched red lines up and down her arms. "I was eating a lot of food, to feel better," she said. "I started eating ice cream all the time to not let it all get to me, but I don't want to get fat. So I just solved it by cutting."

The Mayo Clinic defines cutting as "self-injury," also called "self-harm," as "the act of deliberately harming your own body, such as cutting or burning yourself," "an unhealthy way to cope with emotional pain, intense anger and frustration." Cutters typically say that they do it to alleviate their emotional pain, which is sometimes hard for others to understand, since cutting itself is painful. But "while self-injury may bring a momentary sense of calm and a release of tension," the Mayo website says, "it's usually followed by guilt and shame and the return of painful emotions. And with self-injury comes the possibility of more serious and even fatal self-aggressive actions."

A 2008 study in the *Journal of Consulting and Clinical Psychology* found that 56 percent of adolescent girls reported doing some form of self-harm in their lifetimes. This number is staggeringly higher than the results of studies in the 1990s, which found self-harm among girls to be as low as 3 percent in a given year.

Sierra said she was not the only girl she knew who was cutting. "So many girls do cutting in my school. This girl and me, we were cutting together. She got in a fight with another girl and the girl told her, Go kill yourself. And so she posted on her Facebook page that she was done and she was going to do it. They called the cops and she ended up in the hospital."

Sierra was a tiny white girl with cornflower-blue eyes and limp platinum hair streaked with brown highlights; she had a southern drawl and made a soft slurring sound when she spoke, an effect of her retainer. She sat on her bed, wearing jeans, a dark T-shirt, and many bracelets and rings, her arms clasped around her thin legs. The afternoon sun was coming through the windows and shining on her face, showing up the powder she had sprinkled over the tiny pimples across her chin.

Her stepfather, Donny, was sitting somberly on a straight-backed chair against the wall; he was tall and lanky with long salt-and-pepper hair, which he kept in a ponytail. He used to be in a band in the '80s, he said, but now he was a truck driver. Sierra's mother was the hostess at a restaurant. Her father was back in Michigan.

Sierra said that when she was a little girl in Michigan, her mother doted on her, dressed her up in Disney princess dresses, and showed her off. She couldn't account for why—for as long as she could remember, as far back as kindergarten—she had been bullied. "All my life. And I'm just like, What did I do wrong?" Her voice cracked. "Is there something I don't know about myself that everybody else does? It just started happening and it never stopped happening and it is still happening now."

In fifth grade, her parents divorced, and she moved to Virginia with her mom and Donny. She thought it might be different there, but it wasn't. "These girls would pick on me and shove me and say I was buck-toothed because I had, like, big teeth, and they called me Rat Face."

The bullying got worse when she went on social media. It was in fifth grade that she went on Facebook for the first time. She couldn't say what it was about social media that she loved so much; she just did. "I like joking around with my friends," she said. "And, like, you get to show people pretty pictures of yourself, and even if they say you're ugly, you can be like, Oh, really? Well, here's the proof. I am not. I look good."

She was on Facebook, Twitter, Instagram, and Ask.fm, as well as other sites. While we spoke, she kept going on her phone and checking to see if anyone had liked anything she'd posted, or if anyone was saying anything mean; if so, she would delete those comments.

It was "a lot of work," a constant chore, she said, as there were often mean comments, usually from girls. Social media caused her a lot of "stress," she said, as she was constantly having to edit away the wrong kind of attention and let through only the right sort, such as comments from "nice" girls who called her "pretty" and "funny" and said, "We need to hang out."

But even when people were mean to her on social media, she said, she still felt its draw. Despite all the "drama" she endured online, she put herself out there again and again. It wouldn't seem that someone with Sierra's experience of bullying would want to rush to join a site like Ask.fm, with its reputation for attracting bulliers, but that's just what she did.

"I get these things on there like I sleep around and all that," she said. "Like, You fucking sleep around too much. You're the school prostitute. Or, You're really fucked-up. Or, Oh, you have a boyfriend? Better warn him you're a fake ho. Just like your mom, why is she so obsessed with Disney? I think you get your obsession from her. They said they were going to come and kill my whole family. They said, Nobody likes you, go kill yourself. They kept saying, Go kill yourself, go kill yourself. Please do us all a favor and kill yourself. And I was like, Why would you say something like that, especially if I actually went and did it?"

"I was working two shifts," Donny said, "and her mom was working, too, and we didn't know what was going on. We knew she was being picked on, but we didn't know the extent. And then they said they were gonna kill her. And, you know, there's just no excuse for that."

After she finally told her mother and Donny about the death threats she'd received, they reported them to the police. (This was after months.) "It stopped for a while and then it just kept going," Sierra said. "Like someone will say something I said, or they think I said, and then it will just start up again, and they'll say stuff to me online."

The "rumors" about her that started online spilled over into gossip at school, "and nobody likes me because they think they're true. They say like I smell like fish. My ex-boyfriend, he started the rumor saying that I had AIDS and herpes and that I gave him herpes and had sex with him and I was like, No, that's not true."

It had all made her defensive, apt to fire back quickly and sometimes be mean herself, she admitted. "Sometimes I will just say something kinda mean 'cause I expect they're gonna say something to me first." And it had made her want to post "cute" pictures of herself, so her "haters" could see how wrong they were about how she looked.

"im cute at least I think so don't giv a fuck wht people think," said the profile on Sierra's Instagram account. There were close-ups of her in a tank top showing cleavage; selfies staring in the bathroom mirror, making the duckface—"looking cute," said her own comment about herself. Sticking her tongue out like Miley Cyrus, sticking out her butt on the top of the sink and looking behind at herself in the mirror. The famous sink shot.

Underneath her pictures she posted self-congratulatory comments: "Loving my smile in this one." "no edit needed cuz im cute." "looking adorable I really love my smile." "I'm gorgeous." "the sexiness."

She commented on a picture of herself posing with a friend: "With this awesome bitch getting turntup," meaning drunk or high, "tonight."

Sierra's Instagram pictures didn't fail to attract appreciative comments from boys, sometimes boys she didn't know: "Them mother fucking titties doeee!!!!" "Damn . . ." "Can I get it?"

"Have you got Kik?" one boy asked. "Yeah but I don't know you," Sierra responded. "We can get to know each other," said the boy.

One evening when Sierra was alone in her bedroom she posted a picture of herself on Instagram, "from the side of me, 'cause I was looking cute. Just like the butt." In the picture, she's wearing a miniskirt that stops just below her behind and looking over her shoulder at herself in her screen, Kardashian-style.

Soon after she posted the picture, she started getting mean comments from a girl she knew, and they had a fight in the comments section below, which I'm sorry to say is similar to fights I've seen on girls' social media accounts all over—in the meanness, profanity, slut-shaming, and threats.

Sierra read it out loud: "She said, 'You have no ass girl, stop trying to take pictures like you have one, it's not cute, you look like a ho, O.K. stop, sorry-not sorry . . . you look stupid, all your pics trying to show off what ass you don't have, that outfit makes you look like a cheap prostitute that stands on the corner.'

" 'I'd rather have a small ass than a big one,' " Sierra responded. " 'I may not have an ass but that doesn't matter, I can take pics of whatever angle I want O.K., and no, I don't look like no ho, my skirt rides up so get over it.'

" 'Mm hmm,' " the girl said, " 'yes you do and maybe if you pulled down your damn skirt, ever think of that? Trying to be a show-off it's not cute honey take a seat and put on some clothes it's winter not summer.'

" 'First of all it don't feel like no wintertime,' " Sierra said, " 'it's warm out and I'll pull it down next time happy, good.'

" 'Mmm and you wonder why people don't like you and think you're a ho,' " said the girl.

" 'Just shut the fuck up and grow up,' " Sierra replied, " 'just 'cause you're mad at someone . . . doesn't mean you have the right to bully them, and fuck you for being mean to someone that's no excuse. You need to grow up.'

" 'Really wow that's funny you can talk so much shit on here,' " the girl said, " 'but when I was in your face all you could do was say shut the fuck up. Wow. You're lucky Cameron," a boy in their school, "grabbed me because I was about to swing on your ass but for real-for real the next time I'm not gonna let him hold me back. Come say something to my face and see what happens. You're gonna be on the floor crying. I'm not being a bully, I'm saying it like it is.'

" 'You're the childish one,' " Sierra wrote. " 'I'm not gonna fight you, you're just a waste of my fucking time, bye.'

" 'So you a bad bitch, huh? O.K., I got you, you just wait . . . you're gonna learn how to talk shit about me if you can't back your shit up.'

" 'Just get over it, I'm done O.K.?'

" 'Then get the fuck off my fucking shit you fucking dumbass bitch, if you're gonna talk, you're gonna take your fake ass somewhere else, dumbass,' " said the girl.

" 'LMAO,' " laughing my ass off, commented a friend of the girl's, jumping in and commenting. " 'Don't tell her to shut the fuck up, she not the one that dress like a damn whore, ho, prostitute, slut, if anyone needs to shut the fuck up then it's you boo-boo, trust me . . . she'll beat your ass and leave you there to fucking die.' "

The fight escalated when they went back to school. Other people got involved.

"They must be jealous of her," Donny said, looking at the picture of Sierra on her phone. "Look at her," he said, trying to defend her. "Any man would say she looks hot."

Williamsburg, Virginia

I asked Janie how her experience with cyberbullying had affected her.

"Well, I couldn't trust anybody anymore," she said in her measured tone. "It changed how I acted toward people. I wasn't as friendly as I used to be. I didn't care if I had friends. It just ruined everything, ruined all my friendships. I lost basically everybody—even friends I've known since I was one year old. I lost even my best friend."

Her mother, Betty, had been just sitting listening, letting Janie talk, but now she said quietly, "I think Janie is being very calm in how she tells you this. Her reaction was actually much bigger than she's letting on. She would be strong at school and then come home and curl up on the bed and cry for hours. She didn't want to leave the house, to do anything, didn't eat a whole lot.

"She would not make eye contact with anyone," Betty said. "She completely distanced herself from everyone. This is a child who was the star of the field hockey team and can play any sport without fear. But she was rolled up on the bed wanting to be held and reassured. I didn't want to leave her alone because she was so upset."

Betty showed me pictures of Janie taken at the time; she looked thin and drawn, depressed.

Betty didn't know what to do, she said; and so she did nothing. She'd always thought, even hoped, that Janie's being gay was "just a phase," and she saw the problems Janie was having with her ex-girlfriend in much the same way.

And for a long time, Betty didn't really know what was happening to Janie on social media because Janie didn't show it to her. Betty couldn't really understand at first why Janie was so upset about it anyway. She didn't see how anyone could get so upset about some silly stuff that was being said on "some online thing." She only knew that Janie's life was being disrupted and their family life was being disrupted, and it had been going on all year. All through the eighth grade.

"Janie didn't feel like at first I was understanding enough," Betty said with chagrin.

And then one day Janie sent her this text, which Betty allowed me to see: "This is why kids that get bullied kill thereselves because no one helps them and no one deals with the situation and they make them go be around their bullier that's why they kill thereselves because this is all the people that are supposed to help do . . . How would you feel mom if I didnt tell anybody about those messages and you found me one day dead and I did kill myself and you looked on my phone and saw those how would you feel!"

After receiving this, Betty sat down and read over some of the correspondence that had gone on between Janie and the other kids. "I was horrified," she said. "These were things no one should ever hear anyone say about anybody. It wasn't just girls. It was boys and girls. It was kids I have known since they were little babies."

She went to the school administration, but, she said, "they were resistant to deal with it because it was quote-unquote 'a relationship' and they didn't want to be involved in that. I let them read the correspondence that had gone back and forth. The resource officer"—meaning the local police officer assigned to the school—"was brought in and his feeling was more should be done than what the school wanted to do. The school wanted it to be our responsibility to take care of it. I went to the school superintendent as well, and he did not want to deal with it. So, schools will say they have a 'zero tolerance' for bullying, but they really don't want to deal with anything."

Now that Betty was keyed in to what was happening in Janie's life, she began noticing some things on her own. She started attending the sports practices where Janie still interacted with her ex-girlfriend; they were still on the same field hockey team. And she could see that the father of Janie's ex, who was assistant coaching, "was glaring at Janie. Oh, I called it down when it got out of control."

There was resentment, Betty said, because "the girls were playing horribly, they weren't working together. It became Janie's fault because she would turn around and cry or the girl would cry." And then Betty noticed some of the other mothers whispering about *her*. "My parenting was called into question," she said, tight-lipped.

She said that one of the other coaches at the school took her aside one day and told her she should "really look into what Janie had said" to the other girl online—"which of course I had," said Betty. "It just outraged me that, no matter what Janie had said or the other girl said, this woman was taking sides in a fight between two students. It just wasn't the comment of a responsible adult.

"They had a graduation ceremony and I witnessed the staring, the glaring, the getting together with hands over mouths"—Betty put her hand over her mouth, as if to whisper behind it—"the commenting as we went by. It was in the school gymnasium. They all sat around us and made comments and snickered. We all clapped for Janie and there were comments made as she went up on the stage."

Betty decided that Janie could not return to the school. "I couldn't have her there for four more years. I knew she would never be able to become the person she could be. So we changed her school."

In order to do that, Janie had to move out of her home and go live with her grandmother in a nearby town. She no longer lived with her mother and stepfather. She saw her mother almost every day. Betty said, "It's a lot of driving."

During all of this, had they ever considered going to the police? I asked. "I made the decision not to contact the police," Janie said. "I didn't want one mistake that she," meaning her ex, "had made and everybody else has made to ruin their whole life."

"She wanted them almost protected," said Betty. She began to cry. Janie stared ahead.

"But the good that's come out of all this," Betty said, wiping her eyes, "is our relationship is one hundred and ten percent stronger than what it was." She had realized, she said, "you need to be accepting of your child for the way she is. It's not my business what she likes or doesn't like as far as that preference. What matters is she's a bright child. She is a wonderful person."

I asked Janie what her goal was moving forward.

She said she wanted to join the navy. "I need to get away," she said. "I just want to help the country and join something bigger than myself."

New York, New York

Montana was sitting in the makeup chair in the apartment of a man she knew, a makeup artist she'd met at a summer theater program. He was a gay man in his fifties with a companionable way about him; he was black and burly and wore a woolly sweater. His apartment was full of arty knickknacks and his desk strewn with beauty products—eye shadows, lipsticks, foundations, concealers, and brushes. Let's call him Robert.

Montana was telling me about when she first started realizing she was a girl, and how that felt.

"One time we got a new air conditioner and it came in this great big box," she said. "And my brother put me in it and shut me up and wouldn't let me out. That's kinda how it felt. Like you're stuck in a box.

"And then when I was seven I told my brother, 'I'm a girl,' and he said he was gonna murder me."

"When you were seven years old?" Robert said, aghast.

Montana said, "Yeah. My brother always wanted me to play boy games with him, like throw the ball around, and play video games, and I'd say, I don't wanna do that, I'm a girl. And he got really mad and he said, Stop saying you're a girl. If you keep saying you're a girl, then I'm gonna kill you. You shouldn't live."

Robert made a sympathetic sound. "Gender roles," he murmured. "*They* don't seem in any danger of dying."

Montana's head was covered with the end of a nylon stocking and her eyes were closed. Robert was contouring her face. "She's got such nice high cheekbones," he told me, passing a brush down the side of Montana's nose. "This isn't really that much of a challenge. And those pretty eyes and long lashes."

Montana said softly, "Thanks."

It was clear that Robert was just a friend to her, and Montana had told me as much. "He helps me," she said. "We talk about stuff." He was the one person she knew who accepted her for who she was.

"See, my family is Puerto Rican and Italian," Montana went on. "And they're both very macho cultures. Especially uptown. Like downtown, you walk around down here and nobody says nothing to you."

"Oh, believe me, they *say* things," Robert said. "You just gotta catch them on the right night, when they've been out to the bars!" He laughed his hearty laugh.

Montana opened her eyes and looked up at him. "Really? They say things to you?" Clearly she thought Robert was invincible.

"Oh, I can relate to the bullying," Robert said. "Growing up gay in the South in the sixties they didn't even call it 'bullying.' It was just what you did to gay people because they were *sinners*." Again he laughed his big laugh, which was beginning to seem like a kind of social ointment he had developed in a world in which he'd had to have many difficult conversations.

"But we've come a long way, we've come a long way," Robert added, dabbing concealer under Montana's eyes. "Now they're letting us get married. God help us!" He laughed again.

"And now you have people realizing you have to respect the rights of transgender people—respect everybody," Robert said. He was being encouraging. "I remember Bruce Jenner on the Wheaties box. Who would have thought you'd see him on the cover of *Vanity Fair* looking like Ava Gardner!"

Montana shifted. "I get so judged all the time," she said hesitantly, "I don't have the right to judge anybody. And I don't *judge* Caitlyn— I think what she did was brave. But, like, I read some of the things online about, like, why did she have to come out dressed like that?"

"Dressed like what?" said Robert.

"Like in her underwear."

"You slut-shaming?" Robert laughed again.

Montana said, "No, I just think putting a woman in a sexualized outfit is like saying all that matters about her is her sexuality. I don't think being a woman has anything to do with the way you dress—and if anybody should know that it's me."

"Well, maybe Caitlyn likes dressing like that," Robert said. "I thought she looked good!"

"Yeah, she looked good," Montana said. "But she looked like *society's idea* of good. Like that's how a woman should be. She looked like her family looks—like the Kardashians. Was it her choice? Or was it society's choice? Like, why does a girl have to be girlie?"

"Girl," Robert said, laughing, "you're a feminist."

"I am a feminist," Montana said. "I am definitely a feminist. Every girl has to be a feminist, and if she's not, she's against her own kind."

Robert said, "Mmmm-hmmm." Now he was applying blush. "But you know," he said, "I think it's different when it's Caitlyn wearing her unmentionables on the cover of a magazine—she's a grown woman, she can do what she wants; and isn't feminism supposed to be about women doing what they want? I think it's different when it's a sixty-five-year-old woman than when it's some thirteen-year-old girl. We have some girls coming in the store"—Robert worked in retail—"and they are no older than my coffeepot and they are dressed like straight-up Las Vegas showgirls. Now I know *that* sounds like slut-shaming, but I just think about what my grandmother would say. And I wonder what their parents are thinking. And the way they talk to each other! It's like they have no home training whatsoever. They talk like little gangsters." He laughed again, shaking his head.

"It all goes together," Montana said. "Society wants to sell them things, so it makes them grow up faster. Sexism serves capitalism."

Robert said, "Oh, my!"

"And then it treats them like sexual objects so they have no power and they don't have to pay them as much or give them their equal rights," said Montana. "That's why I can't understand these girls that bully each other on social media, 'cause the society is bullying girls all the time."

"That's very true," Robert agreed.

"Like they bully transgender people for wanting to be girls because they look down on girls!" Montana exclaimed, opening her eyes. "It's like the Madonna song, 'What It Feels Like for a Girl—' "

"Oh, I knew Madonna was gonna come into this conversation!" Robert said. "At least I hoped!" He laughed.

"It says, *'For a boy to look like a girl is degrading 'cause you think that being a girl is degrading,'*" Montana said. It sounded as if she had repeated the lyric over and over again.

"Mmm-hmm," Robert murmured. "But people weren't degrading Caitlyn Jenner, were they? I thought they were celebrating her."

"They were celebrating her because she fit into the box!" said Montana, making the shape of a box with her hands and holding the shape tightly in the air. "'Cause she got dressed up like Kim Kardashian! It's like, okay, if you can fit in this box, we will let you in!"

"This girl is too much," Robert said, chuckling, gently applying mascara to Montana's lashes. "Sitting in my makeup chair railing against the establishment."

Montana laughed.

As he continued doing her eyes, Robert started singing, in his enviable basso profundo: "*'Do you know what it feels like for a girl? . . .'*"

"You know what I think?" Robert said after a while. "I think you're a very lovely young lady."

Montana said, "I am?"

Robert had given her a long, silky button-down blouse to wear over her jeans. Now he took the nylon off her head and carefully brushed out her hair. He stood her up and took her over to a full-length mirror.

"Well, what do you think?"

Montana smiled. "I think I look like me."

Robert put on some Madonna and Montana spent the afternoon chatting with her friend.

New York, New York

After the incident at the pizza restaurant, Hannah and Zora went and sat on a bench in Central Park. They had found each other by texting. Hannah was crying when Zora joined her.

"I hate Alex," Hannah said.

They sat for a while and watched the people going by. Couples holding hands. Nannies with strollers. Zora went over to a pretzel cart and brought back two ice-cream bars.

"Oh," said Hannah, wiping her eyes. "I shouldn't eat ice cream today. I already had pizza."

"But if I keep holding it, it will melt all over my hand," Zora said, smiling.

Hannah smiled back and took the ice cream. "Thanks."

They sat licking the treats and watching a bad balloon clown trying to get tips.

"You know Alex didn't mean any of those things she said," Zora said finally. "But that's Alex. Alex our friend who says awful things sometimes."

"And is a snob and a racist," said Hannah.

"And is a snob and a racist and *kind* of a mean girl." Zora laughed. "But not really. Like, she's just not being brought up well. Everybody deserves a second chance."

"Yeah," said Hannah.

They decided they were going to send Alex a Snapchat. They took a picture of themselves making funny faces—"Oh my God, good one!"—and sent it to her phone. They giggled, waiting for a response. But Alex didn't Snap them back.

Chapter Four

16

Los Angeles, California

She wanted it to be like the scene in the Lana Del Rey video for "Blue Jeans"—"hot and slow and epic." The scene where strangers meet and fall into an easy intimacy, making love in a pool—"and they look so hot and it's just, like, totally epic." A boy at her school—she didn't want to talk about him now; he'd broken her heart; but "like, whatever." She'd "deleted him" from her phone. "I was stalking him too much, seeing him doing fun things on Instagram, and it hurt."

They'd been instant-messaging on Facebook, and one night he told her he loved her. And then, "I found out he was talking to, like, four other girls." And now she wanted to do something to get over it, maybe to get back at him. "I mean, I should have known. All men are basically whores." When he didn't turn out to be her "one true love"—"like Bella and Edward, or Bella and Jacob, you know?"—she decided she had to "lose it to someone," so why not someone she would never have to see again? And yet, she hoped it would be somehow like the Lana Del Rey song. *"I will love you till the end of time,"* it goes.

The guy she was supposed to meet that day—the guy from Tinder, the dating app—"I know, like, five guys who've done it; girls use it, too, but some pretend like they don't"—he was cute and had tattoos on his upper arms. He looked "James Franco–ish," but younger. On Tinder you could meet people in your age group. Emily was sixteen; the guy was seventeen.

Alone in her room the night before, reading her friends' Twitter feeds and watching YouTube videos (Selena Gomez and "baby animals being cute"), she had started feeling lonely, restless, and bored. "Sometimes I just want to talk to a guy so bad." So she downloaded the app and started swiping through the pictures of boys in her area. She "hearted" his picture, and within a few minutes he'd hearted hers, and then they were instantly texting.

"Ur hot," he wrote. "U wanna meet?"

"When?"

They arranged to rendezvous at a shopping mall in Los Angeles not far from the neighborhood where they both lived. "Of course it was going to be a public place. And if it turned out he was really some gross old man, I'd just run away." But there he was, standing by his car, looking almost like his picture . . . Almost. There was something different about his face—it was "squishier. Like, he was almost fat." But now here they were, and she didn't know quite how to get out of it.

He smiled and kissed her on the cheek. He smelled like Axe body spray. She was sorry she'd spent so much time getting ready for this. "I even waxed." He wanted her to get in his car, but she knew she shouldn't. They started walking around the mall, "talking about nothing, nothing. It was awkward, totally weird." He asked if she wanted to sit down, but there was nowhere to sit except in restaurants, so they wound up going inside a Pottery Barn and making out on a couch. Later she posted something on her Tumblr blog about the difficulty of finding love.

Online

Technological innovations have always made their way into how teenagers have sex, fall in love, and date. The quill and the pen begat the love letter. "Don't ever think of the things you can't give me," Zelda Sayre wrote to F. Scott Fitzgerald, whom she met at age seventeen at a country club dance in Montgomery, Alabama. "You've trusted me with the dearest heart of all—and it's so damn much more than anybody else in all the world has ever had."

"[Your] photograph is all I have," Fitzgerald wrote to Zelda (he was twenty-one when they met). "It is with me from the morning when I wake up with a frantic half dream about you to the last moment when I think of you and of death at night."

The telephone enabled teens to talk with their crushes into the night, telling them of their hearts' and bodies' desires. The car made it possible for them to go on drives and "park" in remote locations where they could neck, and more. Movies led to the creation of spaces where teenagers could neck in the dark, while before them on giant screens, implausibly beautiful human beings played out romantic scenes, kissing and falling in love and sometimes having sex.

"Is this what it's like to love somebody?" Natalie Wood's character asks James Dean's in a tender moment from *Rebel Without a Cause*. (Wood was sixteen when the movie was shot.)

"I don't know," Dean says.

"What kind of a person do you think a girl wants?" she asks.

"A man," he says.

"Yes, but a man who can be gentle and is sweet, like you are," she tells him.

He softly laughs.

"And someone who doesn't run away when you want them, like being Plato's friend"—Plato being the vulnerable boy played by Sal Mineo—"when nobody else liked him. That's being strong."

He says, "Oh, wow." And then: "I'm not gonna be lonely anymore— ever, ever. Not you or me."

"I love somebody," she says with wonder.

Our Western idea of romantic love stems from the Middle Ages and courtly love, a literary conceit in which chivalric knights wooed noble ladies through poetry and acts of bravery. The notion is full of questionable class and gender norms and not mentioned here in a nostalgic sense; but it's important to note when thinking about the changes in our idea of love and romance brought about by our use of technology, as well as changes in the ways we have sex. What are sex and love in the Internet age? And what does this mean for girls?

When the Internet and social networking became widely adopted by teenagers in the 1990s, it affected how they connected with each other sexually in unprecedented ways. "We are in uncharted territory," when it comes to sex and the Internet, says Justin Garcia, a research scientist at Indiana University's Kinsey Institute for Research in Sex, Gender, and Reproduction. "There have been two major transitions" in heterosexual mating, Garcia says, "in the last four million years. The first was around ten thousand to fifteen thousand years ago, in the agricultural revolution, when we became less migratory and more settled," leading to the establishment of marriage as a cultural contract.

"And the second major transition is with the rise of the Internet," Garcia says. Suddenly, instead of meeting through proximity, community connections, and family and friends, people could meet each other virtually and engage in amorous activity with the click of a button. Internet meeting is now surpassing every other form. "It's changing so much about the way we act both romantically and sexually," Garcia says. "It is unprecedented from an evolutionary standpoint."

And yet this massive shift in our behavior has gone almost completely unexamined, especially given how the Internet permeates modern life. While there have been studies about how men and women use social media differently—how they use language and present themselves differently, for example—there's not a lot of research about how they behave sexually online; and there is virtually nothing about how girls and boys do. While there has been concern about the online interaction of children and adults, it's striking that so little attention has been paid to the ways in which the Internet has changed the sexual behavior of girls and boys interacting together. This may be because the behavior has been largely hidden or unknown, or, again, due to the fear of not seeming "sex-positive," mistaking responsibility for judgment.

And there are questions to ask, from the standpoint of girls' and boys' physical and emotional health and the ethics of their treatment of each other. Sex on a screen is different from sex that develops in person, this much seems self-evident, just as talking on a screen is different from face-to-face communication. And so if talking on a screen reduces one's ability to be empathic, for example, then how does sex on a screen change sexual behavior? Are people more likely to act aggressively or unethically, as in other types of online communication? How do gender roles and sexism play into cybersex? And how does the influence of porn, which became available online at about the same time as social networking, factor in?

When boys and girls having sex online is depicted in pop culture, it's almost always in a comical way, as in 1999's *American Pie,* in which teenage boys are seen watching on a webcam an unsuspecting girl (Shannon Elizabeth) getting undressed. "God bless the Internet," says one of the boys. This mega-hit movie set a normalizing tone for how many Americans were to view teenage cybersex ever since: boys will be boys—even when doing something unethical and creepy—and girls just laugh along with it, which they are seen doing in the movie.

Psychologist John Chirban believes that sex via screens makes boys more likely to objectify girls, and to see them in much the same way they view the women in porn. "Girls are more often driven to develop relationships and personal connections, and boys don't quite get that as early as girls," Chirban maintains. "Boys might get interested in the pleasure of a sexual orgasm, and they are more likely to see the girl on the other side of the screen as a means to that end than the girl is likely to see the boy that way. If the boys are also watching porn, they're used to the idea that images of women on a screen are there to use as an excitement toward having orgasms."

As soon as social networking was being widely used by teenagers, in the mid- to late '90s, they were using it as a place to "cyber," or have cyber sex. Teenagers have always been interested in sex, of course, but now there was a way for them to have sex, a new kind of sex, without having to actually arrange dates or engage in the often complicated and difficult business of having relationships. "Everybody cybered in AOL chat rooms," says a young woman in New York, age thirty-three, talking about the private online spaces one could create on AOL Instant Messenger, which appeared in 1997. "We would spend hours chatting with boys, sometimes more than one at a time. It got really steamy in those rooms. Nobody's parents had a clue what we were doing."

Parents might have had some idea, if they'd only looked into it, as adults were doing exactly the same things. In the late 1990s and early 2000s, adults were cybering in AOL chat rooms, too, finding sex partners on Craigslist, and hooking up with people they met on online dating services such as Match.com and Kiss.com. "On AOL, it was kind of a game with your friends to try and 'hot chat' with adults and make them think you were older," says a young woman in L.A., age thirty-one. "My girlfriends and I learned a lot from doing that," she adds with a rueful laugh. "These guys had no idea how old you were—there were no pictures or controls on who you talked to."

When webcams came out, kids started putting on shows for each other and participating in mutual masturbation, live. "We did webcam shows on MSN," says a young man in New York, age twenty-five, referring to the now discontinued instant-messaging service MSN Messenger, which appeared in 1999. "It started in seventh grade. You'd show your weiner in the webcam. We played strip poker. It was always about playing games. But then it would get too exciting and somebody would bust a nut."

On the feminist website Broadly, in 2015, the U.K.-based writer and musician Alanna McArdle wrote of her experience webcamming as a middle school girl. "I had an arrangement with around five or six boys in my year at school when I was 13 years old," McArdle wrote. "I would log on to MSN Messenger almost immediately after I got home from school. They would usually ask me to strip, sometimes half-naked, sometimes completely.

"After a blissful year of camming," which her parents knew nothing about, one of the boys in her school told others of their online interaction and, she said, "I was a pariah . . . I began to self-harm and developed the body dysmorphia that planted the seeds of disordered eating in my late teens. I had been a confident and precocious child, but suddenly I questioned everything about myself . . . The boys around me were expected to be sexual. But my own desires and enjoyment? They were unacceptable."

It was the judgmental reaction to what she had done "that destroyed my perception of myself and my sexuality," McArdle said. "I *wanted* to be sexual. I *chose* to engage in sexual activity. To me, stripping on webcam wasn't just an informed choice that I made, but one that was affirmed by informed consent."

One can respect McArdle's feelings about her own experience while still noting that it was she who was the one doing the stripping for the boys, and not the other way around; and one can wonder whether exposure to online porn was informing the boys' choice to ask her to perform for them nude.

"It definitely was a rush," says a young man in New York, age twenty-eight, "to get a girl to take her clothes off on the webcam. It was something that could only happen on the screen. You would never have the balls to ask her face-to-face."

Jennifer Powell-Lunder, a clinical psychologist who specializes in work with tweens, teens, and young adults in Westchester County, New York, believes that the sexual interaction between girls and boys on screens is largely controlled by boys. "Something about social media is making girls more submissive to boys," Powell-Lunder asserts. "Boys in our culture are judged on physicality. From research we know that the boy who is perceived as the strong one is the one who dominates. But on the Internet, anybody can anonymously act as if they're the strong one. So the anonymity is awesome for boys because it gives them the opportunity to act as if they're a top dog. It's a very powerful thing for them to have this secret way of being; it's like Clark Kent syndrome—you're Superman on social media, but you're mild-mannered Clark Kent in real life."

As for girls, Powell-Lunder says, "girls in our culture are judged on their intimate relationships, on their ability to develop intimacy. So because guys are putting it out there that they're the strong ones, girls feel like they can't respond by being dominating. The way they 'win' is through attracting relationships, so when these guys say, Do this, the girls will do it because they want to attract the guys, and because they have the belief that the guys are top dogs because of how they're behaving online. When girls approach boys online," Powell-Lunder adds, "even when they do it aggressively, often you see them asking if they can do things for the boys, like give them blowjobs—it's not, Come over here and do something for me."

Another possible reason for this willingness of some girls to acquiesce to boys' sexual requests and demands online may be the increased availability of girls to boys through social media. I started to think about this early in my reporting, in 2013, when I was on a New York City bus and started talking to a teenage boy I saw Snapchatting. A girl had sent him a provocative picture of herself (not a nude, just a sultry shot of her face). "Gotta wheel the bitches in, gotta wheel the bitches in," said the boy with a familiar sort of bravado. "Nowadays you can do it so easy," he said. "There are so many apps and shit that just, like, hand you the girls. They don't even know that's what they're doing, but really they're just giving teenagers ways to have sex."

Not only ways to have sex, but more people to have it with. When social media moved onto smartphones after 2007, teenagers became more sexually available to each other than ever before. There had never been a way for them to express their sexual interest in one another at any moment of the day, no matter where they were; it was as easy as sending a text. "You can be sitting in class getting a boner 'cause some girl is texting you that she wants to suck your dick," said a teenage boy in L.A. "It's kind of distracting."

"Like a kid in a candy store" seems to apply to how some boys I've talked to view the accessibility of girls on their phones. And this increased availability of options, according to many girls, seems to be causing some boys to undervalue the importance of any particular girl, and to treat girls overall with less respect. "Guys you know from just, like, having one class together will be like, Do you like to suck dick?" said a seventeen-year-old girl in New York. "And if you say no, they just move on to the next person." So how is a girl who is interested in boys to compete for their attention in this crowded space? It wouldn't be surprising if some girls thought pictures that are provocative, nudes and semi-nudes, would be one way of getting their attention.

The effect of the increase in options on dating life can be seen nowhere more acutely than in the changes brought about by dating apps. Mobile dating went mainstream around 2010; by 2012 it was overtaking online dating. In 2015, there were nearly 100 million people on dating apps, according to a study by the research firm Global Web Index. Teenagers don't use dating apps as often as adults—their access to a pool of their peers every day in school seems to make them less likely to seek out strangers for dating and sex—but they are using these services, including OkCupid, Skout, Grindr, and Tinder, in considerable numbers. By Tinder's own account, in 2014 more than 7 percent of its users were between the ages of thirteen and seventeen (the app is designed so that users seventeen and under can only connect with each other, but one might reasonably ask how advisable it is for thirteen-year-olds to be "matching" with seventeen-year-olds). If the total number of people on Tinder is truly close to 50 million, as *The New York Times* reported in 2014, that means that more than 3 million thirteen-to-seventeen-year-olds are on Tinder alone.

But whether or not teenagers are actually using dating apps, they're coming of age in a culture that has already been affected by the attitudes the apps have introduced. "It's like ordering Seamless," says Dan, a twenty-six-year-old in New York, referring to the online food-delivery service. "But you're ordering a person." The comparison to online shopping seems apt. Dating apps are the free-market economy come to sex. The innovation of Tinder was the swipe—the flick of a finger on a picture, no more elaborate profiles necessary and no more fear of rejection; users only know whether they've been approved, never when they've been discarded. OkCupid, Happn, Hinge, and other dating apps soon adopted the function.

"Sex has become so easy," says John, a twenty-six-year-old New Yorker. "I can go on my phone right now and no doubt I can find someone I can have sex with this evening, probably before midnight." Of course, not every young man or teenage boy is going to have as much success with online dating as John—or want to; but even the possibility of such success through technology seems to be having an impact on not only sex and dating, but gender equality.

"It's rare for a woman of our generation to meet a man who treats her like a priority instead of an option," wrote Erica Gordon on Elite Daily in 2014.

"Apps like Tinder and OkCupid give people the impression that there are thousands or millions of potential mates out there," says David Buss, a professor of psychology at the University of Texas at Austin who specializes in the evolution of human sexuality. "One dimension of this is the impact it has on men's psychology. When there is a surplus of women, or a perceived surplus of women, the whole mating system tends to shift toward short-term dating. Marriages become unstable. Divorces increase. Men don't have to commit, so they pursue a short-term mating strategy. Men are making that shift, and women are forced to go along with it in order to mate at all."

But the opening up of dating options is something girls can avail themselves of as readily as boys; and there are many girls who say they're just as interested in "short-term mating strategies" as boys are. "Not every girl wants a boyfriend," says Erika, an eighteen-year-old girl in New York. "Sometimes you just want to have sex, and there's nothing wrong with that." Increased choice would seem to suggest more power in sex, love, and dating, for both girls and women. It's one of the successes of feminism that girls are no longer expected to marry whomever their parents say, for example, or marry at all; and so the fact that they now have a broad spectrum of choices of whom to meet or date or have sex with, through the Internet, would seem, in theory, a good thing for them; and in some ways it must be.

Conversely, we've seen historically that women who are in demand by men have attained more rights and freedoms in societies in which women overall suffer due to gender inequality. In the nineteenth century, white women in the American West had opportunities unavailable to women in eastern states (while women of color in both places were still cruelly disadvantaged)—more liberal divorce laws, equal pay for teachers, and, most important, the right to vote. The West was the first place in America to see women's suffrage. In nearly every western state or territory, women were enfranchised years, sometimes decades, before women won the right to vote in the East. Women in the West experienced more equality because there was a shortage of them; their labor was needed and valued, and so were their bodies, to put it bluntly, for sex and breeding. Historians have theorized that western states "sweetened the deal" in terms of rights in order to attract women's immigration to their lands, as well as to reward the women already there for helping to shoulder the hard work of pioneering. Susan B. Anthony herself was said to have believed that western men were more "chivalrous" than eastern men. Perhaps they had to be.

Online, men often show no signs of feeling the same pressure to be respectful. The behavior of men on social media, in a sexual context, is by now rather notorious. There are websites and Tumblr blogs devoted to it, such as Straight White Boys Texting, TinderLines, and TerribleOkCupidMessages, where contributors post the more outrageous sexts they've received via text and dating apps. There are thousands of examples, one more vulgar and ridiculously offensive than the next. ("Love the hair do you do anal?" "Damn girl is your body an

orphanage? Because I wanna abandon my children in you," and so on.)
One of the marked characteristics of such messages is how quickly and
even comically they become sexual, an indication of how little sense
the sexter seems to have that he is addressing an actual person. ("Hey,
how are you?"—woman. "Buttsecks?"—man. "Excuse me?"—woman.
"Anal?"—man.) There's been less said about how this type of behavior
is seen in boys as well as men, or what effect it is having on girls. "You
want to laugh but sometimes you feel sick," says Yvonna, a sixteen-year-
old girl in Louisville.

Online dating is "truly an evolutionarily novel environment," says
David Buss. "But we come to this environment with the same evolved
psychologies." And women and girls may be further along than men
and boys in terms of evolving away from sexist attitudes about sex.
"Young women's expectations of safety and entitlement to respect have
perhaps risen faster than some young men's willingness to respect
them," says Stephanie Coontz, who teaches history and family studies at Evergreen State College and has written about the history of dating. "Exploitative and disrespectful men have always existed. There are
many evolved men, but there may be something going on in culture
now that is making some more resistant to evolving."

Los Angeles, California

"Social media is destroying our lives," said the girl at the Grove.

"So why don't you go off it?" I asked.

"Because then we would have no life," said her friend.

The girls had been celebrating a birthday at the busy L.A. mall and
now were on their way home. They carried bags of leftovers from the
Cheesecake Factory. There were four of them: Melissa, Zoe, Padma, and
Greta. They stopped to sit down and talk awhile at an outdoor table near
the Gap. It was a steamy Saturday night and the mall was thronged. A
salsa band was playing on a nearby stage; parents watched as little girls
twirled around in princess dresses.

The girls were sixteen, with long straight hair, two blond and two
brunette. They wore sleeveless summer dresses, flats and sandals.

Melissa, Zoe, and Greta were white and Padma was Asian Indian. They all went to the same magnet high school in L.A. Zoe's parents were teachers; Melissa's father was a lawyer and her mother was a stay-at-home mom; Padma's parents were doctors; and Greta's father was in real estate. All the other girls' parents were married.

Greta, they said, was Instafamous, having thousands of followers on Instagram. She showed me a gallery of her Instagram pics; some were of Greta smiling, holding her dog, and some were of her in tank tops and crop tops, doing the duckface. In some of these pictures, Greta stared into the camera with the kind of intense expression seen on the faces of models and Hollywood stars. Some of her followers, Greta said, were people she knew, and some were "random dudes in Italy and Arabia.

"Almost every person I meet comes up to me because I have close to five thousand followers on Instagram," Greta said breezily. "It's almost like a title people associate me with"—meaning "Instafamous."

She relayed all this as if she thought it were ridiculous. The other girls listened with slightly strained expressions.

I asked them what social media accounts they were on.

"I have Facebook, a YouTube, Twitter, Instagram, Snapchat," Melissa said, "Vine . . ."

"Path, Skype," Zoe added.

"Tumblr," said Padma.

"I have a Twitter, but I don't use it except for stalking other people," Greta said.

The other girls smiled knowingly.

"I think everyone does it," said Greta. "Everyone looks through other people's profiles, but especially being teenage girls, we look at the profiles of the males we find attractive and we stalk the females the males find attractive. Like Hunter Hayes," she added, referring to a twentysomething country singer with boyish good looks. "He's beautiful and going to be my husband someday. I mean it." She laughed. "I just, like, go on his Twitter and look at what he's saying and pretend he's saying it to me."

"Stalking isn't really *stalking*," Melissa explained. "It's just a way to get to know them without them knowing that you're doing it. It's not like you're following them around and finding out where they live and looking in their windows."

"It's a way to get to know them without the awkward, like, Oh, what do you like to do? You already *know*," Padma said.

"You can know their likes and dislikes," said Greta. "Oh, they like this band. So you can, like, casually wear that band's T-shirt and have them, like, fall in love with you or something. Or you can be like, Oh, they listen to *that* music? Ew. Go away."

I asked how they knew when someone liked them.

"There's a certain etiquette, certain signs, especially when it comes to liking photos," Greta said.

"When a boy likes your [Facebook] profile pic or almost anything you post, it means that they're stalking you, too. Which means they have an interest," said Zoe.

"If they like your Instagram pictures or favorite your tweets," Padma offered.

"But the thing with social media is, if a guy doesn't respond to you or doesn't stalk you back, then you're gonna feel rejected and upset," Melissa said.

"And rejection hurts," said Padma.

"On Snapchat," Melissa went on, "I hate it when you send a picture of your face to a guy, and you say like, Hey, and they obviously see it, and it's like, Did I look ugly? Is that why you didn't respond?"

"What if they were just busy or something?" I asked.

"That's no excuse," said Melissa. The other girls laughed. "No, really," she said, "because I feel like sometimes they don't respond because they *know* it'll make us feel insecure."

"They'll go like two days," Padma explained. "Like this guy, when I said, Why didn't you respond to my text? He was like, Oh, sorry, I was with my dad. So he clearly read it? And chose to ignore me?" She sounded miffed. "Just, like, why would you spend all that time constantly texting me and then ignore me when I'm the one who texts you first? It causes a lot of relationship issues 'cause girls are like, Why didn't you text me *back*?"

"But then if you ask them that, they say you're needy," said Melissa.

"Or 'psycho,' " said Padma, frowning.

"Well, we *are* kind of needy," Melissa said after a moment.

"I think social media makes girls more needy," said Zoe.

Studies have shown that social media use may be contributing to rising anxiety levels in teenage girls; but there hasn't been much attention paid to the question of whether the way girls and boys are interacting on social media is having a similarly negative effect on girls' sense of security and self-esteem.

"I mean we all, like, overanalyze it," Greta said. "It goes both ways. I love it that, like, if I'm mad at a boy he can see that I've seen his message and he *knows* that I'm ignoring him."

"It causes stress, though, when it's you," Melissa said.

"And depression," Padma concurred. "When they ignore your texts, and then you're like, Well, why am I even *alive*?"

"And so then you're just gonna go and, like, look for another person to fill that void and you're gonna move on to stalking someone else," Melissa said.

"That's how men become such whores," Greta said.

They didn't seem to need an evolutionary psychologist to tell them that an increased array of options was affecting boys' behavior—as well as their own.

"When somebody doesn't answer back you're like, Okay, well, *he* doesn't like me, but who does?" Melissa said, elaborating the point.

I asked them how they made the transition from social media interaction to face-to-face communication. How did you go from liking a Facebook profile pic to having a conversation?

They blinked.

"You talk to them on Facebook, you do chat with them," Melissa said.

"You start texting," said Zoe.

"Boys never start anything in person," Melissa said. "They just always text you."

Who made the first online overtures, girls or boys, or was it equal? I asked.

"It's mostly boys," said Greta.

"But sometimes if a guy's too shy, then you have to start it," Padma said. "It's always this panic moment when you're like, Should I?

Shouldn't I? So you type it," a message or text, "and it just sits there for a while and you debate it and then the second you hit send—" She clutched her chest to illustrate panic.

"Or you make your friend hit send for you," Zoe said.

They smiled again.

"'Cause once you send one message it kind of starts it all," Padma said.

Starts what? I asked.

"Texting," they said.

"There's this boy, Seth," Greta said, "and when he liked my profile picture, I knew it was like, Hey, 'sup, you cute. Then we sat next to each other at a party and he held my hand. We were cute. And we ended up exchanging numbers, and then we texted continuously for about two weeks about pygmy elephants."

But through all their texting about this curious subject—"it was just something funny and random to talk about," Greta said—they never talked on the phone, never again met in person. And then it petered out.

"I'm not sure why," said Greta. "But then I found out he stalked my YouTube channel, so, like, that's a plus. But the one thing I didn't like about him," she added, "was he didn't follow me back on Instagram. Social media causes *soooooo* much anxiety."

The other girls nodded.

I asked if they thought communicating on social media made it harder to connect with someone emotionally.

"Yes," they said.

"One hundred percent," said Greta.

"You can't truly tell someone's emotions over text," said Zoe.

"The term 'texting relationship' is used a lot," Greta said. That was a relationship that took place entirely over text—a kind of online dating that existed only online. They said there were girls who had online "boyfriends" they had never met.

"Dating online is a joke, I think," said Zoe.

I asked them if they thought boys were as focused on social media as girls.

"Maybe not *as* much," Melissa said. "But they definitely are on it a lot 'cause they know we're on it and it's how they can talk to girls."

"Guys actually take the Facebook-talking situation way too far," Zoe said.

"They can get *very* aggressive," said Melissa.

"Like when guys start a Facebook thing, they want too much," said Padma. "They want to get some. They try with different girls to see who would give more of themselves."

"It leads to major man-whoring," Greta said.

"They're definitely more forward to us online than in person," Zoe said. "Because they're not saying it to our faces."

"Boys can be more confident online," said Greta.

"That's completely true," Padma said. "If they tried to say the same things to us in person, there's a high possibility of them getting kicked in the balls!"

Her eyes flashed.

"This guy Seth, who is normally timid in real life, sends girls messages asking for nudes," Greta said.

She held up a text exchange on her phone in which Seth had asked her to "send pics"—meaning nudes, a request Seth had punctuated with a smiley face. Greta had responded "Lololol" and "Hahahaha" and "Nope."

"It wasn't THAT funny," Seth had texted back.

"My friend, she was VC-ing"—or video chatting—"this guy she was kind of dating," Melissa said. "He sent so many nudes to her, but she wasn't trusting that he wouldn't show the pictures to other people. So she Skyped him and showed him nudes that way. He took a screenshot without her knowing it. He sent it to so many people and the entire baseball team. She was whispered about and called names. It's never gone away. He still has it and won't delete it."

I asked them why they thought girls sent nudes, or even posted provocative pictures of themselves, if they knew they could be spread around.

"More provocative equals more likes," Greta said offhandedly.

"It attracts more guys and then it makes other girls think about doing it just for the attention," said Padma. "They're attention whores."

"My father thinks all my photos are provocative," Greta mused.

"I think some girls post slutty pictures of themselves to show guys the side to them that guys want to see," Zoe said. "It's annoying."

"Girls call them sluts. Boys call it hot," Padma said.

Greta shrugged. "I call it hilarious."

Washington State

"Misogyny now has become so normalized," says Paul Roberts, the *Impulse Society* author. "It's like we've gone back to the *Mad Men* days. We can't even see the absurdity and the inequity of it, it's so pervasive. When the male gaze was digitized, it was almost as if it was internalized. With smartphones and social media, girls had the means of producing the male gaze themselves, and it was as if they turned it on themselves willingly in order to compete in a marketplace in which sex was the main selling point.

"And the social media companies aren't going to do anything about it, as long as it's driving traffic. It has so much to do with the drive for the fastest return that can possibly be generated, which has been the [corporate] mentality since the eighties. All you need to know about a social media company is that it's the hits, the clicks, the number of images seen is all you care about, as long as you're driving traffic; and if that traffic involves teenage girls doing self-destructive or character-eroding things, well, we won't think about that. It's people running around looking for anything to generate volume: Oh, teenage girls are taking their clothes off? And that's getting a lot of hits? Then let's turn a blind eye to the consequences. Oh, your daughter's on Tinder? Well, she's just meeting friends. It's all about high-volume usage. I don't think it's necessarily a cynical, let's destroy women thing—it's how can I get my next quarter's bonus?

"And I think that to the extent that the digital social media society normalizes impulses—think it, post it," Roberts says, "we've also created a context for more and more provocative propositions, whatever they are: Look at my boobs. Do you want to hook up? It's moved the bar for what's normal and normalized extreme behavior; everything outrageous becomes normalized so rapidly. You realize how insane things are today when you think about the relative rate of change. When I was in high school, if I had gone around saying, *Here's a picture of me, like me*, I would have gotten punched. If a girl went around passing out naked pictures of herself, people would have thought she needed therapy. Now, that's just Selfie Sunday."

Los Angeles, California

When I returned to my hotel that night after talking with the girls at the Grove, we started exchanging messages on Facebook. They were having a birthday-party sleepover (it was Melissa's birthday), so they would type something on the thread and disappear and then return. When I asked them what they were doing, Padma said, "Having cake." Greta said, "Of course we're all on our phones." Whenever they were free, they would tell me more about their experiences on social media.

"O.K. so my freshman year of high school," Padma wrote, "this sophomore Jaden (ya I regret even his stupid name) messages me on Facebook saying, Hi, because he knows me through mutual friends, and he would talk to me every single day. And one day he asked for my phone number and because I talked to him so much and got to know him I gave it to him. And so then we were texting and he asked if it was going anywhere, like what type of relationship, and I asked him back, and he said he would like a relationship with me, so I said we could try. And that led to us being kinda flirty and talking in person and seeing each other round school, and then he kinda kissed me and then he told everyone else that I kissed *him* and all he wanted was a hug.

"And I was beyond pissed at him," Padma wrote, "because of all the lies he told me and I still hate him to this day . . . And at the time he was telling me all his 'feelings'? He did the same thing to two other girls. And he hurt me so bad that I made Melissa talk to him, to hurt him, like to get a little taste of his own medicine. But then he ended up doing the same thing to her and he caused friction with us as friends.

"And he still does cause friction between us," Padma wrote, "and he's now a major man whore and he needs to leave my school because he has hurt so many girls that I didn't know of before. I've blocked him on Facebook and deleted his number."

"Last year," Melissa wrote, taking up Padma's story, "I met Jaden through Padma. She liked him. Later he hurt her and lied about kissing her. I wanted to help her. So to help her get back at him, I added him as a friend and started talking to him on Facebook. I was planning to play him the way he played Padma and a bunch of other girls. We talked every day for months and he ended up asking me out. So then I started ignoring him and going offline whenever he started to message me. I was messing with him the best way I could . . ."

"But after a while," Melissa said, "I fell for him too." Why? "I don't know . . . We had a thing for a while. We talked every day, and he called me every night to say goodnight. He told me that he loved me and I was completely into him. Buuuuuttttttt I didn't want to hurt Padma because she's one of my best friends. And then when I was finally ready for a real relationship with Jaden, he decided to hook up with this girl Skylar. He started going out with her to make me jealous. I found out on Facebook."

"I was upset," Melissa wrote, "but Jaden convinced me to continue our thing at the same time." How? "I don't know," she said. "He said he didn't want to be tied down by one person and he couldn't choose and this was what everybody did," seeing more than one person, that is, "and I guess I didn't want to lose him.

"So I would see all his relationship with Skylar, their relationship pictures and statuses about how much they love each other on Facebook," Melissa wrote. "And it was awful to see them post on each other's walls. After months of him cheating on her with me—and, I found out, like four other girls—he started going offline on me and ignoring my Snapchats and texts. Then all of a sudden, he would call and Snapchat me until I answered. And then he would stop responding again. He messed with my head so much. He still does. He still tries to talk to me.

"But now I have a boyfriend who actually cares about me," Melissa said. "But when Jaden found out about my new boyfriend, he started talking to me again and started picking up the way we left off. He's still trying to mess up my relationship. And yet he STILL hasn't broken up with her," meaning Skylar, the other girl. "He made my entire 10th grade year horrible and filled with DRAMA."

Padma wrote: "It's been hard for Melissa and me to stay friends and trust each other again. But we are better now and we see we must unite against THE MAN WHORES."

In the Media

What's not often talked about in discussions about the hypersexualization of girls is how this trend has been concurrent with the hypermasculinization of boys. In 1984, psychologists Donald L. Mosher and Mark Sirkin published one of the first studies using the term "hypermasculinity" to describe the behavior of college-age men who associated masculinity with "calloused sexual attitudes towards women," "violence as manly," and "danger as exciting." Since then, hypermasculinity has come to be understood more broadly as beliefs and behaviors which betray an exaggerated observance of traditional male gender roles. Further research has found that images in the media have an influence on hypermasculine behaviors and beliefs. In movies, video games, TV shows, advertising, and other forms of media, boys and men see images of males being strong and successful in the context of overpowering or degrading women. There's probably no better example than the punishing, unfeeling men seen in the most popular online porn.

Hypermasculinity has also been shown to have an influence on men's physical aggression toward women. A study published in the journal *Psychology of Men & Masculinity* in 2002 found that "hypermasculinity may be a risk factor for perpetrating violence against women and that these men ['high-hypermasculine men'] may have a lower aggression threshold." Meanwhile, intimate partner violence has been increasing on college campuses at a time when the rate of domestic violence nationwide has been in decline. According to the Justice Department, "estimates of dating violence among college students range from 10 to 50 percent," with women between the ages of eighteen and twenty-four at the greatest risk for intimate partner violence overall.

Machismo is nothing new. It seems no accident, though, that it became such an exaggerated part of American pop culture during the backlash against feminism of the 1980s and '90s. In Hollywood in those years, women were being demonized in ways rarely seen before in the history of film. There was a wave of hit movies about sinister, often lethal women: *Fatal Attraction, Basic Instinct, Misery, Single White Female, The Temp, Disclosure*. Meanwhile, men in the movies in those same years were near caricatures of hypermasculinity. The films of Sylvester Stallone and Arnold Schwarzenegger provide plenty of examples on their own, from the Rambo movies to *Cobra* to *Conan the Barbarian* to *Predator* to *The Terminator*. Pro-military movies came into style for the first time since the Vietnam War, with *Top Gun* and the *Iron Eagle* films.

Online porn consumption soared, as did the popularity of video games such as Grand Theft Auto, which debuted in 1997. The game has managed to cause controversy with each new installment; versions III through V allowed players to murder prostitutes. In 2013, Carolyn Petit wrote on Gamespot.com, "GTA V has little room for women except to portray them as strippers, prostitutes, long-suffering wives, humorless girlfriends and goofy, new-age feminists we're meant to laugh at."

The 1990s also saw the rise of "bro culture," a term once used to describe the lifestyle of frat boys, but now a fairly common young male ideal. The definition of "bro" is fluid, but the typical image is one of a politically incorrect, flippantly sexist, porn-consuming, booze-guzzling young man who seems determined not to grow up. Lad culture, bro culture's cousin in Britain, brought soft-core porn magazines such as *Maxim* and *FHM* to American shores, with cover images of young female celebrities in porn-star poses, from Jennifer Love Hewitt to Danielle Fishel, Topanga on *Boy Meets World*.

In music, gangster rap became a best-selling genre, glamorizing a view of women as "bitches" and "hos," the dancing eye candy in hypersexualized music videos. By the 2000s misogyny had become so unremarkable that rape jokes were mainstream comic fare. Comedian Daniel Tosh—host of the bro-ish Comedy Central show *Tosh.0*—ruffled some feathers in 2012 when he said of a female audience member who had heckled him for making a rape joke, "Wouldn't it be funny if that girl got raped by, like, five guys right now? Like right now?" Many comedians defended him.

One of the most seductive and influential expressions of hypermasculinity in pop culture has been *Entourage*, which ran from 2004 to

2011. The life of the fictional main character, Vincent Chase (Adrian Grenier), seemed to function for many boys and young men in the same way the world of Kim Kardashian does for girls—"Vince" was a fantasy of fame culture, a Hollywood movie star, handsome, rich, and decked out in spiffy clothes, spinning around in luxury cars and hanging out with his bros in his Hollywood Hills mansion, where he had lots of casual sex with a steady stream of models and "perfect 10s," none of whom had much personality and to whom he bore no responsibility.

"For teenagers everywhere, the show acted as a live-action *Maxim* magazine, delivering hot women, broad humor, and escapism in popcorn-light doses," wrote Brendan Gallagher on Complex.com. "This series is a celebration of masculinity in its most shallow manifestations. Money and power buy sex. If you don't have these things, you are worthless. When women or gay men get power, they must act 'straight' or their 'weakness' will be mocked. Once they do conform to heteronormative power dynamics, the show labels them icy bitches and bitchy queens."

On another cable channel, Don Draper was using and abusing women, and critics were celebrating the show for exposing the sort of sexism that women had endured in the past, and had supposedly overcome.

Facebook

In the months after I met the girls at the Grove, I followed them on Facebook and some of their other social media accounts. In just a short time after I left L.A., I was surprised to see the change in Padma's selfies. It was especially unexpected since she had been so vehement in her disapproval of girls who posted pictures which she said made them look like "sluts." She'd called such girls "attention whores" and said that seeing them post provocative pictures "kills me inside." But she'd also said, "Boys call it hot."

Ever since she'd joined Facebook in 2009, when she was in sixth grade, Padma had always posted pictures that could be described as wholesome; they'd showed the life of an American girl who participated in dance recitals and soccer games; there were pictures of her with her fresh-faced friends, all dressed in casual clothes, smiling and hugging and mugging for the camera. These pictures would get a few likes, or no likes.

And then one day a picture appeared of Padma wearing what looked to be a lacy bustier. Her hair was cascading down over her cleavage. She was staring into the camera with a defiant, sultry expression. She wore a lot of makeup.

"The hotness though," said the comments from both boys and girls. "Looking good!" "Sexy." "Hot." "Gorgeous," "Gorgeous," "Gorgeous." This picture got almost 100 likes.

After that, the pictures on Padma's feed showed her in increasingly provocative poses. There was a picture of her at the beach in a bikini. "#pornstar," wrote a boy. "Put on some clothes," wrote another boy. "I didn't say you could post hot pics." "You're not my dad," Padma flirted back. She posted a picture of herself in a T-shirt which said "FLAWLESS." "Photolicious," commented a boy. These pictures would get between 50 and 100 likes.

I wondered if Padma's seemingly conflicted feelings had anything to do with the fact that she'd been cyberbullied. She'd told me that, in sixth grade, she'd been harassed by a girl on Facebook. "It's one thing when people bully you in person," she said, "but then when you go on the computer it's kind of like you can't escape. They can find you anytime, anywhere; they always have you there to bully. There's people who just take it too far, like as if torturing you in person isn't enough— they have to do it when you're not even near them. Like this one girl called me all these names and then she'd go on her Facebook and get everyone on her Facebook to unfriend me." She was emotional when she talked about it, causing the other girls at the table to grow quiet.

And even though this had happened years ago, I wondered if it had left a kind of scar; and if, like Sierra in Jamestown, Padma had finally broken down and wanted to somehow prove to everyone how "hot" she really was. Was this part of how girls become hypersexualized, first by having their self-esteem destroyed? And what lasting effects was this going to have when these cyberbullied girls became women?

The picture that got the most likes of all was the one where Padma tamed her beautiful black hair. It no longer looked like her natural hair, thick and full. It looked flat and thin and unnaturally shiny, as if it had been submitted to many treatments in a salon. It looked like TV hair.

Commenters wrote: "Your hair looks so much better like this." "You look so good." "Oh please keep it this way." "You are so perfect now my little slut."

"SLUTTTTTTTT," Padma wrote. "I LOVE YOU."

Lakeside, California

On August 5, 2013, Californians started getting AMBER alerts on their phones regarding a missing sixteen-year-old girl, Hannah Anderson, and her eight-year-old brother, Ethan. A multi-agency manhunt was under way, stretching from British Columbia to Baja California, Mexico, for the suspect in their kidnapping—forty-year-old James Lee DiMaggio, a family friend the kids called "Uncle Jim."

On August 10, an FBI agent shot DiMaggio dead in the wilderness near Cascade, Idaho, where DiMaggio had taken Hannah. Ethan and the children's mother, Christina Anderson, had already died, on August 4, in DiMaggio's home in Boulevard, California, their bodies burned in an arson fire. Their deaths, and the fire, were blamed on DiMaggio. Christina had died from blunt-force trauma, apparently inflicted with a crowbar. Ethan's body was so badly burned that medical examiners couldn't determine the cause of death.

This horrifying case was one of the first times social media became such a prominent factor in a crime story involving a teenage girl. For in the days after she was returned safely home, Hannah—a blond white girl from Lakeside, California—went rogue, going on social media and answering hundreds of questions about her experience posed by users on Ask.fm.

"Do you know why he did it?," meaning DiMaggio, one Ask.fm user asked. "Because he's a physco [sic]," Hannah replied. "Are you glad he's dead?" asked someone else. "Absolutely," Hannah said.

"Your hot," another user wrote.

Hannah said, "Thanks."

In the same thread, Hannah posted a picture of her freshly painted nails. "When did you get your nails done?" someone asked. "Yesterday," she said.

The apparent nonchalance with which this sixteen-year-old girl was willing to discuss the details of her traumatic ordeal on an anonymous site was perplexing to many in the news media and on social media as well. It quickly gave rise to speculation as to whether Hannah's detachment could perhaps be an indication of some complicity in her own kidnapping and the crimes against her mother and brother. People started trolling, asking whether Hannah might have actually been having a sexual relationship with DiMaggio. Inadvertently fueling such gossip, Hannah said, on *Today*, "He had a crush on me," confirming what she had already told the world on social media.

San Diego County Sheriff Bill Gore had said in an interview with the *Los Angeles Times* that "everybody, the FBI, our investigators, everybody are convinced that there is no way [Hannah] was anything but the worst kind of victim in this." Still, Facebook pages and Twitter and Reddit threads started to appear in which commenters evaluated the particulars of the case, pointing out inconsistencies in Hannah's story—her claim, for example, that DiMaggio had drugged her with what she thought was Ambien before abducting her, knocking her out, while some saw in a blurry video released from a security checkpoint when they were driving to Idaho Hannah possibly awake in the passenger seat beside him. However, the main thing which seemed to be making followers of the story uneasy was Hannah's avid social media use so soon after the tragedy. Why would a teenage girl want to chat about such personal and dreadful events online? And why was she posting selfies on Instagram?

In the days and weeks after she came home, Hannah was posting selfies—there she was at cheerleading practice, at dance rehearsals, and driving in her car, smiling merrily into her cell phone camera. She seemed ebullient, always smiling and smizing with heavily made-up eyes. "You are like the definition of perfect," commented fans. "You are honestly flawless." "Your eyebrows are perfect! Do you tweeze or wax them?" "You are STUNNING!" "I love love love your style!"

"Aw. Thanks," replied Hannah, with a smiley face.

Social media experts were quick to point out that this was just what kids do these days—they talk about everything online; they seek solace for their pain; and they post a lot of selfies. Eric Rice, a professor of social work at the University of Southern California, told Mashable: "In some ways this is a normal response in the contemporary era for teens. This is just a way of storytelling, through social media, which is fairly normal and a response to trauma."

"It just helps me grieve," Hannah explained on *Today* when asked why she was discussing the tragedy on social media. "Like, [to] post pictures to show how I'm feeling. I'm a teenager. I'm gonna go on it."

In fact, what she was doing wasn't all that different from the online behavior of many adults. The in memoriam post about a deceased parent, friend, or beloved pet has become a social media convention. And such posts always get a lot of likes, however heartfelt they may actually be. The poster is showered with condolences and achieves a kind of social media boost.

But somehow it also brings to mind that scene in 1995's *To Die For* when Nicole Kidman's character, Suzanne Stone, makes a display of grieving for the news media at her husband's funeral, busting out a tape player and blaring Eric Carmen's maudlin 1975 hit, "All By Myself," as she poses, looking stoic and tragic. In the film, it's a satirical moment, meant to reveal how the character has no shame in using the murder of her husband (which she in fact orchestrated) to try, however clumsily, to craft a sympathetic public self, and to increase her fame. "Suzanne used to say that you're not really anybody in America unless you're on TV," says another character in the film.

In the days and weeks after her rescue, Hannah gained thousands of followers on Instagram as she posted pictures of her deceased little brother and mother, alongside lengthy messages expressing her grief: "I already miss you guys so much," she wrote. "But god needed two perfect angels with him up there to get me home and that's exactly what you guys did."

She was getting hundreds of likes on all her photos as well as scores of supportive comments from new followers around the world: "God bless you!" "Stay strong!" "Millions of people love you, girl." Her followers called her "a fighter," "a role model," and "an inspiration." Girls, in particular, swarmed to support Hannah. "I wish I could be as strong

as you," one girl said. There was now a hashtag used for Hannah—
#hannahstrong—which Hannah tagged on her own social media
pictures.

When an Ask.fm user told her she was "worldwide trending on
Twitter," Hannah replied, "lol."

She was famous now, and she was performing the role of the star,
giving her fans what they wanted—which in the new stardom of social
media meant more, more, more of her. But Hannah was also continuing to get hate. Commenters persisted in suggesting that she was somehow culpable in her family members' brutal deaths, alleging that her
relationship with DiMaggio had been inappropriate. Others criticized
her for how she had behaved at her mother and brother's memorial
service, posing for pictures, including a selfie in which she and a friend
were seen pointing their fingers like guns. Some even sounded off on
the way Hannah carried around a Starbucks Frappuccino at the event.
Hannah was being cyberbullied.

It wasn't her first experience with online bullying. In the months
before her kidnapping, she'd been called a steady stream of abusive
names on Ask.fm: "ugly," "whore," "cunt," "bitch," "a fucking ugly
whore."

"Everybody is so mean to you," one commenter observed. "Tell me
about it," Hannah said.

But on Ask.fm, she also showed a resilience to such attacks. She
seemed to take it all in stride, giving back as good as she got. "Keep
talkin shit your pretty funny and pathetic," she told one cyberbully.

On Ask.fm, Hannah presented an image of herself as a sort of in-
the-know party girl. She posted about having rented a "party bus" for
her sixteenth birthday—just like it sounds, it's a rented, chauffeur-
driven bus on which high school kids party, typically with alcohol and
drugs. By her own account, she had given lap dances to many of the
passengers. "Damn on that last party bus you really showed you can
dance little mama," an Ask.fm user commented.

She'd been open about her sexual activity, as well, on Ask.fm.
"Have you ever fucked a black guy?" someone asked. "Yupp," she said.
She'd posted sexy selfies which had received appreciative, sexualized
comments from boys. She'd received graphic sexual advances, most

of which she laughed off. She'd expressed sadness over how she had been "played" by guys. "Why does every guy play you?" someone asked. "Good question," she replied.

El Capitan High School, where Hannah was then in eleventh grade, is housed in a sprawling redbrick building just off the road which runs through the center of town. Lakeside is a middle-class town of some 20,000 people about twenty-one miles east of San Diego. It's hot and flat, with a few shopping plazas and small suburban houses on streets dotted with trucks and parched palms. All around you can see the foothills of the Cuyamaca Mountains, which look so bare and rocky, you feel like you've landed on the moon.

When I went to Lakeside a couple of months after Hannah's rescue, some senior girls in the parking lot of El Capitan remarked on how Hannah had "put herself out there" on social media, referring to how she had talked about her sex life. "She didn't have the best reputation," said one of the girls.

But these same girls also spoke of a "double standard" in their school which got a girl who was open about her sexuality called a "slut," while "if a guy gets a lot of action, it's, Go you."

"The boys here are pigs," said one of the girls. "They're immature. They see a girl twerk at a party, they think, I'm gonna take advantage of her."

"A few boys are okay," the second girl said.

"Like two," said the first.

Regarding Hannah, the first girl said, "Everyone's just looking at her now, like no one wants to say anything," because of what she had been through. "The school told us not to say anything about it to her, but people think it's weird that she seems, like, really happy—"

"Like, *prancy*," said the second girl.

"Like if my mom died I wouldn't be all happy like that," the first girl said.

How were kids reacting to Hannah becoming Instafamous? I asked.

"She's working it," said the second girl with a shrug. "But, you know? Anybody would."

Hannah's life in Lakeside before she became a social media star seems like it was hard. "Why are you always bitchy and sad all the time?" an Ask.fm user asked around a month before her kidnapping. "Your not hot shit," this user went on, "and your annoying when you just try to get attention all the time."

"Get a life. And fuck off," said Hannah.

Hannah's mother and father, Brett Anderson, had recently separated, and Brett had moved to Tennessee for work. Kids from her school said that Hannah had been upset about the breakup of her parents and missed her father. (After the death of her mother and brother, Brett moved back to the area to be with her.)

The apartment complex where she had lived with her mother and brother looked bleak and run-down. Some residents had blankets in their windows instead of curtains. The neighborhood was not especially safe.

According to Andrew Spanswick, a friend of Jim DiMaggio's (DiMaggio was an old friend of Hannah's dad), "Uncle Jim" had sometimes helped Christina Anderson financially. A friend of Hannah's had reportedly said on Ask.fm that DiMaggio had helped with "rides [and] school supplies and stuff." "Jim told me about how he cared about those kids," Spanswick said when I spoke to him on the phone. "Jim was a stabilizing force in their lives," he maintained.

Spanswick, the CEO of a group of rehab centers, had been defending DiMaggio in the media—an unpopular position, given the seriousness of what DiMaggio had been accused of doing.

In 2011, DiMaggio set up a life insurance policy of $112,000 with Hannah and Ethan's grandmother as the beneficiary; Spanswick believes the money was intended for Hannah. "Hannah's father was gone and Hannah was fighting with her mother," Spanswick said. Hannah had confirmed at least part of this, in her appearance on *Today*, when she said, "Me and my mom didn't really get along a year ago." She talked about writing letters to DiMaggio about her troubles, and said he had written her back.

DiMaggio was "like my second dad, we were almost best friends," Hannah said on *Today*. The two had gone on trips alone together; but on Ask.fm, when a user asked Hannah why she had wanted to travel alone with an older man, she replied, "My mom pushed me to go," according to one report. She had posted pictures from some of the excursions on Instagram. One in particular was now feeding contin-ued speculation about the nature of their relationship. On a picture of herself posing in short shorts, Hannah had commented, slightly mis-quoting a line from the Miley Cyrus song "We Can't Stop": "Red cups and sweaty bodies everywhere, hands in the air cause we don't care. #L.A. #Letsgooo." "The Lakeside Lolita had Uncle Jim twisted around her little finger," said a commenter on Fox5SanDiego.com, in a typically sexist comment.

When it comes to women and public shaming, even famous women have something in common with high school girls. Over the years, whenever I've interviewed some famous woman who's had prob-lems with the media, she has invariably expressed her awareness of a double standard in which her youthful indiscretions were harshly judged, while the "bad" behavior of her male counterparts was forgiven or even celebrated. It was only in their coupling with some famous men that two of these women managed to wipe their media slates clean. Angelina Jolie was doing the kind of humanitarian work she's devoted her life to years before she started dating Brad Pitt and was accused of being a "homewrecker"; it was only after she bore their kids that she gained a near saintly reputation in the media, condemnations of her wilder past finally shushed. Nicole Richie's image did a similar 180 almost as soon as she married and had children with rocker Joel Madden (who, despite having a lot of tattoos, has a rather clean-cut image).

Hannah's image similarly seemed to take a turn for the better when she showed herself to be in a committed relationship with a catch. On Instagram, she started posting pictures of the two of them together—he was a tall, white, handsome football player with a megawatt smile, a defensive tackle for the El Capitan Vaqueros named Dylan Vockrodt. Hannah started dating him about a month after she was rescued, she said on Ask.fm, where she'd gone to tell everyone about it. Dylan didn't seem to mind. "I look ripped," he commented on one of her pictures. "Those guns," he said, meaning his muscular biceps.

Hannah posted Instagram pictures of the two of them kissing and cuddling. "You and Dylan are so cute!" an Ask.fm user gushed. Hannah posted pictures of herself in her cheerleading uniform and Dylan in his football uniform, pictures of them hugging and mugging and looking like the perfect high school couple. She posted pictures of them acting silly together and frolicking on the beach—the latter a favorite shot in coverage of famous couples in tabloid media. She posted pictures that suggested she and Dylan had had a sleepover at her grandmother's house; there he was, sweetly cooking her breakfast in the morning. "Awww," said fans. But Hannah assured Ask.fm users that she and her new boyfriend had slept in separate rooms. She was no longer the party girl giving lap dances on a party bus.

And all of these pictures were accompanied by the sort of breathless commentary that is the language of relationships played out on social media: he was her "one true love," the "man who saved my life." "I never thought it would be you."

Hannah's girl followers loved her new romance. They said: "Well you and Dyl are a match made in heaven huh?" "Relationship goals!" "OTP!" "Such a adorable couple!" Hannah posted pictures of herself and Dylan in their finery at their homecoming dance. And with all this posting, Hannah's hate abated. Her story shifted from one about "the Lakeside Lolita" to one of a girl triumphing in the face of adversity and being rewarded with the love of a strapping young man. It was as if, by presenting an image of herself in an idealized, all-American relationship, she had sanitized her past, even transformed herself into a classic American prom queen. She'd re-created herself as the perfect girlfriend, the perfect girl, on social media.

She very well could have taken as a model the way celebrity couples advertise their relationships online, seen the likes and followers and general goodwill that such posting brings. The broadcasting of bliss is part of what makes people love Kim and Kanye, Beyoncé and Jay Z. When Taylor Swift posted an Instagram shot of herself in a bikini getting a piggyback ride from her new boyfriend, Scottish DJ Calvin Harris, the picture got more than 2.5 million likes and over 76,000 comments: "CUTEST COUPLE EVER!!!!!!!!!" Swift's followers soared in the months after the revelation of her new committed relationship, and she became the most followed person on Instagram, beating Kim Kardashian. (At the end of 2015, Swift had more than 58 million Instagram followers and Kardashian had more than 54 million.) An article in *Billboard*, "Taylor Swift & Calvin Harris: Their Instagram Love Story," noted that the couple "have very much controlled the narrative of their relationship through Instagram," evading paparazzi and strategically clueing in fans as to the state of their togetherness through pictures posted on each other's Instagram accounts.

On Kanye's thirty-eighth birthday, Kim posted a photo of the two of them in stylish black-and-white. "Happy Birthday to my best friend in the entire world!" she wrote. "You are the most amazing husband and dad! You inspire me every single day! . . . You have a heart of gold!" The post got more than a million likes.

On Dylan's eighteenth birthday, Hannah posted a video montage of their romantic moments with a message that sounded almost as if Kim had written it: "Happy 18th birthday to the love of my life, the man that stole my heart almost two years ago! I love you way more then you can imagine and I'm so thankful your mine . . . Happy birthday love bug. Your legal now."

But social media fame has its own set of dangers. In the summer of 2015, Hannah posted on Instagram an image of what looked to be a profile page for Dylan Vockrodt. However, Hannah warned her followers: "There is some weird person pretending to be Dylan flirting with girls and trying to get nudes from people . . . Dylan and I are happy and love each other and not letting anyone come between us."

Williamsburg, Virginia

When I was in Williamsburg one evening, I met some girls in the Barnes & Noble at the New Town mall. They were all wearing soft sweaters, jeans, and sneakers, except for Dasha, who wore a blue blazer and gold-studded boots. They were black, all with straight shoulder-length brown hair, except for Diandra, who had black and golden braids. Nina wore glasses. They were all sixteen, except for Dasha, Nina's sister, who was fifteen.

They were students at the same high school, a big bustling school with winning sports teams. Diandra, Dasha, and Chelsea were competitive cheerleaders there. Nina used to be a cheerleader, but now she ran track. The girls said they liked their school, they thought it was "a good place." Nina and Dasha's mother was an executive assistant and their father a hospital administrator. Chelsea's mother and father were teachers, and Diandra's dad worked in construction, while her mother was a stay-at-home mom. All of their parents were married.

They couldn't talk to me then, they said, because they had to ask their parents. So the next day, at a Starbucks in a shopping plaza off Pocahontas Trail, we met again. All of their mothers accompanied them, as did one of their fathers. One of their grandmothers came. Their family members sat at a table nearby, having coffee.

It would have been like any other day at a coffee store, with the hissing of the espresso machines in the background and patrons at tables tapping at their phones, except for what we were talking about: the arrest of a sixteen-year-old local girl for allegedly putting naked pictures of herself on Twitter (the same girl mentioned earlier).

I asked the girls if they had ever heard of a girl doing that before.

"It's not common for them to put it on Twitter *themselves*," Diandra said. "But it's common for them to send it to someone else."

"And then it ends up on there because of that person they send it to," said Dasha.

"People will send nude pictures confidentially to their boyfriend," Nina said, "and then when they break up, the boy will be like, Well, I would like to confirm that we are not together anymore. So they just put it out there" on social media. "They send it to someone and that someone puts it on Instagram or Twitter. Like they have—"

"Pages on it," Diandra said.

"They have pages on it," Nina said. "They have a page with a whole bunch of nude pictures of every girl that's ever sent out a nude before."

"There's lots of pages," Dasha said, "and they put it on there and they 'at' them"—meaning that girls whose nudes were shared were notified by others with an @ sign with their usernames.

"They 'at' their names, like they don't care about their feelings," Nina said. "It will just be up there for everybody to see."

"And *everybody* sees it," said Diandra.

I asked them how often this happened.

"A *lot*," Nina said. "Like every few weeks."

This was the first time I was hearing of this. Later, I would find out from the girls in Boca and the Bronx and other places about slut pages. I still remember how striking it was to me to hear these four very composed and decent girls talking about something so outrageous as if it were normal, with their parents sitting just a few feet away. I had come to James City County thinking that the arrest of the girl who posted her pictures on Twitter was something remarkable. But it wasn't remarkable, it was only ironic that she had been arrested, when, from what these girls were telling me, boys at their school routinely shared nudes of girls without adults even noticing, much less taking any action. What was remarkable was that it was normal to the girls, and that they spoke of it as if it were something that just was.

"It bothers me though," Nina said. "What bothers me is you see how you can't trust."

"A girl will send a naked picture to somebody," Dasha agreed, "and they trust that they won't send it out."

"But I don't understand why they think they *can* trust," said Diandra. " 'Cause once they've done it, somebody can just be like, Oh, I don't like her anymore, I'm over her. And they can send it to a page."

"For *everybody* to see," said Nina, shaking her head.

"And people make rude comments on the pictures," said Diandra.

"People will say like, Oh, I know whose body that is," Nina said. "And sometimes they will even add their names."

I asked them how the girls in the pictures reacted to the exposure.

"Sometimes they try and just delete everything," Diandra said.

"Some don't care," said Nina. "They act like they like the attention. Some are just like, Oh, yeah, I know my body looks good, so I don't care if everybody sees it. And some are really shocked that it's even up there. It depends on the girl."

"But most of them do care," Diandra said, "because if you have a picture of your body on Instagram, then it will be hard for you to get another relationship, because the boys'll be like, Oh, no, I don't want to be with you because everybody has seen your body; it's not just mine. It's everybody's because everybody already saw it. So it affects a person a lot, not just at that one moment but, like, their whole life."

It was shocking to hear of all this for the first time, the information conjuring up connections that went back to the Victorian era and Puritan Boston and the Bible: they were talking about a woman, a girl, being "ruined," something that's not supposed to happen anymore, more than 100 years after the so-called first wave of the feminist movement. In some countries today, "ruined" girls and women are still stoned. It's a horrible reality, not to be diminished. But there's an element to some girls' experience on social media that's not unlike a kind of stoning, a virtual stoning.

The girls said that, while it was mostly boys sharing nudes of girls, there were also boys who put "dick pics" on their accounts, which got forwarded to slut pages as well.

"They'll post a picture and say like, Oh, yeah, I'm big," said Nina. The other girls laughed. "They put it on their Instagram, and then someone will say in the comments like, Oh, no, you ain't even that big"—the other girls giggled—"and then they get their feelings hurt. So this is with everybody. It's not just girls or boys" posting nudes. "It's both."

Was there a difference in how a girl was seen for sending nudes, versus a boy? I asked.

"Oh, *yes*," they said. "There really is."

"A girl who sends naked pictures, she's a slut, but if a boy does it, everyone just laughs," Nina said.

The same double standard applied to a girl who had sex versus a boy who had sex, they said. If a boy had sex, nothing negative was said about him.

"Nothing at all," Dasha said. "It's like boys, they get props, but girls, they have a title if they do things."

"Labels," said Nina. "Like girls will be called a ho or thot. The boys just wanted to be able to say that they had that person and then they'll go and tell their friends, so they say they did all these girls."

The other girls said, "Yep."

The double standard over having sex was more commonly known; and yet it was still surprising to hear them talk about it as if it were a fact of life, like bad weather, about which nothing could be done. When and how had sexism gotten so bad in the lives of girls?

Sometimes, they said, it was considered "okay" for a girl to have sex, but only in the context of a committed relationship. "Sometimes they judge a girl on how long she's been dating the boy," Dasha said. "Like if you're dating for like a year and you do it, they don't really call you anything because you've been dating the boy for a year. But if you've just been dating for like a month or so and you have sex with them, you're considered a ho."

"Just because a girl did it one time they're considered a ho, even though it could have been their first time doing it," Nina said.

And once the label was there, it stuck for all of a girl's high school years, they said.

"And people keep bringing it up and bringing it up," said Chelsea.

"It's not fair," Dasha said.

"But, I mean, I don't think that you *should* have sex with a guy that you've been dating for like two months or so," Chelsea added gently.

"Yes, to me, there's a time frame that should go by," Nina said.

"I don't know," Dasha countered. "Put a label on you?" She cocked her head. "It's just, like, I don't *agree* with you, but I don't agree with them putting a label on you, either. You did it, you did it." She shrugged.

"But you should *know* them," Diandra contended. "You should know them, like, really, really well, and you should actually both trust each other."

"Yeah, okay," Dasha conceded. "If he's not willing to wait, he is obviously not the right person."

"Like he can't just, like, force it on you," Nina said. "If you say no, he has to respect that. If he actually is waiting for your time when you're ready, then that's different than somebody that's pushing it on you and always bringing it up. Then it just shows that that's all they want."

I asked them if they knew any boys like that.

"A *lot*," Nina said.

The other girls said, "Yeah."

"Because they're trying to make themselves seem like they have all the girls," Nina said.

I asked them to describe the boys in their school.

"Childish," said Diandra.

They laughed. She giggled.

"It's certain groups," Diandra said. "There's certain boys who are just like trying to bring up their number [of sex partners] higher than anybody else in their group. And that's when it hurts the girls. It hurts them because they really trust these people—they really trust them with everything they have. And once the trust is gone, they feel like they can't trust anybody ever again."

"And that's how a lot of girls just feel like they just don't care anymore," said Nina. "That's why I think some girls just start having sex with a lot of people, because they think that, I mean, regardless, everybody's going to talk about me, so why not just do it?"

They were highly aware of the inequality in girls' lives. Girls could be called sluts, they said, not only for having sex but for how they dressed. "The boys have a *lot* to say about how people dress," Nina said. "If a girl wears short skirts or something, then the boys will notice them and then try to get something from them," meaning sexually.

They were aware, too, of how impossible standards of beauty exerted pressure on girls. "Like how you have to wear makeup," Chelsea said. "Like with models, there's a lot of stuff going on with computers, so they don't even really look like that. But they make you think they do and then you want to look like that, too. I think that's why some girls will show off their bodies, to show off what they have."

"And like the way they make you think you have to change yourself, like lose weight or gain weight, instead of just being yourself," said Nina.

"I think it's making us, like, lower," Diandra said. "It's bringing us down as females . . . Like, just be you. Because every day it's like you have to wake up and put on a mask and try to be somebody else instead of being yourself. And you can't ever be happy."

Los Angeles, California

In other corners of the country, the slut-shaming of girls continued. "We know this girl Ursula that had a list of guys she had given blowjobs to, like forty-five people," said Sarah. Everyone laughed.

Sarah and her friends Elena, Jeff, and Grace, all teenagers from the Valley, were having dinner in L.A. one night before going to a movie.

Over burgers and fries at an outdoor café, they started talking about the girls at their high school they called "bad."

"Ava's like that, too," said Jeff. "She asked me out and then took my head and, like, shoved it in her bra."

"She gave Richie a handjob in the back of the bus going to band competition," Sarah said.

They talked about girls who had made sex tapes; girls who had sex with different guys at parties every weekend. "Was that the same weekend she went to the emergency room [for drugs]?" Grace asked.

"Remember when Anita got semen on Maya's jacket?" Jeff said with a smile.

"And then Maya posted it on her [Facebook] wall," Sarah said, laughing.

"She asked to borrow Maya's jacket and she wore the jacket, and she gave this guy a blowjob at a party while she was wearing the jacket," Jeff said.

"And then she gave the jacket back to Maya without washing it, so Maya took a picture of the jacket with the stain and posted it on Anita's wall: 'You didn't wash my jacket,'" said Sarah.

They laughed.

"Which was so mean, but I love that she did that. I was like, Oh my *God*," said Jeff.

Tinder

On a sunny day in L.A., I sat with Emily at a table at the Grove and she showed me how to download Tinder. She'd deleted the app from her phone after her bad experience with the boy she'd met up with who hadn't looked like his picture.

"I realized it was too risky," she said. "'Cause you're never gonna know what they really look like. It's all based on looks. Like, Do I like you from your picture? So it's kind of dumb that people post pictures that don't even look like them in person."

She logged on to Facebook, and within a matter of seconds she was on Tinder, swiping through the profiles of boys. "They're all ridiculous," she murmured, swiping. There were pictures of boys smiling and skateboarding and snowboarding, boys holding bottles of beer and smoking bongs. Emily swiped right on every picture, indicating interest, and within minutes she was getting matches. Her picture, now centered in a little circle, came rolling toward a boy's picture in another circle, and collided with it, with a little *ding*. "See," she said, "it's like a game."

Within a few more minutes she was getting messages. She scrolled through them, opening them up. Most were simple greetings—"Hey beautiful," "Hello gorgeous," "What's up"—and then one of them said, "Body pic?" Meaning that the boy was asking to see a picture of Emily's entire body, that her face was not enough for him to make his assessment of her.

Another message said, "You have nice boobs."

"Yeah," Emily said, "that's why I went off it. You get a lot of rude stuff like that."

She said that she was still "in love" with the boy who had broken her heart: "even though I know it's stupid, I can't make the feelings stop." She said the boy was still posting pictures of himself on Facebook and Instagram with other girls. "It doesn't make me feel good to see that. It's like a knife in my stomach every time I see that because he really made me think he cared. I told him everything, like even stuff about my family," while messaging him at night. "I felt like we were in love. He said he loved me."

I asked her why she didn't just unfollow him.

"Because," she said, "then he'll know I care."

She said she'd found out the boy was unfaithful when "my friend saw his chat boxes open on his computer and he was talking to these other girls at the same time as me. I should have known better" than to be with him, she said. "I thought I knew him. But when I think about it, I really only knew him from Facebook. I stalked him."

She said she was trying not to check Facebook as much, so she wouldn't see the boy's pictures, but being off social media had made her feel "anxious, like I don't know what's going on." Being on social media also made her feel anxious, she said. "You can lose yourself in all the posting. It's like everything's just always in your face. Sometimes it gets boring, and sometimes you feel jealous and left out, like people post like party pictures and you weren't there. It makes you feel like a loser.

"That's part of why I think I went on Tinder, to be honest," she said. To feel better about herself, to get matches, to feel wanted.

"Everybody's always gotta post," she continued. "We went to breakfast a few days ago, me and my friends, and when we got there my one friend was like, Okay, I call Instagramming this breakfast. I call the Instagram shot. We were literally just going out for breakfast and she wanted to Instagram the moment. And then we had a plan to go to the museum later, and this other girl was like, I call Instagramming a picture of us at the museum."

Why couldn't you all just post pictures at the museum? I asked.

"Because you all have some of the same followers and if you all post the same pictures you look stupid," Emily said.

"There's so much pressure to be on social media," she said. "Like if you're not, it's like you don't exist. Or people feel like you're judging them for being on it. Like, what, are you looking down on this generation? But I think somewhere deep inside they know it's weird to be on it all the time."

Her phone dinged and she saw she had another match on Tinder. She checked her phone. She stared at it a moment. "Oh, wow," she said. "I actually know this person. He is actually kind of cute. I might message him. I don't know."

Los Angeles, California

Zoe lived in a suburban neighborhood in west L.A. full of oaks and evergreen trees and Spanish Colonial Revival bungalows built in the 1920s. When I went to see her almost a year after our first meeting, Zoe was still sixteen, now almost seventeen. After just this short space of time, she seemed older and more grown up than when I'd met her with her friends at the Grove.

She was barefoot, wearing a purple flowered romper. She had a friend over, Gabby, an Asian girl the same age as she. Gabby had long dark hair and bright dark eyes and wore a romper, too, a black one with flowers. Gabby's parents did marketing for a large corporation.

They sat on the porch and talked about how, even since they had been in middle school, it seemed like there was more focus on social media. Zoe said, "It increases every single day. We're passing down our technology to even younger kids. Girls our age live on their phones. We feel like our social lives are in our phones, and as long as we feel that way, people will keep making apps to make us rely on it even more.

"It's changed even since we were thirteen," she said. "Now you pretty much can get anything from your phone. It can be anything, like ordering a pizza; you don't have to talk to anyone anymore. You don't have to write anymore. We're typing pretty much everything on our phones. My parents talk about how when they were teenagers they would have to go and actually have a conversation to hang out with someone; now you just pick up your phones and have a conversation online."

"I find most of the time I'm with my friends I feel so disconnected with them because of technology," Gabby said. "They're always on their phones to play a game or see what someone is doing somewhere else. A phone is almost becoming like a person—like you can tell Siri anything, you can ask the Internet anything you want."

"Apple is even adding human characteristics to your phone to make you feel closer to it," said Zoe. "We've been watching movies about robots for years, but now we've actually created a robot that we all have a connection to—and now we have to include that 'person' in our lives or we feel like we can't be ourselves."

"I hate it," Gabby said.

I asked them how many minutes or hours a day they were on their phones.

"Too much," Zoe said with a laugh.

Gabby said, "It's hard to say, because it's kind of normal to be on your phone so often. I think I probably check my phone every five minutes?"

"I cannot imagine counting my texts," Zoe said. "I'm texting when I don't even realize I'm texting. I'll read something and reply and I'll have no idea what I said, it's almost unconscious."

"And yet when you have a conversation with someone you tend to remember everything about it," Gabby said, "even the way that they said everything."

They both said they got their phones in sixth grade and had immediately run up their parents' accounts with texts. "I got a navy Razr," Zoe said with a smile. "I thought I was so cool. But now I babysit for a girl who is seven years old and she just showed me she got an iPhone."

"That's like normal to them now," said Gabby.

It was funny to hear that, at age sixteen, they sounded so appalled at the speed with which younger kids were adopting cellular technology; they sounded like parents.

"My mom used to always tell me to write letters to people," said Gabby, "and now she's like, Just text them, so she's kind of affected by it, too; it's not just teenagers, it's everyone."

"My parents always talk about how they never talk on the phone anymore," Zoe said. "They can't believe it."

I asked them why they thought social media was proving so addictive.

"It's the ease and the speed of everything," Zoe said.

"And like on Instagram," said Gabby, "it's really easy to see how many likes and followers you have, and I think a big part of social media is competition for likes and followers."

"We've transferred high school popularity into social media measurements," Zoe agreed. "The popularity contest—it's never been a good thing, and now that we have the actual numbers, we've become greedy. We want more attention. I think people have become obsessed with this attention. It's become an addiction to gain as much as we can. It's depressing how self-conscious we are about these things."

I asked them if kids they knew ever talked about all this—did they ever say, Hey, this is really strange what we're doing, being on social media all the time?

"I feel like we know it," Gabby said, "it's there; but we don't have conversations about it, like, Am I doing this too much? We all do it, so we don't question it. That would mean you might have to stop, and no one wants to stop. Also I think the temptation of being able to self-promote, where it doesn't show who you really are as a person, is just too strong—you can be whoever you want to be on social media. You can promote the good things about your reputation, and be this amazing person, and nobody's ever gonna know what's underneath all of that. And that's very appealing to people."

"It's giving everybody a cover image of who they really are," said Zoe. "Sometimes the people with thousands of followers can be the complete opposite of who you think they are. But some people still believe in the image and take it way too seriously; they think they know people from the image they put out; but you only really understand a person if you have actual conversations with them."

They said it was common now for kids who had never met to know one another from social media; to be at a party, for example, and recognize a girl from another school from following her on Instagram; also to know things about her from what she had posted; even to have gossiped about her, had opinions about her, or maybe judged her.

"It's kinda scary," Gabby said, "it'll be like, Oh, did you see what she posted? Did you see this person's Snapchat Story?"

"If you bring up any person's Snapchat Story, most likely someone will know what you're talking about," said Zoe.

"Everything just revolves around these Internet people we create," Gabby said.

"And everyone is super-aware of everyone's ranking on these sites," Zoe said. "I don't think we would be so addicted to it unless everybody else was—if everyone wasn't talking about it all the time. It's become so normal to talk about Instagram."

The talk turned to girls who posted provocative pictures, as it almost always did when talking to girls about social media and girls.

"It was really eye-opening this summer to see all the girls in bikinis and all this stuff," Gabby said. "They want people to notice them, and they do everything they can to get people to like them.

"It's really hard to see that," she added. "But it's just so normal. Everyone says, Wow, look at her. It really takes away from wanting to know about people and their personality and wanting to get to know someone."

"People have become caught up in how much attention they're getting," Zoe said, "and it doesn't have to be good attention, it can be bad attention; but it feels like girls have become more absorbed with getting attention through these networks for some reason. We see how an icon like Miley Cyrus changed her look dramatically and got so much attention for it. We look up to a person who receives attention like that. We're trying to clone ourselves in a certain way; and some girls figure, Oh, by showing my ass on Facebook I'm getting attention, I'm getting talked about, people are noticing me and in some way that's good. We position ourselves to look the best that we can look by propping up our boobs or doing whatever it will take."

I asked them how the boys they knew thought about girls who posted provocative pictures.

"I have a lot of guy friends," Zoe said, "and someone will mention the name of a girl, and the first thing they say is, Oh, like that girl with the big ass."

"That's what they recognize someone for," Gabby said with a frown.

"It's depressing," said Zoe, "because guys have come to recognize women from images on the Internet. Guys look at this as like a different kind of porn, almost. It's self-generated porn."

I asked if the guys they knew watched porn.

"Oh, yeah, definitely," Zoe said. "They talk about looking at porn; it's just the thing you expect from a guy, it's like normal, nobody questions it or looks down upon it."

"But looking at porn, you view women as something that they're not," Gabby said. "It's the way that they're 'supposed' to look and it just makes everyone have these high expectations of people."

"I think it's exhilarating for boys to see a girl they actually know looking porny" on social media, Zoe said. "Guys even seem to enjoy it better than porn when they see girls they recognize or they know in real life—they seem more interested in it. It's like a feeling of power, maybe? Like they think these girls are doing it for them? And a lot of guys now are interested in girls based completely on what they look like on social media," she said. "No one is actually liking anyone for who they are, they're just interested in them for their image or how many likes they have."

They said there was a lot of sharing of nudes in their school. "All the time," said Gabby. "And it always spreads."

"You hear story after story of people taking a picture that was meant for one person and that picture being spread," said Zoe. "It's a drastic amount of people."

"This crazy thing happened in our school," Gabby said. "There was this guy that got hold of all these pictures of girls and made an Instagram account and posted all these girls' nudes"—it was another slut page. "It got flagged and taken down," she added.

I asked them what happened to the boy who posted the account. Did any girls ever confront him about it? Did he ever get called out?

"It's unfortunate," Gabby said, "but something girls have to deal with is we get jealous of each other and feel the need to judge each other. It's much easier to pick on a girl who sent nudes and say, Oh, why did she do that, or, She's a slut, than to stand up to the guy who posted the pictures of her. She seems to be so vulnerable and easy to take advantage of, and no girl wants to be in that position. So girls don't really stand up for each other or themselves as much as they should. We're scared of standing up for girls in general even though we know how that feels and we know how that hurts, and we'd give anything to know someone's standing up for us, but sometimes girls aren't that brave and they don't want to be picked on as well."

"When you see a naked picture of someone in your class," Zoe said, "I know a lot of girls that judge; people who say it's all their fault; but people don't consider how these things are being spread around and how cruel people are actually being to each other. It's bullying; it's sexual assault, almost. It is sexual assault. But no one will say that or act like that's what it is.

"I have a friend, a guy, who has a friend I'm not a fan of," she went on, "and every time a girl's name will come up he'll say, Oh, I have nudes of her. That's the first thing he'll say about a girl."

And how did she respond to that? I asked.

"I don't say anything," Zoe said. "Even though I know I should."

"When guys share these things," or nudes, "there's no shame in it for them," Gabby said. "They don't think about how it could shame a girl or hurt a girl or affect them even in really terrible ways. And nobody blames the guy—they blame the girl for even sharing nudes in the first place. The boy doesn't get blamed for sharing. In our school it happens all the time. It's just so normal now—so guys don't think about these things; they don't even care to question what they're saying or doing."

"Yeah, guys, honestly," Zoe said, "will not even know a girl at all and assume she's a complete slut because she wears short shorts, for instance. Guys don't really consider how much girls actually go through, especially in our teenage years. Guys really aren't aware or thinking about how we as women are being harassed or how often we are being mistreated by guys all over."

"I think girls want to be seen as a great person to guys," Gabby said, "so when a guy calls her a slut or a whore it really hurts them 'cause they feel like it's coming from someone who's important or who they want to impress. Girls just have to realize they're just words—guys don't know what they're saying when they say those things."

I asked if boys ever stood up for girls who were harassed or slut-shamed.

"I've never met a guy who's stood up for any girl who's been in any situation where she's being sexually harassed in any way," Zoe said. "They're almost blind to it; they just assume it's always the girl's issues and for her to deal with."

"I think boys definitely care more about their reputation than they do about saving someone's feelings," Gabby said. "They won't stand up for someone in fear of them being the one who's picked on or who's hurt."

"And it's not just at school," Zoe said, "it's out in the street. I've been catcalled and men are standing there and they say nothing. I'll walk down a busy street and I'll be honked at, I'll be whistled at by random guys—they don't even consider us as human beings, even though in our society we're supposed to be equals. I certainly do not feel like an equal even though in our society we're supposed to be equals. I feel like I am looked down upon in that I can be misused and mistreated in any way, shape, or form. But I definitely feel like I deserve a voice in how I wish to be treated and how unfair it is to be looked down upon because of being a girl."

In 2014, the issue of catcalling became a subject of national concern with the release of a controversial video, "10 Hours of Walking in NYC as a Woman" by Hollaback, an organization dedicated to raising awareness about street harassment. The Hollaback video showed a young woman walking around Manhattan for ten hours as she was catcalled and harassed more than 100 times. The video was widely criticized for showing harassment by mostly men of color—an awful mistake on the part of the organization, which served to distract attention from a widespread problem. In 2014, a national study by the organization Stop Street Harassment found that 65 percent of women said they had experienced some form of street harassment. Fifty-seven percent said they had experienced verbal harassment, and 41 percent said they had experienced physically aggressive forms, such as being groped or followed. Half of all women reported experiencing street harassment by the age of seventeen.

In her book *Bossypants,* Tina Fey wrote that when she was attending a workshop for women as part of her research for writing the movie *Mean Girls,* the women were asked about the moment when "they knew they were a woman," and most said it was when they were harassed on the street. "The group of women was racially and economically diverse," Fey wrote, "but the answers had a very similar theme. Almost everyone first realized they were becoming a grown woman when some dude did something nasty to them. 'I was walking home from ballet and a guy in a car yelled, Lick me!' 'I was babysitting my younger cousins when a guy drove by and yelled, Nice ass.' There were pretty much zero examples like 'I first knew I was a woman when my mother and father took me out to dinner to celebrate my success on the debate team.' It was mostly men yelling shit from cars."

The psychological effects on girls of street harassment can be profound. A 2008 article in the journal *Social Justice Research* reported that "the present research suggests that stranger harassment . . . is a frequent experience for young adult women, and that it has negative implications for their well-being . . . Sexual objectification is a clear component of both sexual harassment and stranger harassment. In both cases, women are treated as objects to be looked at and touched, and not as intelligent human beings."

"I think [street harassment] makes girls hyperaware of their bodies and at an extremely young age," says Kathryn Stamoulis, an adjunct professor of psychology at Hunter College and psychologist in New York who specializes in treating adolescents. "A girl's confronted with this idea that a woman's body is an object or a tool for a man's arousal or amusement; she becomes very conscious of 'how am I appearing to men.' Then her value can get very tied up in that once she starts looking at her body as a means of someone else's pleasure. This is tied to lower self-esteem, anxiety, depression—it's all related to not valuing all the good things a person has to offer and placing all her value on her sexuality or appearance. Teenage girls are already navigating their emerging sexuality with their peers—to then have this unwanted and outside sexuality thrown at them in this one-sided way with street harassment is just really heartbreaking on a lot of levels."

In 2014, girls all over the world started posting on social media about their experience with street harassment, using the hashtags #catcalling, #streetharassment, and #NotJustHello. The sentiment underlying the posts of many girls was echoed in one, from a teenager with the handle @ankestroobs: "To the guys catcalling me: please don't do that to any woman ever again. It made me feel insecure, scared and uncomfortable." Social media was a place where girls could protest street harassment; ironically, it was also a kind of virtual street itself where girls were continually being harassed, without much attention being paid to the possible emotional consequences.

I asked the girls how it was in school—did boys respect them in class?

"A lot of the time boys want to be know-it-alls and act like they have something that should be heard and needs to be listened to more than girls," said Gabby. "If a girl talks up a lot, they want to one-up her."

"I feel as though I have more equal rights *in* the classroom," said Zoe. "Outside the classroom, even boys who will treat you as an equal in the classroom will be disrespectful outside of it."

Gabby said, "Nobody has any idea this is going on."

I asked them if girls in their school ever talked about feminism.

"They do," Zoe said, "but a lot of them won't talk about it too much because there are a lot of guys who disagree with feminists. I know guys who think the definition of feminism is being anti-men, which is not true—it's one hundred percent about equality. We're fighting for equal rights for women, not to have more rights than men. I have a guy friend who said that feminists think it's okay for women to hit men. Where is he getting this stuff? Where do guys get this stuff where they think women want more rights than men?"

"They get it off the Internet," Gabby said. "From like Reddit threads and the meninists," the antifeminist movement. "And I saw this debate online that said, 'Do women have more rights than men?' And eighty percent said yes they do."

They began to laugh.

Chapter Five

17

The Hamptons, New York

It was a house party in the Hamptons; it had taken Sydney a month to convince her mother to let her go. Her mother was so overprotective, she hadn't even let Sydney go down to the lobby of their building by herself until she was thirteen. She was always encouraging Sydney to look hot and cute—she made her dress up as Britney Spears for Halloween one year; she said she thought it would be "cool"—but then she wouldn't let her show off how hot and cute she was by letting her go to parties with kids from school. Sydney had to sneak out. She knew it was wrong. But her mother was such a maniac when it came to watching over her. It was all because Sydney had been cyberbullied in eighth grade. But that was another story.

And so it took a month of coaxing and cajoling to get her mother to say okay. It wasn't like Sydney to whine or demand. She knew how to convince her mother of something. Every girl did, if she was a girl. Her mother liked to hang out with her, so she would do that, to soften her up. They would snuggle in bed together and watch reruns of *Sex and the City* and laugh. Sydney liked Carrie the best, and her mother liked Samantha. Her mother confessed, "That was me," when she was younger. But she told Sydney, Don't be like that; don't be like me. Dating lots of guys, it won't make you happy, she said, looking at Sydney with her worried eyes. "Oh, Mommy, can I just go to the party?" Sydney said, repeating how it was at a very nice girl's house and the parents would be there and they were very rich people, so it was likely to be a nice place and lots of nice kids were going.

It was Sydney's first time on the Hampton Jitney, the bus to Long Island, and all the way she imagined how it would be. There was a boy from another school going, named Tim, who she kind of had her eye on. He seemed nice, he was quiet and calm, and he kind of gave her "the look." All the way out to the Hamptons Sydney ignored Clara and Stacy, who were drinking vodka from a flask and acting like it was so cool. It was Clara's grandfather's flask or something, and she kept acting like that made it special because it was made of silver, but Sydney would never want to drink vodka out of that old thing, and anyway, she didn't like vodka. She didn't like to drink. She didn't like a lot of things her friends liked to do; she just knew she might like this boy named Tim.

Would they talk? Would they kiss? Would they walk along the beach—such a cliché. But it might actually happen. Would he hold her hand? No, that was silly. Nobody held hands. Did they?

When they got to Megan's house, it quickly became clear that her parents were not home and weren't going to be there all weekend. "Oops," said Megan. "Yay!" said Stacy. Megan was drunk, but this was not unusual. There were already about thirty kids there—it was an enormous house on the beach. There was a big porch where people were standing around with red Solo cups in hand and drinking. There were a lot of boys. A lot of attractive boys. Senior boys.

But she didn't see Tim.

Some senior boys were talking about college. "Yo, I'm in early decision at Columbia," Sydney heard one boy say. "Ya, dude, I'm on the waitlist. Fuck, I don't want to go to fucking Duke." "I wanna join"—the first boy said the name of a Columbia fraternity. "It's so sick. When you join you have to show how much you're worth by buying a new Rolex and throwing it in the East River." "Sick!" They laughed.

Sydney looked around for Tim.

Finally she spied him inside by the fireplace, talking to some girl. But that was okay. He didn't know she was there. She'd seen the girl on Facebook. She was just a rando. She had only like 300 followers. Sydney walked past them, pretending to be on her way to the kitchen. She paused beside them, pretending to look at Megan's baby pictures above the fireplace; but she didn't know if Tim had noticed her. He kept on talking to the rando.

In the kitchen there was a boy lying on the floor, having a molly moment, his face all red; he was perspiring and twitching. "I feel like I'm on fire," he told the girls crouched beside him, the type of girls who always take care of boys. "You're gonna be okay," said one of the girls, stroking his hair.

Tim, Tim, Tim.

And then suddenly there he was in the kitchen, getting some ice from the freezer. Sydney felt paralyzed. He was coming over. "Hey," he said. She said, "Hey."

She wasn't exactly sure how it happened, but then suddenly there they were, making out in the kitchen. Just like that, right there. They'd never really had a conversation, just seen each other at parties, just given each other that look. And now here they were, kissing, as if they'd been doing it forever. As if they'd been married for several years and just suddenly saw each other in the kitchen and thought, I have to kiss her, I have to kiss him, this wonderful woman, this man, that I'm married to. It felt so intimate.

A little while later, Sydney saw Tim on the porch making out with the rando. His hands all up in her shirt. Sydney went and sat on the beach and looked at the waves. When she was on her way home from the party on the Jitney the next day, she got a text from Tim. "Yo, I'll get you next time," it said.

Online

"Hooking up" wasn't invented by millennials, or American college kids, or Tinder. It's been a long, lusty road since the 1848 founding of the Oneida Community, the utopian religious commune in Oneida, New York, which practiced "free love." Its founder, John Humphrey Noyes, a socialist preacher credited with coming up with the term, rejected conventional marriages "in which men exerted rights of ownership over women."

The history of free love in America is intertwined with feminism. Some nineteenth-century feminists questioned whether women could ever be free in the context of marriage as it was practiced at the time, when most men had control over their spouses financially and socially, and often were afforded license to physically discipline them. Mary Gove Nichols (1810–1884), a free love advocate, saw traditional marriage as antithetical to women's rights. And so the answer, for some, was intimate relationships outside of marriage, or marriages which allowed for the free choice of other sexual partners. But "free love," for these feminists, was never intended to mean sex without a sense of responsibility or a consideration of consequences. In 1870, Noyes repudiated the term for how it was being misinterpreted to mean, basically, what we now know as "hooking up." "Free Love with us does not mean freedom to love today and leave tomorrow," Noyes wrote.

"He fucked me and left," said a 2015 Yik Yak post in New York.

In 2000, Tom Wolfe wrote that " 'hooking up' was a term known . . . to almost every American child over the age of nine, but to only a relatively small percentage of their parents, who, even if they heard it, thought it was being used in the old sense of 'meeting' someone. Among the children, hooking up was always a sexual experience, but the nature and extent of what they did could vary widely." Today it's understood among kids and virtually everyone else that "hooking up" means having a sexual encounter without any expectation of a relationship. But through all of the hooking up that's been going on in American life for centuries, it was only in the 2000s that the phrase "hookup culture" came into use, concurrent with the spread of social media and online pornography.

"Hookup culture" is not a phrase that's used to describe a blissful state of free love in which men and women enjoy each other sexually in an atmosphere of mutual respect. It's not free love as envisioned by utopians and feminists of the past. The term has acquired a negative connotation, based on reports from young people experiencing hookup culture themselves, as well as many studies of its effects. For years, especially since the mid-2000s, with the emergence of websites and blogs, young women have been voicing their dissatisfaction. ("Really fuckin hate this hookup culture," said a Yik Yak post in New York.) Young women talk about bad sex and a lack of intimacy, about the scarcity of relationships, and the persistent double standard in which women who hook up are judged while men who do the same have scored. When it comes to women's sexuality, we still seem to be locked in a struggle between the Victorian and the modern eras, seeing women as modest or promiscuous, often accommodating no middle ground. ("Guys: liking casual sex doesn't make a girl a slut," said another Yik Yak post.)

In 2013, blogger Mackenzie Newcomb penned a letter to "Mr. Last Weekend," which lambasted a hookup partner who had apparently called her a "slut." "When I was younger I used to think of the word as nothing but a tribute to sexual liberation," Newcomb wrote. "I can tell you this, with the exception of a few nights on vodka that probably weren't in my best interest, I assure you I always hoped that _____ and I would have an arrangement that lasted longer than the next morning . . . I didn't want to feel like something someone could just throw away the next day."

In 2014, Charlotte Lieberman, then a recent Harvard grad, wrote a piece for *Cosmopolitan* in which she relayed an experience with another type of guy often seen in young women's tales of hookup culture—one less openly hostile but passively aggressive in his refusal to commit to even a basic plan. "We were at a party," Lieberman wrote, "when he approached me and said, 'Hey, Charlotte. Maybe we'll cross paths tomorrow night? I'll text you.' I assumed the *maybe* and his general passivity were just ways to avoid feeling insecure about showing interest. After all, we are millennials and old-fashioned courtship no longer exists."

When "Nate" never texted, Lieberman texted him; but he didn't answer. "When I saw him in class," she went on, "he glanced away whenever we made eye contact. The avoidance—and occasional tight-lipped smiles—continued through the fall semester." Eventually Nate told her, she said, that "he just hadn't been interested in dating me. *Wait, who said anything about dating?!* But I didn't have the energy to tell Nate that I was sick of his (and many other guys') assumption that women spend their days plotting to pin down a man and that ignoring me wasn't the kindest way to tell me he didn't want to lead me on. So to avoid seeming *too emotional, crazy,* or any of the related stereotypes commonly pegged on women, I followed Nate's immature lead: I walked away . . . This anecdote sums up a pattern I have experienced, observed, and heard about from almost all my college-age friends."

It could also describe the experience of many high school and middle school girls, who talk about similar dealings with boys—boys who never want to make a definite plan; who seem to be leaving all their options open; and who seem to assume that girls are waiting with bated breath for boys to appear at their door, or at least to text them. "They're so funny," said a seventeen-year-old girl in the Sheep Meadow in Central Park, where she was sitting with a friend. "They'll text you something like"—bro-ish voice—"Hey, maybe if you're around later I *might* be around, or like, *maybe* we can get together."

"Could they just be insecure?" I asked.

"Noooooo," said the girls. "They have like three other girls they're talking to, so they're waiting to see which one will say yes," the first girl said. "Which one will hook up," the second one clarified. "Or, like, do whatever."

"But we see through them," the first girl said. "We know *exactly* what they're doing." "Yeah, but it's still totally annoying," said the second girl, "because if you actually like someone and want to hang out with them, it would be nice to know if they actually like you back, or what."

Lieberman's piece was in part a response to two widely discussed articles, both portraying hookup culture as a boon for female empowerment. In *The Atlantic* in 2012, Hanna Rosin wrote of young women at "an Ivy League business school" who used young men for their sexual pleasure in order to focus on what they really cared about—academic achievement and career advancement. "To put it crudely," said Rosin, "feminist progress right now largely depends on the existence of the hookup culture." Kate Taylor's 2013 piece in *The New York Times* about female undergraduates at the University of Pennsylvania similarly claimed that young women "saw building their résumés, not finding boyfriends (never mind husbands), as their main job at Penn . . . In this context, some women . . . seized the opportunity to have sex without relationships, preferring 'hookup buddies' (regular sexual partners with little emotional commitment) to boyfriends."

This vision of empowered women as sexually efficient Amazons has been circulating in popular culture at least since the 1930s, as in *Female*—a steamy, pre-Code 1933 film in which Ruth Chatterton plays the hard-charging boss of a car company who uses men as sexual playthings. It's a long-standing female stereotype, as well as a sexual fantasy, that of the shallow, powerful woman bent on material gain, a woman who is able to enjoy copious amounts of casual sex without any need or desire for an emotional connection, much less a relationship. It's also a type of dominating woman found in "businesswoman porn."

By contrast, a 2013 feature by Raisa Bruner in the *Yale Daily News* told of the SWUG, or the "Senior Washed-Up Girl," a sad figure on campus, a veteran of four years of campus hookup culture, who now faced "the slow, wine-filled decline of female sexual empowerment as we live out our college glory days. Welcome to the world of the ladies who have given up on boys because they don't so much empower as frustrate, satisfy as agitate."

In 2011, Lisa Wade, a professor of sociology at Occidental College who specializes in gender studies, gave a lecture about a study she had conducted on the attitudes of college students toward hookup culture; many young women in the study reported that hooking up left them feeling emotionally taxed rather than empowered. "Many of the women in our sample, specifically, felt that they had inherited a right to express their sexuality from the women's movement of the sixties and seventies," Wade said. "So they embraced sex . . . and the right to say 'yes' to sex. They saw college as an opportunity to enact their liberation. And it was going to be glorious . . . But many of our female respondents felt disempowered instead of empowered by sexual encounters. They didn't feel like equals on the sexual playground, more like jungle gyms."

Does hookup culture privilege men and boys? Many girls and young women seem to think so. "When it comes to college dating today, guys seem to be in a position of power, calling the shots on sex and romance," Lieberman wrote. "My friends on other campuses around the country, especially ones where women outnumber men, agree that guys seem to hold the dating power. And even the brightest, most ambitious college women are permitting them to dominate the sexual culture."

"For young women the problem in navigating sexuality and relationships is still gender inequality," says Elizabeth Armstrong, the University of Michigan sociology professor. "Young women complain that young men still have the power to decide when something is going to be serious and when something is not—they can go, She's girlfriend material, she's hookup material . . . There's still this pervasive double standard."

"It's such a game, and you have to always be doing everything right, and if not, you risk losing whoever you're hooking up with," said Fallon, a Boston College undergraduate, one night in New York, where she was working at a summer internship. By "doing everything right" she said she meant "not texting back too soon; never double texting; liking the right amount of his stuff" on social media.

"And it reaches a point where," said her friend Jane, "if you receive a text message" from a guy, "you forward the message to, like, seven different people: What do I say back? Oh my God, he just texted me! It becomes a surprise. He *texted* me! Which is really sad . . . We call it 'text by committee,'" she added.

"If he texts you before midnight, he actually likes you as a person. If it's after midnight, it's just for your body," said Amanda, another Boston College undergrad. It was not, she said, that young women didn't want to have sex. "Who doesn't want to have *sex*? But it feels bad when they're like, *See ya.*"

"It seems like the girls don't have any control over the situation, and it should not be like that at all," Fallon said. Girls talk about how boys say they want "no label" on their relationships, and no commitment.

The double standard in hookup culture is also apparent when it comes to orgasms. A 2013 study by researchers at the Kinsey Institute and Binghamton University found that women were twice as likely to have orgasms in the context of serious relationships than in casual encounters. A survey conducted by sociologist Paula England of New York University, involving more than 20,000 students at twenty-one colleges over more than five years, found that about 30 percent of women had an orgasm during their last hookup with intercourse in contrast to more than 60 percent of men; nearly 60 percent of women in the survey reported having an orgasm the last time they had sex in a committed relationship. Complaints about the elusiveness of orgasms are almost a genre on Yik Yak in New York. "Nobody has ever given me an orgasm," said one post. "The only person that can really get me off is me." "Same," someone commented, with an emoji of a crying face.

According to some young women, young men in hookup culture

often don't pay much attention to their physical needs; and this may be because, as one young man frankly put it, "We don't know the girls." Apparently, though, many young men are willing to receive oral sex from women they barely know. A 2012 review of research on hookup culture in the *Review of General Psychology* reported on a study which found that in 55 percent of first-time hookups, only men received oral sex, while just 19 percent of such encounters saw women enjoying the same privilege.

And it may also be that both young men and young women are taking their cues from porn. In the most popular online porn, women are most often seen serving men's needs, rather than the other way around; there are a lot of blowjobs; and the act of intercourse is, again, often an exercise in "pounding," from which the women have noisy orgasms, in contrast to many women's actual experience.

"When you have sex with a guy, they want it to be like a porno," says a nineteen-year-old girl in New York. "They want anal and oral right away. Oral is, like, the new kissing." "The cum shot in the face is a big thing," said another New York girl, age seventeen. One young woman described sex that feels like "running through a mash-up of porn videos."

"Boys call having sex with a girl the most disgusting things, like 'hit it and quit it,' 'pump and dump,' 'fuck and chuck,'" said an L.A. girl, age nineteen. "'Smash and dash.' That says it all right there." (Interestingly, "pump and dump" is also the name unethical stockbrokers use for the practice of defrauding investors with cheap stocks with falsely inflated prices; the stockbrokers in the scam reap profits, while the investors lose their money. Early in his career, Jordan "The Wolf of Wall Street" Belfort was a notorious pump-and-dumper.)

"I think a lot of being able to climax during sex has to do with your own self-confidence," says Paige, an undergraduate at the University of Delaware, "and so oftentimes you can be completely unaware of it, but you're keeping yourself from letting go and experiencing that situation. Also, like . . . couples aren't exactly the norm anymore, and I mean, how are you going to have such an intimate experience with some random person?"

Some girls and young women say their anxiety about sexual and emotional intimacy also comes from having grown up communicating on social media, so "we don't know how to talk to each other face-to-face." Some say they don't always know how to voice their desires to their sex partners, with whom they may have communicated mainly through messaging and texting. "You form your first impression based off Facebook rather than forming a connection with someone, so you're, like, forming your connection with their profile," said Stephanie, a Boston College undergraduate. "You find yourself, like, naked with someone you mainly know from social media."

Young men say they sometimes feel let down in hookups, too, disappointment often related to how sex in real life doesn't compare to the easy gratification of masturbating to porn. Reports of a curious increase in erectile dysfunction among young American men have been attributed to porn consumption, among other things, including chemicals in processed foods and the lack of intimacy in hookup sex. Ben, a student at an Ivy League school, when asked what he attributed it to, texted: "The phenomenon of the disappearing boner is purely a result of excessive porn use. It's a much talked about thing at [his school]. Essentially you can cherry pick the most arousing stuff online whenever you want every day. Like if you ran on ten cups of coffee a day forever and one day you only drank two cups—analogous to the arousal from random non-intimate sex with a real person who is not a porn star, who is literally designed by a surgeon to trigger arousal cues—even though it's still coffee it's not that stimulating in comparison. Just an overflow of easily accessible mega stimulation that sets the 'what gives you a boner' bar absurdly high."

The question of why some young women are tolerating bad sex, sex that privileges men, may have some ominous answers. Lisa Wade said in her lecture, "Many of our female students recalled consenting to sexual activity they did not desire because they felt it was their only option, even in the absence of physical coercion, threats, or incapacitation . . . Options such as saying no, asking him to masturbate, leaving the situation, or abandoning the friendship or relationship did not seem to occur to them. It was almost as if they felt that it was the natural order of things . . . like water flowed downhill, women must release men's sexual tension. Ironically, then, women were engaging in sex because they felt that the playing field was even, but it was not." One study mentioned in the *Review of General Psychology* survey reported that "78 percent of individuals overestimated others' comfort with many different sexual behaviors, with men particularly overestimating women's actual comfort with a variety of sexual behaviors in hookups." And, another study in the survey said, "not all hookup encounters are necessarily wanted or consensual. Individuals occasionally consent to engage in a sexual act but do not necessarily want sex.

Hookup culture is often heard described by girls and young women as "a contest to see who can care less." "And guys win a lot at caring less," says Amanda, the Boston College student. But it would seem a hollow victory. According to studies, men as well as women experience negative feelings about their casual encounters, from anxiety to depression to regret, with women having possibly more thoughts of worry and vulnerability than men, one study said." Eighty-three percent of college-age women and 63 percent of college-age men in another study said that they would prefer to be in a traditional romantic relationship. So what are the factors behind the alienation of hookup culture? Gender inequality? Technology? Porn?

"I'd love to be able to just, like, text a boy and be like, Yo, I like you, you like me, let's get together and hang out and do stuff," said Marina, a seventeen-year-old girl in New York. "But that does not work with boys. It. Does. Not. Work. 'Cause then they think they have the power, and that's what it's all about—who's got the power."

Of course, not every girl experiences hookup culture as a power imbalance, and there are young women who love hookup sex and do find it empowering. It's not that uncommon to hear young women say they can "fuck like a guy" and not care about having any kind of emotional intimacy. But that very formulation—"fuck like a guy"—suggests having sex in a way that is coded as hypermasculine, unfeeling, with no respect or regard for the other person in the encounter. It's seen as hypersexualized behavior on the part of women, but it's also a kind of hypermasculinity dressed up in a porn-star package. Girls and women objectifying boys and men feels like mirroring behavior, reflecting misogyny.

"I think it got old to be hurt," said Maya, a nineteen-year-old girl in New York. "It got old to be the victim. For girls, it's not getting us anywhere. It's not building our case. It's not getting us any more respect. So it's like, if you can't beat 'em, join 'em."

New York, New York

Sydney had a weekend job at a clothing store on Broadway. It was one of those big busy chain stores with loud techno music and bright fluorescent lights. Her job was to go around and fold things that had been unfolded and replace items that had been tried on but not been purchased. She worked silently and efficiently, keeping her head down. She was wearing a crop top and booty shorts.

She had on a lot of lipstick and eyeliner, which made her look older than seventeen. A male shopper, a guy in his thirties, stopped her to ask a question while she was working. He seemed to be flirting with her. Sydney shook her head at something he said and went in the back of the store. He left.

As we were walking together to the Popover Café on Amsterdam Avenue after she was done with work, I asked her what the guy had said. "Oh," she said with a shrug, "we get hit on all day. The girls they hire are really attractive and they make us dress like this." She indicated her attire. "When they hired me, they said, 'Dress for the hot weather'—which we know means, like, wear nothing. The guys in the store don't have to," she added.

She was a white girl, blond and attractive, as she said. She lived on the Upper West Side and went to a public school. She'd been a private school student until the year before, when her parents stopped being able to afford her tuition. Her father had been a top executive in a major corporation until he was laid off in the financial meltdown of 2008. When she changed schools, she said, she was faced with the problem of having to decide what to wear every day. At private school, she'd had a uniform.

"And I couldn't believe what the girls wore," she said, meaning at her new school. "They dress like sluts. They wear, like, tube tops, bandeaux, and those high-waisted short shorts that show all your butt cheeks—excuse me, you're not at the beach. But if you don't dress like that you're considered weird, and you will get shunned. My mom sees me go out like this for school and she asks me like, What are you doing? To someone who isn't in your shoes, it's hard to understand."

We sat down in the restaurant and ordered lunch. Sydney asked for a popover with strawberry butter.

I asked her why she thought this particular clothing style had come into vogue. "Everything on TV and websites tells you to look like this," she said. "Like they say this is how to get a guy. I feel like it makes girls hate each other, to be honest," she said. "Like girls aren't companions to each other anymore—everything is a competition. I think social media makes it worse.

"Everything is based off looks," she said, "and how many likes you get. So like a lot of girls post pictures with literally nothing on, or bikini shots. They do way too many selfies, and it's like, You need to stop. Girls see that and then they want to compete for more likes and hotter pictures. Guys see that and then guys judge girls so much by the kind of photos they have up. Like on Ask.fm they say your name and ask, like, 'smash or pass' "—an intensification of hot or not, "smash or pass" asks whether or not someone wants to have sex with you. "And boys answer, 'smash' or 'pass,' " Sydney said. "It makes you feel awful. I hate it."

Did she think it affected how boys and girls acted toward each other when they dated? I asked.

"There's no such thing as dating anymore," Sydney said. "I watch really cute, like, high school movies and we don't have that. It's so sad. Like I wonder, What's it like to go on a date?" She seemed to actually be asking. "There are couples," she said, "but the way they get together is they hook up at a party and he'll ask for her number. They make out and then it goes from there."

So the first contact they have is making out? I asked.

"Yeah," she said. "It all starts with hooking up. There are a lot of parties. Kids pretty much just go crazy at other people's houses when their parents aren't there. And sometimes somebody will rent out a space and get a DJ. People hook up with more than one person; the guys try to hook up with as many girls as possible."

At one party? I asked.

She said, "Yeah. The boys have lists and stuff. This kid in my grade has this list of ninety-two girls he's hooked up with."

I asked if that ever seemed awkward, hooking up with more than one person at the same event.

"It's like dark and there are a hundred kids there," Sydney said, "so it's not considered a big deal. Hooking up is just making out. But it's not like they know each other. The 'in' thing for girls to do is to really just go nuts at parties, just go insane. They feel like the more they drink and the crazier they act, the more guys will come to them; but no, they're just gonna abuse you."

Crazy how? I asked.

"Dancing around, flashing their boobs. They just want the attention, to have everyone's eyes on them. I don't go to a lot of parties, but you're considered uncool if you don't go to parties like that," she said.

"The big thing is theme parties. Like Pimps and Hos, Executives and Whores, or Business Slutty. The guys dress up in suits and the girls wear, like, nothing." At a later interview, when these parties came up again, Sydney said she attributed their surge in popularity to *The Wolf of Wall Street*. "That movie is every guy's favorite movie right now 'cause they treat girls like prostitutes," she said. At one point in the Martin Scorsese film, about the rise and fall of hard-partying '80s stockbroker Jordan Belfort, Belfort crows that with money, you can buy "better pussy." "All the boys are saying it's so amazing," Sydney said, "'cause there's so much nudity and the guys all rule and the women are just there to serve them. They all want to live like a billionaire, surrounded by beautiful naked women."

Why did girls agree to dress up like hos? I asked.

"Boys think it's hot. Some girls just do whatever they think boys want," she said. "Boys text them like, Come over, and girls will come over because if they don't the boys will call them a prude. And if you complain about it, you're a feminist and all the guys will run away from you. They'll say you're crazy." What was wrong with being a feminist? "They make fun of feminists in TV shows and movies," she said, "like in *Legally Blonde,* the feminist girl is an annoying lesbian. They make feminists look crazy, like they're so against men and angry.

"There *are* feminist girls," Sydney said. "They express themselves, they stick up for themselves, and they, like, put feminist things on social media. But a lot of girls don't do that and I admit I'm one of them. 'Cause if you do, guys will say, You're PMS-ing. They're so cocky. They think they're so much better than us and smarter than us. But they're not. They're always at each other's houses doing nothing and smoking weed. They smoke weed before school. They have these crews with gangster names. It's ridiculous. They'll text you like, Heyyyyy. What are you doing tonight? What are you doing later? That means they want to hook up with you. They act so nonchalant."

I asked her if kids she knew were having sex.

She said, "No. A lot of people I know haven't done that yet. That's when you have a boyfriend, you do that. Some girls do, but they wait until they actually like someone."

What did girls do when they liked someone? I asked. How did couples become girlfriend and boyfriend?

"People stalk each other on Facebook," Sydney said. "Some kids talk online. But some boys are talking to like twenty other girls. That's happened to me before. It sucks. It's so gross, just grimy. You go on Facebook and you see that a guy is flirting with another girl like she's his girlfriend. I know a lot of people who have gone through that. I don't know if it's considered 'cheating,' 'cause it's just online, but you're leading the other person on; you're being mean.

"It totally affects me," Sydney said. "I have trust issues. I don't trust people very easily."

She said that she had been cyberbullied in sixth grade. It had happened on a social media site for little kids. "It was this thing where you create a profile of a cartoon character," she said, "and this stranger started talking to me and saying really creepy things. I didn't know who it was at first. It turned out it was one of the girls at my school," a Manhattan private school. "She was saying, like, all this sexual stuff. I don't even know how she learned how to talk that way. I was eleven years old and I didn't know how to respond. And then she and her friends took screenshots [of the conversations] and spread them around and started calling me a slut.

"I was completely traumatized," Sydney said. "I had to switch schools." She went to another private school then. "I became insanely insecure." But nothing ever happened to the girls who bullied her. "I begged my mom not to bring the school into it. I didn't want to be that girl that tattletaled."

And then a few years later, she said, she saw her bulliers on Facebook. "They kept stalking me and I was curious, so I friended them back." That's when she found out that these girls had become "famous."

"In New York every kid knows each other, and some kids are famous," she explained. "Everyone's obsessed with the feeling they have fame. They post pictures of themselves at certain parties. They friend certain kids. There's so much social climbing. A lot of kids are friends with certain kids who could help benefit them in some way, especially on the Upper East Side. Even at my school, there's like the certain crowd that I do not want to be a part of, but if you're not a part of it, you're nobody."

She spoke of a girl who had social-climbed by liking "famous" kids' pictures on social media. "She liked her way to the top. She started getting invited to parties and then posted pictures of herself at the parties and now she's completely changed; she dresses so differently now— she dressed normal before and now she dresses so provocatively. She posted bikini pictures on Instagram and got like ninety-two followers in one day; it was mostly guys. She posted her fake ID to show that she likes to party and now she likes to get completely wasted." Now this girl, who had been her friend, was friends with the girls who used to bully her, she said.

Her former bulliers were now two of the most visible girls in the Manhattan high school scene. They were the type of girls who "go clubbing with twenty-one-year-olds" and get invited to "events." On her phone, Sydney pulled up the girls' Facebook accounts, where they had posted pictures of themselves partying in nightclubs and posing, hand on hip, Paris Hilton–style, surrounded by Euro-looking men. These pictures got a lot of likes.

"They think they're like the Kardashians," Sydney said. "They promote themselves on social media and try and get endorsements.

"Girls like this, they wanna live too fast, and they experience way too much in way too little time," she said. "They put everything on Facebook and Instagram 'cause if they show more things they're doing it looks cooler." She said the names of some of the "famous" girls and guys "who do, like, insane amounts of drugs and stuff 'cause they have the money for it. The kids who have more money do more insane stuff 'cause they have the ability to and then they bring their friends into it.

"In Manhattan, there's so much wealth, there's so much one percent," Sydney said. "It's all around you and you're constantly being reminded that you don't have things these other kids have. On social media, too. On Tumblr there's 'The Rich Kids of Instagram,' which is these kids trying to show off their wealth, and it's so not okay, it's revolting, but it still makes me feel bad about myself—kind of like I'm not part of it." She said it gave her FOMO.

The smug-faced teens of "The Rich Kids of Instagram," a notorious Tumblr blog, had been widely mocked for posting over-the-top images of themselves reclining on private planes and posing beside luxury cars, holding up credit card receipts from five-figure shopping trips and popping bottles of Champagne on yachts. And yet the blog spawned an E! reality TV series, *#RichKids of Beverly Hills,* and a novel, *Rich Kids of Instagram: A Novel.* "I've taken so many [fucking, bleeped out] selfies on my cell phone today, it's like embarrassing," a *#RichKids of Beverly Hills* cast member says in the first minute of the first episode of the show. As vulgar and silly as these characters may seem, their material display is not so different from the rich celebrities of Instagram who advertise their wealth in very similar ways. Kim Kardashian posts pictures of herself on shopping sprees, on yachts and private planes.

"I heard about this girl who webcams to get money to buy clothes," Sydney said, grimacing.

"I hate high school so much."

New York, New York

I met Sydney's mother, Anne, one day for brunch in the East Village. She came into the restaurant, an unassuming place, wearing a cape and four-inch heels. She carried a significant handbag. She wanted some reassurance, she said, that I wasn't going to identify Sydney in my book. I assured her I wouldn't. "You have to understand," said Anne. "These girls can make your daughter's life *hell*." Her eyes, so like Sydney's, still looked haunted by Sydney's experience with bullying.

"I blame *Gossip Girl*," Anne said. "When we were kids we weren't *innocent*, but we weren't that mean. Were we?

"I blame MTV," she said. "That's when kids started seeing things they shouldn't see on television. I walked out of *Kill Bill*. I couldn't take the violence. There were people in the movie theater with their kids, and as I walked out I said, 'How can you take your children to watch this?' I said it out loud. I did.

"Read *A Clockwork Orange*," she said. "It's all there, what's happening with kids today." Anthony Burgess's 1962 novel famously depicts a dystopian future in which marauding gangs of teens engage in "ultra-violence" and rape. "He predicted it—it's all sex and violence," Anne said. "When it's all sex and violence, there can't be any childhood." Interestingly, Burgess repudiated Stanley Kubrick's 1971 film version of his book, saying that it "seemed to glorify sex and violence."

"*We* dressed sexy," said Anne. "But not when we were *eleven*. And now you see parents putting their daughters in these tiny little microminis. In *thongs*. What the hell are they thinking? It's like child porn.

"*We* wore tight jeans and halter tops," she said. "We were all trying to look 'foxy,' remember? We had to lie down on the bed to get our pants to zip up. We knew what we were doing. We wore tube tops.

"We did drugs," she went on. "I think we did more drugs than kids do now. We had *sex*. I ran away with an older guy. I met him at a concert. I came *back*, but I was gone for weeks. We hooked up. I think we *invented* hooking up. We did gender-bending things. David Bowie was my god. But it was different. Wasn't it? Why does it feel like it was different? Why does it feel like everything is going to *hell*?

"Are we just getting old?" Anne asked, blinking her startled blue eyes. "Have things always been this *corrupt*?

"Sydney went to the Hamptons one weekend," she said. "The stories that she came back with are so appalling. It was a house party. There weren't enough beds. So the boys made the girls who wouldn't sleep with them sleep on the floor. Chivalry is dead! The trust-fund-Wall-Street-entitled class are a bunch of monsters. There's no feminism anymore—men treat all women like whores, and the girls are all willing sluts that will do anything to get something from these mon-sters. It's very frightening."

Boca Raton, Florida

"Being a parent of a teenager today, it's hard to advise them," Debby said. "We didn't grow up with social media, so we can't understand what they're experiencing. It's easy to tell them how to pick a college and things like that, but we didn't have this constant barrage of stuff, so it's hard to know how to navigate it. So we're doing it together."

Debby and her daughter, Billie, were having coffee at the Starbucks in the Glades Plaza in Boca one hot bright afternoon. Debby was in her forties, Billie was seventeen. They were white, with matching cascades of curly brown hair and big brown eyes. Debby wore jeans and a silky top, Billie wore a sundress and flats. Debby was a stay-at-home mom, she said, and Billie's father was a sales manager.

"What I see in teenagers now is they advertise what they're doing all the time," Debby said, "and it can cause a lot of hurt feelings." She told of how, before a homecoming dance, some of Billie's friends had gone shopping for dresses together and posted the pictures on Insta-gram. "And Billie was like, They didn't even ask me. It's so devastat-ing," Debby said. "Before, you might not have even known that they went, but now everyone posts everything so you so have a thousand more ways to get hurt."

"It's okay," Billie said quietly. "I had my dress already."

Billie went to a public school, a magnet school for high achievers.

"Her friends are in all the AP classes," Debby said proudly. "They're the nerdy girls."

"Yeah, we're the nerds," Billie said with a laugh.

"They don't go to parties," Debby said. "So we haven't had any prob-lem with drinking or drugs. We are very close and she knows that I support her no matter what. We've talked about this many times—I say, I know you're a teenager and you're gonna make some stupid mistakes. But you don't have to hide it from me. I would rather know about it and help you than punish you."

"Most moms don't know what's going on," Billie said. "I'm glad that you're cool with it and I can come to you," she told her mom. She sounded sincere.

"She has girls at her high school that post pictures of themselves smoking pot out of a bong online," Debby said. "And I'm like, Are you kidding me? Where are their parents? They have these rave parties and the girls wear booty shorts and a bra; they're all but naked. And they have no bones about sharing what they're doing—they put it all out there."

"They think it's cool," Billie said with a shrug. "They get like two hundred likes." She said there were girls in her school who posted provocative pictures and sent nudes to boys. "And the boys screenshot them and send them around."

"She would never do that," said her mom.

Billie told the story of a girl, "a very popular girl," who, in the eighth grade, was photographed "sucking a guy's dick. The guy's friend took it. She was kneeling in the grass in this guy's backyard. It was so bad. You could see her but not him. Someone posted it on Facebook and people shared it—mostly boys. Everyone was talking about it. The whole town knew."

"Awful," said Debby.

"People post, like, bikini pics, beach pics, gym pics," Billie said. "It's Florida, so there's a lot of skin exposed all the time, and there's always an excuse for girls to show off their bodies. That's when they get the most attention from boys, when they get the most likes. They're trying to feel like they're worthy."

"Well, you have done that before," Debby said gently, "when you felt—"

"But I was in a group with friends," Billie countered quickly. "It was not anything sexual."

Debby said, "But like when you were on the catamaran with Laurie—"

"That was *different*," Billie said firmly. "I've never done a sink shot or anything like that. Sometimes you're just in a bikini and your friends just take a picture."

She said that girls in her school revered "Kendall and Kylie" for their social media fame. "Everyone loves them and follows them because they don't have a normal life—they don't go to school, they travel and model. They made an empire."

"It's really sad," Debby said. "Posting pictures all the time. What kind of life is that?"

"I do post pictures," Billie said, "but it's like me and my friends at academic awards ceremonies."

Debby said that she attributed Billie's critical perspective on social media to the fact that she hadn't gotten an iPhone until she was sixteen. "Kids are getting them at *six*," Debby said. "I always thought it was ridiculous to buy such an expensive phone for a young person. But then I started to feel bad because that's how they socialize, so if she didn't have one it would be like not having a social life. I didn't want her to feel isolated and left out."

"You have to have an iPhone," Billie said. "It's like Apple has a monopoly on adolescence."

With some ups and downs in its sales to teens since 2007, Apple has remained on top, still the number one provider of smartphones to kids. In the fall of 2015, 67 percent of teenagers owned iPhones, and 74 percent said the next smartphone they purchased would be an iPhone, according to the investment bank Piper Jaffray's biannual "Taking Stock with Teens" report. Has there ever been another brand that so infiltrated the tastes and habits and buying aspirations of the young? Apple has a stronger hold on teenagers than Studebaker or Clearasil or even Nike ever had, and a more profound influence in their lives. It would seem to follow that the company has a responsibility to assess the impact its products are having on the lives of teens, especially girls.

Soon after she got her phone, Billie said, she saw her first dick pic. "It was on a Snapchat Story. There are dick pics everywhere."

"I didn't even know what a dick looked like at that age," Debby said.

"Boys think it's hot to show their dicks," Billie said.

"I don't think it only happens to teenagers," said Debby, with a confidential tone. "I have a lot of friends who are getting divorced and are single right now, and they are on Plenty of Fish and Tinder and all those things," meaning dating apps, "and you could not believe the things men are sending them. It's a whole new world out there."

Billie said, "Dick pics are degrading."

I asked her what dating was like in her school.

"People post pictures of their relationship to get likes and show off," she said. "They post pictures on Instagram of each other making out and going out to fancy dinners in Miami."

"And lying in a bed together and putting their hands in each other's pants," her mother said. "They're sixteen years old and they're grabbing each other's crotches! Where are these parents? What room and what bed are they lying in?"

"They have sex here at like thirteen," Billie said. "They do everything, so it's not a big deal for them to be posting pictures of them lying in bed together."

She said it was common for boys to ask for nudes on text or to say, "Kik me," meaning go on Kik Messenger to exchange nudes. "They're horny," she said; "frankly, they're just horny."

"And when the girls post sexy pictures they reward them by telling them 'hawt,'" Debby said with a frown.

"Like, Your body's perfect," said Billie. "Damn, boobs. Those tits. Dat ass. Or they say, You're beautiful, with a heart [emoji]. Sometimes girls just fall for it.

"I guess I am a feminist, sort of," Billie said tentatively. "Okay, I am a feminist. I don't want to be anyone's property. I don't like seeing guys rub their groin on people—it looks like they own that person. They grind up next to girls at parties. It's a grindfest. It makes me so uncomfortable. Some girls are willing. I wouldn't ever let them. So they don't come up to me and try it. I guess I'm not approachable."

"She puts up a vibe, like keep your distance," her mother said approvingly.

"You have to earn my respect," Billie said. "But sometimes I feel like I can't be . . ." Her voice trailed off. "I feel like the guys don't like me," she said after a moment.

"Because you don't fit into these categories!" her mother exclaimed.

"I guess," Billie said.

"This is what I tell her," said her mother. "When the right one comes, he's gonna love her and never let her go."

Billie smiled; but she didn't look convinced.

"A boy started texting her," Debby said. "He'd followed her on Facebook and he told her, 'You're so pretty, I want to take you out.' So they started texting, and then all of a sudden he started asking her the most inappropriate questions."

"They were things you wouldn't ask someone in person," Billie said. "What's funny is I think he thought that's what he was supposed to do. Like he actually thought that was how he would make me like him."

In his profile picture on Facebook, he appeared to be an average-looking white boy, a year older than Billie, age eighteen. He wore a baseball cap. He looked like any number of boys you might see in any number of high school cafeterias.

Their texting started innocently enough.

"Hey, what's up?" he wrote.

"Nothing much, what about you?" she replied.

"Just chilling in art class."

"I have English."

"Honors?"

"AP."

The boy seemed impressed. "Oh shit haha," he responded.

"What do you want to do tonight?" he asked.

"Don't you have homework?" she replied.

"No."

"It's a weeknight."

"So."

"Lucky. I wish that could be me," Billie said, meaning she had homework to do. "Can I be you?"

"You can have me," said the boy.

Debby exclaimed, "And they've never even met!"

"I thought we were just going to get to know each other," Billie said. She said she had never sexted.

After that, she didn't respond to him for a while.

"What?" the boy texted repeatedly. "What?"

After a few days, they started talking again. Billie said, "I gave him another chance. I guess I thought like maybe it was a mistake, a one-time thing," meaning his forward comment.

So they started talking about Billie's gym routine. The boy seemed very interested in Billie's athleticism. "I work out a lot," she said, "and he kept asking, Do you have a six-pack? And I said, No, I'm just fit and strong. But he just kept asking about it. And so I said, Why do you want to know? Do *you* have a six-pack? And he said, No, I'm really skinny."

"Oh my god I'm just skinny you could probably beat me up," he wrote.

She didn't answer that.

Later he asked, "What are you doing now?"

She didn't answer that, either.

"What's the furthest you've been?" the boy suddenly asked.

"I don't want to talk about that," Billie replied.

"I'll tell you if you tell me," texted the boy. "Can I ask if you're still a virgin?"

Billie didn't answer.

"We can still chill tonight?" he asked her.

Billie wrote him. "You're making me uncomfortable. I'm sorry but I'm not into hanging out anymore."

"What are you serious?" wrote the boy.

Billie didn't answer him.

"I'm sorry for asking," the boy said. "I'm sorry it made you uncomfortable."

"That's okay," Billie answered, "but that doesn't make me feel any more comfortable."

"So there's no way to hang out?" he said. "How can I make you feel more comfortable?"

When she didn't respond, the boy went on: "I'm not the guy you think I am. I've barely done anything with a girl and that's why I asked you because I didn't want you to get disappointed with me. I haven't done anything with girls! I'm not experienced like other guys. If you still feel uncomfortable I understand but I really want a gf," a girlfriend, "and I think you would be the perfect one." Here he added a string of heart emojis. "Please give me a chance. Why can't we hang out?"

"No," Billie wrote.

"But he kept pressuring her," Debby said. "Why *did* you ever talk to him again?" she asked Billie.

"I don't know," Billie said. "I guess I felt bad."

She had never had a boyfriend before, she said; she'd never had a texting relationship, either.

"I told him, I don't want to rush into anything," she said. "I said, Let's get to know each other first. I finally said, Okay, I'll meet you in a public place, so he couldn't, like, advance on me."

"When do we chill?" he asked her.

"Over the weekend," she said.

"What about today?"

She told him the weekend was better.

"Will you cancel?" he asked.

"Only if you act disrespectful," she answered.

"I won't baby."

"He called me 'baby,'" Billie said with a frown.

"And he never had met her in person!" Debby pointed out again.

The boy kept on texting, asking Billie when they could "chill." Billie evaded the question. She told him, "I have a lot of homework to do and I'm taking my grandma to lunch and to a movie."

"Are you with your grandma?" he asked later that day. She didn't answer.

The next day he wrote, "What are you doing?"

"I have to volunteer later at a home for adults with disabilities," Billie said.

"Do you have a Snapchat then?" the boy asked, possibly looking for an exchange of nudes.

Billie said, "I blocked him."

"This is my opinion," Debby said. "We didn't have access to porn. Now the guys all watch porn, so they have this very unrealistic expectation of how they're supposed to behave and what they're supposed to get out of it. And there are plenty of girls who will give them just what they want."

Livingston, New Jersey

"I guarantee you," Teresa said, "any girl who doesn't get a lot of guys *wishes* she could."

We were sitting in her car in the parking lot of the Starbucks where the kids in her school hung out in the afternoon. Livingston is an afflu-ent town of around 30,000 people, about an hour and a half from Manhattan. The Starbucks parking lot was full of Mercedes and Range Rovers belonging to kids in Teresa's class. Her car was a BMW, which she said her father had bought for her as a congratulatory gift when she lost twenty-five pounds. "His whole attitude toward me changed," Teresa said. "He didn't look at me like I was pathetic anymore."

She was sipping her drink, a Venti iced skinny hazelnut macchiato with sugar-free syrup. She was smoking a Marlboro Gold and blowing the smoke out the window. She was wearing a pair of Dolce & Gabbana sunglasses. Her lip gloss shimmered.

"And I guarantee you," she went on, "every girl wishes she could get three hundred likes on her pictures. Because that means you're the girl everybody wants to fuck. And everybody wants to be the girl everybody wants to fuck.

"Every girl who isn't that girl secretly hates herself," Teresa said. "I know because I used to be that girl. On Facebook they called me horrible names. I had to delete my account for a while. But I have no sympathy for fatties," she went on. "Just get your fat ass in the gym and work out. It's not that hard."

I asked her if she thought it was sexist that so much emphasis was placed on girls and women being hot. "No," she said. "That's what people who are jealous say. It's healthy to be thin. It's empower-ing to be hot. Being hot makes you feel fucking amazing. Anybody who isn't hot is just fucking jealous. Did you see 'Dear Fat People'? That Nicole Arbour video? I fucking loved it. She said what everybody really thinks."

In 2015, Arbour, a Canadian comedian and YouTuber, drew criti-cism for her "Dear Fat People" video in which she mocked overweight people, claiming fat-shaming is "not a thing." "Fat people made that up," said Arbour, a thin white blonde. "That's the race card with no race." She spoke of encountering an "obese" family in an airport who "smelled like sausages" and had "Crisco [coming] out of their pores like a fucking Play-Doh Fun Factory." The video has been viewed nearly 8.5 million times on YouTube.

In a video response, Whitney Way Thore, star of the TLC show *My*

Big Fat Fabulous Life, retorted, "Fat-shaming *is* a thing; it's a really big thing, no pun intended. It is the really nasty spawn of a larger parent problem called body-shaming, which I'm fairly certain everyone on the planet, especially women, has experienced." But Arbour refused to take her video down, saying of her critics, "What they are saying is a ridiculous outrage to a comedy video that has a bit too much truth in the jokes for their personal taste."

"Being hot gets you everything," Teresa went on. "You'd be amazed how many things I got when I turned into this."

Like what things? I asked.

"Like people not looking at me like I was disgusting anymore," she said. "Like people looking at me like I was giving them a boner." She laughed. "Like every time me and my girls go out, we get free drinks. Guys just *buy* us stuff."

She said that she had slept with five guys in the last year since her transformation. "And I don't regret a single one. Girls who judge me should just stop judging other girls for having fun and for doing what they want. Like, You're just fucked-up about sex. Get over it. Or better yet, Get laid and chill.

"When I'm ready for a relationship, I'll have one," Teresa said. "Right now I'm just having fun. And there's nothing wrong with that. I'm a teenager. These are my ho years."

I asked her if the guys she slept with treated her with respect. "You should ask me how I treat *them*," she said. "I play them before they play me."

She showed me her phone, tapping and scrolling through texts. She showed me some conversations in which she was sexting with boys. "I can fuck any one of 'em whenever I want," she said, chuckling.

Brooklyn, New York, and Gainesville, Florida

"Nothing would be wrong with hooking up if the students I spoke to seemed really empowered and excited about it," says Donna Freitas, the author of *The End of Sex: How Hookup Culture Is Leaving a Generation Unhappy, Sexually Unfulfilled, and Confused About Intimacy.* For her book, Freitas conducted an online survey of 2,500 college students and interviewed over 100 more on seven college campuses. But the culture she describes is not so different from what many high school students are also experiencing. Or it may be what awaits them, in a few years, if nothing changes.

"The more I talk to students," Freitas says, "the more the culture of hooking up seems really problematic for them. Both young women and young men are seriously unhappy with the way things are; they're really ambivalent about the sex they're having. According to everything they see in pop culture, they're supposed to be having a great time; but it's rare that I find a young man or young woman who says hooking up is the best thing ever. In reality it seems to empty them out.

"There's this sort of soullessness fostered in hookup culture, there's a learned callousness. Sex is something you're not to care about. It's almost like their job to get it done. One word I keep hearing from students is 'efficient.' They're so busy, so overscheduled, hooking up is an efficient way to get sex 'done.' And you have to show that you're doing it. The reason for hooking up doesn't seem to be pleasure, fun, or intimacy; it's all about performance, gossip, and being able to update about it on social media."

But posting about hookups on social media comes with its own perils, especially for girls, Freitas says. "One night can make or break your college experience. One wrong photo, one misstep, one tagline or comment, and you are done. I hear this over and over—it goes online and it's viral. Young women are terrified of getting a reputation, but they feel like they have to participate in hookup culture and advertising their hooking up on social media.

"Social media speeds us all up," Freitas says. "We're constantly expected to be on it, to be updating. We're almost doing it without thinking. And that's really playing into how we act sexually. Students hook up with someone after friending them on Facebook or following them on Instagram. They wake up the next day in bed with someone they haven't had a conversation with. We need to give them the tools to have a conversation about what they want and what they expect from this encounter.

"I see students getting better and better at hookup culture," Freitas says. "They're getting better at not caring. And I think that's really troubling. Everybody is becoming a sex object, a sex toy; it's an exchange, an agreement. The mainstreaming of porn is tremendously affecting what's expected of them. They're learning sex through porn. What it means to have sex, a lot of the time, is to mimic what they see in pornography. Alcohol is one of the criteria of the hookup," Freitas goes on. "This is *Mad Men* sex, boring and ambivalent. They drink like they're Don Draper to drown out what is really going on with them. Alcohol has long been liquid courage. What I think has changed is why kids drink. This is about, How can I medicate myself so I don't feel? What I see is, I've got to drink so I can gear up to do this thing. I've got to get this over with and alcohol is a way to get through it.

"Conservatives sort of love all the stuff that I'm saying," Freitas says, "but it's really hard to get liberal women to have this conversation because people are very afraid to critique hookup culture for fear of being called anti-sex. There's this sense that you give up your feminist cred if you critique what people perceive as a sexually liberated practice. Big-time feminists won't go near hooking up because they see it as sexually liberated. But I'm looking at it on the ground, and it doesn't hold up as sexual liberation. Hookup culture is an incredibly antifeminist culture. It's the antithesis of empowerment and choice."

In 2015, in *The Independent Florida Alligator*, the school newspaper of the University of Florida, Ann Manov, an undergraduate, wrote a column headlined "Don't Twist the Meaning of Sexual Liberation." "What's sexual liberation?" Manov asked. "Women's rights to Planned Parenthood, abortion and contraception are under threat"; but meanwhile, even " 'progressive' men's" sense of sexual entitlement is thriving," she said.

"It's a poli-sci student lecturing me that it's illogical not to sleep with him," Manov wrote. "It's him, after he cheats [on] me, saying, 'I would never date you.' . . . It's playing the umpteenth side chick for a . . . Ph.D. student who says love is a lie and I'm being irrational . . . It's people I've barely met asking me my bra size. It's a friend's boyfriend messaging girls on OkCupid—'But just for sex, so it's OK.' It's a girlfriend telling me she wants to be a born-again virgin. It's her Tinder non-boyfriend refusing to use a condom . . .

"This isn't sexual liberation," Manov said. "It's asking us to f— like men and shut up . . . Women are raised to seek male approval. So even if we don't want to screw a guy, we still want him to want to screw us. The market is rigged: What does 'want' even mean? . . . I don't want to cum with strangers. I don't want my feminism . . . to translate into that impersonal, inevitable 'Well, I guess it's time to undress.'"

Santa Clarita, California

Amanda tried to kill herself in eleventh grade. Her boyfriend had broken up with her so that he could play the field before graduating from high school, he said, and after some months of turmoil, Amanda took an overdose of one of her mother's prescription medications. She was hospitalized briefly and had gone into therapy.

We talked one day at the home of Kim Goldman of the Santa Clarita Valley Youth Project. We sat on her porch overlooking the mountains, eating strawberries at a wooden table.

Amanda was a white girl, tall, with long dark hair and soft brown eyes. She was growing up in a wealthy area, but her family was not rich, which she said could be hard. "When my dad found out my mom was pregnant, my dad broke up with her," she said. "For a long time my mom was a single mom. We didn't have anything." Now her mother was married to Amanda's stepfather, a security guard, and things were better. "But you still always feel like you don't measure up," she said.

Amanda met her ex-boyfriend, Tom, when she was fifteen and he was seventeen. "He and I were like best friends from the start," she said. "He was the person I talked to about everything. When he broke up with me, the reason he gave was that there were three weeks left of senior year and he just wanted to 'live it up.' He said he wanted to have sex with as many girls as he could. Like, he said there were girls he wanted to bang and he might never get another chance.

"It's still a struggle to me today to get past that," Amanda said. "I already had trust issues because I was abandoned by my real dad. I'd never had sex before Tom; he was my first. Like it hurt me really bad when he broke up with me. My whole world fell apart. I loved him so much."

She'd had a rough high school experience, beginning in ninth grade, when she was cyberbullied on Facebook by a girl at her school, along with the girl's mother. "She"—the mom—"was saying I was a slut and all I do is lay on my back, but I've only been with one person," said Amanda.

"This girl and me, we just weren't friends anymore and she would talk crap about me, and I would talk crap about her, and it got onto Facebook. And then her mom got in the mix and her mom was talking crap about me—like her mom was saying that I was a slut and just opened my legs for everyone."

Amanda's parents reported the cyberbullying to the police, she said, but they were told nothing could be done because no direct threats were made. Feeling isolated and depressed, Amanda got into drugs, ecstasy and weed, and started hanging out with the "scene" kids, kids who are into hard-core punk rock.

"All I talked about was sex, drugs, money, and partying," she said. "I'd post pictures on Facebook of me smoking weed and partying. The druggies wouldn't judge me, so I felt safe with them. My mom found out I was doing all that stuff when I was in tenth grade. She caught me doing ecstasy. It caused a lot of problems between us." Her home life became stressful.

When she started dating her boyfriend, Amanda said, she finally felt as if she had "something to live for." "We were like the one couple in school that everybody knew, that everyone was like, You're so cute. You're gonna be together for a really long time." And now that she had a steady boyfriend, she said, no one called her a slut. "People see you with a steady guy and they're like, Oh, she must be okay, 'cause he likes her—she got a guy.

"I've only had one sex partner," Amanda said. "I know a lot of people that have slept with multiple guys 'cause they were drunk or high. To me that's gross. You don't sleep with random people. I hear so many guys in my school be like, Yeah, I had sex with this girl and that girl. They brag about it. I feel so bad for the girls. Guys talk about it like it's sports. There's this term for a girl—they call it a 'homie hopper,' 'cause she goes from friend to friend. There's this one girl in our school that's slept with multiple guys and she was never dating any of them and they call her that.

"There's a girl I know, I talked to her once in English class in ninth grade and she was pregnant, and I was like, Who's the dad? And she said she didn't know. She was open about it. I was like, How many guys have you had sex with lately? and she was like, Ten, and I was like, Well, is one of them the dad? And she was like, Yeah, probably, I don't know. I was like, You don't care? She said, I don't care about the guys. And I was like, You don't care that you had sex and shared your body with ten other guys? And she was like, No, not really."

Amanda attributed her boyfriend breaking up with her to the influence of his friends and the fact that it was "cool for a guy to have a lot of different girls." "All his friends were like, Dude, you have a girlfriend. You can't do anything," meaning have sex with other girls. Amanda said he confessed to her that after breaking up with her, he slept with the "homie hopper."

"Boys have no respect for girls," Amanda said. "They'll be like, Damn, that girl's hot, I'd fuck her. They'll be like, I'm gonna get some of that. They're very cocky. I wish it was the days when boys would have to get to know you before you have sex with them."

Boca Raton, Florida

Billie and her friends Sally, Madison, and Michelle had dinner one night at Rise, a sushi restaurant in a shopping plaza in Boca. They came together in Billie's car. Sally was an Asian girl with long dark hair and bangs, and Madison and Michelle were white girls, brunette and blond. They wore sundresses and tank tops and cotton skirts and flats and sandals. Sally and Madison were Billie's "nerdy" friends, and Michelle was the one Billie had told me was "fun, and a little wild." Sally's and Madison's fathers both had civil service jobs, and their mothers were stay-at-home moms. Michelle's mother had her own business and her father was an engineer. All of their parents were married, except for Michelle's, who were divorced.

They were a close-knit squad, they said; they had their own finsta, one only they could see. "We post funny things and try and make each other laugh," Billie said. They had a group chat where they communicated with each other all day, every day.

They were sitting at a table in the casual family place in front of heaping plates of sushi, laughing, showing me an Instagram picture Billie and Michelle had taken. Billie was dressed up like a guy and Michelle in an overtly sexual outfit; they were doing the duckface, arms around each other's shoulders. It was some kind of parody picture, like "Kim and Kanye, like when you think you're the sexiest couple," Billie said. "We sent it to him!" Michelle said, giggling. She was referring to the guy she'd been hooking up with, Kyle, who, she found out, had a girlfriend named Morgan.

"I liked him since like the first day of school freshman year," said Michelle. "I thought he was smart. He was really sexy. He seemed like he had his stuff together. We would text about homework all through sophomore year, text about chemistry homework, flirt with each other over text.

"So this year we hooked up." They slept together, Michelle told me later, saying, "He actually got mad at me when I said I was nervous and he pressured me, like, Just do it, we like each other. And so we did.

"And then, okay, after we hooked up he ignores me," said Michelle. "He ignores me for a few weeks. He was like, Don't tell anybody. I still didn't know he was with this other girl.

"So then I was in his car one day and her name," Morgan, "came up on his [phone] screen and he was like, Oh, don't worry about her, she's obsessed with me. So after that I would ask him about her, but he would make it like they were just on and off. And then I didn't want to have anything more to do with him. I stopped returning his texts.

"So I wake up one morning and I go on Instagram and I see he followed me and he liked a picture of me in a bikini. And I'm like, *Really*?" She frowned. "So I go back and look at his profile picture on Facebook and see this other girl Morgan commented, 'So handsome babe.' Which made me really mad. So I commented, *'So handsome babe,'* under her, like mocking her, 'cause he's liking my photo and he's obviously with *her*. So he deletes my comment immediately.

"So he's been hooking up with me *and* her, and now he's liking my bikini picture, and deleting my comment!" After she made the comment, she said, "he blocked me on Facebook and Instagram.

"Me and him and her, we're all in the same first hour" at school, she said. "It was me, him, and this other girl in class together that same morning—it was so awkward.

"So I start texting him. I was mad. I was being really angry at him. And he starts saying really sexual things to me and he sends me a picture on Snapchat of his dick and he says, Did you miss it? And he says, Do you want to hook up with me? So I asked him, What are you *doing*? And he says, I want to put you in a good mood. So he's obviously trying to calm me down by coming on to me so I won't say anything to her."

"Or maybe just the whole situation is making him horny," Billie suggested.

Michelle said, "That, too. And then I'm so like not returning his texts. But then he was being so confusing. I did text him again and he would not answer. So he's shitting on me *again*. And so then this girl he's dating, Morgan, she posted a picture of herself with him on Instagram and she's like, My babe. Billie saw it and sent it to me. And I'm like, Oh my *God*. So me and Billie, we imitated the picture and we sent it back to him on Snapchat." This was the picture they had showed me.

The girls giggled. Billie made the same bro-ish duckface from the picture.

"So he texts me like, I'm not okay with this," said Michelle. "And I said, You're with *her* and you're trying to get with *me* and I'm not okay with *that*. So the next day in school I saw this girl Morgan. I had never talked to her before. So I go up to her and I'm like, Are you dating him? And she's like, Yeah, we've been on and off for a while. And I said, You know, he's been cheating on you with me. And she starts, like, crying and freaking out. I showed her the dick pics and all the texts and she's crying and going crazy. So he comes outside—'cause I texted him—it was in the courtyard of school—and there was a *beatdown*. She's smacking him. I took a video."

Michelle pulled up the video on her phone. It showed a teenage girl beating a teenage boy. You could hear the slaps and the cracks on his skull and the girl screaming and crying. "You're a fucking asshole!"

The other girls at the table watched the video—they had seen it many times before—gasping and cracking up.

Michelle put down her phone when it was over.

"But now they're back together," she said with a shrug. "She was texting me like, He's so disgusting. But she took him back. He's being so nice to her—he took her on all these crazy dates and everything. He added me back on Snapchat just so I could see all these pictures of them together. There's pictures of them at the beach and he's like hugging her."

New York, New York

One day, some months after I met Sydney, she was meeting her friends for lunch at Serafina, an Italian restaurant on the Upper East Side. It's a casual place with yellow walls and waiters who look like aspiring actors. Tourists with shopping bags from the Metropolitan Museum of Art were sitting at tables next to families with toddlers playing on iPads. There was a five-year-old's birthday party going on, with bobbing balloons and mothers snapping iPhone pics and children begging for ice cream.

Sydney's friends looked a bit mortified by this juvenile atmosphere as they were led to their table. They were all very fashionable in the way of Manhattan girls, all age seventeen. They were slim and slinky and wearing eyeliner wings and sheer sleeveless tops, short shorts, and ankle boots. It was a sort of hipster, fashionista version of provocative.

They sat down and ordered salad and one plate of pasta and split it among them. "I'm not hungry," they said. "I had a big breakfast."

Sydney said nothing during the entire conversation, not a word. She'd been very talkative when I met with her before. But this was a powerful squad, a bona fide clique which, she said, "terrorized" girls in her school, and they seemed to make her watchful and wary.

I asked them to tell me about their school, and they started talking about how it was full of "mean girls"—which was a curious thing since this was how Sydney had characterized them.

"Girls in general are mean," Jenny said. She was a white girl who looked like Snow White. Her parents were both actors.

"So mean," said Lydia. She identified herself as "Blewish," black and Jewish. Her mother owned a fashion company and her father was a writer. "Not *us*."

"It's not *just* girls," Isabella said carefully. She was Asian and Latina, tall and Bette Davis–eyed with a wavy bob. Her father was a social worker, her mother a stay-at-home mom. "At our school, *people* can be really mean to each other," she said. "Like there's this girl—well, she happens to be overweight—which is *fine,* a lot of people *are*—but a lot of boys in our school tend to tease her or make fun of her."

"She stalks celebrities and she was named 'The Stalker Girl,'" Lydia said flatly, as if to suggest that the teasing had some justification.

"Like, she had a fascination with celebrities," Jenny chimed in. "She has a few boy bands that she's really into. She follows them on Twitter and stalks them."

"She'll wait for them outside hotels," Lydia piled on. "It's really intense. She'll be like, I met Nick Jonas. She knows their license plates. She knows when their car comes out of the hotel, I mean."

"I think she signed up with a special website that notifies her where the celebrities are. There's a whole community of stalkers," Jenny said. She and Lydia tittered.

"I mean, I like celebrities, too," Lydia said. "But I wouldn't *stalk* them. That is highly creepy."

"But there was an instance," Isabella pressed, "where one of the boys, like, hacked her Gmail account and e-mailed some other boys from our school, like, Do you want to go to prom? Like to humiliate her. It was like bullying. And she posted on Facebook about how she was upset. And I commented, Are you okay? I hope she didn't think I was being sarcastic."

The other girls were silent a moment.

"I've never seen an instance where people are bullied," Jenny said with a sniff.

Her two good friends, who were sitting at the table with her, had been cyberbullied in the past. (Isabella later said she had been cyberbullied in sixth grade on Myspace.)

I asked them more about the behavior of boys. For example, did they comment on the way girls dress?

"The problem is with *girls* slut-shaming," Lydia said, a tad impatient. "It's all coming from girls. If a girl wants to dress slutty, I'm all for it—do you—but there are girls that slut-shame on other girls. It's disappointing, 'cause you're a girl, too.

"Like if a girl hooks up with three boys in one night," she went on, "that's a problem for girls. But if a boy does the same thing, they're celebrated. It's like, Oh, congratulations, that's great. Boys don't shame each other—they *high-five* each other. But for girls it's like, You're a slut, why would you do that? Girls call each other names—like thot and slide," another word for slut.

"So only girls slut-shame? Not boys?" I asked.

The girls said nothing. Sydney stared at her salad.

I asked them to tell me more about the parties at their school. "They're not *all* Business Slutty," Lydia said, shooting Sydney a disapproving glance. "A lot are just regular parties. It's called a 'free.'"

"They're almost like every weekend. Everyone goes," Jenny said. "Sometimes kids rent a hotel room, at like the Plaza or Trump Tower. Everyone who's invited knows each other. If not from schools, then from social media. Like you'll see a girl and be like, Why do I know her full name? And you'll realize, Oh, she's been in pictures with my friends on Facebook or Instagram. So you smile at each other even though you don't know each other. It's actually really creepy."

I asked what happened at the parties.

"Drinking, drugs, smoking pot, cheap liquor, beer and vodka," Lydia said matter-of-factly. "Molly."

"It's not unusual to go to a party and be like, I can't go in 'cause the police are there," Isabella said.

"Some girls act just ridiculous at these parties," said Lydia. "I've seen two girls hook up with one guy. These girls came out of the bathroom once screaming, like, We just hooked up in the bathroom!" She made a face.

"There's this group of three best friends and one of them wasn't there and she liked this boy and her two friends hooked up with that boy at the same time," Jenny explained.

"It was so mean," Isabella said. "This other girl had feelings for the guy. I think they were drunk."

"It's *girls* initiating it usually," Lydia said. "It's one way girls mess with other girls, by hooking up with guys they know they like."

Isabella seemed to be getting antsy, as if she wanted to correct something about all this. "But boys mess with girls' heads, too," she said. "Like I've certainly experienced this: you kiss someone or you hook up with someone, and the guy doesn't say anything about it to you after. In the beginning, when I was first getting involved with guys, it used to, like, really bother me—that guys just talk about how many girls they get with, but then if a girl hooks up, they say, She's such a slut, she's so easy. When I was first getting involved with guys, I was so upset by it. I was so upset. I got like anxiety issues about going to parties 'cause I felt there was this pressure to hook up. So when I was thirteen I just started to hook up with random guys and it was really overwhelming to me. I didn't know at first that, like, I could kiss a guy one night and then he wouldn't ever text me or talk to me again." She looked around the table tentatively, as if nervous about having revealed all this.

The other girls said nothing.

"I've never experienced that because I've always had a boyfriend," Lydia said dryly. "I've never been 'out there.'"

"But boyfriends are rare," Isabella countered softly.

"There are a *lot* of boyfriends and girlfriends," Jenny said. "They just don't, like, go out on *dates*—it's just, like, cuffing season."

Cuffing season? I asked.

"That's a period of time in the winter," Jenny explained. "You know, like when people stay in a couple because it's cold out and they want to nest. Boys say, I'm cuffed, I'm whipped," meaning handcuffed, pussy-whipped.

I asked her if she thought the phrase was sexist.

"They *want* to do it," Lydia said, referring to boys. "They don't *have* to be cuffed. They do it because they like the girl."

Isabella suddenly seemed ready to explode. "I don't feel like guys ever have to take any responsibility for what they do," she said, her voice trembling with emotion. "I feel like guys get away with not having to contact a girl, like, after they do stuff with them. And then it's like, Oh, that's just how guys are. I've heard that so many times—like, Oh, that's a guy, you just have to deal with it. No, I don't have to deal with it at all. Like some of my closest girlfriends have told me, like, Don't expect anything from guys. And I think that's just like—really? Like, you know what, no, I *am* going to expect something."

She looked around again. Jenny and Lydia seemed annoyed. Sydney was staring at her pasta.

"Yeah, but there is a lot of pressure on guys, too," Lydia responded quietly after a moment, narrowing her eyes. "Like saying, Don't expect anything from him, he's a guy—that's categorizing guys. *That's* sexist. Like, Don't expect anything from him? What does that even mean? Him being a guy shouldn't mean he can't have emotions or can't get attached to anyone."

"I—I didn't mean it like that," Isabella said quickly. "I was just saying some girls will say that after guys hook up with someone and never talk to them again."

"Well, what do these girls expect?" Lydia said. "Just going to parties and hooking up with people—not every girl does that. *I* wouldn't want to meet a guy that way."

Isabella looked deflated. "I'm not saying I do that *now*," she said, "but when I did it in the past, I didn't like how the boys acted after. I didn't like the feeling of boys having all the control—of like having to wait for them to call you or text you. I feel like their brains are wired differently and they don't even realize the effect that they have on a girl sometimes—they should, but they don't."

"A lot of the time they *don't* realize what they're saying or doing," Lydia agreed. "My close guy friend hooked up with this girl and he ended up telling everyone that she was a horrible kisser. And that is something you *don't do*—it was so wrong and it really hurt her and I made him feel horrible for it. I was like, I can't even look at you right now. And now people see her differently. But *he* didn't know what he was doing."

Isabella wrinkled her brow.

"Nobody's teaching them respect," Jenny said after a moment to Isabella. "And without respect, there's this whole thing where girls can be treated as sexual objects. And if you're a sexual object, why would anyone have to worry about your feelings? If boys were taught respect, these things wouldn't happen."

"That's exactly what I was trying to say," Isabella said.

"I know," said Jenny.

Isabella smiled, relieved.

Boca Raton, Florida

Dinner at Rise went from sushi to mochi and fried green tea ice cream. The girls talked and laughed.

"It's amazing how much we're just talking tonight," Madison said. "Like, nobody is on their phones."

"I like it so much better," Billie said. "Phones just destroy conversation."

"Especially with boys," Sally said. "They never talk to us."

"They don't have to," Billie said. "They don't have to engage in a conversation. They can just text."

"They can text four girls at once," Sally said. "I'm not just faulting boys—girls do it, too. But think about it. You can have a live chat going on FaceTime and be texting and Snapchatting someone else."

And how did this affect how girls and boys viewed each other? I asked.

Billie said, "It reduces respect. 'Cause it's not a respectful way of communicating with someone. No one is special or has your full attention. It's like you're dealing with four or five options and seeing which one will pan out."

"Social media just rushes everything," Sally said. "I feel like no one's waiting till they're ready to have sex."

I asked them if people at their school were having actual sex, not just cybersex. They laughed.

"Are you kidding me?" said Michelle. "People are having sex *in school*. There's condoms all over the place."

"I walked in on two girls in the bathroom once," Billie said.

"I walked in on a girl and a boy," said Madison. "It was oddly quiet, and I see this girl's feet and boy's feet standing in the corner of the big stall. I just left."

"Can't you wait till you get home?" Billie joked.

"Sometimes they put a sign on the door that says OUT OF ORDER," Madison said. The other girls laughed. "But you can tell someone wrote it and it wasn't a printed thing," she added.

"I hooked up with a guy at school junior year," Michelle confessed. "He was this hot football player—gorgeous blue eyes. We were taking the same drama class. We made out in the theater. I just wanted to make out with him. Guys at our school are not datable."

"Nobody dates. It's just hooking up," said Madison.

"After parties, it's like, Who got with who? What's the scoop?" said Sally. "Monday morning you get the gossip."

"'Oh, I was drunk, I don't remember it,'" Billie said, repeating an oft-heard phrase.

"There's parties every weekend," Madison said. "People get drunk, hook up. Seniors are like, Let's live it up. We're all going off to different colleges, I'm never going to see you again, so let's just, you know, do it."

I asked if they thought porn had anything to do with all this.

They all said, *"Yes."*

"Boys look at porn all day," said Billie.

"They watch it during class," said Madison.

"Whenever you text a guy and ask, What are you doing?, they say they're watching porn," said Sally. "Some guys in my class were actually watching it while someone was doing a presentation. This girl Jennifer was giving a presentation and these guys put their phones like that"— she held her phone up to show the screen. "They were like, Oh, Jennifer, I have a question, and they raised their phones and it was a porn video. She couldn't even concentrate. It was so sad. I felt so bad for her."

Didn't the teacher see? I asked.

"The teacher didn't even know," Sally said. "She was at the back. The boys were sitting in the front of the class."

"Disgusting," said Michelle.

I asked why no one told the teacher.

The girls all looked around at one another. "If you tell on them, they'll never let you forget it," said Billie.

It was a classic case of sexual harassment. I asked if this had occurred to them.

"Actually, yes," said Madison. "But boys do stuff like that all the time—like in my history class this kid watches porny videos that his girlfriend sends him and he shows them around. Guys watch it right there in class. They just think it's funny. I don't know if they realize it's *harassment.*"

They said their school was a competitive one, "a pressure-cooker school." "Everybody competes for grades." Kids competed with one another to get into Ivy League schools. "Like you only matter if you get into a really good school," said Billie. The girls all said they wanted to be doctors, surgeons, pediatricians; they said they'd been inspired to go into the sciences from watching *Grey's Anatomy*—a show with several strong female leads who are doctors in a hospital. So these were empowered, privileged girls, girls who saw themselves as future doctors. And yet they didn't feel they could speak up when they were being sexually harassed in a high school classroom.

More than forty years after the Equal Employment Opportunity Commission began enforcing Title IX, issuing regulations against sexual harassment in publicly funded schools, the sexual harassment of both girls and boys in schools has quietly gone mainstream. A national survey in 2011 by the American Association of University Women (AAUW) of students in grades seven to twelve found that "sexual harassment is part of everyday life in middle and high schools. Nearly half (48 percent) of the students surveyed experienced some form of sexual harassment in the 2010–11 school year, and the majority of those students (87 percent) said it had a negative effect on them. Verbal harassment (unwelcome sexual comments, jokes, or gestures) made up the bulk of the incidents, but physical harassment was far too common. Sexual harassment by text, e-mail, Facebook, or other electronic means affected nearly one-third (30 percent) of students . . .

"Girls were more likely than boys to be sexually harassed, by a significant margin (56 percent versus 40 percent)," the AAUW report went on. "Girls were more likely than boys to be sexually harassed both in person . . . and via text, e-mail, Facebook, or other electronic means . . . Girls' experiences tend to be more physical and intrusive than boys' experiences. Girls were more likely than boys to say that they had been negatively affected by sexual harassment . . . Not only were girls more likely than boys to say sexual harassment caused them to have trouble sleeping . . . not want to go to school . . . or change the way they went to or home from school . . . girls were more likely in every case to say they felt that way for 'quite a while' compared with boys.

"Too often, these negative emotional effects take a toll on students' and especially girls' education, resulting in decreased productivity and increased absenteeism from school," said the AAUW report. "Thus, although both girls and boys can encounter sexual harassment at school, it is still a highly 'gendered phenomenon' that is directly and negatively associated with outcomes for girls . . .

"Girls were much more likely to experience unwanted sexual jokes, comments, or gestures . . . more likely to say that they were shown sexy or sexual pictures that they did not want to see . . . and that they had been touched in an unwelcome sexual way . . . Girls were also more likely to say that they had been physically intimidated in a sexual way . . . and were forced to do something sexual." The AAUW found that the prevalence of sexual harassment was statistically similar among students of different racial and ethnic groups. It found that very few students would admit to harassing others.

"A boy tried to unzip my pants." "I was called a whore because I have many friends that are boys." "Someone had lewd photos on their phone—they asked if I wanted to see them and even though I said no, they showed them to me anyway." These were some of the incidents the AAUW reported. The study found that whether a girl becomes a victim of sexual harassment has much to do with her physical appearance. Girls "whose bodies are really developed," "who are very pretty," "who are not pretty or not very feminine," or who are overweight were the most likely to suffer sexual harassment.

And yet, despite the high numbers of girls experiencing sexual harassment in schools, only 12 percent said they ever reported it to an adult. "Some researchers claim that sexual harassment is so common for girls that many fail to recognize it as sexual harassment when it happens," said the AAUW report. A 2014 study, published in *Gender & Society*, of students between the ages of twelve and seventeen in a Midwestern city also found that girls failed to report incidents of sexual harassment in school because they regarded them as "normal." Their lack of reporting was found to stem from girls' fear of being labeled "bad girls" by teachers and administrators, who they felt would view them as provoking how they were treated. They also feared the condemnation of other girls, some of whom were shown to be unsupportive, accusing them of exaggerating or lying. Many girls saw everyday sexual harassment and abuse as "normal" male behavior and something they had to ignore, endure, or maneuver around. "They grab you, touch your butt and try to, like, touch you in the front, and run away, but it's okay, I mean . . . I never think it's a big thing because they do it to everyone," said a thirteen-year-old girl in the study.

But another important question is, What is making some boys think sexual harassment is normal? In the AAUW study, when the small percentage of students who admitted to sexually harassing others were asked why they did it, 44 percent said, "It's just part of school life," and 39 percent said, "I thought it was funny." "People misunderstood that sexual harassment is about sex—it's really about control, and power, and abusing it," said Anita Hill in the documentary *Anita*.

"It's just become so common," Billie groaned, referring to boys looking at porn in school. "And, like, what are you supposed to say? It's bad enough when they compare us to porn stars and look at their pornstar accounts on Instagram at lunch. But when they're, like, looking at a girl they know—that *we* may know—a girl our age"—now she was referring to boys looking at nudes—"how can we, like, object? Either we're slut-shaming or we're jealous or a prude."

"They look at their pictures and talk about who they want to, you know," Madison said. "Like whose butt is bigger, whose chest."

"We're used to it," said Michelle. "This all started in sixth grade. They started asking for nudes. I don't know if they had any idea that it's *harassment*—I don't know if they do now. They're just doing it 'cause they're horny and they want to see naked girls."

"Girls get accused of doing all the messed-up stuff on social media, but guys do it, too," said Billie.

I asked them what they thought of the argument that girls taking and sending nudes was empowering for them.

"I don't buy it," Sally said. "If you felt good about your body, you would conserve yourself for somebody you think really deserves that. There's other ways of showing off your body than showing everything. Like, some things are better left unshown."

Michelle made a face. "But I think a guy should respect a girl no matter how much skin she's showing," she said. "They're still human beings—they still have a brain, a personality. You don't know anything about them. You can't just, like, say disrespectful things about them. They're still a person."

"I agree," said Billie. "But boys *don't* respect girls who show off their bodies—they think it's hot, but they don't respect them. It's the *boys* that find it empowering because they think it's being done for them."

They talked about a girl in their school who wore provocative clothes—booty shorts and tops showing "side boob," they said—and flirted with male teachers in order to get better grades, or so they believed. "She calls this seventy-year-old teacher 'babe,'" said Michelle. The other girls laughed.

And does it work? I asked. "No, she gets bad grades," said Michelle.

"See, no guy respects that," Billie said. "Maybe if they've been raised by like the biggest, most feminist mom, but how many of those moms exist?"

"Most moms have no clue what boys are like," Madison said.

"No, and we don't want to tell them, 'cause they'd be too worried about us," said Michelle. "And, seriously, like some moms don't want to hear it. They blame everything on girls. They're just like, Oh, look at what she did to my precious son, she sent him nudes. They don't know that, like, their son is hooking up with their daughter and sending pictures of his dick to other girls." Now she was talking about Kyle again.

"Like that weekend Billie sent me the picture of him and his girlfriend," she went on, "he had stayed over at my house the night before. So he was hooking up with me and then posting 'couples' pictures with *her*. And he was telling her mom over wine, I'm in love with your daughter. He was making plans with her mom about how he could still be with her when they went to college. He leaves her house at four o'clock—I'm at Hollister shopping—and he calls me right after he left. Like right after!" It was something she and Morgan had ascertained when they compared notes. "He said all this stuff to her mom and then he left her house and was trying to get with me."

She held up his text from that day: "I'm hard and horny lol and I just want you."

The other girls shook their heads.

"High school boys suck, they really do," said Madison.

Sally looked down. "Well, not all," she said.

"Oh, that's right!" said Michelle. "Sally knows a good guy."

Sally said, "He is a good guy." She smiled.

She had liked him since freshman year, she said. In the spring, she added him on Snapchat—"I was scared, but I did it. But then," she said, "he didn't add me back," so she was scared that he wasn't interested. Two whole days went by. "So I took back my request." She was in agony. "He's a very smart, respectable boy. I thought I had no chance."

And then her little sister, who was thirteen and, Sally said, "much more into social media than I am, took my phone and added him again and he added me back. I was like screaming, running around the house, I was so happy." Ever since, she said, they had been Snapchatting. "Texting is one thing," Sally said, "but Snapchat is so much more personal. You're sending someone a picture of where you are and what you're doing—what you can see with your eyes.

"First he sent me a picture of his dog," she went on, shyly, "and then I sent him a picture of my Pillow Pet. It was just funny and cute. He sent a selfie, then I sent a selfie.

"Now," she said, "we go to lunch together."

"So in the midst of all this hypersexual stuff you're having a real romance," I said.

Sally smiled. "It's a fairy tale. I'm hopeful, yes."

"It's not social media that's the problem," Billie observed, "it's the way we use it, it's the people behind it."

"When he followed me on Instagram, I got so excited," Sally said. "Or when he likes my pictures, I feel like he's sending me a message, like, I'm thinking about you."

"I see the way he looks at her," said Billie, smiling.

"He's cute," said Michelle.

Sally laughed, joyful.

The other girls giggled.

"I like this guy," said Madison.

"Yeah, me, too," said Sally.

"His posts are about, like, history and things," said Michelle. "It's cute, it's funny."

"We're Facebook friends, too," Sally said.

I asked if they had gone on an actual date.

"Well, no," Sally said. "I think he's shy. So I'll probably have to ask him out. I think I might text him, What are you doing this weekend? Or Snapchat him. I'll just put it out there, you know? Social media is definitely a good way to ask someone something like that, 'cause you can always check if they're online."

They already had one another's phone numbers, she said, as they all shared numbers in school for homework purposes. "It always starts with homework," said Michelle. "Some guy will text you like, Do you have the chemistry notes? And the next thing he's asking you for nudes."

They laughed.

"I have a question," Sally said. "If you send someone a Snapchat, you can see if they open it up or not, you know, with the arrow or the square? So he Snapchatted me a couple days ago and we FaceTimed for two hours and then I sent him back a Snapchat the next day and he opened it up but he didn't respond. And my thirteen-year-old sister said, Oh, that's bad, you can't Snapchat him for the rest of the week unless he does it first! And I'm like, Oh my God, that's crazy. She said, You need to have the square and not the arrow."

The other girls pondered that a moment. "Well . . ."

"This is all we do," Billie remarked, "is analyze this stuff, like tea leaves."

"You sister is so critical of you," said Michelle. "Why is she always telling you what to do?"

"She's just trying to look out for me," Sally said, "because she knows I don't know about social media."

They started talking about how their younger sisters—they all had one except for Billie—were social media mavens on a scale they couldn't even imagine: "They're *all* about social media."

"My sister posts selfies every day," Sally said. "She cares so much about how she looks. I could care less when I was her age. I'd wake up, go to school. I didn't put on makeup. They skip the awkward stage."

"They're really self-conscious," said Michelle. "They're so picky about what they post—if they have forty-nine likes on a picture they have to delete it because it's not enough."

"They're always comparing themselves," said Madison.

"In middle school now, the way they dress and use makeup," Billie clucked. "In middle school I had a flip phone. I just pulled my hair back in a ponytail. I was so gawky."

"My sister is complaining to my mom that she has yellow teeth!" said Michelle. "She has an iPhone and she's freaking out about how she looks in selfies. She uses the app to whiten her teeth."

"A lot of these girls are getting eating disorders and they don't even know that these models are Photoshopped to make the thigh gap or whatever," said Sally.

"I was watching an interview with a girl who posed for *Playboy*," said Michelle, "and she was like, I did not even recognize myself. That's how much they edit them."

"We're so fragile," Sally said. "We're very vulnerable now; being a teenager, you're already so susceptible to all this stuff. And just looking at social media and having these expectations placed on you—what you need to look like, dress like. It's a lot of pressure to put on girls and it's really taking a toll on girls and you can see it."

Chapter Six

18

Tucson, Arizona

She was lying on top of a grainer, headed for Tucson, when she realized she hadn't looked in a mirror in weeks. It seemed so silly, to think of that now. She wondered what she looked like. And then she realized she didn't care.

She used to be one of those girls who puts pictures of herself on Facebook. In her album there was a photo of her as a girl of twelve, smiling broadly in sporty clothes; she was wearing glasses, looking expectant and eager to please, standing next to a piano in a suburban living room. And then there was a selfie taken a few years later, when she was fifteen; she was wearing something tight and red. Eye makeup heavy. It all seemed so far away.

A grainer was a train car that carried dry goods like grain or sand or clay; it had a ladder going up the side, that was how you climbed up. That was if the bulls, or the rail yard police, didn't catch you. But she'd gotten pretty good at knowing how to evade them. She had a *Crew Change*—that was the underground guide of train riders; she'd gotten it off a kid in San Francisco in exchange for beer. She was a traveling kid, a homeless girl, and had been since she was sixteen.

The best part about traveling, she said, was the trains. She loved "absolutely everything" about trains, "the noise, the speed, the distances, the way they shake." The way you could scrunch into the corner of a boxcar with your head on your backpack and listen to the *chunk-chunk, chunk-chunk,* of the wheels against the rails, lulling you to sleep.

She said, "People try to find that sound on YouTube just to listen to it when they can't drift off right away." To her it was the sound of dreams, of traveling. She'd stretch out and look up at the stars.

She didn't know the names of the constellations, but she wished she did. She thought one of them might be Artemis, the goddess with the bow and arrow, who'd kill anybody who tried to do her harm. (Artemis does not appear in the stars.) "I wished I had a bow and arrow," she said. She'd look for Artemis at night, the train moving beneath her like a big friendly whale, the dark trees and mountains sliding by like ocean landscapes. "I feel like it's heaven. You get to skip most of Babylon and see the pretty parts of the world that most people don't see 'cause they're taking the highway."

The whistle would wake her up. The sound of a train whistle was an unforgettable thing, like a man's bellow or a woman's scream. She would have fitful dreams. There were things she was running away from, but she preferred to think of her exit from society as a choice she made in the spirit of adventure.

Everything had slipped away slowly, and then all at once. She'd lost her home, her phone. The phone was the last thing to go. Without it she felt untethered. At first it was a bad feeling, anxious-making, and then she had felt freed. There were things she had to get away from, and she realized one of them was her image in the selfie.

Online

In October 2015, Essena O'Neill, an eighteen-year-old model from Coolum Beach, Australia, caused a sensation by renouncing social media. It made headlines all over the world because the blond and beautiful O'Neill was a social media star, with more than 600,000 followers on Instagram and more than 300,000 subscribers on YouTube.

"I'm quitting Instagram, YouTube and Tumblr," O'Neill said in an Instagram post. "Deleted over 2000 photos here today that served no real purpose other than self promotion. Without realizing, I've spent [the] majority of my teenage life being addicted to social media, social approval, social status and my physical appearance. Social media, especially how I used it, isn't real. It's contrived images and edited clips ranked against each other. It's a system based on social approval, likes, validation in views, success in followers. It's perfectly orchestrated self absorbed judgment. I was consumed by it."

Before deleting her account—which she renamed "Social Media Is NOT Real Life"—O'Neill rewrote the captions on her remaining photos, saying what had gone on behind the scenes, revealing they had been staged, often sponsored by brands. "NOT REAL LIFE," O'Neill said on a photo of herself posing in a tight white gown. "I didn't pay for the dress, took countless photos trying to look hot for Instagram, the formal made me feel incredibly alone." "And yet another photo taken purely to promote my 16 year old body," she commented on another photo. "This was my whole identity. That was so limiting. Made me incredibly insecure. You have no idea."

O'Neill decried the pressure on teenage girls to attain an image of perfection. "A 15 year old girl that calorie restricts and excessively exercises is not goals," she said in another edited caption. "Anyone addicted to social media fame like I once was, is [not] in a conscious state." "Trying to make my stomach look good," she commented on a bikini shot, which she explained had been the result of more than 100 tries. "Would have hardly eaten that day. Would have yelled at my little sister to keep taking them until I was somewhat proud of this. Yep so totally #goals."

O'Neill also appeared in a series of YouTube videos, pointedly barefaced—unedited in real life, so to speak—as she elaborated on her message. In these videos, as well as in interviews and on blog posts, she said: "I spent hours watching perfect girls online, wishing I was them . . . Then when I was one of them I still wasn't happy, content, or at peace with myself . . ." "Everything I did was for views, for likes, for followers. I did shoots for hours just to get photos for Instagram . . ." "I was addicted to what others thought of me, simply because it was so readily available. I was severely addicted . . . I didn't even see it happening, but social media had become my sole identity. I didn't even know what I was without it."

With this outpouring of self-revelation, O'Neill said, she wanted to inspire young girls to become conscious of the ways social media was influencing their self-esteem and their behavior. In other interviews and social media posts, she said: "I just want younger girls to know this isn't candid life, or cool or inspirational. It's contrived perfection made to get attention . . ." "If you find yourself looking at 'Instagram girls' and wishing your life was theirs . . . realize you only see what they want . . ." "I urge you to try no social media, no viewing anyone online for a week." "Go outside, go to a park, go to a beach, go somewhere there are people around you . . . What I'm doing here is a statement that real life isn't through screens."

O'Neill had done a powerful thing: she'd said what many people were already thinking, or had thought at some point as they posted another selfie or edited picture that made their life seem more perfect and glamorous than it actually was. There were already many girls who knew that the photos of social media stars were manipulated, and manipulations—in fact, they were replicating the same techniques in their own social media posts. There was already a heavy sense among girls that there was something insidious about their social media obsession, as well as a feeling of helplessness as to how to escape it.

"I never paid attention to Essena O'Neill but I really admire her bravery and honesty now," tweeted @caranvr. "essena o neill is one of the truest and realest people ever, i feel like my life has changed because of her movement i'm not even kidding," tweeted @amateurlarry. "Essena O'Neill: 'social media isn't real please stop worshipping me.' Me: *worships her even more*," tweeted @lindslaaay. The actress Sophia Bush tweeted, "My GFs&I spent the better part of yday discussing Essena O'Neill's awesome serving of social truth." Ironically, and yet unsurprisingly, before she shut down her accounts, O'Neill had amassed tens of thousands more followers.

Her Instagram edits quickly spawned copycats, social media users emboldened by her example to post pictures of their "real" selves, or to rewrite photo captions in order to express the truth behind their posts, using the hashtag #socialmediaisnotreal. "I have changed into someone who validates their self esteem and self worth on likes/comments on my photos and I'm over it. From now on, I will be posting unedited photos . . . Not just me trying to look like something I'm not in real life . . . Welcome to a new era," wrote Baylynne Williford, an Instagram user, next to a shot of herself smiling and looking to be wearing no makeup.

But nothing on social media ever seems to stay uncontentious for long, and soon there was an O'Neill backlash. It had its own hashtag, #IAMREAL, and it was being spearheaded by other social media celebrities. Australian model Gabrielle Epstein, twenty-one, also blond and beautiful, wrote on her blog, "Of course Instagram isn't real life. Everyone, myself included, chooses the highlight reel of their life to present on social media—we all know that . . . However, that doesn't mean I have ever pretended to be someone that I am not on Instagram." It was a contradictory sort of statement, which would actually seem to support O'Neill's questioning of the authenticity of an online self.

A more personal attack on O'Neill came from two of her former friends, the twin YouTubers and singer-songwriters Nina and Randa Nelson, age twenty-two, who refer to themselves as "influencers." In a fifteen-minute video, widely circulated in the media, the two railed against her, calling her rejection of social media a "hoax." The sisters revealed that they had been the hosts of a recent trip O'Neill made to L.A., where O'Neill had said she'd observed other social media personalities acting in a way she found "fake." O'Neill hadn't named anyone's name, but the Nelson twins took her comments as a personal affront.

"How were any of us fake to you?" they asked, finishing each other's sentences. "*That* is fake. She thinks she's doing this whole real thing on the Internet, but to me it's just as fake as an edited image . . . I think the person who is fake here is Essena." They sounded a bit like middle school girls cyberbullying someone on social media.

"It's still one hundred percent self-promotion," said the twins, noting how O'Neill's rejection of social media was only gaining her more fans. "And also what's wrong with self-promotion?" they asked.

"Just because she sees views and likes and followers as validation doesn't mean we do," they said. "If you're celebrating your body . . . people need to stop hating on other girls for that . . . don't be jealous just because somebody is confident in a bikini." It was the slut-shaming Escher painting, in which girls hate on girls who hate on girls who hate on girls—and an example of one of the pernicious elements of social media O'Neill had been complaining about coming back to attack her.

The twins also gossiped about their former friend, alleging she had actually become despondent while visiting L.A. after a breakup with a young man. "The reason she's so down is because of this breakup with this guy," they said, revealing that the young man was someone O'Neill had met through them. He was quickly identified as "Los Angeles heartthrob Blake Michael, nineteen, best known for his work in the Disney sitcom *Dog with a Blog*," according to the *Daily Mail*, which noted, "Mr. Michael has more than one million followers on Instagram and is popular on both Facebook and Snapchat." Michael and O'Neill had apparently dated for a few weeks.

O'Neill had perhaps opened herself up to this kind of scrutiny when she mentioned in one of her vlogs that, while in L.A., "I was dating a guy that was way more famous than me . . . way more successful, had an amazing car, beautiful beyond words. And he was fucking depressed! . . . I was surrounded by all this wealth and all this fame and all this power—and yet they were all miserable. And I had never been more miserable."

Her Taylor Swift–style allusion to her allegedly depressive lover was not the wisest step in terms of maintaining her credibility; but she is a teenager (as Swift was when she wrote those difficult-breakup songs that got her called boy crazy), and one who had just experienced L.A. in all its glitzy glory. "I was . . . extremely lost in the 'celebrity construct,'" O'Neill blogged. The *Daily Mail* reported that the Nelson twins said that "O'Neill began to 'hate L.A. and I guess everyone along with it' when her L.A.-based relationship broke down." With these claims, the story began to turn. It was no longer about a girl with a critique of online culture. It was about a girl who'd had her heart broken by a cute boy. And that was a much more familiar and perhaps more palatable story.

Is it really impossible to imagine that it was experiencing L.A., the heart of fame culture, that made O'Neill reassess her pursuit of fame online? It wouldn't be the first time that someone was thrown into self-examination by the shallowness of Tinseltown.

The media in America was not much more sympathetic to O'Neill. A piece in *The New York Times* spent more time doubting her message than relaying it to its readers. The piece didn't mention any of O'Neill's online supporters, though it did say "some Facebook users, skeptical of Ms. O'Neill's declarations, view her turn against Instagram as just another means of self-promotion." The *Times* interviewed an expert, a "researcher at Snapchat" named Nathan Jurgenson, who argued that "intentional construction of our identities is not an activity unique to the online world." Jurgenson said, "All of identity theory is about talking about how we perform, so it's a little bit strange when people who have studied that literature hear people go 'oh everyone's performing now,' and it's like, no, that's all the self has ever been."

"All the self has ever been"? Identity theorists might agree on that, but Descartes might not. Or Kant. Or the Buddha. "What is a self?" is a question that's been explored and debated by philosophers for centuries, with no consensus that all "self" is "performance."

Jurgenson's dismissiveness of O'Neill was a defense of social media by someone who had an interest in protecting it, as the employee of a social media company (and a company, Snapchat, which was being widely used for the exchanging of nudes among teenagers). It ignored the reams of studies that have been done supporting much of what O'Neill was saying: studies questioning whether social media makes people addicted, anxious, and depressed, more craving of approval and more superficial; studies asking whether communication over screens is less rich and empathetic than communicating face-to-face. Jurgenson and the *Times*, as well as many other reports on O'Neill, also ignored the other main element of her message—that social media is a place where girls and young women are hypersexualized and feel pressure to sexualize themselves.

Other criticisms of O'Neill were more blatantly sexist. On a Facebook post, also widely quoted in the media, former YouTuber Zack James, the CEO of a social media advertising company, Rise9, addressed O'Neill by saying, "Social Media isn't a lie, you were the lie." Calling social media "mankind's greatest communication tool," James said, "Allowing yourself to become pressured into a false life that you're uncomfortable with is the result of your own actions and intent." He informed O'Neill that her critique "further shows your lack of attempt to understand yourself"—thereby reducing her analysis to a personal failing, and disregarding her intelligence, which, whatever you thought of her message, was evident in how she expressed herself. More backlash came from still other social media users, who called O'Neill a "poser," a "liar," and a "fake."

When I asked Alex Kazemi what he thought about all this, he said,

"I think regardless if she is being fake or genuine, look at the reaction. It comes from a place of threat." Kazemi is a twenty-one-year-old Vancouver-based writer and filmmaker, Internet famous for his short film *Snapchat: Mudditchgirl91* (first released as a Snapchat Story), about a teenage girl who acts out sexually online and ponders self-mutilation.

"Social media is like Scientology," Kazemi said. "If you leave it, you are shunned or disconnected, but if you stay on it, you are normalized and not posing as a threat. Snapchat feels insulted, because she left them. Those girls," the Nelson twins, "feel catty because it's like, What makes you any better than us?"

And was O'Neill just being "fake"? Was her exposure of her own falseness on social media an act of self-promotion after all—a clever form of rebranding? For even as she denounced her own online presence, she announced a new one, with the launching of a website, Let's Be Game Changers. She said the site would be dedicated to promoting her true passions, including environmental preservation, veganism, and gender equality. She was reportedly also writing a book.

As for her critics, O'Neill wrote, "PEOPLE SAY GOSSIP AND RUMOURS TO AVOID THE REAL PROBLEMS: paid posts, endless shoots, edited life. Is it real? Is it what our generation should be doing with our time?"

"I think that's the darkest aspect of this story," Kazemi said, "this possibility that she's saying these very real, very disturbing things for a very fake, superficial outcome, exploiting the issues to essentially loop back to what she's supposedly fighting against, and benefit from it."

But is it possible to do anything on social media that is not self-promoting? It's one of the questions O'Neill raised; and the answer would seem to have come as soon as she asked it, with the increase in her followers and fans. Even calling out the enterprise of "likes" as a sham gets you likes. This speaks to not only the culture of social media but its existence in a broader culture of fame, in which so much focus and value is placed on the self and the promotion of self, self as a brand.

Kazemi experienced a real-life cautionary tale along these lines with his Snapchat film; what he conceived as a sort of exposé of social media, fame culture, and porn was soon absorbed into all those things and, he believes, transformed into an example of the very thing he meant to condemn. "*Snapchat: Mudditchgirl91* was a social experiment," Kazemi says. "It was meant to hold up a mirror to a culture obsessed with the way things look. At a time when Instagram stars post a Windex bottle beside a skull lighter, and thousands of people gaze at it and like it for its 'aesthetic,' I wanted people to see three minutes of the unspoken reality of the way people are using Tumblr. Teens exploit themselves before they even get a chance to be exploited by older people; girls playing up to porn categories like 'barely legal' is considered normal, and they think it's artistic. It was perfect that a site like *Playboy*"—which called it "The Weirdest Snapchat Story of All Time"—"exposed the video to millions of viewers, because them sexualizing the situation just proved my point on the huge problem with what makes clickbait.

"People have a hard time separating who people are outside of Instagram and who they are on Instagram," Kazemi says. "And so I thought that if I took a girl like Internet Girl," a real online celebrity, Toronto-based Bella McFadden, "who posts self-sexualized, provocative photos, and has made a brand for herself based off of industrial-nu-metal shock"—referring to the hard-core, post–heavy metal music style popularized by Marilyn Manson—"if I got her to pretend to make a Snapchat account and perform a real-time fictional Snapchat Story for her followers, would they be able to tell that something was off? That she was in character? Or would they just grab a snack and watch this possibly mentally ill girl lose her mind as entertainment, in the same way we as a culture are the audience for the meltdowns of female celebrities like Amanda Bynes?

"Vice," the news outlet, "ended up posting about the film on their official Snapchat channel," Kazemi says, "and the account gained over fifty thousand followers." Marilyn Manson tweeted, "I have no idea why, but I know I like it." Kazemi says, "Boys were posting messages [to McFadden/mudditchgirl91] like, 'I'm going to rape you,' and men were sending dick pics, and kids were sending me pictures of themselves imitating and fetishizing the satirical scenes in the movie.

"Hollywood tried to get involved," Kazemi says, offering him deals to produce the film as mass entertainment, "and that's when I pulled the plug, rather than using this account in the future for my own self-promotion or for Bella's. I had the real-time character post a live sui-

cide note"—*The Real-Time Suicide Note of Snapchat: Mudditchgirl91*—"to
raise awareness of the psychological danger of garnering instant attention and fame too fast. The Snapchat account and all other mudditch
girl91 accounts were deleted.

"Two weeks later, Bella got an online spread in *Nylon* magazine.
People were still trying to use her as clickbait and trying to make her a
star. My message was washed away into the depths of the Internet, right
along with the movie.

"Why do some people today still have Twitter and Instagram han-
dles with the name mudditchgirl? I don't know. I think people today
just think that if you do something shocking, anything shocking, you'll
be rewarded with likes and sexual attention, which is why they saw the
character as something they aspired to be."

Beverly Hills, California

"Growing up in L.A. is unlike growing up in any other place in the
world," Leilah said. "You're growing up in an environment where everyone knows someone famous, or is someone famous."

We were sitting in her bedroom. She lived in a Spanish Revival
house in the Hollywood Hills on a steep, winding street with homes
hidden behind cockeyed driveways and boxy hedges. Her bedroom had
a bulletin board crammed with mementos of her high school years.
There was a test on which she'd gotten 99 percent, snapshots of herself
with friends, and the bright red bow from when her father bought her
first car. There were books and art supplies and stuffed animals on the
shelves and desk and bed. There was nothing that alluded to celebrity,
not a magazine or a photo.

She was a white girl, age eighteen, tall with long dirty-blond hair, a
round open face with wide blue eyes. She wore a beige cotton dress and
no makeup.

"Celebrity and fame are just kind of the norm in our day-to-day lives,"
Leilah said. "Every Westside academy," meaning the private schools in
the western part of L.A., "has a number of Academy Award–winning
parents. So every time there's an awards show, you see someone's dad

or mom or aunt or uncle, either winning an award, or there would be a pan to their table." Her own mother and father were executives in the movie business.

"Parents are by definition uncool," she said, "so when your friend's mom or dad is famous it doesn't seem all that amazing. When you see some major star getting a snack out of the refrigerator at night when you're on a sleepover, he doesn't seem that big of a deal anymore. He's just somebody's dad eating an apple.

"My friends in the Valley think of L.A. as this wonderland of stardom and fame, but it's not anything like that," she said. "The idea that everyone has of Los Angeles is actually much different than it really is. It's really not that glamorous. I think L.A. kids are more aware that fame is an illusion. So it's kind of uncool to say you want to be famous."

And yet everyone was on social media.

"Everyone knows how many followers everybody else has," Leilah said. "The amount of followers you have on your Instagram speaks to your popularity. It's very present in our lives, like thinking about how to get more likes on Instagram. Girls make sure they post their picture at the right time of day when people are online or they'll add a good filter. They'll go to a certain restaurant and post a picture saying, I like this restaurant, I like the food here, but really they're thinking this is going to make a good Instagram picture."

And, she said, everyone idolized Kendall Jenner. "I think it's because she's the same age as me and my friends and because she almost seems just like a normal teenage girl. And although she has fame and celebrity, she seems to be 'just like us.'" It was the Kardashian magic trick, becoming famous for the illusion of being real.

"I'm not that active on social media," Leilah said. "I do have an Instagram, but I don't try and get followers. When I was younger I would look at social media all the time and check how many likes I got on every picture. I was very conscious of my activity on Facebook, making sure I posted pictures on a regular basis. Now I don't think I've posted anything in two years."

What had changed? I asked.

"It was gradual," she said. She'd started to realize that social media was bringing out in her things that she didn't like. She said it made her "jealous." "A lot of social media is just the best part of everyone's lives, and it can make you jealous of what someone else's life is like. It can be very overwhelming, every five seconds seeing someone's new profile pic on Facebook and they look perfect and they get a hundred likes."

She said she'd started to catch herself thinking of ways to present herself in order to get likes. "It seemed so icky. I try to stay off it now because it's not a real representation of your life. You may post a picture with your makeup done and your hair perfect, but on a daily basis that's not what you look like."

She said she tried not to stalk people anymore, not to look through anyone's pictures. "I think that now, before you ever get to know some-one, you know far too much about them, just clicking through a few pictures. It's not real, and yet it melds into the actual reality of a relation-ship. Like somebody will say, Last month I went to visit my grandma in Wyoming, and you say, Oh, that's very interesting; but you already knew that because you looked on their Instagram profile and you saw that they posted a picture of them with their grandma.

"Social media is this weird, kind of half reality, half fantasy world. It's almost like you know people's secrets, and they never know how much you know. There's something sort of sinister about it. It's like you're spying. I have to consciously say, No, I'm not going to look through these pictures. But it's very tempting when you have this access."

She said she tried to keep off social media as much as possible now in order to "stay in the moment." "I think that making a conscious effort to not be on my phone all the time and enjoy life as it's happening has really helped me stay sane. Gradually being able to separate from social media has helped me in just realizing that the world *isn't* social media. Social media is so present, it feels like it's *there*—but it's not. You may think that that is what reality is, but it isn't. And so to separate from it just keeps me seeing the world as it is, if that makes sense."

She said she knew girls who were "obsessed" with posting, who would never stop checking their phones. "And it's strange, it's like this elephant in the room, but nobody talks about it. I think to sit on your bed for five hours checking your Instagram and Twitter and Snapchat and making sure that you have updated your profile picture—it can make you sick. To always be texting and posting and tweeting twenty-four/seven, to always be on your phone, is unhealthy.

"It's not that I don't like social media," Leilah added. "I do—I'm a teenage girl, it's part of our DNA. But I think I like it too much. I think we all like it too much."

I asked what she thought the answer was.

"I think if girls would have a conversation about the fact that our self-worth is not based on how many likes we got on our last Instagram picture or Facebook profile picture," she said, "and be really honest about the fact that we're all thinking it—we're all thinking, Ooh, yay, I got five more likes on my picture today, and getting excited when we check our phones and see ten more people liked our Instagram pictures—if we could be very candid about it, if we were able to discuss this with friends and be open, I think it would make it less scary."

She had an air of finality, as if she'd said what she wanted to say. The air conditioner in her window whirred.

Tucson, Arizona

Daisy used to have a phone but, she said, she couldn't afford one anymore. "But I don't mind," she said. "You don't spend all that time looking at Facebook."

She was sitting on the corner of Congress Street and Fourth Avenue one sweltering afternoon. The corner was near some train tracks, and a train went by emitting a long, lonely whistle. "Don't you love that sound?" she said, looking up from her sewing.

She was a white girl, age eighteen, small with short straight dark hair sticking out from underneath a scuffed-up baseball cap. She was wearing a tank top, a pair of oversized shorts, and a brown scarf tied around her neck. She was barefoot, dirty, but not as dirty as some of the other homeless kids drifting around Tucson, the ones they called crusty punks. "Well, I'm clean right now," she said. "Somebody let me use their shower."

She was sewing a coyote patch on the seat of a pair of jeans, using dental floss as thread. "After a while your pants or any piece of clothing, they start to get holes," she said with her Southwestern twang, which brought to mind the voice of Sissy Spacek in *Badlands*. She said, "It gets cold with the wind."

Tucson is a city of about half a million people, about sixty miles from the Mexican border. One of its main features, besides heat and cactus, is homeless teenagers. In winter, they come seeking the warmer climate, arriving on freight trains or by hitching rides. They line the sidewalks of Congress Street—the center of Tucson's once seedy, now gentrified downtown—sprawled against backpacks, begging for spare change. Since the 2008 recession, the number of homeless children and teenagers in America has grown dramatically. According to a report from the National Center on Family Homelessness, the number of homeless kids in America reached an all-time high in 2013, nearly 2.5 million. Poverty is the main reason kids become homeless, but some are runaways, escaping homes where there's sexual abuse or violence; and some are tossed out because they're LGBTQ.

Daisy identified as queer, she said. The last time she saw her "wife," a girl named Macaroon, was in San Francisco. They had "stood on a rock in a river" and "just repeated whatever we could remember from a wedding ceremony." Macaroon had given Daisy her name, saying she was as pretty as the flower. And Macaroon was the first person with whom Daisy had ever hopped a train. She'd been living with her grandparents in Colorado when Macaroon proposed they take off. "And I was like, Okay, why not? I wanna see the country," she said. "I wanna see the world."

She had clear blue eyes and a few pale freckles sprinkled across her nose. Her shoulders and neck were burned. Her traveling companions—a square black lab, a wriggling brown pit bull puppy, and a bearded young man named Jack, age twenty-three—were lounging on the ground nearby, trying to stay out of the sun.

"Everything wears down from walking so much," she said, talking about her sewing. "This is one of the most vulnerable areas on my body," meaning her rear end, "so I have to keep it covered. I can't be running around showing my vagina or my ass all day. So I have to sew 'em constantly, and right after I get done sewing 'em, they get a new hole.

"You don't want to flaunt what you have too much," she said. "I mean, wearing tank tops and shorts, 'cause it's hot, you can't really get away from it—everybody's gonna be looking at your legs and your cleavage, 'cause it's just there. Being a girl, it's definitely harder 'cause girls get stared at more. People like to look at a pretty face more than an ugly face. If they see an ugly face they're like, *Ewwww, I'm gonna get a disease*." She shook her head.

"Dudes got it lucky, don't you know," she said, tying knots in the threads on her coyote patch. "They don't have boobs, they don't have vaginas. They're cute, but they don't have as much to flaunt as a female. So they don't get approached the same. I mean, you don't see a lot of guys walking down the street checking out a guy's ass—like, Hey, dude, you got a nice ass."

Hearing her talk, it occurred to me that, all over the country, girls were holding protests so that they could dress in revealing clothes, and here was a girl who had to worry about covering up to keep herself out of physical danger.

"They're gonna come at you anyway," she said. "But there's no reason to give them extra cause. That's why in the winter, when it's cold, sometimes I'll put on a lotta layers and tuck my hair under my hat and try and pretend that I'm a boy.

"I don't like to get into any guy's car anymore," she said, "'cause—this happened to me before I ran away—this guy pulls into this street, I'm just trying to walk home, and this guy's like, Where you going? Like, he pulls into the road so that I have no chance to move unless I go around his car. And I say, I'm going home. And he says, Can I take you there? And I didn't want to walk another mile and a half to my house." So she got in. "So we're driving along and he's like, Do you want to make some money? He asked me, How much for an hour? And so I said, I have a gun and I'm not afraid to use it." She made her face look tough.

"I didn't really have a gun," she said. "Guns, you have to have a permit, and I lose papers too easy.

"I do have this," she said, drawing a switchblade from her backpack. It was carved, black and silver, about the size of a stapler. She let a blade fly open with a click. "This was a ground score," she said. "That's something you find on the ground that nobody claims. I got it in San Diego."

I asked her if she'd ever had to use it. "No," she said. "I mostly use it to cut fruit. That's good, 'cause I'm not really that good at fighting."

She said she ate from Dumpsters, or from handouts from strangers, or with money she "spare-changed." She mostly slept outside, she said. She didn't like shelters; "they're not so safe and anyways there's never any room." She said she'd been all over, seen mountains and oceans, "the grand parts of the country." She saw the sun setting from the cliffs at Big Sur, the green waves crashing, foamy. She saw the huge stone faces of the presidents staring down at her from Mount Rushmore.

She said a moment came when she was on a train when she realized she hadn't looked in a mirror in weeks. There was something happening to her, she said, happening to her as a girl; she didn't care what she looked like anymore, or what anybody thought of how she looked.

"When I was in high school," she said, "I used to do the same thing as everybody else. I'd have to buy pretty clothes and put makeup on and brush my hair and put it up and make it look nice and walk like this"—she did a little parody, sitting, of a "sexy" walk—"and not like this"—she moved her shoulders more naturally side to side—"you know? You have to walk a certain way, you have to talk a certain way, you have to look a certain way. You pretty much have to fit the role society gives you, because if you don't, a lot of men are gonna be like, Oh, she's pretty, but what the fuck is she wearing? Like, *Ewww*, you're not pretty because your clothes are ugly, you're not pretty because you didn't brush your hair—like, Look at you, you don't wear makeup, you ugly-ass bitch.

"Fuck that," Daisy said. "I don't like makeup. Makeup's a cover-up—it's hiding your natural beauty. You're already fucking pretty, why do you have to emphasize it? Like, I'm gonna wear short-ass shorts that show half my butt cheeks and put eyeliner and lipstick and blush and whatever else, man, just to emphasize these here cheekbones and shape of my eyes. *Ooh*"—she sounded sarcastic—"look at my *lips*. People look at your eyes anyway if you're having a conversation with someone and they have any respect . . . you don't have to put on eyeliner to make people look into your eyes . . . You shouldn't."

She said, "I think girls need to be themselves, stop trying to fit in, stop trying to do what everybody else wants you to do." She said she used to use social media, post pictures of herself, and try to get "the likes." But "I don't like social media," she said. "Social media's just really overrated. Like, people just want to stare at themselves and never talk to each other. If people never talk to each other, what's the world come to?

"One time I was in a mall," she said, "and I saw a guy looking at his phone walk right into a glass door." She laughed, shaking her head.

"I don't know why girls put up all those sexy pictures online and all that," Daisy said. "Like, why do they have to have every guy be like, Damn, girl. Why do I need a guy to make me feel pretty? I already feel pretty. I guess I used to not think so. But then I did."

She said she hadn't seen a TV show or a movie in months, hadn't opened a magazine or gone on the Internet to surf the Web. I asked her if she thought that getting away from the sexualized images of women in mass media had made her care less about looking "a certain way" herself.

"I don't know," she said, shrugging. "I just realized I loved myself the way I am, no matter what anybody thinks. I stopped trying to make everybody think I'm pretty or like me, or trying to fit in—'cause, shit, I did try to do that for a while . . . and that never works, never gets you real friends. I stopped talking to a lot of people 'cause a lot of people judged me for it and now I don't care.

"I love myself," she said. She smiled. "When I get hyper, though, I'm fucking nuts."

Panama City Beach, Florida

The girls were twerking around the pool at the Holiday Inn Resort on spring break. The DJ was playing "Blurred Lines," Robin Thicke's 2013 hit that tells a girl, *"I know you want it,"* and it seemed to be a favorite.

A line of girls was squatting, thrusting their hips back and forth, jiggling their butts. Boys jumped out of the pool and shoved their crotches into the twerking girls from behind. The twerkers laughed, grinding back into the boys.

"Spring break, yeah!" shouted a boy.

All over the patio, kids were taking pictures with their phones—pictures of each other, pictures of the twerking girls. They were posting them to social media.

There were little clusters of girls taking selfies, girls doing the duck-face, throwing faux gang signs.

"You look hot," they told each other. "*You* look hot." "We're so hot."

"Show your tits! Show your tits!" chanted boys and girls in the pool.

Out on the beach, there was a sprawling crowd of kids, all milling around, red plastic Solo cups in hand. A volleyball game was going on. A football sailed back and forth. Suddenly a cheer went up.

Everybody looked up at a small plane puttering across the sky; it was trailing a banner with a logo for Trojan, the condom company: REAL. GOOD. SEX.

"We want sex!" chanted boys.

"Woo-hoo!" said girls.

"We want pussy!" said boys.

Girls said, "Yeah!"

Kids were filming the plane.

There was a group of four girls in bathing suits, attempting to take a group selfie, but one of them kept slinking down into the sand. She lay in the sand, laughing.

"Peyton, *stop.*"

Peyton was drunk. She'd been drinking since early that morning, said her friend Hayley, sighing. "Well, we've all been drinking since this morning," Hayley said, "except for me—'cause I was the one driving. I'm the responsible one. I'm the mom."

"You are the mom," said her friend Brooke.

"Peyton is not the responsible one," Hayley said, putting her hands on her hips, looking down at Peyton on the sand. Peyton was contorted with laughter. "Peyton is the one we all have to look after."

"I love you," said Peyton.

"Put your arm around me," Hayley said, trying to pull Peyton up off the ground.

"Okay, Mom," Peyton said, putting up her arms.

Hayley hoisted Peyton off the ground and posed her against her shoulder, like a drunk rag doll.

They'd driven straight through from Detroit, about fifteen hours from Panama City Beach. They were students at Wayne State University College of Nursing, all age eighteen. Their bodies were thin and toned—they said they'd been working out "like crazy," getting ready to spend a week in their bikinis. "And you know there's going to be pictures." They'd arrived at the hotel and checked in and come straight out to the beach. And now they wanted to send a Snapchat to their friends to announce their arrival. They wanted to Instagram the moment. They posed together, smiling their "we're having the time of our lives" smiles. Brooke held a cell phone camera up in front of them.

But Peyton slunk down on the sand again before they could get a good picture.

"Peyton is the one our moms are paranoid about us acting like," Brooke said, looking down at Peyton.

"We're always scared she's gonna wander off without us," said their friend Taylor.

"Do you wander off sometimes?" Hayley asked Peyton.

"A little bit," said Peyton.

"She's the devious one," said Brooke.

"When Peyton wanders off, we have to try and find her, 'cause she obviously will wander off and talk to anyone for a long period of time," said Hayley.

"Just a loooong period of time," said Peyton.

"And you can't trust everyone you meet, can you, Peyton?" Hayley said, leaning down again to pull her up.

"Bad things can happen," Peyton said in a singsong.

Some boys had noticed Peyton's predicament and had come over to watch. They were shirtless, wearing multicolored trunks and funny hats—a cowboy hat, a sombrero. They looked as if they'd been getting in shape, too, pumping iron in preparation for spring break. One had a tattoo on his chest, block letters saying STAY HUMBLE.

One of the boys took out his phone and started filming Peyton.

"Hey, stop," said Hayley.

"Why? It's funny," said the boy.

"No it's not," Hayley said.

The boy kept filming.

"You guys, that is really not okay," said Brooke.

The other boys laughed.

Then Peyton started to feel like she had to throw up. She flipped herself over and went on her knees in the sand. "Uh-oh," she moaned. "I'm gonna be sick."

"Oh, no, not here," Brooke murmured worriedly.

"Come on, get up, I'll take you to the bathroom," Hayley pleaded in Peyton's ear.

"Let her hurl!" said one of the boys.

"Are you filming this?" said his friend, grinning.

"Yeah," said the boy with the camera, "this is hilarious."

Peyton spewed all over the sand with a roaring belch.

"*Ewwwwww!*" said the boys. "Oh my God!" "Nice one!"

"Oh, I'm putting this on the spring break Snapchat Story," the boy with the camera said.

"No, you guys, don't," said Taylor.

"Seriously," said Hayley. "That is seriously fucked."

"She's the one who's wasted," said the boy.

There's been a precipitous rise in drinking among high school and college-age girls, according to studies. In 2013, the CDC identified binge drinking as "a serious, under-recognized problem among women and girls." About 20 percent of high school girls binge drink, the CDC reported, as do around 24 percent of college-age women. "Between 1999 and 2008, there was a 52 percent increase in the number of young women showing up in emergency rooms for being dangerously intoxicated, while the rate for males in the same period rose only nine percent," reported *The Wall Street Journal* in 2013. "Between 1998 and 2007, there was a 30 percent increase in the number of women arrested for drunk driving, while there was a seven percent drop in drunk driving arrests for males." Girls are reportedly having their first drink at a younger age, at around fourteen. No study has really accounted for why.

Is it because of the way images of women drinking have been glamorized in pop culture? (*"It's all a blur last night,"* Katy Perry sings in "Waking Up in Vegas.") Scenes of women clinking glasses as an act of camaraderie and triumph have been mainstreamed since *Sex and the City.* Or is it because, since the '90s, beer and wine and liquor companies have stepped up their marketing to young women?

Is it due to the many pressures on girls—pressure to achieve in school, in sports, and simultaneously be beautiful and sexy at all times?

In a survey by Girls Inc., school-age girls reported feeling an overwhelming pressure to be "perfect"—not only to succeed in school and engage in multiple extracurricular activities, but also to be "kind and caring," "please everyone and dress right," and "be very thin."

Or is there more drinking by teenage girls and young women because, in hookup culture, alcohol diminishes the need for emotional intimacy during sex? Or is it a display of female power, to "drink like a man"—even as female bodies process alcohol at a slower rate, leading to intoxication after fewer drinks?

Peyton wiped her mouth. She stood up shakily, holding on to Hayley. "You okay?" Hayley said.

"Yeah, I'm good," said Peyton.

"Let's go get you some water," Hayley said.

The other girls followed as Hayley hustled Peyton, staggering, into the hotel.

"Thanks for the show!" said the boy with the phone.

Hayley put her middle finger up in the air, not turning around to look at him.

Los Angeles, California

Rachel lived in Beverlywood, in the Westside of L.A. Leilah told me I should talk to her, as she was an unusual girl these days, "really anti–social media." I went to her house one afternoon; we sat on the back patio by the pool. Her shaggy sheepdog padded around. Rachel was eighteen, with long curly brown hair and merry brown eyes. She was barefoot, wearing a sundress; she brought to mind a hippie girl from the 1970s.

"I think the most relevant thing for me was deleting my Instagram," Rachel said. "I didn't like the way that my life was becoming something staged for pictures. I prefer to enjoy what I'm doing for the sake of doing it, not for getting other people to approve of me. And that felt like what it was becoming. There's this expression, 'Do it for the Vine,' and I really don't like that saying because it means we're not doing it to do it, we're doing it to record it and have people press 'like.'

"I started a rule among my friends: phones in the middle of the table on silent whenever we get together for lunch or dinner. Whoever picks up their phone first has to pay the bill. It helps a lot because people now have to actually be forced to pay attention to each other. I went camping a couple weeks ago and everyone was looking for a [Wi-Fi] bar so they could post a picture and finally they gave up—we were out of range. So I put everyone's phones in the car and I said, It doesn't matter if we get service. And for a couple of hours, it was so much fun. We went hiking. And everyone was talking to each other, which is so rare these days.

"And then we came back to the car and everyone just grabbed their phones. The service had reached us, and the rest of the night was spent on phones. We were sitting around the campfire and people were reading things out loud from their phones, and I said, Why don't you guys want to be here in this moment? And they didn't understand. They said, We're present, we're reading current events, it doesn't get more present than that." She smiled at the irony of it.

I asked her if she ever felt like she missed out on anything, not being on social media.

"Yes, but in a good way," she said. "I'll be in conversations with people where they'll be talking about whatever so-and-so tweeted or posted and I don't know what they're talking about, but I also don't care. Sometimes there will be a ten-minute-long conversation where I can't participate because I didn't see that post or I didn't watch that video, but I'd rather not anyway. If I want to get to know someone, I don't want to know the version of themselves that they artificially created and posted online.

"High school is about being cool," Rachel said, "and being cool is being in-the-know. So if you don't have that one app that's popular or you haven't seen that thing online that everybody's talking about, you can be made to feel like you're out of it, and no one wants to be that one that doesn't *know*. But how important is it really to know what Mary posted yesterday on Instagram? If I want to know Mary, I'll call her up and ask her to hang out."

She said she'd also noticed how the pressure to create a "perfect" social media self was influencing girls to focus more on their appearance. "It just seems like the norm now, to be 'into beauty,' and there's no, like, embarrassment about it. Everyone is trying to look like the girls in magazines or the famous girls online and there's so much access to so many different products to make yourself look 'better.' I think it's sort of normal now to *not* look like what you really look like. 'Get this makeup, get this body, wear this bra, and you'll look this much better.' It's a kind of Photoshopping of your actual self.

"I have friends who are very into makeup, and they watch YouTube videos about it to learn how to put it on. They're like, I have to have this blush and this eyeliner. I know a girl who posted before and after pictures of herself as she was giving herself a makeover. She posted about it, saying, like, I don't need that snack, and she showed the workouts that she did at the gym. And she was totally comfortable sharing very provocative pictures of herself, semi-nudes, after she had lost weight, saying, Look how much better I look now. It was actually disturbing. I kept thinking, Why does she need us to see this?

"My brother has a Tinder and is active on it," she said, "and we were looking at the girls on his feed. So I downloaded Tinder onto my phone so we could see the difference between the girls' and the guys' profiles, and the girls were a lot more primped and edited, posing in very seductive ways. The girls were more sexualized, pushing up their boobs and making pouty faces. Some of the guys were in the gym, not wearing shirts, but mostly they were just drinking or holding girls on their arms. I think it's pretty obvious that social media is having a bigger effect on girls than on boys.

"Obviously there's a beneficial quality to social media, having everybody tuned in to more or less the same wavelength," Rachel said. "It's so much easier to share information and exchange opinions. But like any tool, social media can also be misused, and I think right now it's being misused socially. I feel like there are so many ways this technological boom could have gone that would be so much more beneficial.

"I just don't see a place for it in my life. I think my feelings about this come from my family. We're a family that is really close and likes to be really present with each other all the time, and that's not possible if you're focused on what you're gonna put on your timeline. We don't allow any electronics at the table, and when we go on family trips, we leave our phones in our rooms. I'm so grateful for that. I have a close relative who is really attached to her phone, and she'll spend the entire time at family dinners taking pictures of everybody, and then she goes in a corner, creating an Instagram, and then she's checking for likes and she's not part of the conversation. I see that in a lot of people now and I don't want to be that way."

Rachel's family was Jewish, and they kept Shabbat, the tradition of having family meals and refraining from working or using electronics from sundown on Friday until sundown on Saturday. "Doing the family dinner thing on Friday nights brings us together," she said. "We talk about our week and sit and share, and I think that is rare for a lot of families these days. We've prioritized real intimate family interactions, and I think that has made a huge difference . . . When you don't have the skills and the practice of being comfortable with just being, then the phone becomes a sort of crutch. People say, When I'm standing by myself, I'll pretend I'm on the phone or pretend I'm texting—they don't want to be alone. But then your existence, it's not real. Or you're creating a different version of it, and missing out on so much by just staring at your phone.

"I don't have any solutions," Rachel said, "but I think it's time to start addressing the fact that things have gone awry. Social media has created an even bigger disparity between the way you are and the way people *think* you are; and it seems like it doesn't lead to a fulfilling life.

"People are not pursuing happiness with this. They're pursuing an attractive picture."

Sacramento, California

I talked to Zanab on the phone; she was in Sacramento. We met telephonically through a mutual friend. She was eighteen and described herself as a "modern Muslim." Her parents were from Pakistan, but they didn't always speak Urdu in their home, she said, as more traditional families did. She and her mother didn't wear hijab. "I wear short sleeves. I can dress however I want." She said she was on social media—Facebook, Snapchat, and Instagram—"but I'm not constantly updating pictures. It's not like an hourly thing. And actually I hate it.

"My school is very academic," Zanab said. "We come home and start working on homework immediately, so I don't have a lot of time for anything else. And this relates to why I think social media is not that great—not because it's all an ego thing; it's because being on social media takes away from the precious time that you have on this earth.

"As a Muslim I believe one day the end is going to come and I'll be judged for my actions and what I did on this earth. Being on social media takes away from the precious time that you have and that time could be used in much more productive ways—whether religiously, with family, or whatever it is; it's just not a good use of time," she said.

"My perspective isn't so much religious, it's more, I guess, toward productivity and what you can do with your time. I'm only eighteen, I've seen very little of life, and I hope to see a lot more, but what I'm seeing of the kids of this generation after me, it really saddens me because they are all constantly on their phones, Snapchatting, Instagramming, and some of these are kids less than fourteen years old.

"I went to a family dinner two nights ago," she said, "and one of my cousins, she is no more than twelve, she had her iPhone out the entire time while we were at dinner and she was FaceTiming with one of her friends. It was not only a breach of social etiquette—the fact that she even had an iPhone at dinner and was FaceTiming the entire time—but it saddened me, because instead of having a nice dinner with the family and spending time with us, she was doing something else. I know that we would never do that when I was younger. When I am with my family, my phone is never on, I'm never texting people. The constancy of social media is increasing all the time, and you can really see it in younger kids.

"People have no etiquette for using their technological devices anymore. I'll see people at the mosque taking selfies on their phone. They'll be texting in the mosque—that irks me so much. I can't explain how much it upsets me. I'm the same age as some of them and I would never do that. We're in a holy place and you're taking selfies on your phone? Really? How do people think that that's okay?" she asked.

"I have seen girls whose mothers are sitting right next to them when they're on their phones and the mothers don't say anything. My mom and I have discussed this multiple times. We agree it's incredibly disrespectful—you're in the house of God and you're on Snapchat? What's worse is that at my mosque, our imam, he has multiple times asked people to put their phones away, and they don't. He has decided he is going to buy a cell phone jammer to stop the incoming calls."

"People take calls in the mosque?" I asked.

"While we're in prayer!" Zanab exclaimed. "Forget about that they have their ringers on and it goes off while we're in prayer. Two, three, four people's phones will go off even after the imam says turn off your cell phones. It's so sad—and it's not just kids, it's older people; some people just let it ring. What goes through your mind is, How can you think this is okay?

"I saw a lady during Ramadan, she was sitting in the mosque talking on her phone while people were doing prayers—people were in their sanctuary praying and she was talking on her phone! I just looked at her like, Are you serious right now? It's not just young people who are addicted. You try and tell your friends to put it away, but nothing changes.

"I get so mad when I'm out to lunch or dinner with my friends and they're playing on their phones," Zanab said. "I think it's so rude when you're talking to someone and they're texting. I don't understand what runs through people's minds. You don't see it as much in Third World countries. There's more human, face-to-face interaction there—people *have* phones, they just seem to want to talk to each other. People in America don't like interacting face-to-face anymore. That's how people used to communicate before they had phones, by actually talking. I'm like, Hello, remember conversations?"

Brooklyn, New York

"I found Jesus on the Internet," said Kira. She gave a little laugh. She was joking, sort of, but not really. Here's what happened:

She was a private school girl; she'd recently graduated from one of the top private schools in Manhattan. She had made excellent grades and competed in sports and enjoyed, for the most part, her school experience. But there was always a certain tension, she said, because she was one of the few black girls in her class.

"It's not that anyone is openly racist," she said, sitting on the front stoop of her family's home in Fort Greene, Brooklyn, one summer day. She was wearing jeans and a T-shirt and flat sandals. Her hair was pulled back in a stylish bun. "But things would always come up where it becomes clear there is this divide between you and the other girls in terms of your experience," she said.

"Like you'd hear someone say something a little strange about a pop star, like Beyoncé; they'd say something like, Oh, how can Beyoncé say she's a feminist when she's dancing around like a stripper, or something like that. And they don't understand that to black girls, black women, Beyoncé is a symbol of something greater than just what she's wearing. She's an incredibly powerful businesswoman who has a very strong perspective on female empowerment.

"But you can't get into a big argument every time," Kira said. "You have to pick your battles. You have to be with these girls for four years, and so you don't want to constantly be fighting over every little thing."

Then something came up that Kira felt she could not ignore. It was in July 2014, when Eric Garner was killed by a New York City police officer who put him in a chokehold while arresting him on suspicion of selling cigarettes on the street. "This was such a clear-cut case of police brutality and also racism," Kira said. "It was so traumatic to see this man be literally murdered before our very eyes. I couldn't watch it but one time. It was just so disgusting that this happened.

"And we would have never known it happened without phones," said Kira. "So that's the first thing I want to say about phones. With everything bad that's happening with phones, they are the one thing making it possible for people to really see the racism. I feel like God has given us these phones to help us bear witness to our struggle. I think a lot of people had no idea just how bad it was before all these videos of police shootings."

And in the months after the Garner killing, there were other shootings, other videos. "It seemed like every day you would go on Facebook and see another unarmed black person being murdered," Kira said. "So that's another thing I want to say about social media: it raises awareness. People would never have seen these things without the Internet and social media. They would never have seen Phillip White or Walter Scott being killed. I think the one that got to me the most was Tamir Rice."

Rice was the twelve-year-old Cleveland boy who was shot point-blank by a police officer in a park, where Rice had been playing, in December 2014. A tip had come in to 911 that there was "a guy . . . with a pistol" in the park; Rice had a pellet gun, a toy. "They shot him for no reason," Kira said. "He was just a child and they murdered him. And the police called this 'reasonable.' I think that one affected me the most because I have a little brother who is thirteen. He was twelve at the time, same as Tamir."

She'd been following stories about the Black Lives Matter movement that had been growing in the wake of more police shootings. She'd been reading tweets with the hashtag #blacklivesmatter on Twitter. The Black Lives Matter movement, which would prove to be so effective in the coming months, was begun by three black women—community organizers and activists Alicia Garza, Opal Tometi, and Patrisse Cullors—as an online campaign. "And that's another thing about social media, okay?" Kira said. "It's a tool for activism. All these people all over the country, all over the world, were galvanized by this organizing that was going on on social media. You could go on Twitter and find out exactly where you could go to a protest. You could hear a thousand voices talking about what was happening and how it was affecting different people. Some people are using social media to promote themselves. But other people are using it as a way to try and really change our society for the better."

In December 2014, she said, she joined the Millions March NYC protest. "The media said tens of thousands of people were there, but to me it seemed like it must have been a lot more than that." She marched up Sixth Avenue and then down Broadway, "and then when we got to the Brooklyn Bridge, I participated in a civil disobedience. The police said we couldn't go across, but we did it." She was energized by the protest, she said, by the feeling of being a part of change. "It was good to see so many white people out there," she said. "I actually didn't expect that. There were people of all races."

But when she went to school on the Monday morning after the protest, she was shocked to find that some of her classmates were not even aware that the protest had happened. "An historical event takes place in your city and you don't even know?"

When she talked about it to other students, she said, there were some "strange reactions. Like some people didn't understand why you 'need' to protest. They didn't say it this way exactly, but it was like, Your life is fine, what are you complaining about?

"If people aren't aware that there is institutional racism, and these police shootings affect every black person, how do you explain it?" she asked. "Where do you begin? How do you explain that this could happen to my little brother at any time? Or *me*—black women get killed by police, too, although you don't hear as much about it. That's why they made #SayHerName"—a hashtag created to raise awareness about the deaths of Sandra Bland, Natasha McKenna, Janisha Fonville, and other black women who died as a result of police shootings or while in police custody.

Kira tried, she said, to engage in dialogue with her classmates. "But almost every conversation was very frustrating. One girl even said, like, Why can't they forgive? And I'm like, Why can't they forgive? Why can't the police stop shooting?"

She started to feel tired a lot of the time, she said, "which didn't make any sense, 'cause I was getting lots of sleep. If anything, I was sleeping more." She started to wonder if she was depressed. "And I've never been a depressed person, like nothing ever gets me down." She suddenly felt, a few times, a shortness of breath when she was sitting in class or walking through the halls. She started to wonder if she was developing anxiety; there was so much going on—applying to colleges, taking SATs, "all that senior stuff." And then it finally occurred to her that "I can't breathe" were Eric Garner's final words. "It's one of the chants we do at protests—'I can't breathe.' And here I was literally feeling like I couldn't breathe." She then identified her anxiety as coming from something else; from "the reality of my school life versus the reality of what I was seeing online, all this murder of black people."

And then, she said, "I hit my bottom," in June 2015, when Dylann Roof, twenty-one and white, killed nine black people in Charleston,

South Carolina, at one of the oldest black churches in the country. "This was a place that was important in the Civil Rights Movement," Kira said. "He'd killed all these devout Christian people—even the preacher," Clementa Pinckney, "who was also a state senator. Six women and three men." She stayed up all night, she said, reading about the shooting on the Internet, "and crying.

"And, I don't know, there was just something about it that made me want to go to church. My parents are not very religious. We have a church, and we go on holidays with my grandmother. But after I read about that, I just felt the need to go."

It was the place, she said, where "black people have always gone to find strength and solace in the struggle."

Panama City Beach, Florida

When I was in Panama City Beach, I bought some GoPro footage for sixty dollars from a guy I'll call "the Bro." I had seen the Bro walking up and down the beach with a GoPro camera strapped to his head. He was staying in my hotel. The Bro was a towering hunk of a boy, age eighteen, who went to Michigan State University. He wore a backward baseball cap and a backpack from which there was a plastic tube extending into his mouth; it carried beer. As I sat in my hotel room watching his work, I thought if the Bro didn't go into finance, as he told me he planned to after graduating from college, he had a future as a pornographer.

There were many sequences of the Bro walking up and down the beach asking girls to pull down their bathing suit tops, which they usually did, Girls Gone Wild–style, after giggling and making him promise that he "wouldn't put it on the Internet." There were close-up shots of the shaking behinds of girls twerking. "Let me get the butt," the Bro would ask, at which point the girls would laughingly back up into his camera. He filmed himself fingering the crotch of a girl as she twerked by the side of the hotel pool.

There was footage of the Bro and his buddies, black and white boys together, talking about how they had met some "white hos" who "liked the long d," or dick.

And there was footage of the Bro and his friends having an assignation with these same girls, whom the Bro had described to me as "up-for-anything sluts."

Teenagers have been filming themselves having sex since at least the mid-1990s, when digital camcorders went into mass circulation. They were only doing what they saw adults doing—making sex tapes, making porn, which they could now view online whenever they wanted. The leaking of the sex tape of Pamela Anderson and Tommy Lee in 1997 glamorized the practice. "Where are we?" Anderson asks Lee in a moment from their footage. "We're on some big-ass yacht," says Lee. At first seen as shocking, the graphic images of these two celebrities having sex in a luxurious locale (on their honeymoon in Cancún in 1995) were soon distributed across the Internet, watched by millions of adults and kids. By today's standards, the Anderson-Lee sex tape seems mild; they're married and in love and rather tender with each other. Their private footage was never meant for public viewing. "The tape was, without question, physically and illegally taken from Anderson and Lee's home," said *Rolling Stone*. The leaking of their sex tape normalized not only sex tapes themselves but their nonconsensual sharing. Afterward, sex tapes became a routine occurrence in celebrity news, and in teenage life as well.

In the Bro's footage, you see four girls, all barefoot in bikinis, dancing around his hotel room; they're waving around a large plastic water pistol and spraying it into each other's mouths; it's full of vodka. "Spring break forever, bitches!" one of the girls says, seemingly quoting from *Spring Breakers*, the 2013 movie starring Selena Gomez and Vanessa Hudgens, both Disney Channel stars when the girls in the room were little.

Spring Breakers, in the half-century-long tradition of spring break movies (the first was 1960's *Where the Boys Are*), is about a group of soul-searching, sexually curious college girls who travel to Florida for spring break. In the 2013 incarnation of the tale, they get some guns, knock off a fast-food joint, and then become the "bitches" of a drug-dealing rapper named Alien, played by James Franco, with whom they have a threesome before making off with his money in a stolen car.

The movie, directed by Harmony Korine, was hailed by reviewers as a triumph for its dreamlike cinematography ("a trippy, fluorescent whirl of boobs and bongs"—*Us Weekly*) and parody of youthful American decadence ("the pursuit of happiness taken to nihilistic extremes"—*The New York Times*). It also had an inordinate number of butt and crotch shots not unlike those in the Bro's GoPro footage. *Rolling Stone* said the film had a "kind of girl-power camaraderie that could almost be called feminist," while *The Guardian* declared that it "reinforces rape culture . . . It's 90 minutes of reinforcement of the party girl image, the kind of bad girl who's 'just asking for it.' " The film did well with college students.

"We got a cheerleader in the house!" one of the boys in the Bro's GoPro footage crows.

"Wooooo!" say the girls. "Yeah, baby."

"You can record this," says one of the girls.

"Oh, we're recording, don't worry," says the Bro from under the camera, which is still strapped to his head.

We watch as the girls lie down next to each other on the bed and squirt liquor into each other's belly buttons. "One-two-three!" The boys swoop down to do "body shots" off the girls, slurping liquor from their stomachs. "Yeah!"

Then the boys and girls switch places; now the boys are lying side by side, getting liquor shot into their belly buttons by the girl holding the water pistol. The perspective of the Bro, the cameraman, has changed. Now, instead of looking down at the girls, he is looking up at them.

They're smiling. The girl poised to do a body shot off the Bro's stomach is dark-haired and voluptuous, in a hot-pink fringy bikini. She grins at him with big white teeth.

"You're going lower, way lower," the Bro tells her, suggesting that she should travel to places below his belly.

"Three-two-one!"

The girls bend down and do their body shots, and then they all come up but one—the girl in the hot-pink bikini, who continues traveling from the Bro's belly button all the way up his torso, licking and kissing until they are finally making out.

"Wooooo!"

The other girls in the room hoot and holler and slap the pink-bikini girl's behind.

"Shake that ass, bitch!" they say, continuing to spank her as she and the Bro make out. Then the footage cuts off.

I thought about the scene later when reading some pieces on the subject of drinking and campus rape. The girls in the Bro's GoPro footage were clearly into what was going on. They were also drunk.

Drinking is a complicating aspect of the campus rape debate, which, among other things, has made it very charged. In 2013, when *Slate* columnist Emily Yoffe wrote an essay headlined "College Women: Stop Getting Drunk," she was excoriated. Yoffe argued that with studies claiming a connection between binge drinking and rape on college campuses, young women should be warned about the dangers of drinking. "Young women are getting a distorted message that their right to match men drink for drink is a feminist issue," wrote Yoffe. "The real feminist message should be that when you lose the ability to be responsible for yourself, you drastically increase the chances that you will attract the kinds of people who, shall we say, don't have your best interest at heart."

On Jezebel, Erin Gloria Ryan expressed her outrage at Yoffe's piece: "DON'T write a piece about rape prevention without talking about rapist prevention." On *Salon*, Katie McDonough accused Yoffe of victim-blaming: "Our culture is swimming with examples of women—in movies, television and real life—who are 'punished' for their 'bad choices' with sexual violence. 'Bad choices' include wearing a short skirt, staying out too late, getting too drunk, trusting too much." In 2014, *Wall Street Journal* columnist James Taranto did blame women for their rapes, arguing that intoxicated rape victims should be held equally accountable as their intoxicated rapists—and that they are not, he said, is "self-evidently unjust." As unjust as rape? you want to ask.

Spring break and the specter of rape have been conjoined since *Where the Boys Are*. It was billed as a comedy, but—tellingly, in one of the first Hollywood movies to explore the changing sexual attitudes of American youth—it's really about a sexual assault. Toward the end of the film, the "insecure" girl in the group (Yvette Mimieux) is raped by a cavalier college boy who suffers no consequences for his crime. Mimieux's character is portrayed as having made those "bad choices" McDonough mentions. She's the only one in her group who actually has sex (willingly so, before her rape); the rest of the girls, who

remain chaste, are rewarded at the end of the film with committed relationships with boys they've met on their trip. The film was in keeping
with a long Hollywood tradition of shaming girls for being sexually
active.

In 1991, the reliably hard-hearted Camille Paglia praised *Where
the Boys Are* for its verisimilitude, saying it "still speaks directly to our
time . . . The victim, Yvette Mimieux, makes mistake after mistake,
obvious to the other girls. She allows herself to be lured away from
her girlfriends and into isolation with boys whose character and inten-
tions she misreads." Paglia dismissed "the theatrics of public rage over
date rape" as feminists' "way of restoring the old sexual rules that were
shattered by my generation. Because nothing about the sexes has really
changed." In other words, boys will be boys, and girls must maneuver
accordingly.

The girls I met on spring break were very aware of the potential for
rape in the hypersexualized atmosphere. Many of them carried their
own plastic containers, which they called "chug jugs," in order not to
have to accept drinks from boys, who, they feared, might roofie them,
or drug them with a "date rape" drug, most commonly Rohypnol. But
their chug jugs tended to be half-gallon-sized and were filled with what
they called "jungle juice," a potent cocktail consisting of a haphazard
blend of alcohol and juices. They sipped from the jugs all day long,
getting drunker and drunker. "I don't want to be raped," a nineteen-
year-old girl named Mariah said. "I don't want to be drugged. That's
why I am gonna be really careful with my drinking here. If it was back
home, I would be comfortable getting passed out, I know my friends
would take care of me, but here, I don't know what would happen if I
was passed out."

It was the way she phrased this that made me start thinking about
rape in connection with social media, and porn. She talked about "getting passed out" as if it were something that just happened to her, as if
she were passive in the experience. There were moments in other interviews when an impression of passivity among girls came up: the girls in
Montclair saying how they felt they had to placate boys who asked them
for nudes, lest there be retaliation; girls all over saying they felt there
was nothing they could do when nudes were put up on slut pages; Lily

in Garden City and others saying they felt they had to put on makeup and dress a certain way in order to attract boys and fit in with girls; the girls in Boca saying that they felt they couldn't speak up against sexual harassment; Jennifer Powell-Lunder saying outright, "Something about social media is making girls more submissive to boys."

When I spoke to Donna Freitas, she said that, in her interviews on campuses, "these young women's sense of their own agency is incredibly detached; they tell me, And then I found myself in someone's bed having sex. There's little actual choice or volition when you are drunk, and there is this expectation among everyone that if you are walking with a boy to your dorm room after a party, sex will necessarily happen."

Freitas talked about interviewing a girl who described a night when she went home drunk with a boy and she "woke up and, she said, He was masturbating in my mouth. She was talking about this like this was a usual occurrence, and I think it is." The girl was surprised when Freitas referred to the experience as a sexual assault. "She had no idea that that's what it was," Freitas said. "I'm not sure some young women know what consent is anymore." It's ironic that there has been such outrage in the media about young women crying rape, when in actuality there seems to be a lack of understanding among some young women and girls about whether their encounters are rape or not.

"We've learned to be distant from our bodies," Freitas said, something she attributed in part to our increased interaction on screens. Her words tied in to what Rachel and Leilah in L.A. were saying about how being on social media made them feel less than "present" and "in the moment." "We're interacting with another virtual persona, profile to profile," Freitas said. "Kids think they can hook up with someone like they're friending someone on Facebook, but afterward they realize it wasn't like friending someone on Facebook, because they say, I have this pit of emotions in my stomach. But I'll do it again to get rid of the feelings, I'll use alcohol to tamp down these feelings."

There's been a lot of talk, in the current discourse around feminism, about women having "agency," or independence of choice and action, self-definition and self-direction. There's so much emphasis on acknowledging the need for this, and in honoring girls' and women's capacity for this, that there's never much questioning of whether they actually have it. Agency isn't something that's always necessarily present in someone's decision-making. In fact, it's the nature of a sexist society to rob a woman of her agency long before she becomes a woman, when she's still a girl. Women's identities crystalize in cultures that are in many ways dead set against their interests. Girls are exposed to expected norms of behavior long before they're able to decide whether these norms are what they choose to inhabit. Feminists since the 1960s and '70s have been aware of the challenge of women having true agency in a society that teaches them to be subordinate and passive, or hypersexual, or whatever undermines their ability to achieve equality and respect.

That's why, when antifeminists accuse women of being complicit in the sexist stereotypes they also object to, feminists can legitimately argue that women might make different choices—they might have agency—were it not for the constant images and messages in the media, advertising, and so forth promoting sexist norms and role models. There's also the risk for girls and women of being punished for refusing to comply with what's expected of them. For feminists, the answer to the problem of agency has long been that of women discovering their own "voice." And so now, if we are always insisting that no matter what girls want to do is what they need to do, and what they should do, then we are denying the possible influence of sexism on their decision-making—we're denying the existence of sexism. If girls aren't educated about what sexism is and encouraged to consider its effect on their own lives, then how can they have the critical tools with which to discover their own agency, and their own voice?

I thought about all this while watching the Bro's GoPro footage, which seemed like *Spring Breakers* redux. I caught the girls sometimes looking seductively into the camera, as in porn, where women are often seen looking intensely into the eyes of men when they give them blowjobs. Kim Kardashian does this in her sex tape, when she's giving oral sex to Ray J.

Later, when I saw the Bro by the pool, I asked him what had happened after the camera had turned off. I told him I was a little worried about whether the girls had been able to stay in control of the situation.

"Dude," he said, giving me a look. "Those bitches were wild. They wanted to make a porno."

Tucson, Arizona

The offices of Youth on Their Own (YOTO), an organization providing support for homeless kids in Tucson, have a closet full of things they need to survive and get along: bottles of water, packaged food, bedrolls, backpacks, blankets, clothing, soap, tampons, sanitary napkins, and school supplies. Many homeless kids go to school, the only stable place they know.

The majority of the kids YOTO serves are girls. And because of the demographics of the area, many are Latina and Native American. Native American girls are disproportionately likely to become homeless and run away, according to the National Center for Children in Poverty. The principal reason is the high incidence of domestic violence, sexual assault, and rape on reservations, where there's often no accountability for the perpetrators. According to the Justice Department, one in three Native American women will survive rape or attempted rape, about double the national rate. About 40 percent of Native American women will be victims of domestic violence, according to the National Congress of American Indians.

Sarah Deer, a professor of law at William Mitchell College of Law, a 2014 MacArthur Fellow, and a citizen of the Muscogee (Creek) Nation, says that Native American girls who are labeled as runaways often are actually the victims of human traffickers. "Fourteen-, fifteen-, sixteen-year-old girls," says Deer, "especially when there's a history of drug and alcohol issues, a troubled childhood, they write it off as a runaway, when in fact you find, if you dig deeper, there is predatory behavior and someone targeting these girls and trying to prostitute them. They sell them on Craigslist, on the Internet. The only thing that will happen when the girl comes back is they will say, Oh, she ran away. No one will believe them."

At YOTO I met an Apache girl, Arlene. She was eighteen, with shiny, thick black hair and caramel-colored eyes, wearing a crop top and jeans. She'd grown up on the reservation of the White Mountain Apache Tribe. The Apaches have lived in eastern Arizona for thousands of years; they fought with a legendary fierceness against the settlers and Spanish and American military forces that came to take their land, until finally they were overcome. Now what's left of their original territory is a place for tourism—fishing, camping, gambling. Tourists hike on their land, have barbecues, and hunt elk.

"We live in the woods," said Arlene. "We have a trailer, not bigger than this room." We were sitting in an air-conditioned conference room of about 300 square feet. "Four of us stayed in there—me, my brother, my mom, and my mom's husband. We had no electricity, no running water or gas. We had to go get water from a faucet somewhere. We used a generator whenever we didn't have candles. We used to cook over a fire; we didn't have a stove. We had an outhouse. I didn't like it because if you live in a normal house you can walk down the hall to the bathroom, but we had to put on a jacket, sweats, and walk outside just to go.

"Every time my mom would get drunk her husband would beat her up. He beat her up all the time. He never hit me or my brother. But my brother would get mad and get violent sometimes. When he was sixteen, he killed someone. He's in jail now.

"I started drinking when I was about thirteen. Why I started drinking was because I was mad. In a way I wanted to forget about everything, just give up on everything; in another way, I wanted to get people mad so they could start caring about me. I would drink vodka. There's certain places, certain houses, hot spots," on the reservation, "where people sell alcohol and drugs. They don't care how old you are, as long as you have the money. I would go to this house all the time; they would give me a fifth of vodka. For money I would sell my stuff, steal from my mom, sell her DVDs. I sold her camera.

"I went to this house one day with my dad—my dad was drunk; he left me there. There was this guy—he used to see me around and say stuff to me, tell me to go meet up with him and party with him. He was like thirty-five. This house—anyone can go in there; people sleep in there; anyone could walk in. It's a place where people party. I was sitting there on the couch outside—and I was really drunk and this guy told me to drink with him. And I was like, Okay. Then he gave me a pill. He said, Take this. I didn't care about anything. So I was like, Okay, whatever. I was so mad, so upset. I wound up waking up in this room—it was, like, little flashes. Where am I? I was laying on this bed. I didn't have any clothes on. I didn't see him anywhere."

He had raped her.

"It's fine," she said. Her breath was coming shallow and rapid.

"I told my mom what happened and she was like, Oh, yeah. She didn't say anything—just Oh, yeah. She didn't say anything to help me feel better. She didn't want to listen."

Native women, says Deer, have learned to "suffer in silence." "Why report a crime to a system that may re-victimize you, that won't hold anyone accountable?" she says. "The cycle just repeats itself—mothers, daughters, sisters, nieces, go through the same thing down through the generations because these women don't have a legal system to turn to." (In 2015, a new federal law went into effect which for the first time allows Native American tribes to prosecute some crimes of domestic violence committed by non-Natives in Native country. While the law was a welcome step forward, many feel that it still falls short, with its very limited parameters.)

But Arlene did report her rape to the FBI. "I reported it," she said, "and they said they would do whatever they can. I've had an FBI agent investigating me ever since I was in the fifth grade. I was in a foster home, and my foster dad used to do stuff to me when I was nine, ten. So did a friend of my mom's. They were letting him stay with us. My mom was passed out. When I told my mom about it, she was really mad. She thought I was lying. I didn't bring it up anymore. My mom wouldn't listen; she thought I was being dramatic. I wasn't. I was just telling her what had happened, how I felt. She said there's nothing you can do about it, so don't even talk about it.

"I was in treatment for alcoholism and trying to kill myself and running away. I've tried to commit suicide ever since I was eleven. I tried to overdose. I used to cut myself. Once or twice I was really serious; the rest of the times I was just really mad and didn't know what to do. I was in treatment for a year. They were working on my cases against my former foster dad and my mom's friend. I went to all the trials. The FBI man and I, we were really close, so when I was in the hospital," after she was raped by the thirty-five-year-old man, "he came into the hospital. I told him everything that happened with the guy at the party house. I told him I was drunk. He and his partner, they put it in a report, but they said they couldn't really do anything 'cause I was drunk; they said people would say I could be lying, exaggerating. I felt stupid."

She had moved back into foster care.

After she'd gone, I said to Dane Binder, YOTO's program director, who had sat in on our meeting, that Arlene's experience seemed extraordinarily hard. He said, "It's actually pretty common."

Later I looked up Arlene on Instagram. She had done many selfies, puckering up for the camera, blowing kisses, showing cleavage, posing in tight skirts. "Hot yo," "Damn someone looks nice," male followers commented. I expressed my sadness at seeing these images to a female friend in her thirties. She disagreed. "No matter what she's been through, she wants to own her sexuality," she said. "This sounds like her trying to figure that out—how to own her sexy." Was it that? Or was Arlene being abused all over again? I wasn't sure.

New York, New York

"The hos have come out for Halloween!"

The four NYU girls, freshmen, age eighteen, were stumbling through Washington Square Park. They were on their way to a party in someone's apartment. They stopped along the way to take an Instagram picture under the Washington Square Arch.

"We hos! You know we hos!" they said, dancing around.

They posed for their group selfie with their different phones, striking seductive poses. Then they stood in a huddle together, bent over the phones, posting their pictures.

They were dressed as a sexy cat, a sexy devil, a roller derby queen, and a Disney princess.

I asked them if I could talk to them.

"If you can stand some dirty talk!" the devil said, slapping me with her devil tail.

" 'Cause we dirty hos!" said the princess.

They were already drunk—"We started drinking at four!"—and they said they had forgotten the address of the party. The cat fumbled in her purse, where she said there was a "flyer." Only she carried a purse—"I'm the designated cell phone carrier!"—because the others didn't want to ruin their costumes with the encumbering look of a bag.

I asked them whether they were wearing their costumes ironically or in earnest. Hadn't "slutty" Halloween costumes become a cliché?

"'In Girl World, Halloween is the one night a year when girls can dress like a total slut and no other girls can say anything about it,'" said the sexy devil, quoting *Mean Girls*.

The roller derby queen said, "It's fun!" She did a little turn on her Roller Blades.

"Don't slut-shame us!" the princess said.

I said I hoped I wasn't.

"You're slut-shaming by even asking the *question*," the princess said. "Why can't we dress however we want? What makes one way of dressing slutty and one way *not*?"

"Yeah, what's 'slutty'?" said the sexy cat.

"This is a SlutWalk!" said the sexy devil, prancing up and down, shaking her hips. A SlutWalk, of course, is a march or protest, as well as a movement, seen since 2011, in which women wear "slutty" clothes in order to protest rape culture, specifically the way it blames rape on a woman's clothing or appearance.

"I'm so proud of you for being a slut and looking hot," the princess said.

Some other girls teetered by on heels. They were dressed as . . . sluts?

"Lemme guess," the princess called. "You're sluts!"

"You know we're big sluts!" said one of the girls.

Everybody laughed.

"Yeah, sluts! Go sluts!" A group of boys dressed in costumes had joined the party.

"Go fluts!" said the one dressed as a vampire, through his plastic vampire teeth.

"Hooray for sluts!" said the one dressed as the Dude from *The Big Lebowski*.

"Yeah," said the girls, less enthusiastically.

"You're my perfect match, sluts," said another boy. "I'm Tinder." He pointed to his shirt, on which he had drawn a heart and an X. He wore the Tinder logo on his head, a flame made out of red construction paper. "You wanna swipe right on me?"

"How long did it take you to come up with that?" the sexy devil asked.

"This already sounds like one of my Tinder conversations!" said Tinder Man.

"Why don't you come with us, sluts?" said the Dude. "I know a really slutty party we can take you to where you can get really slutty."

"Thank you, no," the sexy devil said. "We have a party to go to already."

The sexy cat found the flyer in her purse, and the girls hurried out of the park.

"Go sluts! Go sluts!" the boys chanted after them.

Tucson, Arizona

Night descended on Tucson and the temperature dropped. Daisy put on her green army jacket, her socks, and a pair of sneakers. Jack woke up. They chatted awhile and decided this was the night they were going to California.

"We're gonna hop out for the West," Daisy said. "Get on a train and see how far it can take us."

They made their way to the rail yard, which was enclosed with a chain-link fence. They walked along, looking for a good place to jump over. They were trying to stay out of sight, which was difficult while traveling with two dogs, the lab and the rambunctious pit bull puppy.

There were a couple of trains already stopped in the yard. One of them said EMP WESTBOUND on its side. "I wonder if that one's going west," whispered Jack. "It says *west*," Daisy said. "I know," said Jack, "but that don't mean it's going west right *now*." "Then why's it say it?" Daisy asked. They were bickering, like any couple.

They'd met in Golden Gate Park, in San Francisco, they said, about six months before. "First time I saw her," said Jack, "she had the gay pride flag on her back, so I was just like, whatever," meaning he thought he didn't have a chance. Then they saw each other again and "got all shwilly," drunk. Daisy had told me earlier she "liked to hold his hand"; and she said she found it easier traveling with a guy. "That's just how it is," she said. "If you're with a guy, there's less chance of getting raped."

Something about the way she said this made me want to ask her again why she ran away. Then she told a story of sexual abuse that had happened in her home when she was fourteen. It was a family member, a man. The police had brought her home. Then she ran away again.

I asked her if she'd ever talked to her mother about it. She said her mother didn't believe her. "For a long time she blocked me on Facebook," she said. "She wouldn't answer my phone calls, wouldn't answer my texts. So I just left her alone."

She and Jack waited in the dark until the flashlights of the bulls vanished. Then they got the two dogs over the fence, ran across the yard, and disappeared into the train.

Panama City Beach, Florida

In Panama City Beach, in March 2015, a nineteen-year-old girl was gang-raped in broad daylight on the beach as she lay unconscious in a lounge chair. Cell phone footage of the crime was retrieved in a police investigation. The video shows a crowd of hundreds of spring breakers, boys and girls, watching, not intervening, a few feet away; some are filming. "She isn't going to know," one of the rapists reportedly joked.

When police tracked down the victim, she said she didn't remember anything about it. She said she thought she might have been drugged. Three arrests were made, two of students at Troy University in Alabama. One of the young men is alleged to have known the victim since middle school; they traveled to spring break together.

In porn, videos of a "passed out girl" getting gang-raped are not uncommon. On Pornhub and PornTubeMovs, there are links to videos titled "Passed Out Girl Fucked at Party" and "Passed Out Girl Gets Raped by Three Men."

Chapter Seven

19

New Albany, Indiana

It was the night of another party with all her friends, the same sort of party they'd been having since high school. They were doing all the same things—drinking, listening to music, joking around, trying to hook up. This one was in someone's basement. It was always in a basement or a backyard or in someone's dorm room, now that they were all in college. There was always an air of expectation, involving the promise of sex. Who would hook up with whom, who hadn't hooked up with him or her before?

"In this town everybody's pretty much fucked each other," Meredith said. "It starts in high school, freshman year. There's not much to do around here but drink and fuck and get on Twitter."

But everybody knew Meredith probably wouldn't hook up, because she just didn't. "Meredith still has her V card," said her friend Ethan approvingly, putting his arm around her. "He's a fuckboy," said Meredith.

She liked to joke to her friends that "the name of my sex life is *The Virgin Suicides*." It wasn't that she couldn't get a guy; she'd had plenty of opportunities. "All the guys around here are so easy. They try and get in every girl's pants." In college, there was the expectation you would hook up, and that made her a curiosity to those who didn't know her, at first.

"They say like, Well, why not? They look at you like, What's wrong with you? They act like maybe you're a prude." But after they got to know her, they knew that this was not the reason.

It wasn't that she refrained from sex on religious grounds. "My family goes to church and all that, but I'm not like some Jesus person." She knew all about the "purity myth." "I don't think being a virgin is some badge of honor or makes you any better. I mean, when the Jonas Brothers had purity rings, me and my friends just laughed."

When she was in high school, she'd had a crush on Rob Pattinson, the handsome *Twilight* star. She'd had a pillowcase with his face on it that she slept on every night. "I just liked the way he was so in love with her," meaning Bella, the gloomy high school girl played by Kristen Stewart. "I liked how he respected her and protected her." It's true—he was a vampire. "But that made them have to wait," she said. "It was all this sexual tension all the time and it made it romantic. I'm a hopeless romantic."

Now, everything went so fast because of social media, she said. "And it's like you don't know who you can trust 'cause everybody's talking to like three different people at one time. So many relationships start and end because of social media. It causes so much conflict nowadays. People are just too friendly with each other all the time, and some are sneaky."

She liked movies like *The Notebook* and *Dear John,* where the lovers loved each other and no one else. "The guy is just so in love with the girl and the girl gets to decide what happens and there's this really long time before anything does happen, and there's this build-up of feeling." But she'd never seen anything like that in real life. "Now it's just like, DTF?" Down to fuck. "Yeah, let's go. And maybe they wind up dating. But I've seen so many girls get their feelings hurt and so many girls get bad reputations.

"I'm just afraid if I lose it to someone who doesn't really care, something bad will happen. Or it'll just be so disappointing. I'm afraid I'm gonna get my feelings hurt, and it will be just awful."

She'd dated guys, she said, but "they've all been douchers," douchebags. "I don't want to waste it," her virginity, "on some random guy. They all have STDs from these girls around here. Nothing verified, but I'm sure. They don't use condoms."

She looked around at the party, sipping her beer, wondering how or when it would ever happen for her.

In the Bedroom

In the 1980s, when HIV/AIDS was spreading and taking thousands of lives, American high schools instituted sex education classes stressing the use of condoms. There was AIDS hysteria and legitimate AIDS fear, and "safe sex" became a national obsession. With the ascendance of the Moral Majority and the Republican right, sex ed in American schools also encouraged abstinence. Teenagers were still having sex, but they seemed to get the message, using condoms more often. Widespread condom use may have had an effect on the teen pregnancy rate, which dropped by more than 30 percent between 1990 and 2004. Condom references in pop culture abounded; in the 1992 Cameron Crowe movie *Singles*, there's a party scene in which a basket of condoms is prominently displayed. "They're free," the hostess says cheerily. Condoms were party favors.

Throughout the 1990s and 2000s, antiretroviral drugs, used to control HIV infection, became more and more effective. The disease was by no means cured, but it became possible for people with HIV to live long and relatively healthy lives. With this welcome advance in medicine, the fear of AIDS receded; the disease was no longer the constant subject it once was in the media; and condoms became less evident in pop culture. In *Sex and the City* and *Entourage*, two hit shows from the 2000s about sexually active women and men, there was rarely any mention of condoms. In one episode of *Sex and the City*, the female characters do discuss them, sheepishly admitting that they don't always use them.

In a 2014 survey by the Trojan condom company on the attitudes and behaviors surrounding condom use, only 35 percent of adults reported always using condoms when they had sex. The study found that among those with repeat partners who reported not using a condom each time, close to 50 percent said they stopped using them in the first month of their encounters, and 62 percent by the second month. In 2015, a study by the CDC on the sex habits of teens was widely reported as saying that "contraception use" among teenagers "remains high." But what the CDC study actually said was that the majority of teenagers used condoms "the first time they had sexual intercourse." Of the 34 percent of teenagers who reported having had sex in the previous three months, 41 percent said they did not use a condom the last time they had sex. Use of the morning-after pill by teenage girls increased over the past decade from 8 percent in 2002 to 22 percent between 2011 and 2013, suggesting a decline in condom use or other forms of birth control overall.

Meanwhile, STDs are on the rise, which would suggest declining condom use as well. Half of the 20 million new STDs reported between 2011 and 2013 were among young people between the ages of fifteen and twenty-four. Young people of those ages contract gonorrhea and chlamydia at four times the rate of the general population, and people in their early twenties have the highest reported cases of syphilis and HIV. One in four American women is currently infected with HPV, the human papillomavirus (the transmission of which condom use can greatly reduce, but not entirely prevent, as HPV is spread by skin-to-skin contact as well as by sexual intercourse). Some strains of HPV can cause cervical cancer. In 2010, the U.S. Department of Health and Human Services reported that "four in ten sexually active teen girls have had an STD that can cause infertility and even death."

Medical professionals and sex educators use the terms "condom fatigue" and "prevention fatigue" to describe a reluctance to use condoms by those who have grown weary of the safe sex message. Some experts attribute condom fatigue to the fact that younger people have no memory of the worst years of the HIV/AIDS crisis in the 1980s and early '90s. "The young people today know HIV as a manageable, chronic disease," Laura Kann, an expert in youth risk behaviors at the CDC, told *Time*. "It's not something that can kill you in their eyes. So that leads, most likely, to an attitude that it's not something that they have to protect themselves from."

When I asked, "Do you use condoms?" of some young men in their early twenties in New York, active dating app users who said they had multiple sex partners every month, one answered, "Fuck no." And another, "I'm not from the eighties. Everyone thinks that you have to use condoms, but in this day and age there's just not that risk out there."

"I think it's also the alcohol," says Eriauna Stratton, twenty-four, formerly the vice president of Voices for Planned Parenthood at the University of Kentucky. "As the resident adviser in my dorm I saw so many really drunk girls, especially freshman girls. Once a girl was brought back to the dorm by a stranger. We had to call an ambulance. She had alcohol poisoning; we were afraid she might die. I think the alcohol is leading them to not use condoms. They're not sober enough when they have sex to think of protection."

Beth Kaper, a sex educator in Scottsdale, Arizona, who teaches students in fifth grade through college, says, "You can see the decreased condom use in the rise in chlamydia. Teenage girls are being infected at alarming rates." The highest rates of chlamydia infection in the United States are among girls and women ages fifteen to twenty-four. "Chlamydia is a silent disease," Kaper says. "Usually girls don't have any symptoms, so they don't go to the doctor, but if you don't get it treated it can lead to infertility. The guys can get it, but it usually doesn't affect their fertility.

"Young women aren't protecting themselves," says Kaper. "They get hooked into the social aspect of having sex. The peer pressure now is ten times worse." She attributes this increased pressure in part to social media. "Social media, as it's used," she says, "is encouraging very sexual behavior at a very young age. And they're not learning to be intimate in any other way than a sexual way. They think intimacy is sex. We try to give them alternatives, explain that holding hands is intimate, talking to each other, spending time together. There is so much oral sex— usually it's girls giving it to guys. One boy said, 'Well, Mrs. Kaper, it's a great way to get to know someone.' It's something so casual to them."

There seems to be a correlation between the reduced use of condoms and a lack of conversation around the subject of condom use. The research by Trojan found that "nearly 40 percent of people who didn't use a condom during their last sexual experience reportedly did so without discussing it first." Is this also due to condom fatigue? Or another sign of the diminished communication brought on by sexual relationships mediated by screens? In hookup culture, where partners are often relatively unknown to each other, or even anonymous, is it surprising that some aren't having conversations about contraception?

This would all seem to tie in with a 2015 report by the Rhode Island Department of Health, which found a connection between rising STD infection rates and high-risk behaviors associated with casual sexual encounters arranged on dating apps. Several other studies have also found that people who meet sexual partners online engage in riskier sexual behaviors.

Lastly, there's the widespread feeling that using condoms makes sex less enjoyable, especially for men. In 2013, Bill Gates presented a challenge to inventors to come up with "a Next Generation Condom that significantly preserves or enhances pleasure" as a way of promoting "regular use." Though "male condoms are cheap, easy to manufacture, easy to distribute, and available globally," said a news release from the Bill & Melinda Gates Foundation, "including in resource poor settings, through numerous well-developed distribution channels, . . . the primary drawback from the male perspective is that condoms decrease pleasure as compared to no condom, creating a trade-off that many men find unacceptable. Is it possible to develop a product without this stigma, or better, one that is felt to enhance pleasure?"

The bigger question is why aren't teenage girls and women insisting that boys and men wear condoms? Why are women acquiescing to the preferences of their male sex partners, gambling with their own health and well-being? The research by Trojan also found that men are more likely to be the ones expected to purchase and provide condoms in heterosexual encounters, despite the fact that 75 percent of those surveyed agreed that men and women are equally responsible for bringing up condom use. So why are women leaving the question of condoms up to men? Why, again, are they being passive?

Notably, condoms are not used in porn. Since 2012, when California passed Measure B (the County of Los Angeles Safer Sex in the Adult Film Industry Act), requiring porn companies to use condoms when filming all vaginal and anal sex scenes, the majority of the porn industry has moved from Los Angeles to Las Vegas, where there are no such restrictions.

"Thousands of [porn] performers have been infected with thousands of STDs over the last few years according to the Los Angeles County Public Health Department," wrote Michael Weinstein, president of the AIDS Healthcare Foundation, a vocal supporter of Measure B, in 2012. "That is not a small issue . . . These performers are not disposable. As important is the effect that the films themselves have on public health. The fact that most straight porn is made without condoms sends a horrible message that the only kind of sex that is hot is unsafe."

Jeffersonville, Indiana

It was the Fourth of July, and the three girls were walking in the town parade. Mikayla's grandmother was running for an office in the county government, and they were supporting her by strolling alongside her candidacy golf cart. Mikayla's grandma waved to the town. The golf cart rolled slowly up Main Street.

The girls, Mikayla, Ashley, and Meredith, all nineteen and white, listlessly waved American flags on sticks. They were wearing short shorts and T-shirts, Converse and flip-flops and sunglasses.

People sat on the sidewalk, on folding chairs, watching the parade go by. Balloons bobbed around on strings. Little girls in red-white-and-blue dresses called "Bubble gum!" at a man who was tossing handfuls from a classic car.

"God bless America!" a woman yelled. "Woo!"

The girls seemed to be getting bored.

Ashley started checking Tinder on her iPhone.

"This guy matched me," she said, walking along. "I'm gonna say, 'Hey good-looking, what's cooking?' He looks like Peter Pan."

"Oh my God, he *is* Peter Pan," Meredith said, checking out the guy's profile pic. "He goes to my school," Bellarmine University in Louisville. "We see him eating in the student lounge all the time. He's pretty cute in person."

"He says, 'Let's do dessert,' with a winky face," Ashley said, rolling her eyes. "He sounds boring as fuck." She was a dark-haired girl with a rock 'n' roll vibe; she had a stud in her lip and wore a T-shirt with a picture of Machine Gun Kelly, the white rapper.

"I just got a message," said Meredith, checking Tinder on her own phone now. She was tall and rangy with shoulder-length dark hair and the jaunty air of a female comedian. "He wants to know my Snapchat."

"Tell him your Snapchat," Ashley said, unimpressed. "Ugh, this other dude won't leave me alone. I need to find a dude I can say is my boyfriend 'cause this dude keeps sending me pictures of his big huge donkey dick . . .

"Oh, no!" Ashley suddenly exclaimed. "I just passed a cute boy with long hair and forgot to swipe!"

Meredith said, "That always happens."

Ashley said she liked "tattooed guys." "I wanna marry a rock star."

The girls swiped at more guys' pics on their phones. Mikayla, blond and olive-skinned, suppressed a yawn.

"Why are you on Tinder when you have a pregnant girlfriend?" Ashley asked, seeing a picture of someone they knew on her screen. "Who would date him?"

"Someone who wants to be a stepmom," Meredith said.

"Meredith has the best Tinder story," said Ashley.

Meredith grinned. "On my first Tinder date," she said, "the guy got pulled over and his license was suspended and he didn't have the right tags on his truck. And the cop said he'd had a DUI." Still, she kept dating the guy for a month. "Then he broke up with me," after she wouldn't have sex with him, she said. "The next day on Facebook I saw he had a new girlfriend already."

New Albany, Indiana

"I just think that boys are really disrespectful now," Ashley said. "Like, I feel like they can do anything, and say anything, and it's okay, and it's not okay at all. And I know it's kind of hypocritical 'cause I touch the 'd.' "

The others laughed. Ashley was known to be a "wild child," and one of the reasons was her habit of grabbing boys' crotches. She said she did it because "they do it to us. If they can do it, why can't we?"

They were sitting on couches in a dorm room at Indiana University Southeast, a regional campus of IU in New Albany, Indiana. New Albany is a bedroom community of some 36,000 people on the Ohio River, just across the water from Louisville. It's surrounded by farmland. It has an abundance of fast-food restaurants. "We eat McDonald's like every day," Ashley said.

New Albany was the town where the five friends in the room had grown up; they'd known one another since middle school. They were Ashley, Meredith, Kelsey, Natalie, and Natalie's boyfriend, Matthew.

They were eating rainbow-colored Popsicles.

"Boys will grab your ass," Ashley said, "just grab you, and you'll turn around and they just act like that's okay. And their friends'll be like"—bro voice—"*Yeah.* But that's *gross.* Boys feed off each other. I feel like they do it to look cool for their friends."

"And like, having 'ten stats,'" Natalie said, meaning sex partners numbering in the double digits. Natalie was white, small and blond, and wearing a Teenage Mutant Ninja Turtles T-shirt. "That's cool to them," she said. "Like having fucked ten girls. Like, guys I went to high school with had competitions" to see how many girls they could have sex with. "The basketball team was notorious for competing on how many girls—like, I know one guy who is up in the *eighties.* Like, that is a bizarre number to fathom."

"I don't even know eighty boys to fuck," said Meredith.

"And, like, flipping is an option," Natalie went on, referring to the practice of passing a girl from boy to boy during a sexual encounter.

"Like running trains on people," Meredith said. "That's taking advantage of girls when they're drunk. I guess she doesn't have to be drunk, but they tag each other; one gets in there and finishes"—she smacked her hands together to indicate a callous attitude toward "finishing"—"and then he tags his friend and they're like, Yeah, and then *he* does it—"

"Like takes advantage of her when she's drunk," explained Ashley.

"Like takes advantage when the girl is drunk and unaware that it's happening," Meredith said. "It's happened to girls at our school."

I asked if what they were essentially talking about was gang rape. They said, "Yeah."

The scenario they described was much the same as what allegedly happened in 2013 at Hobart and William Smith Colleges in western New York, in 2013 at Vanderbilt University, in 2014 at Johns Hopkins University, and at other schools around the country, as reported in the news: a girl gets drunk, and a group of boys rape her, sometimes recording the acts on their cell phones. "It's sick how normalized rape is while drinking," tweeted a teenage girl, @nicolepaigeh, in 2014.

Security cameras from the night of the alleged rape at Vanderbilt show Brandon Vandenburg, his teammate on the Vanderbilt Commodores Cory Batey, and two other young men carrying the unconscious victim to Vandenburg's room. At least five people reportedly saw this, but no one seemed to think there was anything odd about it; at least not enough to report it. Seeing girls passed out on campus and being carried into dorm rooms by boys apparently wasn't that unusual.

Kelsey started talking about Steubenville, the notorious case from 2012, in which an unconscious sixteen-year-old girl was raped by two high school football players and sexually assaulted by others, some of whom shared pictures and video of the acts on social media, in Steubenville, Ohio.

"The guys 'had a future' and the girl 'ruined the future' for them," Kelsey said with a frown. She was a dark-haired white girl; she wore a black sundress.

"She 'ruined the future' for them," she went on, "but she's the one that got raped." She was referring to when CNN reporter Poppy Harlow lamented on-air that the boys accused of raping the girl "had such promising futures—star football players." "What's the lasting effect, though, on two young men being found guilty in juvenile court of rape essentially?" asked CNN anchor Candy Crowley.

"They turn it around on girls," Meredith said. "Like, she shouldn't have been drunk, she shouldn't have been acting like that—"

"She shouldn't have been wearing that," said Ashley.

"Yeah, like she was asking for it, she was dressed like a whore," Meredith said. "If you're a guy," she added sternly, "just have some fucking sense—don't do it."

"Why should it matter what she was wearing?" Kelsey asked.

"Well, when they raped her they took her clothes off, so it didn't matter what she was fucking wearing," said Meredith grimly.

I asked Matthew how the guys he knew would view the subject of this conversation. He was a white boy, brown-haired, square-jawed, and preppy, wearing boat shoes and salmon-colored shorts.

"It depends on the guy," Matthew said. "Like, I know guys that would think [running a train] was the ultimate goal. I know guys that I grew up with that their"—air quotes—" 'goal' is to 'Eiffel Tower' a girl."

"I don't even know what that is," said Kelsey.

Matthew smiled uncomfortably. "It's when two guys have sex with a girl and they high-five"—he brought his arms down in a V, smacking his hands together for emphasis—" 'cause, like, one's at one end, one's at the other, and they make the Eiffel Tower," or a tower shape, above the girl. "It's like a life goal of theirs."

"Pluggin' her up," Meredith said.

"Pluggin' her up," said Ashley.

They laughed, outraged.

What they were describing were common scenarios in porn. Hundreds of thousands of results come up in an Internet search for "Eiffel Tower porn." "College dudes doing the Eiffel Tower" is the title of a video on the porn site BurningCamel, on which college kids post self-generated pornography. "Running a train" porn, where multiple men have sex with one woman, is another popular theme, with millions of links. "Running a train on bitches," "Running a train on this MILF," and "Running a train on teen" come up in searches.

"Guys, like, joke about it," Matthew said, referring now to "running a train," "but when it comes right down to it, it's just so, like—I don't even know how to explain it." He made a disgusted face.

"It's nasty," said Meredith.

"It's fucked-up," said Ashley.

"We don't partake in it," said Natalie.

"But we know people that do," said Kelsey. "They brag about it."

"The not-funny part is when it happens and the girl doesn't even want to do it," Matthew said.

"In all honesty sometimes the girl is willing," said Meredith, "but it's still gross. It's gross when girls get taken advantage of, but it's gross when some girls want to do it."

I asked her why she thought it was "gross" for girls.

"Because they're just doing it for the guys," she said. "They're doing it 'cause they think that's what the guys want . . . Some girls are like, Let's do the map, or whatever."

She was referring now to an expression describing when a girl offers up the three orifices of her body—"mouth, asshole, and pussy," or "the map"—for a guy to enter.

"Stop!" shouted Ashley, laughing.

"Girls say, Let's do the map?" I asked.

"And we know who. And it's pretty sad," said Kelsey.

"It's just what a person likes," Matthew said with a shrug. "As a guy, I don't see going to a party, getting drunk off my ass, and seeing who I can hook up with, how fast—that's not something I seek to do. But if you ask five of my closest guy friends, that's *all* they like to do."

"Like *all* of them," said Kelsey.

"Like all of them—literally," Ashley said. "Like almost every dude is like that."

"Like literally now, even me being with a boyfriend," Natalie said, "I will get a text that says, Wanna fuck? I keep them to show him," Matthew, "so he knows who it is."

"And it's guys I grew up with, known since first grade," said Matthew.

"It's one man for himself," Natalie said. "There's no bro code. 'Yo, wanna fuck?' It's bad."

"I took a women-and-gender class," Kelsey said, "but we never talked about some of the most downright ornery stuff that goes on." In other words, what was happening in the real lives of the girls she knew was not being covered in her college women's studies class. "For example," she said, sitting up straighter, "for guys it's okay if they fuck like ten girls, but if a girl does it, we're a whore."

"We're a run-through," Meredith said.

"We're a run-through," said Kelsey, counting off the insults on her fingers, "we're dirty, blah blah blah. But if a *guy* does it—"

" 'Oh my God, props,' " Ashley said in a "bro" voice.

"Yeah," said Meredith, throwing faux gang signs.

" 'You're the man,' " said Ashley.

" 'He is awesome,' " said Kelsey.

" 'He pulls bitches,' " Natalie said.

"And that's stupid," said Meredith.

"And it really is like that," said Kelsey.

"On Tinder, like on social media," Meredith said, "you'll be going through looking at it, and some guys, literally their little biography will say straight up, like, If you don't wanna fuck, don't message me."

Kelsey gave a rueful laugh. "It's so messed up."

"They'll tell you, Come over and sit on my face," said Ashley.

"Like, Don't bother swiping if you're not looking for a hookup," said Meredith. "And it's just so disgusting."

Matthew looked skeptical. "Do you think through the generations it's changed, though?" he asked.

"I think it's *out* there more," Meredith said. "There's more ways now to say it and be up-front about it."

"I don't think guys have changed," Matthew said. "I think it's just out there more because of social media."

Newark, Delaware

It was a Friday night, and the girls of Haines were having a "pre-game," a drink before going out to bars. "Haines" was the nickname of their house on Haines Street, just off Main, a popular hangout, they said, for "cool girls."

It was a rickety-looking two-story house with two porches in front, peeling and worn from many years of college kids plowing through.

"Cheers!" said the girls, all white and nineteen, doing vodka shots, followed by swigs of Diet Coke.

They were students at the University of Delaware, which traces its history back to 1743. Three of the college's first ten students went on to sign the Declaration of Independence and one to sign the Constitution. It's a publicly and privately funded university with a quality of education said to be on par with an Ivy League school. The campus is picturesque, with redbrick Georgian buildings and a wide green central lawn. Delaware has an active Greek life, and is consistently ranked as a top "party school."

A YouTube video from 2012 shows scenes of a Delaware frat party: you see kids drinking from beer bongs; kids grinding up against one another, dancing; girls making out with each other; a boy fingering a girl's crotch as she dances. "Why do you love Delaware?" an off-screen interviewer asks. "Because of the fuckin' bitches here!" says a boy. "We're all fucking pretty," says a girl. "We're all hot," says another girl.

"You look sexy tonight," the girls of Haines told each other. "You look hot."

They said they were a "pretty well-known squad."

"Everybody just says, We're going to Haines," said Rebecca, a tall girl in a black bustier and short shorts. She had long blond hair, canny eyes, and a smoky voice. "We're such a group of stoners," she said. "Boys come over to smoke a blunt and chill and have a good convo and don't hit on us and don't worry, Does this girl know what she's doing? Does she want my dick? No—we're just friends with them."

"Everyone knows we're a squad," said Sarah, an artsy-looking girl in harem pants.

The girls in the kitchen were all in their going-out clothes—bandeaux and bustiers and halter tops and long, low-cut dresses and stylish short shorts. They were all sorority girls, except for Rebecca, though they lived together off-campus rather than in a sorority house.

They snapped selfies together, Instagramming and Snapchatting themselves in their "hot" looks. They consulted one another on what they should write as captions. "Glam squad?" "Oh no, that's so over-used."

There was a lot of long, dark hair and long earrings swinging around and the sound of girl chatter and laughter and the clean smell of shampoo and perfume. "Oh my God, what is that *dress*?" someone asked. Eve—a thin dark-haired girl with angular features—had entered the kitchen wearing something short and tight, black and strappy, shades of *Fifty Shades of Grey*.

"It's funny," Eve said, "all my girlfriends who saw me in this outfit tonight were like, You look sexy, you look great, but then my friend Jake, when he saw me, the first thing he said was, Are you trying to get railed tonight? And I was like—" She blinked rapidly, showing annoyance.

"Getting railed," she explained, was "getting fucked, having sex with someone, in a really not nice way. It's interesting," she said, "when you hear girls talk about how you dress, they use confident words, like 'hot.' And then you hear that from a boy and it's like, Should I change?"

"It's the double standard," Rebecca said blandly, pouring out glasses of Franzia white wine.

"I feel like girls dress for girls, not for guys," said Ariel, who wore short shorts and a silky black halter top. "My boyfriend says, You always dress the hottest when I'm not with you. I like to look cute because that's my image on the line when I go out."

"Cheers," said the girls of Haines again, clinking wineglasses.

"But most of us here," Rebecca said, "our friends are all *guys*. We're very much guys' girls and not girlie girls."

What was a "guys' girl"? I asked.

"Guys like us," Rebecca said, "because we're not like girls—we're like *them*. This is the house guys come over to to chill, and not the house where the girls are just being dramatic and *naah-naah-naah*"— she made the face of a girl being "dramatic."

"I always say that I don't want to be a girl," said Lally, a petite blonde, only slightly embarrassed by the confession. "I *want* to be a guy. I don't like being a girl. I used to hate it."

"Except for the clothes," said Rebecca, after a brief silence.

They laughed.

In 2009, the Urban Dictionary defined a "guys' girl" as "a mix between tomboy and girly girl . . . The guys talk openly in front of her and she wouldn't be out of place going to a strip club with them. A guy's girl enjoys the freedom guys have in farting, eating disgusting food, and in how they discuss sex, but still likes to look and feel like a woman."

A guys' girl was the antithesis of a "girlie girl," said the girls of Haines. Girlie girls were "bitches," "uptight." And not good friends.

"In every sorority there's one group of catty bitches who think they run shit," said Eve. "Everyone puts those people on a pedestal."

"It's so insane," Sarah agreed.

"The way that girls talk about you," Lally said, "you can't even have a true girlfriend, because she's a bitch. She's just a *bitch*. But not these girls," she said.

"I used to *hate* being a girl more than anything," Lally went on, "but then I fell into the right group. I wanted to be a guy because I don't want to deal with drama, I don't want to have to deal with who's gonna be my friend today—are they gonna be mad at me again? About like stuff that's so stupid and petty to think about. You don't have to think about that stuff with these girls."

"That's why when we found each other it was so great," Ariel said, "'cause it was like, Yo, you're basically a *dude*. We can hang out and not be catty, not give a shit about what that person wore last night."

The impulse to act "girlie" could come up in texting, they said, and the way it made girls anxious about how to respond to guys. "Like, when I'm texting a boy," Sarah said, "the first thing I do is to type out a paragraph—well, guys don't give a fuck about eighty percent of what I'm trying to say. I have a lot going on in my head and I know that a lot of it is complete *nonsense*. But I have people here who will point that out to me. Being a girlie girl is being someone who's gonna get really tightly wound and not realize that."

Hearing them talk made me think of Bethany Mota, YouTube sensation and self-proclaimed girlie girl. For the girls of Haines, defining themselves against the stereotype of the girlie girl seemed like a brand of feminism: they saw themselves as the opposite of such girls, girls who fulfilled undermining stereotypes. But in defining themselves against one stereotype, were they only becoming entangled in another, one based on male approval? Semantically, in their self-definition, guys' girls belonged to guys. They were "cool girls," it seemed, because guys thought they were cool.

"And also," Rebecca said, "look at this house. It's not, like, a girlie place. We're all really dressed up right now, 'cause we're going out and we wanna look good, but we're not always in makeup. We'll be in our sweatpants. Free the nipple!"

She was referring to the Free the Nipple movement, dedicated to desexualizing women's bodies, particularly breasts, and exposing the double standard of how male versus female bodies are viewed.

Somehow this set off the Miley Discussion.

"She Instagrams like it's Snapchat," said Eve. She meant that Miley's Instagrams were as personal and intimate as Snapchats.

They talked about Miley's infamous performance at the MTV VMA Awards in 2013.

"I thought it was hilarious," Sarah said. "The foam finger? Like, What the fuck is happening?"

"She was making a name for herself," said Rebecca.

"She was doing whatever the fuck she wants," said Eve. "And we just made her more famous and more rich and more popular and more known—and guess what? That's awesome—*she's* awesome."

"It was the best business move ever," Rebecca agreed.

"She has a great team behind her," said Sarah.

I asked them if they thought Miley was a guys' girl or a girlie girl. "Oh, a guys' girl, *definitely*."

New Albany, Indiana

The afternoon of the Fourth of July, Meredith, Ashley, and Mikayla went to a party at "the quarry." The quarry was in Falling Rock Park, in La Grange, Kentucky, about thirty minutes from New Albany. It was a shale pit, the size of a small lake, filled with blue rainwater, surrounded by trees and rectangular rocks stacked at angles like giant pieces of French toast. There were sandy parking areas around the perimeter where kids were milling about next to their cars.

Mikayla was wearing a red-white-and-blue bikini with a spangling of stars. Ashley's bikini was black with gold beading, and Meredith had on a one-piece with an orange T-shirt over it. They wore their sunglasses.

They parked beside a cluster of cars where they saw some of their high school friends—boys and girls in bathing suits, all holding swim noodles and plastic rafts, cans of beer and red Solo cups.

The backs of the cars were open and filled with coolers. Kids were mixing drinks, pouring juice and liquor into soda bottles, chugging.

Music was playing, wafting across the air: *"Man, let's get medicated—"* The sun beat down. The New Albany girls got out of their car and called to their friends, who nodded and waved.

Mikayla's new boyfriend, Jim, was already there, a white boy in black-and-white trunks. He came shambling over and kissed her. They'd met at Little Five, the annual bicycle race at Indiana University at Bloomington, where Jim was a student.

"We had a beer pong contest to see if we would kiss," Mikayla said. "And I won."

"And they've been married ever since," Ashley said, fluttering her eyes.

"I feel like I've known him forever," Mikayla later tweeted. She was madly in love; and in the culture of social media, it was something she felt she constantly had to share. She tweeted and Instagrammed about their relationship almost daily, posting selfies of them together with comments like, "I'm so lucky to have this man in my life & to be able to call him my boyfriend." She posted photos of them cuddling and kissing and cutting up. "I am one lucky girl and I am so proud to be your girlfriend," she said in a comment. "I have no idea what I'd do had I not met you b," or baby, friend.

The girls mixed drinks over the cooler in the back of the car—vodka, rum, orange juice, and Hawaiian Punch. "I can't get too drunk 'cause I don't wanna embarrass myself," Ashley said, pouring vodka into a red Solo cup. "My mom always says you can do whatever you want, just don't be in a porno or act like a slut."

Kids were drinking whiskey and vodka from the bottles, following it with swigs of Red Bull, Monster Energy, and Diet Coke. As the afternoon wore on, they got hotter and drunker, and they started dancing around. Boys danced with pelvic thrusts, undulating next to girls. Some of the girls looked annoyed but said nothing about it.

Boys in baseball hats danced with swim noodles flopping between their legs. A tall, rascally-looking white boy with dark hair named Ethan, in red-and-white-striped swim trunks, was the standout of the bunch. He was slapping girls' behinds, pinching them. They turned around without a word, barely registering what he'd done.

"I'm out here," Ethan kept saying, in his white-boy-doing-a-homeboy voice. He was the one Meredith had called a "fuckboy."

He was also the aspiring rapper among them, the wannabe Eminem. He used to post rap videos on YouTube. Now he was in college, studying business. Seemingly inspired by the freewheeling atmosphere, he started rapping for his friends. They stood in a circle, listening.

"You wanna know about me?" he rapped. "Y'all can go and check Google. She said she wanna ride me, and I ain't talking about this noodle. I said bang, look at my thang, look at my wang. Put it in her mouth, that's how we do in the South. All these thots, put it right in. The pussy I shatter . . ."

His friends were laughing, drinking.

"And my dick was so long when I raped you," Ethan rapped, "you would claim that you were into it . . . Just ask like four chicks here, I'm packing the magnum. Fuck that man, I'm going in raw, they saying awww . . ."

The kids clapped when he was finished.

He was rapping about rape, but no one seemed to mind. Or if they did, they didn't say so. Rape is not an uncommon theme in popular music. Rapper Rick Ross rapped in the 2013 song "U.O.E.N.O.": *"Put molly all in her Champagne / She ain't even know it"*—a scenario that describes a rape preceded by drugging. Other major rappers who have rhymed about rape include Eminem (*"you're the kind of girl that I'd assault and rape"*), Tyga (*"rape your lady"*), and Ja Rule (*"rape your stray ho"*).

In the 1970s, feminists called the normalization of rape in popular culture "rape culture," referring to attitudes in advertising, movies, music, TV shows, and other media that dismiss or encourage sexual assault and rape. Examples could also be statements, such as Fox News pundit Liz Trotta saying, in response to a 2012 Pentagon report showing an increase in violent sexual assaults of women in the military, "Now, what did they expect? These people are in close contact." Or Yale fraternity brothers chanting, "No means yes! Yes means anal!" during a 2010 pledge initiation. Some say rape culture doesn't exist. In 2014, *Time* ran an article saying, "It's Time to End 'Rape Culture' Hysteria." A week later, it ran a piece by Zerlina Maxwell, "Rape Culture Is Real."

Ethan took a bow.

Unaccountably, the boys began chanting: "U-S-A! U-S-A! U-S-A!"

"Happy birthday, America!" someone screamed.

"Hos, hos, hos, hos," Ethan said, indicating some new girls in bikinis were walking by, several yards away. "Shot, shot, shot, *shot*," he called at the girls, gesturing for them to come over, wiggling his fingers at them. He held up a whiskey bottle and said, "Shot, anybody want a shot?"

The girls trotted over.

"Yeeeah!" Ethan said with a smile.

"Yeah!" said the boys.

"Shots for thots," said Ethan.

The girls opened their mouths and let the boys pour liquor down their throats. They wiped their mouths and smiled.

"Let my dick breathe," Ethan joked, meaning there were so many girls surrounding him, he was suffocating.

"United States of fucking America!" said a boy.

"My question is, Who's coming home with me?" Ethan said. "I'm getting loose as shit out here. My signature dance is this," he said, pumping his pelvis back and forth. "Hey, nice cheeks, Orange," he called to a girl in an orange bikini who was walking by.

"Want a shot?" he asked. She came skipping over.

"Cheeks, cheeks, cheeks!" Ethan said. "I knew you would come when I called you."

"She got a fat ass," a boy muttered appreciatively.

"Shot, shot, shot!" said the boys.

"That's nice, tastes good," said Orange, smiling, after downing a shot of their whiskey.

Ashley and Mikayla were watching, shaking their heads.

"Boys are disgusting," said Ashley, frowning.

Then she said, "I'm so glad I have my friends."

She put her arm around Mikayla and they hugged. "Aw," Ashley said, "this is a sweet moment." They smiled, heads together, rocking back and forth.

The friendship of the New Albany girls, in the way of girl group friendships today, was impassioned and entangled in social media. They were connected, they said, all day, every day, through their cell phones and social media. It was unusual for one of them not to have her phone on, not to be communicating constantly with the others, through group texting or reading and commenting on one another's social media posts.

"We love social media," Ashley said. "Literally, that's our entire life. All day I'm checking Twitter. If I don't know where my friends are, I just go to Twitter, 'cause they post what they're doing."

"We tweet each other," said Meredith.

"That's what we talk about—like, Did you see this picture this person posted?" said Ashley.

"We'll screenshot it and then group text each other about it," said Meredith.

"Like, if someone posts an ugly picture, then you're like, Did you see *this*?" Ashley said. "People will try and show me stuff and I'm like"— waving her hand dismissively—"No, I know, I already know. It's weird for me to not be on Twitter."

Twitter was a place where they let one another know what they were doing, often with an attempt at a witty twist ("Trying to take a quick snooze in this chair in the library is the ultimate struggle," Kelsey had tweeted), and how they were feeling ("I'm so stressed it's unreal," tweeted Mikayla), and, in a way, who they were ("All that goes through my head all day is 'what is some super bad shit I can do that no one else would,'" tweeted Ashley). It was where they went to keep threading together their connection, and to make one another laugh. "Why limit happy hour to an hour??" tweeted Meredith. And sometimes it was a place to express, in a sidelong way, their pique with one another. "My friends are a lil fake but I love them," tweeted Ashley, to no one in particular. And later: "I'm over everyone."

One of Ashley's recent tweets said: "Honestly I have no clue what I did before Mikayla."

They continued hugging each other, smiling, whispering in each other's ears.

Some of the boys were watching; and they began to chant: "Make-out! Make-out!"

Ashley and Mikayla broke away from each other's embrace and stared at the boys, perplexed.

"Tongue! Tongue!" the boys said, poking their fingers in the air in time with their chanting. They seemed to see Ashley and Mikayla's "sweet moment" as the prelude to a scene out of lesbian porn.

Ashley turned around and jabbed her finger back at them, mocking them. "Make-out! Make-out! *You* make out!" she shouted.

The boys' chanting died down. They looked confused.

Mikayla laughed. "I'll give you twenty dollars," she told them. "If you make out, then we'll make out."

"Not in the United States of fucking America!" said a boy. "Only girls!"

"U-S-A! U-S-A!" the boys started chanting again. "Girl-on-girl! Guys-not-on-guys! Girl-on-girl!"

"That's *sexist*," Ashley said.

"Kiss! Kiss! Kiss!" the boys screamed.

"Make-out! Make-out!" Ashley and Mikayla screamed back at them.

"Simmer down," somebody said.

Ashley and Mikayla finally gave up, backing down.

The boys cheered and gave each other the pound—the rough bro handshake—congratulating one another on their shouting victory.

Newark, Delaware

At night the girls from Haines went out to the bars. They walked along Main Street, four sexy girls in sexy clothes. "The squad is out," they said. "They know this squad."

It was Lally, Sarah, Rebecca, and Ariel (they were the ones who had IDs). More girls kept passing by, girls in halter tops and bandeaux and bustiers. "Hi, babe!" "Hi!" There was hugging and air kisses between groups of girls.

Newark is a college town, with an area of less than nine square miles and a population of around 31,000. Main Street is the main drag, a long strip of bars and fast-food joints housed in neo-Colonial buildings. It smells like fast food and bacon.

It was early in the night, but there were already pools of vomit here and there, on the sidewalk and the street. The girls walked along, texting, checking out what was happening elsewhere on campus.

Groups of boys came strolling by, wearing polos and button-downs and madras shorts.

"Where you going?"

"I dunno. Maybe Kate's."

Pecks on cheeks were exchanged with boys. They chatted about what bars they were going to, all very nonchalant, as if nobody really cared.

"You wanna see a bunch of drunken girls—wildly drunken girls?" said Rebecca.

Klondike Kate's was packed with girls and boys, all drinking and talking loudly. *"Wanna do a shot?"*

Girls were drunk and reeling, some hitting on guys in an overt way. Rebecca looked disdainful. "Basic bitches, basic, basic bitches," she said.

It was a bar scene you could see on a college campus almost anywhere in America, a loud and noisy party. What was striking was to see some of the girls "literally throwing themselves on guys," as Rebecca said. For the girls it was perhaps an expression of sexual agency. But the self-satisfied look on the faces of some of the boys could make you think of David Buss's assertion that, in the age of the Internet, men are pursuing an increased array of options "and women are forced to go along with it."

The girls from Haines stayed awhile, but the place was deemed too crowded and full of "drunk bitches" to be any fun, so they went home.

They poured more drinks in the kitchen and assembled in their basement, where they often hung out. There was a Chinese lantern hanging over a couple of tattered couches and a coffee table outfitted with several bongs. The walls were decorated with tie-dyed tapestries and white Christmas lights.

They sat cross-legged on the couches, texting and tapping at their phones. There were six girls, all drinking white wine and intermittently doing vodka shots. They were Rebecca, Eve, and Ariel, all from Manhattan; Sarah and Lally, from New Jersey; and Paige, a girl with auburn hair and glasses, from Connecticut.

"Did you *see* those girls literally throwing themselves at guys?" Rebecca asked with disgust.

"I was just like, *Why?*" said Lally. "Why can't you just be *friends* with guys? Friends first, then if you're interested, go for it, more power to you."

"It's mostly the younger girls," Ariel explained. "Especially incoming freshmen."

What did guys think when girls "literally threw themselves" at them? I asked.

"They think, I'm gonna get fucked later, so I'm gonna let it happen," said Eve, "but then they talk shit right after it happens—like, How annoying was she?"

"They just wanna get their dick wet," said Sarah.

"I think it's important for girls to be assertive, though," said Paige. "There's a certain boundary, of course, but if you want something, you gotta get it."

"I went for it with James," Lally said proudly. "I'm a girl with a boyfriend," she told me. "Almost three years."

There was a rustling among the group. Of the six girls, three had boyfriends—Ariel, Paige, and Lally. The girls who did not have boyfriends looked a tad uncomfortable all of a sudden.

"We were off and on and the reason we were off is I don't think *I* was everything to him that I was supposed to be," Lally said. "And now we're on and I can tell he wants intimacy—he *wants* that relationship . . . He kind of got over his college time to fuck around with girls and do whatever he was doing."

She told the story of their relationship in a bubbly rush: it had started with a hookup; and then one day, Lally said, she told the boy, "If I'm just your toy and we're just hanging out, then let me know, because I am building feelings . . . And he was like, No, we're good. And ever since then we've been together," she said, beaming.

The other girls were silent.

I asked if this was a common thing, for a hookup to lead to a relationship.

The other girls said, "Noooooo."

"If you're up-front with them about what you're thinking . . . it magically is a lot easier," Eve said. "They're not such dicks. Because if you just, like, say, Let's be honest"—she took on a very frank voice—"We're just gonna sleep together and I don't wanna have to do the *texting* thing and I'm gonna be gone before you wake up—if you just *say* it"—here she waved her hand—"magically they have more respect for you and are much nicer. It's, Oh, she knows what's going on, I don't have to pretend."

"And if you say, I have feelings for you," Ariel said, "and they say, I don't *want* that, then you save yourself a whole fucking—"

"Shit-show," murmured Paige.

"Girls complicate everything," Eve said, "but the great thing about guys is how they don't give a shit—they get to the point. That's how they always are, and so if you just say what you're thinking, whether or not it's going to go the way you want, if you say it clearly"—she snapped her fingers—"they'll give an answer back. They're not trying to over-analyze and dissect and think into things."

Now Rebecca was looking uncomfortable, as if there were something about all of this that wasn't squaring with her own experience. "But it seems like the girl always has to be the one to say what she's thinking *first*," she said. "Like, By the way, it's totally *fine* if I don't sleep over—you don't *have* to text me. I think that now in college everybody has that FOMO; this is my time to be young, to sleep around, to party. And I think that guys . . . maybe wouldn't treat a girl the nicest because of what the girl might think of him. '*Ooooh*, he double-texted me!' 'He drove me home in the morning.' That's a big deal!

"'He kissed me good-bye!'" Rebecca went on. "Boys are afraid to make it seem like it's more than it is, thinking *we'll* see it as more than it is. But they get it wrong."

It was the same quandary girls everywhere seemed to be dealing with: how to bring boys up to speed with the fact that women might just want to have sex as they do, without the expectation of a committed relationship. Or could it sometimes be having to convince oneself of not wanting to have a relationship at a time when these were becoming more and more rare?

Then Sarah talked about "this kid I'm hooking up with." There were guys the girls said they hooked up with, and guys they were "talking to"—a step down in intensity, it could be going on at the same time as hooking up with another person. "Like, I'm terrified about the idea of being exclusive with him, let alone *dating* him," said Sarah, "but he's someone that I absolutely love hanging out with. I just don't want to make a real choice because that's really scary. But when we hook up he's always like, No, I *want* to see you"—which was a surprise to her, different from the usual thing of guys acting aloof.

"He's very open about wanting it," Sarah said, "which is why I actually ended up liking him, 'cause when I texted him it wasn't like, wait forty minutes. He texted me right back. That's why we're supposed to *have* our phones, because we actually *want* to speak with each other. It's just so refreshing. I don't have to, like, bullshit around with him and it doesn't matter if I want to see him or fuck him or whatever, I can just text him and it doesn't matter. That's why I ended up liking him, because it was never a game."

"I *do* play games," Eve said after a moment. "But I think that's just because I'm bored. I'm *terrible*. If there's no games and I'm not, like, being entertained, you lost my interest, good-bye, on to the next one."

Her delivery was theatrically dismissive; she was their femme fatale, their Samantha from *Sex and the City*.

"Eve is the one who wants what you can't have," Rebecca said, grinning. "She's the no-strings-attached, we-can-fuck-just-to-fuck type of person."

"It's sad," Eve said with a sigh, "because it means I'll never be with anyone—and eventually you have to get *someone*."

"You like to hunt," said Sarah.

"I've been in two relationships," Eve said, "but it's all just entertainment for me. If I'm gonna be married for the rest of my life, I'll have to be with the same person forever. So"—she snapped her fingers in the air—"keep me interested now!"

New Albany, Indiana

"Nobody knows how to have a relationship anymore," Matthew said. It was the afternoon when he and his friends were all gathered in Natalie and Ashley's dorm room at Southeast. "How can anybody have a relationship when everything's so out there in public like that, on social media? How can you know what's just for you, and what's for everybody else?" he asked.

Natalie, his girlfriend, looked at him funny.

"Oh my God, yes," Ashley agreed. "Like I will get a good morning text: it'll be like, Good morning, beautiful, hope you have a wonderful day. And I'll be like, Oh my gosh, that is so sweet. And then I will get on Twitter and see a girl has posted *the same exact words*, like, Look what bae sent; and so obviously he said that to her, too. He mass texted it!"

"That's a fuckboy," Meredith said.

"That's a dude that cannot have a relationship," Ashley said. "Like all he wants to do is fuck girls."

"Self-absorbed," Meredith said.

"Who cares more what his bros think about a girl than what he thinks about her," said Ashley. "Who calls girls sluts and whores but does the same thing."

"And acts like he wants a real relationship but he never really does," Meredith said.

I asked them what percentage of boys they thought were fuckboys.

"One hundred percent," said Meredith.

"No, like ninety percent," said Ashley. "I'm hoping to find the ten percent somewhere. But every boy I've ever met is a fuckboy."

When real relationships did occur, they said, the partners became "obsessed" with what each other was doing on social media.

"You're tweeting and watching, watching everything someone tweets," Ashley said, "and you keep going back and forth watching what they post. We call it 'twatching.'"

"People play with each other's minds," Meredith said. "Like, if you wanna piss someone off, they can see who you're talking to, so you'll just start talking to someone to get the other person mad."

"*They* twatch each other a lot," Ashley said, pointing her Popsicle at Matthew and Natalie.

Matthew said, "Not true."

"In your recent searches," said Ashley, laughing, "you know it says 'Natalie.' You *subtweet* each other," meaning to post mean comments that the other couldn't see. "You *fight* on Twitter."

Natalie and Matthew recounted how they had recently gotten back together after going on a months-long break. During the time of their separation, they admitted, they had "twatched" each other relentlessly on social media.

"She stalked the shit out of him," Ashley said.

"And he would post pictures of other girls and I would tweet about my experience with guys," Natalie said. "I acted like I didn't care. Nowadays, if you care, you're dumb."

"You make yourself look so dumb," Ashley agreed.

"That's when guys are like, Oh, she *cares* about me," Natalie said.

"And then they're like, I can do whatever I want, she's always gonna be chasing after me," said Meredith.

"And if you care too much," said Natalie, "they're like, Oh, she's psycho, she's in love, she's too attached."

Matthew said, "For a guy nowadays, it's either you're whipped or you don't give a shit. It's like there's no in between."

I asked them what they thought was making girls and boys treat each other this way.

"Boys want to have the power," Natalie said, "and girls don't want to get hurt."

Matthew countered, "Nobody wants to get hurt."

But after some time, Matthew and Natalie said, they'd started to miss each other; and they started to be able to admit that they missed each other.

"And we realized we had been taking our relationship for granted and we really like each other," said Matthew. "We learned if you want to keep the relationship, you have to show the other person how much you value the relationship."

They were back together now. But still, they said, they were struggling with the effect of social media on their relationship.

"You just have no privacy, no time apart," Matthew said. "You always know what the other is doing. Like if I see she hasn't tweeted anything for three or four days, then I'm like, What could she be doing for three days that she hasn't posted anything? If she tweets like, I just had McDonald's, then I know she's probably in her dorm eating McDonald's; but if she doesn't say anything, she could be doing anything under the sun."

"That's some crazy-person stuff," said Ashley.

"No," said Matthew, "that's what relationships are like these days. The days of calling your home phone once a night to say good night to your significant other is long gone."

"If she's not tweeting, it doesn't mean she's fucking someone else," said Ashley.

"But you wonder what it *does* mean," Matthew said. "That's what starts to go through your head."

"And then there's when someone doesn't post about you on Woman Crush Wednesday," said Natalie, giving him a look.

Apparently Matthew had sometimes failed to post pictures of Natalie on Woman Crush Wednesday. There was also Man Crush Monday, which Natalie faithfully observed, except when Matthew had been remiss in his duties.

"Woman Crush Wednesday is overrated," Matthew said with a scowl. "Some people in a relationship will do it every single week and if you don't it's like you're in a fight."

"That's why we're trying not to do Twitter, 'cause it makes everything so much harder," said Natalie.

"Like, if you favorite something or you tweet something to someone that is not your girlfriend or boyfriend," Matthew said, "then you're in a war. It looks a lot deeper than it really is, and it brings up a whole new conversation that you don't need to have: Who is she? How do you know her? Do you have her number?"

A few months later, they broke up.

New Albany, Indiana

The kids jumped in the water from high up on the rocks. The girls went gingerly over the side, the boys with great running leaps, doing flips in the air. They lolled on their rafts and inner tubes, basking in the sun, chatting languidly with one another. The water was so clear and clean that now and then you could see a big brown bass wiggling past their legs.

Mikayla appeared, upset. She and Jim had had a fight.

"He just said that he could get whatever girl he wanted here," said Mikayla, fighting back tears. "I guess because all these girls are flocking around because Ethan is rapping and they're handing out shots." She said she thought Jim was being influenced by the other boys. "Look at Ethan," she said. "He would not have done that long rap if the boys hadn't been egging him on like, You're so fucking cool."

"It's bro-chure," meaning bro culture, Meredith said. "I call it 'bro-chure.' It's being with your bros. We also call it Nasty Time."

Mikayla put on a "bro" voice: "Yeah, fuck 'em, who gives a shit about girls? 'Cause we're the fuckin' man. Fuck you all, we're drunk, we don't give a shit."

"Bro-chure," Meredith repeated.

"It sure is," said Mikayla.

"We don't tolerate it," Meredith said.

"We may be the one friend group that's just like, I'm not gonna take that," Mikayla said, referring to how she and her squad were unlike other girls in their refusal to brook sexist behavior. "Meredith's probably the best person I know when it comes to that—she stands for her own. She stands for whatever is right."

"I fuck wit them," Meredith said, grinning from behind her shades, meaning she let boys know when they were out of line.

"And she will tell the boys straight as it is," said Mikayla.

"It's 'cause I'm not dickmatized," Meredith said, meaning she was not hypnotized by sex. "I never will be dickmatized, never," she added resolutely.

"She's the most independent person I know," said Mikayla. "I became friends with Meredith one day and she's the best thing that ever happened to me . . . She inspires me as a woman."

Mikayla took a few steps away, rubbing her eyes.

"She always starts crying when she talks about emotional stuff," Meredith said affectionately.

Meredith was a feminist. I asked her if she thought of herself this way. She shrugged. "Yeah, why not?" she said.

Mikayla came back and I asked her what she was going to do about Jim. She said she wasn't going to have an argument "while we're both drunk."

"He's bromancing," Meredith said.

"They're all the same," said Mikayla.

"But we love them," Meredith said.

"We do?" asked Mikayla.

They looked over at the cars, where the boys were beating one another with swim noodles, slapping each other with loud cracks.

"Boys are stupid," said Ashley, coming over. "Mikayla is my girlfriend."

Mikayla kissed her cheek. They smiled at each other.

Mikayla went and talked to Jim, and when she came back, she was smiling. He followed behind her, holding her hand, looking hangdog. "He said he was sorry and I'm the best, which is right," she informed us.

"I was raised by a southern granma and I know when I mess up I have to apologize," said Jim.

They kissed. Mikayla looked happy. Jim looked relieved.

"Look at Cody," Meredith said, shaking her head. We all looked over at their friend Cody, a tall white boy wearing a lazy grin. He was surrounded by three very young-looking teenage girls who were doubling over, laughing at whatever he said. "Oh my God, *yes*," "I can't *believe* you!" "You are so *funny*!"

"Three at once," Mikayla remarked. "Well, Cody is a babe."

"Bro hos," said Ashley.

Ashley and Meredith started parodying the girls, flipping their hair and prancing up and down. We watched as Cody typed all three girls' numbers into his phone before they skipped away.

The boys by the cars had all started dancing around to the song "My Girl," but instead of "My girl," they sang, *"My thots . . . Talkin' 'bout my thots!"*

"That should be the fuckboy anthem," said Meredith.

Newark, Delaware

At a party one night in Paige's room, Rebecca passed around a video of herself twerking on spring break. The video had been taken that year in Cancún. It was close-up footage of Rebecca's behind undulating in a pink bikini, shot by someone positioned underneath her in the sand.

"Oh my God, this is me on the beach in slo-mo, isn't that *insane*?" she asked.

"That's awesome," said a girl named Liza. "That's a nice shot of your butt."

"Thank you," Rebecca said.

"That's really impressive," Liza said.

The girls made margaritas in a blender and drank from pink martini glasses with straws. "So yummy," they said. Boys sat around the coffee table, smoking blunts. BEST NIGHT EVER said the sparkly gold party letters strung on the wall.

There was a boy there named Kevin, tall and handsome, black, age nineteen, with short-cropped hair, in a sweatshirt, Timberlands, and jeans.

They'd been talking about how there was no dating in college anymore. I asked Kevin why boys didn't ask girls out on dates.

"Yeah, Kevin," Rebecca prodded.

"I guess for the simple reason they don't have to," Kevin said frankly. "To be honest, we don't have to." He sipped his beer.

"I got asked out on a date once and I thought it was a joke," said Sarah. "The guy asked me out, and I was like, Is this real? Is he kidding?"

The girls all laughed, dancing around to Katy Perry.

"You don't have to take a girl on a date in order to hook up with her," Kevin said. "The mind-set on a college campus—things are quote-unquote 'easier' at school. I think guys and girls come to college expecting to hook up."

He said he had not been on a single date since he had been at college. He had taken a girl out to dinner once, he said; "but that was already when we were hooking up. Like, take a girl on three dates, kiss her at the end of the date?" He gave a dry laugh. "No. Guys just don't have to take girls out."

The talk turned to numbers, numbers of sex partners.

"Over fifty," said another guy at the party.

"Well, there are sixteen thousand people here," Kevin said with a laugh.

They all started counting, laughing, remembering hookups.

Rebecca was murmuring something to Kevin off to the side.

"You've been doing what you needed to do," he told her kindly.

"If you say yours, I'll say mine," Rebecca told him. "I'm like at ten, and he's like there, around there," she announced.

"Okay, eleven," said Kevin.

"Are you really *ten*?" Lally said, catty.

"I mean, I'm not gonna count out loud and say *names*," Rebecca said, defensive. "They add up fast."

I asked them about slut-shaming; were girls judged for hooking up?

"Well, it's an obvious double standard," Kevin said. "That's just how it's always been. Why? I don't know. I'm not an advocate of it."

I asked him if he ever used the word "slut."

One of the bros in the room let out a loud *"Burrrrrrp!"*

"Uhhhh," said Kevin, "I don't really want to answer that question. Hmmm."

"Hahahaha," said one of the guys.

"It's disrespectful to call a girl a slut, obviously," Kevin said. "It demeans someone because they are not part of a social norm. But even girls call each other sluts. It's a universal thing."

Rebecca looked grim.

"Eight of ten girls have called another girl a slut," Kevin maintained.

"Ten out of ten," piped up a girl.

"Girls shit on other girls just as much," Kevin said.

"More!" said a girl.

"But in different ways," Rebecca said.

"I hate it," said a girl.

"Girls will slut-shame, too," Kevin said. "Girls are called sluts not just because of how many guys they sleep with but because of *why* they sleep with guys."

"It's fun for guys to have meaningless sex," Rebecca said, "because they wanna just get it in, they wanna de-stress; but, I mean, we're all human beings, we're all very sexual in our nature. And yet for some reason it's seen as more shameful or unacceptable for girls to go out and have meaningless sex. If girls do that, she's called a slut.

"School's hard," Rebecca went on. "We have so much work. Our parents are pushing us to get a job. So that's why we drink and, like, a lot of kids, get blacked out, and we just want to leave our problems and—"

"And make mistakes," Kevin said.

"And make mistakes," Rebecca concurred. "It's YOLO, it's the YOLO lifestyle." You only live once.

"And we in this society glorify people that don't show any signs of being stressed out," Kevin said. "If you look stressed out, it's not a good look. We're encouraged to not express how stressed we are." It was another aspect of hypermasculinity, the shamefulness of showing emotion.

"Guys are taught to hide their feelings," Rebecca said. "Sometimes Sarah will come in and be like, I have to de-stress right now! And she'll scream and cry and just get it out."

"I just need to air it out," admitted Sarah.

Sarah suddenly remembered that her parents had offered to subsidize all their trips down to spring break that year. The girls cheered. "But they're only putting in for travel, not food," Sarah advised.

Rebecca shrugged, sipping her drink. "We'll find a bunch of guys on their bachelor trip that just wanna take girls out and sugar daddy us for the week."

She was joking, I think; but the idea of having a "sugar daddy" isn't inimical to many girls in an era when the dating site Seeking Arrangement claims to have close to three million "sugar babies," male and female. In 2015, Seeking Arrangement released a list of the top colleges where girls were using the site, the top three being the University of Texas, Arizona State University, and New York University. The exchange between a sugar baby and a sugar daddy who meet on a commercial website isn't legally allowed to involve direct payment for sex, but after the two people meet, there is no monitoring of the relationship.

A sugar baby is provided with an "allowance" for her attentions; the average allowance, according to Seeking Arrangement, is $3,000 monthly. It's a kind of soft prostitution that's become normalized by social media and seems to have become more attractive to some young women in a challenging economy. "There's nothing shameful about it," said a young woman in New York, twenty-two. "I can't make enough money in an office job to pay my rent, so if I can make five hundred dollars by having dinner with some guy, I'm gonna do it." Some sugar babies have Amazon Wish Lists where they tell their sugar daddies what they would like to have, everything from jewelry to silverware to furniture to magazine subscriptions.

"It's really common now for girls to say they're 'using' guys for meals or other stuff," said Elizabeth, a college student in Florida. "They act like it's no big deal." A few young women admitted to me that they used dating apps as a way to get free meals. "I call it Tinder food stamps," one said.

"Bow down bitches, bow bow down bitches—"

The girls of Haines sang along to Beyoncé's "Flawless."

New Albany, Indiana

"I'm not gonna lie," Ethan said. "I always tell them, I ain't got no condom, and they're just like, Fuck it, let's do this shit. I'm Mr. Raw Dog, all right?"

"Raw dog" refers to condomless sex.

"Basically, shit happens," Ethan said. We were in his house. There was a party going on in his basement.

His mother was away for the holiday weekend. The basement was dark and filled with kids listening to music, talking, drinking.

"But it gets down to the nitty-gritty when they come back for a visit and I'm with my boys," Ethan said. "That's when you hit them with the old hocus-pocus: they get into bed, then I leave the room and go tag-team my boy, and, boom, he does the ol' hocus-pocus. She don't even know who's who"—meaning he's tricked girls into thinking they were having sex with him when they were actually having sex with him and his friends.

"The girls always find out," Meredith said with a frown. "They might not know right away if they're drunk, but they'll always find out."

"You basically gotta look out for your dudes," Ethan said. "If I know I'm with a disrespectful woman, she's got downright dirty standards, I might as well get a few good friends in on the action."

I asked him if he watched a lot of porn.

"I got caught with porn at age thirteen," he said. "I first looked up 'boobs' on Google when I was like twelve or thirteen. I went on a porn site and saw what a blowjob was and I was like, Damn, I gotta get one of those. And so I went on a hunt, and like in sixth grade I got my first BJ. Today, I probably watch porn twice a day minimum."

"I wanna believe in y'all's species, your race," Ethan said, referring to women, "but I can't right now. I'd have to scan this room, but I'd have to say like forty-five to sixty-five percent of them are thots. A thot is 'that ho over there.' It's a new word for 'ho' or 'whore.' I don't like to disrespect women, but it's necessary."

Why? I asked.

"Because," he said, "they don't respect themselves, you know what I'm saying? I'll bet every chick in here except for two or three has had sex with multiple guys. If you want me to, I'll call them out."

"It's a small town," said Ashley, also frowning. "A lot of people around here have hooked up with the same people because there's not a lot to choose from. The dudes are thirsty as fuck. I've had at least twelve guys in this room hit me up on Facebook, Tinder, Twitter, Instagram—all of it."

"Social media?" Ethan said. "That's where the thots come out. I'm getting calls from girls I ain't even heard of before: 'Ethan, come over here,' you know what I'm saying?"

There was a supporting pole in the middle of the room and Ethan ran to it and swung around it, stripper-style. His friends laughed, cheering.

"At some point I want to get out of here," Ashley had told me earlier. "Like, it's just too small for me. I feel like I can do bigger and better things with my life. Like I would love to be famous," she said. "I think I could be famous. I love the Kardashians. Like, I wish I *was* a Kardashian. I start watching that show and I feel like I am one of them. I start talking like them. I love Kylie Jenner's style. I love reality TV."

She once tweeted: "I feel like I personally know every celebrity."

Her Tumblr blog was artistic and erotic. A lot of it was sort of curated porn, showing images of rough sex between tattooed young men and women; breasts and necks with bite marks.

Some drunk boys were playing a game where they smacked each other in the face. A boy with half-closed eyes was standing bent over, his chin stuck out, waiting for someone to punch him.

"I'll fucking hit you," Ashley said, running over.

She pulled back her fist and punched him hard on the jaw. There was a crack as he went reeling.

Newark, Delaware

At the end of the night, some of the girls of Haines went down to the basement to smoke pot. A bong went around. A wiry white girl named Brit, who they said was "nuts," had come over and was telling loud stories about her night; the rest of them barely listened. They were all on their phones, checking their texts and Snapchat, Instagram, to see what all their friends had been doing. A box of Insomnia Cookies was passed around.

Someone had posted something on Yik Yak about Kim "going off on some random freshman girl."

"Oh," Brit said, and shrugged, "I don't Yak. I use Facebook the most—I *stalk*."

They started talking about their social media use.

"My personal Snapchat is like, 'In my bed throwing up,'" said Brit. "My Special Moments," a Snapchat feature, "are like, throwing up, being drunk, getting hungover, being re-drunk."

"I'd delete my Facebook if I could," said Caleb, Paige's boyfriend, who had joined them. "I keep it 'cause of Paige, 'cause we're in a relationship."

Paige murmured, "I like to look at his pictures."

"I'm such a *stalker*," Brit said.

"I used to leave my job to go water my crops on FarmVille," said Lally, meaning the social media game on Facebook where the user is a farmer who must tend to his livestock and crops.

"Watering my crops on FarmVille got me through the day in high school," Brit said.

Ariel said, "My professor had to make an announcement—he said, You can't leave class to go harvest your crops, and we were like, You *water* your crops, you don't *harvest* them."

They all laughed.

"FarmVille was a while ago," someone said.

They went on thumbing, swiping, checking, texting.

New Albany, Indiana

"We're gonna be like, Will you marry me?" Ethan said, miming texting the proposal on his phone. "And they'll be like, I do," he said, continuing to pretend to text the wedding ceremony.

The party had wound down. There were just around ten kids left. Some of them lay on the floor, passed out, or checking their phones.

Mikayla and Jim lay behind the couches, talking and whispering. Some kids sat around the counter on the swivel chairs. They were Ethan, Ashley, Kelsey, Meredith, a young black kid named Devon, and a chubby white boy named Jared. The counter was littered with fast-food containers.

"Social media is a nightmare," Jared said, "because we all hang out together and ninety percent of the time we're all on our phones. Look at Meredith right now."

They all looked at Meredith, who kept on touching her phone, not looking up.

Jared said, "You just sit there and—" He picked up his phone to illustrate, and then he saw that he had received some texts. "Oh, I'm sorry," he said, swiping at them.

"Ooh, popular," said Meredith.

They tried to calculate how many group messages they received a day from the twenty-one people in their texting group.

"Two thousand?" "Three thousand?" "Three thousand four hundred?" they asked.

"It's stupid," said Jared.

"It is stupid," said Devon.

"I have to turn my phone off when I go to sleep so I don't hear it," Jared said. "It just keeps going off with texts. It wakes me up."

"You lose sleep," said Ashley.

"I love talking to my friends all day—it gets me *through* my day—but it's a love-hate relationship," said Jared. "More of a hate."

Ethan posed a question to the group: "Relationship or single? Which would you rather be?"

"I wanna marry Ethan," Ashley said sarcastically. Apparently they had a history.

"I wouldn't be mad," Ethan said. "You get a decent job, I get a decent job. But let me put it this way, every girl around here is not worth our time."

Ashley stared.

"I take offense at that," Meredith said.

"I do, too," said Kelsey.

"You should—you definitely should," Ashley said.

"What's wrong with us?" Meredith demanded.

"Meredith's still got the card," as in the "V card," Ethan said. "Ashley is a sweet girl, but she just likes to act reckless whenever she's around people."

Ashley gave him a look.

"I have no bad words to say about Kelsey," Ethan said. Kelsey had a long-term boyfriend. Ethan said he would never get serious with any girls in their town because they had "fucked too many people."

"But what about you?" I asked, reminding him of his claims about his sexual exploits.

"I'm on a rampage," meaning sexually, he admitted. "With a scoring average higher than Kobe Bryant." He claimed to have slept with more than forty people.

I asked, "Do you think having such a high number makes you less—"

"Desirable?" he said. "Of course."

"Less human," Ashley muttered.

"Less respectable," said Ethan.

"I was going to say, Do you think it makes you less able to connect with people emotionally?" I asked.

"Yes, of course," Ethan said. "Relationships aren't coveted now. Back in the day, a relationship meant something. Now it's like we're dating but we're not gonna get married, so I'll just cheat. My friends are like, She's not gonna find out—you can have the main course and some appetizers, too."

"I do not think like that," Kelsey said.

"That's like the shittiest thing I've ever heard," Meredith said. "I think it's the thrill of getting away with something."

"I just think everyone wants to have sex with each other," said Ashley.

"It's not just guys!" Ethan exclaimed. "Girls cheat, too. Do you know how much it hurts a guy to get cheated on?" His voice cracked. "My friends were like, Yo, your girl was at her ex's house." He'd been cheated on; he still didn't seem over it.

"Social media makes everything so easy," he said. "If you meet someone on Tinder, Twitter, Facebook, you can just easily start conversing and like, it's so easy now, it's unreal. It used to be you would meet someone and then you'd say something cute or funny and then ask like, Lemme take you out. But now like you meet 'em on Twitter and it's like, Hey, what's up, you tryna come over and chill? I haven't been on an actual date with a girl in probably two years.

"I almost wish we lived back in the day," he said, "like in the seventies, when you had to go knock on the door and ask the dad for permission. That's when the best days were, not even lying." He sounded wistful.

"You weren't even there, so how do you know it was better?" Ashley asked.

"From movies and shit," Ethan maintained. "It was more genuine. Now so many girls are like on Twitter, tweeting and texting you, trying to hang out with you . . . It's not *hard*."

Then Ashley and Ethan hugged; they kissed each other tenderly on the cheek.

"We made out last night," Ethan said. "Not a hundred percent sure . . ."

"Ashley got those marks on her neck from him," said Meredith, looking up from her phone.

Devon gently pulled back Ashley's hair. There were red marks along the sides of her neck. They looked like fingerprints.

"Who did that to you?" Devon asked.

"I think he *grabbed* me," Ashley said, meaning Ethan. She put her hands around her throat in a mime of choking, eyes flying open.

Everybody went, "Oooooh."

"What the fuck," said Ethan, making a face.

"I swear," Ashley said.

It seems reasonable to wonder whether the violence in online porn is having some influence on why hookup sex often seems to involve rough sex. "Any girls out there want to be cock slapped?" said a Yik Yak post in New York. It isn't just young men who bring rough sex into hookups, young women do as well. "I want to be pounded like a slut," said another Yik Yak post. "Some girls literally want to get punched," said a young man in New York, age twenty-five. Aggression is part of sexuality, and no one wants to judge anyone else for his or her sexual preferences. But the fact that women are so often the recipients of the violence in the sexual acts portrayed in porn gives one pause for the ramifications of this in rough hookup sex.

Amy, twenty-six, a young woman in New York, says she believes the rough sex in hookups actually stems from a lack of emotional intimacy: "It's this idea that you have to have this intense sexual experience. It covers up the fact that you barely know each other."

"Okay, favorite movie," Ethan said expectantly. "One, two, three—"

Ashley stared at him, uncomprehending.

"Aw," he complained. "*The Notebook!*"

"Oh, *The Notebook,*" she said lightly. "We do love *The Notebook.* Sorry."

" 'If you're a bird, I'm a bird!' " he said, quoting the movie, dismayed. It seemed like a very romantic film for "Mr. Raw Dog."

"He fucking loves it," said Ashley, grinning.

"I can quote every single line from it," Ethan said. "But," he added bitterly, "movies aren't real. It's all Tinder and Twitter and getting busy."

He got up and went over to join the boys who were doing running jumps onto a bed in a corner of the room. They did cartwheels onto the bed, bouncing and flopping onto the floor, hitting the wall.

Ashley watched him. She looked alone.

"I'm so emotional," she said self-consciously, glancing around. "Sometimes if I see, like, a good hit in baseball, I, like, have to leave. My mom's like, Ashley, you need to be on antidepressants." Her eyes were welling up. "Or like, when people cheer, and everyone is happy, I feel like it's crazy no one else is crying. I get goose bumps like any time someone is happy.

"My friends get pissed at me 'cause I never want the party to end," she said. "I will stay there until there's one person left. I will just fall asleep on the ground. I don't want to leave before the party's over, 'cause what if something cool happens? My friends say I have a FOMO. I just don't want to go home. I just want the party to go on forever."

She looked lost.

Newark, Delaware

The morning after their party, Rebecca, Sarah, Ariel, Lally, Paige, and Caleb were all sitting on the upstairs front porch around the white iron tables. They were eating bacon-egg-and-cheese sandwiches and bagels with cream cheese from a deli on Main Street. They had wet hair from showering and were in sweats and hoodies.

It was an overcast day, threatening to rain, and the mood was subdued. They were nursing hangovers with coffee, orange juice, and ginger ale and Advil and food.

Rebecca seemed especially reserved. Her pale green eyes were puffy and tired. She picked at her bagel.

"So I saw you with *Jon*," Lally said with a little smile. "You were like, Okay, let's make out." She sounded a bit gossipy.

"Oh," said Rebecca, smiling back tightly. "That was so like, whatever . . . We had a good night together. Nothing special. He was a respectable sleeper."

"You *have* to be a good bed-sharer," Sarah said helpfully.

"He was good," Rebecca said, shrugging. "Otherwise I would have told him to go home. But it was late and I felt bad, so I was like, You're fine, you're not gonna cuddle me too much."

"Don't cuddle me—get the fuck *off* of me," Sarah said.

"Who else went out with him?" Rebecca asked, looking around. Others at the table had apparently slept with Jon as well.

There was silence.

"*I* went out with him," offered Sarah.

"I was like, Why not?" Rebecca said. "It was very unexpected. But it happened. It happens when you drink alcohol." She tried to laugh. "When he went home, he said he was doing the 'stride of pride,'" instead of the walk of shame.

"I only had one walk of shame, and I pretended to be coming back from running," Sarah said.

"Hi!" "Hi!" "Oh, hi!"

There were girls clomping up the stairs to the porch, girls in short sundresses and heels, friends of Haines. They were Courtney, Jessica, Danielle, and Cassidy.

"Why are you all dressed up?" "Oh my God, everyone looks so cute!" "How was last night?" "What'd you do?" The sister squad sat down around the tables.

"We picked up some dudes last night," said Courtney, a white girl with tawny skin and hair. "We didn't know them. They went to school with Jesse," another friend of theirs. "One of them was a dickhead. One guy was on the baseball team."

"This kid went to sleep and woke up with the same hairstyle, how the shit did that happen?" said Danielle. She was a white girl in a low-cut red dress, with long brown hair and a Betty Boop voice. "He's here for the weekend," she added. She didn't seem excited about it.

Some of them were checking Tinder on their phones.

I asked why they needed to use a dating app on a college campus, where presumably there was an abundance of guys.

"Sororities and fraternities are like a big thing here," Jessica explained. She was a white girl, athletic-looking, with a blond ponytail. "They meet up, they have their own parties, so it's hard to meet people 'cause guys won't talk to you"—unless you were connected with their frat.

"It's, like, fun to get the messages," Danielle said. "If someone likes you, they think you're attractive."

Rebecca had done "Tinder PR" for Sarah, meaning she had chosen guys and messaged them for her, like a social media Cyrano.

"She swipes right on people who are terrifying," said Sarah.

"It's a confidence-booster," Jessica said.

"It depends what you want to use it for," said Rebecca. "If you want to use it to hook up with someone, that's great, but what I've seen is girls complaining about how, Oh, this guy wants to meet up—he wants sex. And I'm like, That's what it's *for*."

"I'm on it nonstop, like nonstop," Courtney said. "Like twenty hours a day."

"All guys are on Tinder," said Jessica.

"They are," Danielle said. "And they're so rude. You put up a picture and you get all these comments like, Wanna do butt things?"

I told them how I had heard from guys that they swiped right on every picture in order to increase their chances of matching with a girl.

The girls exploded with laughter.

"Nooooo," Courtney said.

"Boys will do anything, do anything, to get it in," Rebecca said grimly.

"Not Caleb," said Paige.

Caleb looked up from his phone, pretending not to know what was being said.

"My boyfriend's perfect," Rebecca teased.

"If you have good girlfriends, you don't really need a boyfriend," Courtney observed.

"But there's a lot of needs your girlfriends can't satisfy," Rebecca said with a grin.

"A lot of guys are lacking in that department, too." Courtney sighed. They laughed.

"We go sex toy shopping together frequently, Rebecca and I," said Paige.

"We help people pick up their first toys," Rebecca said, smiling. "Like online. A lot of guys are super-intimidated by your vibrator—not all guys are, but a lot of them are."

"I need to get a vibrator," Danielle murmured.

"I have three," Paige said.

"I have three," said Courtney. "They're all broken."

"Oh, Courtney," Rebecca said, giggling.

They laughed.

"Yeah, like if you're having good sex, you're having a good *life,* and if you're not, you're *not,*" said Paige. She said she wanted to be a sex therapist.

"I took a human sexuality class last semester and fell in love with it," Courtney said. "I was so excited to go every single week."

"You guys watched porn in class," Rebecca said.

"Yeah, we did, but it's not really about sex, it's about yourself," said Courtney.

"Some people are gonna hate me for this," said Paige, with her girl-ish smile, "but I think porn stars are the best type of feminists because I think that they're all about satisfying themselves and their own personal wants and their own personal needs, and they recognize that they're very sexual creatures and that's just such a natural instinct and feeling for all of us; so I think it's so amazing that they get on camera and do what they love and they don't care about the stigmas around being a porn star—they just care about making themselves happy and satisfied, so I think it's just so great."

I asked her if she knew if porn stars had real orgasms, or were they just performing?

"Oh, it's performance, I guess," Paige said, "so in *that* way I guess it's not necessarily the best thing but—"

"What's a real orgasm like? Like I wouldn't know," Courtney said.

They laughed.

"I wish I did," Courtney said. "I know how to give one to *myself—*"

"Yeah, but men don't know what to do," Jessica said, as if this were well known. She was tapping on her phone.

"Without [a vibrator] I can't have one," Courtney said. "But it's never happened" with a guy. "It's a huge problem."

"It is a problem," Jessica agreed.

I asked if guys they knew tried to give them orgasms.

"If you're in a relationship they do," Jessica said.

"They try but it's still like, they can't get there," Courtney said. "They really just don't know how to do it."

"They think they're doing something right, but no," Jessica said.

"I just wanna, like, *experience*," Courtney said. "It's just so hard voicing what you want. It's so difficult—like, I can't do it."

"You have to be comfortable," Paige said.

"I think that you need to have open communication with people," Rebecca said. "But if they're not down for it, just be like, Okay, I'm not going to do this with you again. But I'm not gonna sit there and not *enjoy* myself. I wanna enjoy myself, but I wanna make sure they're enjoying themselves, too. I would so much rather they *tell* me than just sit there and be like, Oh, this sucks."

"But how do you say that in a sexy manner?" Courtney asked. "Like does it *have* to be sexy, like"—sexy voice—"Honey, no, that's not working."

They laughed.

"Like if he's doing something to you and it's not happening, just put your hand there and be like, How about you do this?" Rebecca suggested.

"Just guide them," said Sarah.

"I'll just text him right now," Courtney said, pretending to text her hookup partner.

Laughter.

"You have to *praise* them," Ariel said. She was an early education major. "It's kind of sick, 'cause that's how I learned to get children to do what you want them to do, and it's the same with guys."

More laughter.

"If it's all, like, negative," Rebecca said, "like, Ach, this isn't working, you're just gonna feel like crap and it'll be awkward and ruin the moment. Move their hand and be like, *Oh*"—sexy voice—"I love when I'm on top, let me go on top."

They talked about how ironic it was that "every woman's magazine tells you how to please a man, but they hardly ever tell you how to get them to please you."

"I've been having sex with the same guy now since the winter," Courtney said, "and he *still* hasn't given me an orgasm."

"You need to talk to him," Rebecca said.

Courtney said, "I think it's because he's always like"—determined bro voice—"I wanna make you come! And then I'm like"—anxious face—"I have to come now! How'm I gonna fucking come like that?"

They roared.

"What about your vibrator?" I asked.

"I broke it," Courtney said.

Bigger laugh.

"Has he used it on you?" asked Rebecca.

"Mmm-hmm." Courtney sighed.

"You need to get a new one," Rebecca said. "Or how about you can use it on yourself while you're with him and then you can use it together—so it's not like *you* doing it."

"Can you make your body *depend* on a vibrator to have an orgasm?" Courtney asked. "Wouldn't it be great if you could just have them without it?"

"Some women have them so easily," Jessica said, snapping her fingers, "and other women don't."

"Fuck the girls that can orgasm like five times without even touching!" said Courtney.

"Apparently it *does* happen," Rebecca said.

"Yeah," Sarah said. "I think they're faking. That's the other thing—faking is so annoying sometimes."

"Guys can sleep around, and either way they're gonna have an orgasm," Rebecca complained. "They're gonna come, and it's gonna be great; but they don't realize it's harder for us."

"I get really tired of faking," Sarah said. "My question is—can they tell? 'Cause sometimes when it's actually happening"—that is, when she was having an orgasm—"they *can't* tell. Once he actually gives you a real orgasm, *can* he tell? It's really useless and annoying that half the time I'm only having sex with him so he can come. I'm really over it at this point. Like, okay, I wanna go back to bed."

"Sex is supposed to be for two people," Rebecca said.

"Yeah, sometimes I'm just bored," said Sarah.

Another laugh.

"I think now women are so much more sexually aware and horny," Courtney said. "Guys probably think girls *aren't* horny, but we are just as horny or even hornier, 'cause we can't satisfy ourselves as much as they can. It's harder to, but we need to do it—it *needs* to happen."

"An orgasm a day keeps the stress away," Rebecca said, smiling.

"I think men have a skewed view of the reality of sex through porn," Jessica said. "Because sometimes I think porn sex is not always great—like *pounding* someone." She made a pounding motion with her hand, her face intense.

"Yeah, it looks like it hurts," Danielle said.

"Like porn sex," Jessica said, "those women—that's not, like, enjoyable, like having their hair pulled or being choked or slammed. I mean, whatever you're into, but men just think"—bro voice—"I'm gonna *fuck* her, and sometimes that's not great."

"Yeah," Danielle agreed. "Like last night I was having sex with this guy and I'm a very submissive person—like, not aggressive at all—and this boy that came over last night, he was hurting me."

They were quiet for a moment.

Newark, Delaware

Eve didn't come out of her bedroom all morning, and when she finally did, she was quiet, padding around the kitchen, making food. She wore no makeup. Her hair was in a ponytail; she was wearing sweatpants and a pair of glasses. She seemed different from the girl of the night before, the brassy girl in the cocktail dress.

Her friends went off to a frat party in the rain, and she sat alone at the kitchen table eating pasta. She never said where she went the night before or what had happened or with whom; she just said that she was "taking a day to herself." She'd been in her bedroom all day watching *Game of Thrones.*

She started talking about how the show was "very pornographic." "It's funny some people look down on porn," she said, "and then they like a show like *Game of Thrones.* Our whole society has become like porn. Nobody wants to look at that."

I asked her if she thought, as Courtney did, that porn was affecting the way people had sex. She said she didn't know; "but a lot of guys are just into their own pleasure," she said. "They don't know how to satisfy the girl, or they don't even try. That's why I don't get the whole one-night-stand thing. I don't believe in one-night stands strictly for the reason that you will almost never find a guy that has you in mind in that situation. It's for him and for him only. We," meaning girls and women, "are a lot more complicated, that's just the way we're designed, and so for someone to take the time to respect that and let both parties be pleased—like that rarely ever happens with a, Oh yeah, I'm drunk, let's go.

"It's not like we have to go get married now," Eve said, "but why do you want it at all if it's not going to be equal? I don't understand.

"But I couldn't tell you what it is that I'm actually looking for," she went on. "I'm just glad that it's accepted now for people to say that, like, this is not what it's supposed to be. I don't want to say that hookup culture is wrong, but—yeah, it's just not working."

She'd had one serious relationship, she said, a boy from high school she dated through college. It ended when the boy became physically violent, she said, punching a hole through a window when he was drunk, "obliterated. I know he never would have touched me" in a violent way, she said, "but when I say I have zero tolerance for something, I'm not fucking around." She told him, "Walk out of my life and never turn around and look back."

She'd been on one date in college, she relayed with a wry smile. "That was like my one glimpse into dating life, and I thought, like, Wow, if only this was the norm. This was like the diamond that will never come again. That incenses me." The boy had borrowed his friend's car, picked her up, and driven her to Main Street, "and we went out to dinner, and it was just so refreshing. Awkward as hell because I'd never done it before, but it was a real-life thrill. I was like, Holy shit, how do I look? Like I couldn't plan on what I was going to say to him . . . It's not like texting . . . Like you're here, this is live, this is now. I need that. I want that. But that doesn't happen anymore. People asked me about it afterward, like, What was it like? And it was like . . ." Her voice trailed off. "It was nice.

"I'm hoping so much that when I leave college and go into the adult world, that it kind of happens again," she said. "In my head I think it's coming. But then I know it's not. It's been so long since that has been the norm that no one wants to be the one to just go ahead and do it. But what I think is funny is, this guy who did ask me out on a date got moved up so high on my list. And I wish boys just realized, like, you know, you could actually be getting so many more girls if you went about this in a different way." The boy who took her on the date and she didn't wind up going out. "But at least I had the chance to get to know someone without just hooking up," she said.

"Do we even know how to fall in love anymore?" Eve asked. "Do we even know what being in love is? Will we ever get there because we have such a screwed-up notion of what it should be, or how you should get there? . . . Everyone wants love," she said, "and no one wants to admit it."

Conclusion

Sometimes, when I was on a reporting trip and I'd come back to my hotel room after a day of talking to girls, I'd have to sort of just sit for a while and take it all in. Whether it was after seeing screenshots of thirteen-year-old girls on "slut pages," or hearing about a fourteen-year-old girl being mocked and bullied online, or finding out about a sixteen-year-old girl trying to deliver a presentation in school as her classmates flashed pornography at her—I had to just sit and reflect. I felt sad sometimes. I think what made me feel the worst was the sense I got from many girls that they felt disrespected.

So much had changed in the lives of these girls compared with girls who came before them. And yet, as they often said, there were no rules for how to behave in this new social media landscape, no guide for them to know how to respond to the way others were behaving and treating them. They were social media pioneers, but it was as if they were commanding their covered wagons without any maps or sextants.

Being a teenager has never been easy. Faces and bodies are changing, hormones raging, emotions all over the place. Imagine adding to that a constant pressure to take pictures of yourself and look "hot" in those pictures and have people like them. Imagine getting a dick pic from a boy, maybe before you've ever held a boy's hand. Or being asked for nudes at a time when you're just trying to feel comfortable in your changing body, and not always succeeding. Imagine developing a crush on someone, who seems to like you back, only to find out that he's been "talking" to other girls, online, even at the same time you thought you were having an intimate conversation.

My own life as a teenager wasn't perfect—no one's ever is—but I was blessed in many ways, especially in the boyfriend I had in ninth grade. Let's call him Sean. I hadn't talked to him in more than thirty years when I called him up one night, after I'd come back to my hotel room after interviewing Sierra, the Jamestown girl who had suffered so much from being bullied and cyberbullied throughout her life. I found myself feeling very troubled by her story, at the way she seemed to have internalized this expectation to look "hot" and so wanted to be liked and loved and considered hot by strangers on social media. For some reason I wanted to talk to Sean about it. I wanted to ask him what life was like when we were kids, and try to remember if we had known anything like innocence.

"Well," he said with a laugh. "Not exactly." He was talking to me from Miami, where he's the dad of three teenagers, a boy and two girls. He reminded me of how kids in our grade were having sex—"I think a lot," he said. He remembered some girls dressing pretty provocatively back then as well. "So you think it's always been this way?" I asked. Sometimes, when I would tell people about what I was hearing in my interviews with girls, this was what they would say.

"Oh, God, no," said Sean. "I think the biggest difference is kids are watching porn." He brought it up on his own. I hadn't told him this was what I thought, too. "It changes how boys look at girls. I mean, how can it not?" he said. He said he talked to his son about porn on a regular basis, telling him not to watch it; "but I know he's probably going to anyway, so I tell him to remember it's not real life. I want him to be able to have a real relationship with someone someday, and the porn kids see just messes with their heads. I can't believe anybody argues with that. It's just common sense."

When I hung up the phone, I realized that the talks Sean was having with his son were the ones we need to have as a nation. I think, for the well-being of girls, and boys, we need to have a national conversation about online porn and its effects on kids. I'm not advocating censorship. I know, as Soraya Chemaly said, that "porn isn't going away." There were attempts early on to legislate the accessibility of online porn, but that's a whole other discussion. Parents need to know their kids are seeing porn, either deliberately or accidentally, and they need to consider porn's influence on their lives—on their view of their own sexuality as well as how they treat each other in a sexual relationship. This is especially urgent in the lives of girls. Because the porn that children and teenagers most often see presents an image of women and young women and even teenage girls that is, frankly, degrading. We can't deny any longer the influence this is having on the lives of girls.

But violent porn that is degrading to women doesn't occur in a vacuum. Its popularity is indicative of a culture in which, despite the welcome gains of women in education and the workforce, women and girls continue to experience sexism and misogyny. The fact that there are still people who would deny this seems indicative of a lack of education. I think we also need to start educating girls and boys about the history of the women's movement, in order to help them develop a better understanding of women's experience and to help them grow compassion—boys for girls, girls for one another. In schools, from the earliest ages, in kindergarten, children should be learning about the history of women in America and their struggle for equality, just as they learn about the history of the Civil Rights Movement. The story of women of all races is left out of American education too much of the time. And I think this has got to change.

Now more than ever, I believe, girls need feminism. They're deeply in need of a set of critical tools with which to evaluate their experiences as girls and young women in the digital age. Feminism, as varied and diverse in its expression as it has always been, is at its core a set of critical tools that enable girls and women to recognize inequality and work toward equality—political, economic, and social. So much of what goes on on girls' phones is unequal, beginning with the "hot or not" contest in which many are continually engaging—a form of sexualization that is potentially damaging to their emotional and even physical health.

Many of the girls I spoke to were struggling with anxiety, depression, cutting, and other issues; and while social media use alone can't be blamed for this, of course, there seems to be evidence that it could be exacerbating some of these problems. Often I witnessed, with girls, a kind of unease, a sort of buzzing, rushing, anxious state as they engaged with their phones, constantly checking, checking, to see what was happening or what was being said about them on social media. In our celebrity- and fame-obsessed culture, their engagement with social media also seems to be making them—and perhaps all of us—more interested in self-promotion. At a time in their lives when girls are just trying to discover who they are, for them to then feel pressured into creating an impossibly "perfect" self online, disconnected from reality, seems, again, a very unhealthy if not damaging activity. Should they go off social media? At least more of the time? I think this is a conversation parents should be having with their daughters.

And social media is a place where, unfortunately, girls are encountering attitudes and behaviors that must be called sexist. They need to be able to identify these things as such, and to know that they're not reflective of their self-worth—to know, in fact, that they are challenges to their success and happiness. They need to be able to understand, and respond accordingly, and sometimes fight back. Which a feminist consciousness will help them to do. "Feminism is for everybody," bell hooks said. Children of all gender identities will benefit from learning about what is also at the core of feminism: self-respect, and respect for others.

We can change the culture of social media. But we need Silicon Valley to help. The leaders of tech, who are reaping such profits from girls' fascination with their products, need to take responsibility for the effect of their industry on girls' lives. Silicon Valley players are smart. We constantly hear how smart they are. If they're also good, they'll address how to stop the exploitation and degradation of girls and all children online. They'll become more active in the fight against the cyberbullying of girls as well as of boys, and of children who identify in other ways. They'll speak out against the harassment of girls and women online, against rape and death threats against women, and the nonconsensual sharing of nudes. A logical first step in changing the culture of Silicon Valley would be hiring and promoting more women in their own industry.

Finally, I think girls need to read. Which they already do; but they need to read more. Early in this book I reported on my conversation with April Alliston, the Princeton professor who talked about how it was with the invention of the printing press that we first saw porn in its modern form. Porn was a reaction to women reading, to becoming more educated and informed. It was meant to degrade women and distract them from becoming educated, in the view of some historians, as a way to keep them from becoming empowered. And so for girls now to model themselves in the image of pornography, one could argue, is for them to embrace their own disempowerment. Girls need to put down their phones sometimes and pick up books.

When I talked to my old friend Sean, he reminded me of how it was when we were discovering first love. He made me remember how we used to walk home from school in the afternoons and do homework together at my house, how we never seemed to stop talking and enjoying each other's company. We never had sex, although we did kiss and so forth. The point of being together was not to have sex, necessarily. It was to become intimate. "Intimacy was more valued then," Sean said on the phone. I so want girls and all kids to have this experience of feeling close to someone, to feel valued and loved. It would not only be nice—I believe it's necessary. Because no matter how much we may feel that this world of social media is real, as Riley, the girl in Montclair, said, it's "a second world." The real world we inhabit together is the one that matters; we need to find a way of navigating ourselves and our children back there, to the world of true and lasting connection.

Acknowledgments

I couldn't have researched or written this book without the honesty and generosity of the girls I interviewed. I thank them all, along with many of their parents, for their candidness in sharing their stories. I trust they know when reading the book that this is only a snapshot in time in their lives. It's a difficult and challenging time for many girls, and their bravery and openness have made it possible for me to talk about issues that affect all girls. I could not be more grateful to them for that.

While researching and writing I had conversations with many people that spawned thoughts and reflection, but conversations with April Alliston, Jeannine Amber, David Buss, Soraya Chemaly, Susan J. Douglas, Donna Freitas, Justin Garcia, Michael Harris, Jennifer Powell-Lunder, and Paul Roberts were especially important in my developing an understanding of the broader themes at work in the stories of the girls I interviewed. I thank them all for sharing their time and brilliance.

Jordan Pavlin, my editor, helped me see how to make the book a reality. I was swimming in interviews with hundreds of girls, which she patiently helped me to crystalize into a narrative. Throughout this process my agent, Kimberly Witherspoon, provided invaluable support and counsel. I thank them both, and feel very lucky to have spun into their orbit.

I wouldn't have conceived of the book were it not for Graydon Carter, who saw a crisis in the lives of girls and sent me off on my first reporting trip to find out what was going on in their lives. I am deeply indebted to him as well as to Dana Brown, my editor at *Vanity Fair*, for their insights, support, and guidance.

I also thank Ellen Feldman, my production editor, for helping to make the book better. I thank Erin Sheehy, Richard Beck, and Benjamin Phelan for fact-checking the book, and Veronica Chambers for reading parts of the book and letting me know about the Willie Mae Rock Camp for Girls.

Many of my friends and family members helped me as well, especially my mother, Alice, whose innate sense of how to parent compassionately has been a true north. I also thank my brother, Noah, and sister, Liz, as well as Spencer, Satsko, Amy, Michael, Austin, Calvin, and Daniel for listening and supporting me when I was having trouble, and sharing their friendship and companionship in this years-long process. And finally I would like to thank my daughter, Zazie. Her kindness and suggestions helped me in so many ways, especially in making me realize every day how dear girls are, and how important it is for us to give them a better world.

Bibliography

Abram, Susan. "Measure B in LA: A 'Thin Layer of Latex Has Produced More Drama Than Sex.'" *Huffington Post*. Last modified November 5, 2013. http://www.huffing tonpost.com/2013/11/05/measure-b-la-_n_4219019.html.

Adichie, Chimamanda Ngozi. *We Should All Be Feminists*. New York: Anchor Books, 2012.

Alice, Slack. "Overexposed: Parents Post 1,000 Pics of Their Kids Before Age 5." *Infosecurity*. Last modified May 31, 2015. http://www.infosecurity-magazine.com/ slackspace/overexposed-parents-post-1000-pics/.

"All-Female Jury Throws Out 'Girls Gone Wild' Lawsuit." CBS Local. Last modified April 7, 2011. http://miami.cbslocal.com/2011/04/07/all-female-jury-throws-out -girls-gone-wild-lawsuit/.

Amber, Jeannine. "Real World." *Essence*, January 2013.

"Annual AAFPRS Survey Finds 'Selfie' Trend Increases Demand for Facial Plastic Surgery Influence on Elective Surgery." American Academy of Facial Plastic and Reconstructive Surgery. Last modified March 11, 2014. http://www.aafprs.org/ media/press_release/20140311.html.

Ansari, Aziz, and Eric Klinenberg. *Modern Romance*. New York: Penguin Press, 2015.

Anthony, Sebastian. "Just how big are porn sites?" Extreme Tech. Last modified April 4, 2012. http://www.extremetech.com/computing/123929-just-how-big-are -porn-sites/2.

Arias, Ileana, Robert Bardwell, Eric Finkelstein, Jacqueline Golding, Steven Leadbet- ter, Wendy Max, Howard Pinderhughes, Dorothy Rice, Linda E. Saltzman, Kevin Tate, Nancy Thoennes, and Patricia Tjaden. *Costs of Intimate Partner Violence Against Women in the United States*. Atlanta: Department of Health and Human Services, Centers for Disease Control and Prevention, National Center for Injury Control and Prevention, 2003.

Arkin, William M. *Unmanned: Drones, Data, and the Illusion of Perfect Warfare*. New York: Little, Brown, 2015.

Armstrong, Elizabeth. *Paying for the Party: How College Maintains Inequality*. Cam- bridge, MA: Harvard University Press, 2013.

Ault, Susanne. "Survey: YouTube Stars More Popular Than Mainstream Celebs Among U.S. Teens." *Variety*, August 5, 2014.

"AVG Study Finds a Quarter of Children Have Online Births Before Their Actual Birth Dates." Business Wire. Last modified October 6, 2010. http://www.businesswire .com/news/home/20101006006722/en/Digital-Birth-Online-World.

Bailey, Beth L. *From Front Porch to Back Seat: Courtship in Twentieth-Century America.* Baltimore: Johns Hopkins University Press, 1988.

Bates, Laura. *Everyday Sexism . . .* New York: Simon & Schuster, 2014.

Bauerlein, Mark. *The Dumbest Generation: How the Digital Age Stupefies Young Americans and Jeopardizes Our Future.* New York: Jeremy P. Tarcher/Penguin, 2008.

———, ed. *The Digital Divide: Arguments for and Against Facebook, Google, Texting, and the Age of Social Networking.* New York: Jeremy P. Tarcher/Penguin, 2011.

Bazelon, Emily. *Sticks and Stones: Defeating the Culture of Bullying and Rediscovering the Power of Character and Empathy.* New York: Random House, 2013.

Bennett, Laura. "Self-Publishing: Kim Kardashian just wants to be seen. This 445-page book of selfies might be her masterpiece." *Slate.* Last modified May 2015. http://www.slate.com/articles/arts/books/2015/05/selfish_kim_kardashian_west_s_book_of_selfies_reviewed.html.

Berg, Barbara J. *Sexism in America: Alive, Well, and Ruining Our Future.* Chicago: Lawrence Hill Books, 2009.

Berkman, Fran. "Why a Teen Kidnapping Victim Turned to Ask.fm for Solace." Mashable. Last modified August 15, 2013. http://mashable.com/2013/08/15/hannah-anderson-ask-fm/#doUWLRp2FGqF.

Best, Joel, and Kathleen A. Bogle. *Kids Gone Wild: From Rainbow Parties to Sexting, Understanding the Hype over Teen Sex.* New York: New York University Press, 2014.

Binge Drinking: A Serious, Under-Recognized Problem Among Women and Girls. Atlanta: Centers for Disease Control and Prevention, 2013.

Boonstra, Heather D. "What Is Behind the Declines in Teen Pregnancy Rates?" *Guttmacher Policy Review* 17, no. 3 (Summer 2014).

Bourin, Lennart. "Gates wants geeks to build a better condom." CNN. Last modified March 26, 2013. http://www.cnn.com/2013/03/25/health/bill-gates-condom-challenge/.

boyd, danah. *It's Complicated: The Social Lives of Networked Teens.* New Haven, CT: Yale University Press, 2014.

Britt, Robert Roy. "Why Men Report More Sex Partners Than Women." Live Science. Last modified February 17, 2006. http://www.livescience.com/7038-men-report-sex-partners-women.html.

Bromwich, Jonah. "Essena O'Neill, Instagram Star, Recaptions Her Life." *New York Times,* November 3, 2015.

Brumberg, Joan Jacobs. *The Body Project: An Intimate History of American Girls.* New York: Vintage Books, 1997.

Bruner, Raisa. "#SWUGNATION." *Yale Daily News,* March 29, 2013.

Bryer, Jackson R., and Cathy W. Barks, eds. *Dear Scott, Dear Zelda: The Love Letters of F. Scott & Zelda Fitzgerald.* London: Bloomsbury, 2002.

Burgess, Anthony. *A Clockwork Orange.* New York: W. W. Norton, 1962.

Burgess-Proctor, Amanda, Sameer Hinduja, and Justin W. Patchin. *Victimization of Adolescent Girls.* Orlando, FL: Cyberbullying Research Center, 2009.

Burleigh, Nina. "What Silicon Valley Thinks of Women." *Newsweek,* January 28, 2015.

Buss, David M. *The Evolution of Desire: Strategies of Human Mating.* New York: Basic Books, 1994.

Carr, Nicholas. *The Shallows: What the Internet Is Doing to Our Brains.* New York: W. W. Norton, 2010.

Centers for Disease Control and Prevention. "Nationally Representative CDC Study Finds 1 in 4 Teenage Girls Has a Sexually Transmitted Disease." CDC. Last modi-

fied March 11, 2008. http://www.cdc.gov/stdconference/2008/press/release-11
march2008.htm.

———. "Reported Cases of Sexually Transmitted Diseases on the Rise, Some at Alarming Rate." CDC. Last modified November 17, 2015. http://www.cdc.gov/nchhstp/
newsroom/2015/std-surveillance-report-press-release.html.

———. "Sexual Risk Behaviors: HIV, STD, & Teen Pregnancy Prevention." CDC. Last
modified September 1, 2015. http://www.cdc.gov/healthyyouth/sexualbehaviors/.

Chidi, George. "Teen charged with distributing underage explicit photos for Tweeting
nude selfies." Raw Story. Last modified February 8, 2014. http://www.rawstory
.com/2014/02/teen-charged-with-distributing-underage-explicit-photos-for
-tweeting-nude-selfies/.

Chirban, John. *How to Talk with Your Kids About Sex*. New York: Thomas Nelson, 2012.

Chow, Kat. "Video Calls Out Catcallers, but Cuts Out White Men." NPR. Last modified November 1, 2014. http://www.npr.org/sections/codeswitch/2014/11/01/3604
22087/hollaback-video-calls-out-catcallers-but-cuts-out-white-men.

Clark, Shelley, Caroline Kabiru, and Eliya Zulu. "Do Men and Women Report Their
Sexual Partnerships Differently? Evidence from Kisumu, Kenya." *International Per-
spectives on Sexual and Reproductive Health* 37, no. 4 (December 2011).

Cloos, Kassondra, and Julie Turkewitz. "Hundreds of Nude Photos Jolt Colorado
School." *New York Times*, November 6, 2015.

Coontz, Stephanie. *The Way We Never Were: American Families and the Nostalgia Trap*.
New York: Basic Books, 1992.

Cornell, Drucilla, ed. *Oxford Readings in Feminism: Feminism and Pornography*. New
York: Oxford University Press, 2000.

Davies, Anna. "Does Social Media Push Us to Cheat?" RedbookMag. Last modified
September 11, 2014. http://www.redbookmag.com/love-sex/relationships/a18734/
social-media-cheating/.

DeAngelis, Tori. "Web pornography's effect on children." American Psychological
Association. Last modified November 2007. http://www.apa.org/monitor/nov07/
webporn.aspx.

de Beauvoir, Simone. *The Second Sex*. New York: Alfred A. Knopf, 1952.

Dines, Gail. *Pornland: How Porn Has Hijacked Our Sexuality*. Boston: Beacon Press,
2010.

Douglas, Susan J. *The Rise of Enlightened Sexism: How Pop Culture Took Us from Girl
Power to Girls Gone Wild*. New York: St. Martin's Griffin, 2010.

———. *Where the Girls Are: Growing Up Female with the Mass Media*. New York: Three
Rivers Press, 1994.

Elliott, Stuart. "Trojan Teams Up with MTV Again to Promote Condom Use, and the
Brand." *New York Times*, September 9, 2014.

Ellis, Kelly. "This Is Not the Last Thing You'll Ever Need to Read About Sexism in
Tech. Not Even Close." Medium. Last modified October 2, 2014. https://medium
.com/@kellyellis/this-is-not-the-last-thing-youll-ever-need-to-read-about-sexism
-in-tech-in-fact-its-not-even-5b8400e913ec#.faap9noif.

The Evidence Suggests Otherwise: The Truth About Boys and Girls. Washington, DC: Education Sector, 2006.

Fahs, Breanne. *Performing Sex: The Making and Unmaking of Women's Erotic Lives*.
Albany: State University of New York Press, 2011.

Fairchild, Kimberly, and Laurie A. Rudman. "Everyday Stranger Harassment and
Women's Objectification." *Social Justice Research* 21 (September 16, 2008): 338–57.

Faludi, Susan. *Backlash: The Undeclared War Against Women.* New York: Anchor Books, 1991.

Farhi, Paul. "NBC in talks for documentary on Hannah Anderson kidnapping/murder case." *Washington Post,* October 29, 2013.

Fey, Tina. *Bossypants.* New York: Little, Brown, 2011.

Flood, Michael. "The harms of pornography exposure among children and young people." *Child Abuse Review* 18, no. 6 (November/December 2009): 384–400.

Flynn, Natalie. "Rx-Related Charges for *Girls* Guy; Civil Suit Settled." E! Online. Last modified April 13, 2007. http://www.eonline.com/news/54888/rx-related-charges -for-girls-guy-civil-suit-settled.

Freitas, Donna. *The End of Sex: How Hookup Culture Is Leaving a Generation Unhappy, Sexually Unfulfilled, and Confused About Intimacy.* New York: Basic Books, 2013.

French, Marilyn. *The War Against Women.* New York: Ballantine Books, 1992.

Friedersdorf, Conor. "The New Intolerance of Student Activism." *The Atlantic,* November 9, 2015.

Gallagher, Brenden. "Nobody's Perfect: *Entourage*'s 25 Biggest Fails." Complex. Last modified May 1, 2013. http://www.complex.com/pop-culture/2013/05/entourages -25-biggest-fails/.

Garber, Megan. "You Win, Kim Kardashian." *The Atlantic.* Last modified May 13, 2015. http://www.theatlantic.com/entertainment/archive/2015/05/kim-kardashian -selfish/393113/.

Garcia, Justin, Chris Reiber, Sean G. Massey, and Ann M. Merriwether. "Sexual Hookup Culture: A Review." *Review of General Psychology* 16, no. 2 (2012): 161–76.

Garcia, Patricia. "We're Officially in the Era of the Big Booty." *Vogue,* September 2014.

Gardner, Howard, and Katie Davis. *The App Generation: How Today's Youth Navigate Identity, Intimacy, and Imagination in a Digital World.* New Haven, CT: Yale University Press, 2013.

Gender Differences in Participation and Completion of Undergraduate Education and How They Have Changed over Time. Washington, DC: U.S. Department of Education, 2005.

"Gender Equity in Education." U.S. Department of Education Office for Civil Rights. Last modified June 2012. http://www2.ed.gov/about/offices/list/ocr/docs/gender -equity-in-education.pdf.

Gen Nexters Say Getting Rich Is Their Generation's Top Goal. Washington, DC: Pew Research Center, 2007.

"Get the Facts on Eating Disorders." National Eating Disorders Association. Last modified 2011. https://www.nationaleatingdisorders.org/get-facts-eating-disorders.

Gevinson, Tavi, ed. *Rookie Yearbook One.* New York: Razorbill, 2014.

———. *Rookie Yearbook Two.* New York: Razorbill, 2014.

Glaser, Gabrielle. "Why She Drinks: Women and Alcohol Abuse." *Wall Street Journal,* June 21, 2013.

Gleick, James. *The Information: A History, A Theory, A Flood.* New York: Vintage Books, 2011.

Greenberg, Barbara R., and Jennifer Powell-Lunder. *Teenage as a Second Language: A Parent's Guide to Becoming Bilingual.* Avon, MA: Adams Media, 2010.

Greenwald, Glenn. *No Place to Hide: Edward Snowden, the NSA, and the U.S. Surveillance State.* New York: Metropolitan Books, 2014.

Grigoriadis, Vanessa. "Kim Kardashian: American Woman." *Rolling Stone,* July 27, 2015.

Grousnell, Lauren, and Laura House. "Friends of Instagram model who 'quit' social media call it a HOAX—as she finally shuts down her accounts." *Daily Mail*. Last modified November 3, 2015. http://www.dailymail.co.uk/femail/article-3302605/Essena-O-Neill-slammed-fellow-YouTubers-Nina-Randa-Nelson-say-quitting-Instagram-HOAX.html.

Gurney-Read, Josie. "'Sharp rise' in number of school girls with emotional issues." *The Telegraph*. Last modified April 20, 2015. http://www.telegraph.co.uk/education/educationnews/11548719/Sharp-rise-in-number-of-school-girls-with-emotional-issues.html.

Hains, Rebecca C. *The Princess Problem: Guiding Our Girls Through the Princess-Obsessed Years*. Naperville, IL: Sourcebooks, 2014.

Harris, Michael. *The End of Absence: Reclaiming What We've Lost in a World of Constant Connection*. New York: Current, 2014.

Hill, Catherine, and Holly Kearl. *Crossing the Line: Sexual Harassment at School*. Washington, DC: American Association of University Women, 2011.

Hinduja, Sameer, and Justin W. Patchin. *Bullying, Cyberbullying, and Sexual Orientation*. Orlando, FL: Cyberbullying Research Center, 2011.

Hine, Thomas. *The Rise and Fall of the American Teenager*. New York: Avon Books, 1999.

Hlavka, Heather. "Normalizing Sexual Violence: Young Women Account for Harassment and Abuse." *Gender & Society*, June 2014.

Holmes, Oliver. "Mobile dating apps spur HIV epidemic among Asia's teenagers, says UN." *The Guardian*, November 30, 2015.

hooks, bell. *Feminism Is for Everybody: Passionate Politics*. Brooklyn, NY: South End Press, 2000.

Horwitz, Sari. "New Law Offers Protection to Abused Native American Women." *Washington Post*, February 8, 2014.

Hunt, Elle. "Essena O'Neill quits Instagram claiming social media 'is not real life.'" *The Guardian*, November 3, 2015.

Izadi, Elahe. "Nearly a Third of U.S. Women Have Experienced Domestic Violence." *Washington Post*, September 8, 2014.

James, Carrie. *Disconnected: Youth, New Media, and the Ethics Gap*. Cambridge, MA: MIT Press, 2014.

James, E. L. *Fifty Shades of Grey*. New York: Vintage Books, 2011.

Kardashian, Kim. *Selfish*. New York: Rizzoli, 2015.

Kearl, Holly. *Unsafe and Harassed in Public Spaces: A National Street Harassment Report*. Reston, VA: Stop Street Harassment, 2014.

Kilbourne, Jean. *Can't Buy Me Love: How Advertising Changes the Way We Think and Feel*. New York: Touchstone, 1999.

Kitchens, Caroline. "It's Time to End 'Rape Culture' Hysteria." *Time*, March 20, 2014.

Kitroeff, Natalie. "In Hookups, Inequality Still Reigns." *Well* blog, *New York Times*. Entry posted November 11, 2013. http://well.blogs.nytimes.com/2013/11/11/women-find-orgasms-elusive-in-hookups/.

Kohlman, Stephanie, Amber Baig, Guy Balice, Christine DiRubbo, Linda Placencia, Kenneth Skale, Jessica Flitter, Jessica Thomas, Fereshte Mirzad, Hillary Moeckler, and Shayne Aquino. "Contribution of Media to the Normalization and Perpetuation of Domestic Violence." *Austin Journal of Psychiatry and Behavioral Science* 1, no. 4 (May 16, 2014).

Konrath, Sara H., Edward H. O'Brien, and Courtney Hsing. "Changes in Dispositional Empathy in American College Students over Time: A Meta-Analysis." *Personality and Social Psychology Review* 15, no. 2 (2011): 180–98.

Krischer, Hayley. "Meet the Instamom, a Stage Mother for Social Media." *New York Times*, November 14, 2015.

Lambert, Molly. "Nicki Minaj Reclaims the Twerk in the 'Anaconda' Music Video." *Grantland* blog. Entry posted August 20, 2014. http://grantland.com/hollywood -prospectus/nicki-minaj-reclaims-the-twerk-in-the-anaconda-music-video/.

Lenhart, Amanda. *Cyberbullying*. Washington, DC: Pew Research Center, 2007.

———. *Teens, Social Media & Technology Overview 2015: Mobile Access Shifts Social Media Use and Other Online Activities*. Washington, DC: Pew Research Center, 2015.

Levin, Diane E., and Jean Kilbourne. *So Sexy So Soon: The New Sexualized Childhood and What Parents Can Do to Protect Their Kids*. New York: Ballantine Books, 2008.

Levy, Ariel. *Female Chauvinist Pigs: Women and the Rise of Raunch Culture*. New York: Simon & Schuster, 2005.

Lieberman, Charlotte. "Why College Dating Is So Messed Up?" *Cosmopolitan*. Last modified February 10, 2014. http://www.cosmopolitan.com/sex-love/advice/a5585 /college-dating-screwed-up/.

Lounsbury, Kaitlin, Kimberley J. Mitchell, and David Finkelhor. *The True Prevalence of "Sexting."* Durham: University of New Hampshire, 2011.

Mabe, Annalise G., K. Jean Forney, and Pamela K. Keel. "Do you "like" my photo? Facebook use maintains eating disorder risk." *International Journal of Eating Disorders* 47, no. 5 (July 2014): 516–23.

Malach, Hannah. "SyracuseSnap: Here's what you missed from the now-banned campus story." The Tab. Last modified October 28, 2015. http://thetab.com/us /syracuse/2015/10/28/syracusesnap-aint-mamas-campus-story-1340.

Males, Mike, and Meda-Chesney Lind. "The Myth of Mean Girls." *New York Times*, April 1, 2010.

Manian, Divya, Jessica Dillon, Sabrina Majeed, Joanne McNeil, Sara J. Chipps, Kat Li, Ellen Chisa, Angelina Fabbro, and Jennifer Brook. "An Open Letter on Feminism in Tech." Model View Culture. Last modified May 22, 2014. https://modelviewcul ture.com/pieces/an-open-letter-on-feminism-in-tech.

Manov, Ann. "Don't twist the meaning of sexual liberation." *Independent Florida Alligator*, November 8, 2015.

Mather, Kate, Andrew Blankstein, and Kurt Streeter. "Amber Alert Suspect James DiMaggio Slain; Girl Rescued." *Los Angeles Times*, August 10, 2013.

Maxwell, Zerlina. "Rape Culture Is Real." *Time*, March 27, 2014.

McArdle, Alanna. "When I Was a 13-Year-Old Camgirl." Broadly. Last modified October 12, 2015. https://broadly.vice.com/en_us/article/when-i-was-a-13-year-old -camgirl.

McChesney, Robert W. *Digital Disconnect: How Capitalism Is Turning the Internet Against Democracy*. New York: The New Press, 2013.

McRobbie, Angela. *The Aftermath of Feminism: Gender, Culture and Social Change*. London: Sage Publications, 2009.

Millhiser, Ian. "School Photoshops T-Shirt That Says 'Feminist' Out of Class Photo." ThinkProgress. Last modified April 16, 2015. http://thinkprogress.org/ justice/2015/04/16/3647792/middle-school-censors-students-t-shirt-used-word -feminist/.

Mills, Nicolaus. *The Triumph of Meanness: America's War Against Its Better Self*. New York: Houghton Mifflin, 1997.

Mintz, Steven. *Huck's Raft: A History of American Childhood*. Cambridge, MA: Harvard University Press, 2004.

Morrissey, Tracie Egan. "Is Kim Kardashian a Feminist Role Model?" Jezebel. Last modified July 31, 2013. http://jezebel.com/is-kim-kardashian-a-feminist-role-model -975647442.

Mosher, Donald L., and Mark Sirkin. "Measuring a Macho Personality Constellation." *Journal of Research in Personality* 18, no. 2 (June 1984): 150–63.

Murphy, Doyle. "Hannah Anderson 'Sick' from Autopsy Reports, Responds to Critics in Latest Ask.fm Posts." New York *Daily News*, October 3, 2013.

Murray, Andrew. *Information Technology Law: The Law and Society*. Oxford: Oxford University Press, 2013.

Nagler, Linda Fregni. *The Hidden Mother*. London: Mack Books, 2013.

Newcomb, Mackenzie. "A Letter to a One-Night Stand." *Mack in Style* blog. Entry posted October 13, 2013. http://mackinstyle.com/2013/10/13/a-letter-to-a-one-night-stand/.

"New Girl Scouts Research Exposes the Impact of Reality TV on Girls." *Girl Scout Blog*. Entry posted October 13, 2011. http://blog.girlscouts.org/2011/10/new-girl-scouts -research-exposes-impact.html.

Newhall, Beaumont. *The History of Photography*. New York: Museum of Modern Art, 1982.

Nicks, Denver. "Hannah Anderson's Horrifying Ordeal: 'He Told Me He Had a Crush on Me.'" *Time*, October 9, 2013.

Notar, Charles E., Sharon Padgett, and Jessica Roden. "Cyberbullying: A Review of the Literature." *Universal Journal of Educational Research* 1, no. 1 (2013): 1–9.

Ohlheiser, Abby. "Meet 'Titstare,' the Tech World's Latest 'Joke' from the Minds of Bro-grammers." The Wire. Last modified September 8, 2013. http://www.thewire.com/ technology/2013/09/titstare-tech-worlds-latest-brogrammer-joke-techcrunch -disrupt/69171/.

Orpinas, Pamela, Caroline McNicholas, Lusine Nahapetyan, and Alana Vivolo-Kantor. "The Myth of 'Mean Girls.'" *StopBullying* blog. Entry posted September 10, 2015. http://www.stopbullying.gov/blog/2015/09/10/myth-mean-girls.

Paglia, Camille. *Sex, Art, and American Culture: Essays*. New York: Vintage Books, 1992.

Palladino, Grace. *Teenagers: An American History*. New York: Basic Books, 1996.

Pascoe, C. J. *Dude, You're a Fag: Masculinity and Sexuality in High School*. Los Angeles: University of California Press, 2007.

Petit, Carolyn. "City of Angels and Demons." GameSpot. Last modified September 16, 2013. http://www.gamespot.com/reviews/grand-theft-auto-v-review/1900 -6414475/.

Pinsky, Drew, and S. Mark Young. *The Mirror Effect: How Celebrity Narcissism Is Seducing America*. New York: Harper, 2009.

Piper Jaffray Companies. "Taking Stock with Teens—Fall 2015." Piper Jaffray. Last modified Fall 2015. http://www.piperjaffray.com/3col.aspx?id=3631.

Pipher, Mary. *Reviving Ophelia: Saving the Selves of Adolescent Girls*. New York: Ballantine Books, 1994.

Prinstein, Mitchell J. "Introduction to the special section on suicide and nonsuicidal self-injury: A review of unique challenges and important directions for self-injury science." *Journal of Consulting and Clinical Psychology* 76, no. 1 (February 2008): 1–8.

Rankin, Seija. "18 Moments from the 2015 Teen Choice Awards That Made Us Feel Super Old." E! Online. Last modified August 17, 2015. http://www.eonline.com/

news/686923/18-moments-from-the-2015-teen-choice-awards-that-made-us-feel
-super-old.

"The Rich Kids of Instagram." http://richkidsofinstagram.tumblr.com.

Riley, Michael. "Empower the Tribes, or Beef Up the Federal Role? Each Side Has Its
Own History of Failure." *Denver Post*. Last modified November 14, 2007. http://
www.denverpost.com/lawlesslands/ci_7454999.

Rinzler, Lodro. "4 Reasons Porn Is Actually Really, Really Good for Women." *Marie
Claire*. Last modified March 9, 2015. http://www.marieclaire.com/sex-love/news/
a13647/why-porn-is-actually-a-good-thing/.

Roberts, Paul. *The Impulse Society: America in the Age of Instant Gratification*. New York:
Bloomsbury, 2014.

Rodger, Elliot. "My Twisted World: The Story of Elliot Rodger." Unpublished ms.,
January 2014.

Rojas, Marcela. "Social Media Helps Fuel Some Eating Disorders." *USA Today*. Last
modified June 1, 2014. http://www.usatoday.com/story/news/nation/2014/06/01/
social-media-helps-fuel-eating-disorders/9817513/.

Rosin, Hanna. "Boys on the Side." *The Atlantic*, September 2012.

———. "Why Kids Sext." *The Atlantic*, November 2014.

Rushkoff, Douglas. *Coercion: Why We Listen to What "They" Say*. New York: Riverhead
Books, 1999.

Ryan, Christopher, and Cacilda Jethá. *Sex at Dawn: How We Mate, Why We Stray, and
What It Means for Modern Relationships*. New York: Harper Perennial, 2010.

Ryan, Johnny. *A History of the Internet and the Digital Future*. London: Reaktion Books,
2010.

Sabina, Chiara, Janis Wolak, and David Finkelhor. "Rapid Communication: The
Nature and Dynamics of Internet Pornography Exposure for Youth." *CyberPsychology & Behavior* 11, no. 6 (2008).

Sadker, Myra, and David Sadker. *Failing at Fairness: How Our Schools Cheat Girls*. New
York: Scribner, 1995.

Sales, Nancy Jo. "Friends Without Benefits." *Vanity Fair*. Last modified September 26, 2013. http://www.vanityfair.com/news/2013/09/social-media-internet-porn
-teenage-girls.

———. "From Model to Mogul." *Vanity Fair*, February 2007.

———. "Tinder and the Dawn of the 'Dating Apocalypse.'" *Vanity Fair*, September
2015.

"Sanctimommy Round-Up!" STFU, Parents. Last modified March 5, 2013. http://
www.stfuparentsblog.com/post/44603020352/sanctimommy-round-up.

Sax, Leonard. *Boys Adrift: The Five Factors Driving the Growing Epidemic of Unmotivated
Boys and Underachieving Young Men*. New York: Basic Books, 2007.

———. *Girls on the Edge: The Four Factors Driving the New Crisis for Girls*. New York:
Basic Books, 2010.

Scelfo, Julie. "Bad Girls Go Wild." *Newsweek*, June 12, 2005.

Schulzke, Eric. "Small Colorado Town Rocked by Sexting Scandal at Local High
School." *Deseret News National*, November 11, 2015.

Segal, David. "Does Porn Hurt Children?" *New York Times*, March 28, 2014.

Shortchanging Girls, Shortchanging America. Washington, DC: American Association
of University Women, 1991.

Siegel, Lee. *Against the Machine: Being Human in the Age of the Electronic Mob*. New
York: Spiegel & Grau, 2008.

Sifris, Dennis, and James Myhre. "The Real Reasons Why People Don't Use Condoms: Understanding Condom Bias, Condom Fatigue and Gender Dynamics of HIV." About Health. Last modified November 19, 2015. http://aids.about.com/od/womenandhiv/a/Why-People-Dont-Use-Condoms-and-That-Includes-Women.htm.

Silverman, Jacob. *Terms of Service: Social Media and the Price of Constant Connection.* New York: HarperCollins, 2015.

Simmons, Rachel. *Odd Girl Out: The Hidden Culture of Aggression in Girls.* New York: Mariner Books, 2002.

Skrzypek, Jeff. "South Florida mom says photos of her infant being used on Instagram in sexually explicit way." WPTV. Last modified November 18, 2013. http://www.wptv.com/news/region-c-palm-beach-county/west-palm-beach/south-florida-mom-says-instagram-photos-of-her-infant-being-used-in-sexually-explicit-way.

Smolowe, Jill. "Mean Girls." *People,* April 28, 2008.

Sollosi, Mary. "See Cara Delevingne take on morning talk show hosts in painfully awkward interview." *Entertainment Weekly.* Last modified July 28, 2015. http://www.ew.com/article/2015/07/28/cara-delevingne-awkward-interview.

Song, Sandra. "Updated: Inside the Deeply Bizarre Snapchat Movie That Has Even Marilyn Manson Freaked Out." *Paper.* Last modified July 22, 2015. http://www.papermag.com/updated-inside-the-deeply-bizarre-snapchat-movie-that-has-even-marilyn-1427608906.html.

Sporn, Stephanie. "Since When Does All-American Style Mean One Size Fits All?" Refinery29. Last modified December 5, 2014. http://www.refinery29.com/2014/12/78964/brandy-melville-one-size-fits-all.

Stapleton, AnnClaire, and Josh Levs. "Alleged gang rape on crowded beach is 'not the first,' sheriff says." CNN. Last modified April 16, 2015. http://www.cnn.com/2015/04/14/us/florida-panama-city-gang-rape-case/.

Steinmetz, Katy. "(No) Condom Culture: Why Teens Aren't Practicing Safe Sex." *Time,* November 12, 2013.

Strauch, Barbara. *The Primal Teen: What the New Discoveries About the Teenage Brain Tell Us About Our Kids.* New York: Anchor Books, 2003.

Talbot, Margaret. "Girls Just Want to Be Mean." *New York Times,* February 4, 2002.

Tam, Eva. "YouTube's Bethany Mota Redefines Being a Celebrity." *Digits* blog, *Wall Street Journal.* Accessed May 28, 2015. http://blogs.wsj.com/digits/2015/05/28/youtubes-bethany-mota-redefines-being-a-celebrity/.

Tapscott, Don. *Grown Up Digital: How the Net Generation Is Changing Your World.* New York: McGraw-Hill, 2009.

Taranto, James. "Drunkenness and Double Standards." *Wall Street Journal.* Last modified February 10, 2014. http://www.wsj.com/news/articles/SB10001424052702304558804579374844067975558.

Tarrant, Shira. *Men and Feminism.* Berkeley, CA: Seal Press, 2009.

Taylor, Jim. *Raising Generation Tech: Preparing Your Children for a Media-Fueled World.* New York: Sourcebooks, 2012.

Taylor, Kate. "Sex on Campus: She Can Play That Game, Too." *New York Times,* July 12, 2013.

Timberg, Craig. "How Violent Porn Sites Manage to Hide Information That Should Be Public." *Washington Post,* December 6, 2013.

Tognotti, Chris. "What Is '#Gamer Gate'? It's Misogyny, Under the Banner of 'Journalistic Integrity.'" Bustle. Last modified September 5, 2014. http://www.bustle.com/articles/38742-what-is-gamer-gate-its-misogyny-under-the-banner-of-journalistic-integrity.

Turkle, Sherry. *Alone Together: Why We Expect More from Technology and Less from Each Other.* New York: Basic Books, 2011.

"2014 Year in Review." Pornhub. Last modified January 7, 2015. http://www.pornhub .com/insights/2014-year-in-review.

Tyre, Peg. "Education: Boys Falling Behind Girls in Many Areas." *Newsweek,* January 29, 2006.

Uhlsa, Yalda T., Minas Michikyan, Jordan Morris, Debra Garcia, Gary W. Small, Eleni Zgourouf, and Patricia M. Greenfield. "Five days at outdoor education camp without screens improves preteen skills with nonverbal emotion cues." *Computers in Human Behavior* 39 (October 2014): 387–92.

U.S. Department of Health and Human Services. "Sexually Transmitted Diseases." HHS. Accessed July 8, 2015. http://www.hhs.gov/ash/oah/adolescent-health -topics/reproductive-health/stds.html.

Vaglanos, Alanna. "30 Shocking Domestic Violence Statistics That Remind Us It's an Epidemic." *Huffington Post.* Last modified October 23, 2014. http://www.huffing tonpost.com/2014/10/23/domestic-violence-statistics_n_5959776.html.

Wade, Lisa. "The Promise and Peril of Hook Up 'Culture.'" Speech delivered at various universities, 2010–2013.

Wallace, Benjamin. "The Geek-Kings of Smut." *New York,* January 30, 2011.

Wallace, Kelly. "Narcissistic parenting: When you compete through your child." CNN. Last modified July 24, 2015. http://www.cnn.com/2015/07/24/health/health -narcissistic-parenting-children-impact/.

Walter, Natasha. *Living Dolls: The Return of Sexism.* London: Virago UK, 2010.

"What Is the Magcon Family?" Magcon Fam. Last modified 2013. http://magconfam .weebly.com/what-is-the-magcon-family.html.

Wiedenkeller, Pat. "Another 'Wall Street' with Woes to Face." *New York Times,* November 2, 2008.

Wiseman, Rosalind. *Queen Bees and Wannabes: Helping Your Daughter Survive Cliques, Gossip, Boyfriends, and the New Reality of Girl World.* New York: Three Rivers Press, 2002.

WNYC. "The Myth of the Safer War." WNYC. Last modified September 11, 2015. http://www.wnyc.org/story/myth-safer-war/.

Wolak, Janis, David Finkelhor, Kimberly J. Mitchell, and Michele L. Ybarra. "Online 'Predators' and Their Victims: Myths, Realities, and Implications for Prevention and Treatment." *American Psychologist,* February/March 2008.

Wolfe, Tom. *Hooking Up.* New York: Picador, 2001.

Wollstonecraft, Mary. *A Vindication of the Rights of Women.* Lexington, KY: Wollstone-craft Books, 2013.

Woyke, Elizabeth. *The Smartphone: Anatomy of an Industry.* New York: The New Press, 2014.

Zahn, Margaret A., Susan Brumbaugh, Darrell Steffensmeier, Barry C. Feld, Merry Morash, Meda Chesney-Lind, Jody Miller, Allison Ann Payne, Denise C. C. Gott-fredson, and Candace Kruttschnitt. *Violence by Teenage Girls: Trends and Context.* Washington, DC: U.S. Department of Justice, Office of Justice Programs, 2008.

Ziv, Stav. "Child Homelessness in U.S. Reaches Historic High, Report Says." *Newsweek,* November 17, 2014.

Zurbriggen, Eileen L., Rebecca L. Collins, Sharon Lamb, Tomi-Ann Roberts, Deborah L. Tolman, L. Monique Ward, and Jeanne Blake, eds. *Report of the APA Task Force on the Sexualization of Girls.* Washington, DC: American Psychological Association, 2007.

Index

400

Index